THE CONGREGATION OF TIRON

SPIRITUALITY AND MONASTICISM, EAST AND WEST

Spirituality and Monasticism, East and West explores the everyday life of monastic individuals and the collective experience of religious communities and it focuses on the nature of asceticism and monasticism rather than monastic institutions, patronage, or property. The series is a home for research on both Western and Eastern Christian communities and also welcomes submissions exploring non-Christian traditions during the period 500–1500 CE.

The series is particularly keen to host research into Sufi orders or lodges, the life of Buddhist, Hindu or Daoist monasteries, and the monasteries of the Eastern Christian churches, including the Nestorian church, as well as new research into spiritual and monastic life in the Roman church. It also welcomes research into gendered differences in spirituality during this period as well as different forms of ascetic practice.

Series Editors

Scott G. Bruce, *Fordham University*
Anne E. Lester, *Johns Hopkins University*

Editorial Board

Anne E. Lester, *Johns Hopkins University*
Massimo Rondolino, *Carroll University*
Darlene Brooks Hedstrom, *Wittenberg University (Ohio)*
Mario Poceski, *University of Florida*

THE CONGREGATION OF TIRON

MONASTIC CONTRIBUTIONS TO TRADE AND COMMUNICATION IN TWELFTH-CENTURY FRANCE AND BRITAIN

BY
RUTH HARWOOD CLINE

British Library Cataloguing in Publication Data
A catalogue record for this book is available from the British Library

© 2019, Arc Humanities Press, Leeds

The author asserts her moral right to be identified as the author of this work.

Permission to use brief excerpts from this work in scholarly and educational works is hereby granted provided that the source is acknowledged. Any use of material in this work that is an exception or limitation covered by Article 5 of the European Union's Copyright Directive (2001/29/EC) or would be determined to be "fair use" under Section 107 of the U.S. Copyright Act September 2010 page 2 or that satisfies the conditions specified in Section 108 of the U.S. Copyright Act (17 USC §108, as revised by P.L. 94–553) does not require the Publisher's permission.

ISBN: 9781641893589
e-ISBN: 9781641893596

www.arc-humanities.org
Printed and bound by CPI Group (UK) Ltd, Croydon, CR0 4YY

CONTENTS

List of Illustrations vii

Abbreviations ix

Preface xi

Acknowledgements xiii

Introduction 1

Chapter 1. The Appearance of Tiron within Church Reform and Monastic
    Reform from the Eleventh Century 7

Chapter 2. The Tironensian Identity 15

Chapter 3. Bernard of Abbeville and Tiron's Foundation 33

Chapter 4. William of Poitiers and His Successors 47

Chapter 5. Expansion in France 73

Chapter 6. Expansion in the British Isles 127

Chapter 7. The Later History 167

Appendix 1. Comparison of the Papal Confirmations 181

Appendix 2. Disputes 187

Select Bibliography 197

Index of Tironensian Places 203

General Index 213

LIST OF ILLUSTRATIONS

Maps

Map 3.1. Bernard of Tiron's Travels 39

Map 4.1. Congregation of Tiron ca. 1119. 51

Map 5.1. Chartres-Blois. 76

Map 5.2. North France 93

Map 5.3. West France. 99

Map 5.4. South France 109

Map 5.5. East France 117

Map 5.6. Tiron and Daughter Abbeys' Dependent Priories. 124

Map 6.1. South Britain. 131

Map 6.2. Kelso Abbey. 142

Map 6.3. Arbroath Abbey 150

Map 6.4. Lindores Abbey 158

Map 6.5. Kilwinning Abbey 163

Tables

Table 5.1. Chartres-Blois. 77

Table 5.2. North France. 94

Table 5.3. West France. 100

Table 5.4. South France 110

Table 5.5. East France 119

Table 6.1. South Britain. 132

Table 6.2. Kelso Abbey..143

Table 6.3. Arbroath Abbey..151

Table 6.4. Lindores Abbey 159

Table 6.5. Kilwinning Abbey 164

ABBREVIATIONS

These publications and other citations given in a shortened form in footnotes are listed in their complete form in the Select Bibliography.

AASS	*Acta Sanctorum*
ADEL	Archives départementales d'Eure-et-Loir
BC	*Bullarium sacri ordinis Cluniacensis*
CNDC	*Cartulaire de Notre Dame de Chartres*
Cuninghame	Cuninghame, Topographized by Timothy Pont
ES	*Early Sources of Scottish History*
GC	*Gallia Christiana* (using the revised "Maurist" version). 13 vols. 1715–1785
IS-ADEL	*Inventaire sommaire des archives départementales antérieures à 1790. Eure-et-Loir*
Kelso Liber	*Liber S. Marie de Calchou, Registrum Cartarum Abbacie Tironensis de Kelso 1113–1567*
Lindores Cart.	*Chartulary of the Abbey of Lindores 1195–1479*
OV	Orderic Vitalis. *Historia ecclesiastica; The Ecclesiastical History of Orderic Vitalis*. Edited by M. Chibnall.
PL	Patrologia Latina (*Patrologiae Cursus Completus. Series Latina*). Edited by J. P. Migne.
Rule	Benedict of Monte Cassino, *The Rule of Saint Benedict*.
T	*Cartulaire de l'Abbaye de la Sainte-Trinité de Tiron*. Edited by Lucien Merlet. 2 vols. Chartres: Garnier, 1883. "T1" refers to the first volume and "T2" to the second.
VB	*Vita beati Bernardi Tironiensis autore Gaufredo Grosso.* Edited by Godefroy Henskens and Daniel Papebroch.
VB, trans. Cline	Geoffrey Grossus. *The Life of Blessed Bernard of Tiron*. Translated by Ruth Harwood Cline.
VCH Hampshire	*The Victoria History of Hampshire and the Isle of Wight*. Edited by William Page. Vol. 4. Victoria County History, 1911.
WCM	*Winchester College Muniments*. Compiled by Sheila Himsworth. 3 vols. Chichester: Phillimore, 1984.

PREFACE

THE JOURNEY TO Tiron began as an intellectual exercise. After I had translated the five romances of Chrétien de Troyes into English verse, I was asked to discern his identity. I postulated that the creator of the Arthurian legend was a gifted cleric, fond of hermits, and well-connected to the House of Blois-Champagne, whose members were prototypes for his characters. Chrétien's detailed descriptions of southern England in *Cligès* indicated that he had visited that country before settling in the court of Champagne. The genealogies of Thibaut II, count of Blois-Champagne, and his illustrious children show royal and episcopal connections in England and France. One genealogy included Thibaut II's natural son Hugh of Blois, a knight wounded in battle who became a monk of Tiron Abbey in the diocese of Chartres. Hugh's career took him to England under his uncle King Stephen, where he was abbot of St. Benet's Hulme (ca. 1141–1146/49) and of Chertsey outside London (1150–1155). Hugh returned to Champagne with his uncle, Henry, bishop of Winchester, upon the accession of Henry II, became prior of Notre-Dame d'Arable (1156) and ended his days as abbot of Lagny (1163–1171). Rich, lame, and castrated, Hugh of Blois seems a prototype for *Perceval*'s Fisher King. I speculated that Chrétien may have been associated with him and thus came to the attention of the literary court of his half-brother Henry, count of Champagne, and Countess Marie, the daughter of Louis VII and Eleanor of Aquitaine. Thus Chrétien de Troyes led me to Abbot Hugh, who led me to Tiron.

When I discussed my research with my Georgetown thesis advisers, Bennett Hill recalled that his mentor David Knowles considered Tiron much more important than Savigny among the twelfth-century reformed Benedictine orders that coexisted with Cîteaux. Thus the topic of my doctoral dissertation was the foundation and first century of the congregation of Tiron, which expanded from obscurity in the forests of the Perche to an international congregation with headquarters in Chartres and Paris and abbeys and priories in modern France and the British Isles. My research entailed translating *The Life of Blessed Bernard of Tiron* by Geoffrey Grossus, a retrospective tribute to its miracle-working and prophetic founder, written and recopied in the abbey's fine scriptorium. After my defence in 2000 my advisers and I concurred on polishing and publishing the *Life* and continuing research on the congregation. In pre-Internet days much travel ensued to libraries in Paris, Poitiers, London, Winchester, and Edinburgh, where librarians provided many nineteenth-century specialized studies of individual foundations.

Time and again I returned to mapping to discern a coherent pattern for my findings. Initial mapping of Tiron's abbeys and priories showed their areas of concentration: riverine expansion in France and coastal expansion in Britain. Scottish studies showed the importance of mapping churches, farms, and townhouses, which indicated their routes to towns and ports. The same approach applied to their properties in modern France.

Tiron expanded into hamlets, but modern electronic resources pinpointed the properties and showed their direction and proximity, usually 10–16 kilometres or a day's walk or hauling distance. The network of trade and communication was largely in place by 1147. Its configuration contextualized the charters describing acquisitions, obligations, and disputes. Tiron enjoyed royal favour and preceded Cîteaux in its expansion. The study of Tiron rebalances the modern perspective of the twelfth-century reformed orders by showing their variety and engagement through crafts and agriculture in the rise of towns and nation-building.

ACKNOWLEDGEMENTS

I AM DEEPLY indebted to my long-time friend and adviser Jo Ann Moran Cruz, Associate Professor of History, Georgetown University, who helped me make a career change from diplomatic translation to a doctorate in medieval history in 2000. Professors James Collins, Dennis McManus, and the late Bennett Hill, my Georgetown University advisers, and Theodore Evergates of McDaniel College, have provided twenty years of sustained interest, insights, and contextualization of my findings during my research on the congregation of Tiron. In particular James Collins noted the rank of Tiron's commendatory abbots and directed me to sixteenth-century sources that showed Tiron's wealth at that time. Giles Constable, professor emeritus at the School of Historical Studies, Institute for Advanced Study, Princeton, New Jersey, gave early guidance. All recognized the importance of the congregation of Tiron when it was widely regarded as obscure.

The librarians of Georgetown University, the Catholic University of America, the Library of Congress, the British Library, the Universities of Edinburgh and Glasgow, the Bibliothèque nationale, the Médiathèque François Mitterand, and the Centre d'études supérieures de civilisation médiévale of Poitiers were exceedingly helpful in providing early published research on individual foundations. Melissa Jones, Meg Oakley, and Megan Martinsen of Lauinger Library, Georgetown University have provided specialized expertise. John Hardacre and Suzanne Foster, the Winchester College archivists, gave outstanding advice concerning the charters of Tiron's local priories. In Chartres, Abbé Pierre Bizeau, the diocesan archivist, and Michel Thibault, the departmental archivist, and in Poitiers, Mirielle Jean, the departmental archivist, offered valuable guidance. In Edinburgh and Glasgow Geoffrey Barrow, Mark Dilworth, and Kenneth Varty guided my research on Tironensian abbeys and foundations in Scotland. Constance Berman, professor emerita of history, University of Iowa, contextualized Tiron's development into an order alongside the Cistercians. Constance Brittain Bouchard, distinguished professor of medieval history, University of Akron, Ohio, answered research questions and offered thoughtful criticisms. George Beech, professor emeritus of Western Michigan University, provided an original candidate for Abbot William of Poitiers. I am most grateful for their interest, time, and expertise.

The maps were designed and produced by Patrick Jones, Cartographer/Lab Manager of the Department of Geography and Earth Sciences, University of North Carolina at Charlotte.

This book is dedicated to my husband, William R. Cline, Senior Fellow Emeritus of the Peterson Institute for International Economics, with deepest love and gratitude. Bill has encouraged me throughout my graduate studies, research, and teaching. He has lent wise counsel and economic expertise to many problems I was unable to resolve. He has travelled with me to major British and continental European libraries but also driven into the countryside to Tiron's abbey buildings and ruins at Thiron-Gardais, Bois-Aubry, Asnières, and Ferrières, and to Kelso, Arbroath, and Lindores in Scotland. Together we have explored the premises and gotten the lay of the land. Bill has travelled the road to Tiron literally and figuratively and supported me unfailingly along the way.

INTRODUCTION

NO ONE TRAVELLING hundreds of kilometres in modern France and Britain to visit the abbatial church of Tiron and the scattered ruins and transformed remains of its abbeys, priories, and churches would immediately realize that in the twelfth and thirteenth centuries they all were part of the congregation of Tiron (ca. 1107–1109 to 1792–1794). This congregation, founded by a hermit some 40 kilometres southwest of Chartres, became noted for its crafts. The Tironensian order expanded to a large and prosperous congregation under a remarkable abbot, and formed a centralized "international" network of exchange and communication between France and the British Isles. The congregation of Tiron survived until the French Revolution and then passed into near-obscurity.[1]

Tiron has also passed into near-obscurity in accounts of twelfth-century monasticism. The congregation of Cluny (founded 910) with its wealth and elaborate liturgies was contrasted with the congregation of Cîteaux (founded 1098) and its emphasis on austerity and simplicity. Cîteaux absorbed a portion of the population growth, coalesced, and expanded into an enormous international congregation during the twelfth century, whereas Cluny was sometimes presented as being in decline. Cîteaux's willingness to accept marginal wasteland, its initial exclusion of women and its rejection of income sources like churches, tithes, rents, mills, or serfs[2] formed an image that was projected onto other reformed orders. Cistercian studies have proliferated and less attention has been paid to other reformed orders. More recent scholarship includes studies of the Carthusians, Gilbertines, Premonstratensians, Fontevraudians, Savignacs, and Tironensians, and revisions have been proposed regarding the Cistercians, which include the participation of women.[3] Published cartularies have made primary sources accessible to inform specialized studies. Studies of French religious foundations in Scotland reflect the "Auld Alliance" between Scotland and France to curb English expansionism and the Anglo-Normans' desire to extend educational and technological advances to a rural economy. They show the variety of the reformed orders, including marked differences from Cîteaux.

Whereas the contrast between Cluny and Cîteaux has dominated the study of reformed monasticism, Giles Constable observes that their differences have been exaggerated. The major dissimilarity was their spiritual orientation: Cluniac monks felt assured of their salvation and were spiritually and economically connected to their communities, particularly through intercessory prayer, whereas Cistercian monks sought individual salvation through direct spiritual experience, isolation from their communities, personal devotion, and imitation of Christ. Cluny was centralized, but Cluniac practices varied under the rule of individual abbots; varying Cistercian practices were

---

[1] Cline, "The Congregation of Tiron in the Twelfth Century," 520.
[2] Lawrence, *Medieval Monasticism*, 161.
[3] Berman, *The Cistercian Evolution*.

eventually unified by visitations and general chapters. Constable notes that Cluniac and Cistercian monasticism evolved over the twelfth century: "In practice, the two models had common roots and overlapped in many respects, and they followed parallel courses of development which tended to converge and to reduce the original contrast between them."[4] Tiron adopted the most fitting organizational features of Cluniac monasticism and the ascetic features of the reformed eremitical monasticism that preceded Cîteaux.

The historiography of twelfth-century monasticism has not given Tiron its due as an expansive reform movement comparable to and yet different from that of the Cistercians. Initially the Tironensians wore different habits and were known as the "grey monks" but as they grew wealthier their distinctiveness blurred in France and they were called Benedictines. Therefore Tiron was not closely studied. In twentieth-century historiography Tiron is sometimes grouped with Fontevraud and Savigny because their founders were colleagues. David Knowles lists the English and Welsh houses of Cluny and the new orders of Fontevraud, Grandmont, Cîteaux, and Tiron, and groups Tiron with Grandmont and Bec-Hellouin.[5] R.W. Southern concentrates on the Augustinian canons and the Cistercians in his study without mentioning Tiron, in *Western Society and the Church in the Middle Ages*. Lawrence mentions Tiron in his study of medieval monasticism, and Constable touches upon Tiron in his study of the twelfth-century reformation.[6] In England and Wales Savigny and Tiron are often considered together, with Tiron presented as a poor relation. In addition to at least twelve abbeys in France, Savigny founded fifteen abbeys in England and Wales before its merger with Cîteaux ca. 1147, in contrast to Tiron's single abbey of St. Dogmaels in Wales. In his study of medieval England, Colin Platt notes that Tiron founded "the merest handful of communities" and, like Savigny, made little impact on England.[7] To a considerable extent Tiron was overlooked in studies of reformed Benedictine monasticism.

Notwithstanding, Bennett D. Hill shared personal knowledge that David Knowles was well aware of Tiron and advised Hill that Tiron was much more important than Savigny.[8] Although smaller than Fontevraud and Savigny, Tiron was a prominent and prosperous monastic congregation with a fief in downtown Paris and an income comparable to some bishoprics. Tiron provides a more nuanced example of a reformed order with enduring royal and aristocratic patronage, long-distance travel, and involvement with trade and political developments on both sides of the English Channel.

Much of what we know about Bernard of Abbeville, abbot of Tiron, is derived from the foundation story, the *Vita B. Bernardi Tironiensis*, a retrospective work commissioned by and dedicated to Geoffrey II of Lèves, bishop of Chartres (r. 1116–1149). Its

---

[4] Constable, "From Cluny to Cîteaux," specifically 239.

[5] Knowles and Hadcock, "Houses of the Order of Tiron," *Medieval Religious Houses: England and Wales*, 102. Knowles, *The Religious Orders in England*, 2:165.

[6] Lawrence, *Medieval Monasticism*, 156. Constable, *The Reformation of the Twelfth Century*, 50–51 and 218.

[7] Platt, *The Abbeys and Priories of Medieval England*, 39.

[8] Personal communication from Bennett D. Hill to Ruth Harwood Cline and Jo Ann Hoeppner Moran-Cruz.

nucleus is a saint's life written ca. 1147 by a monk named Geoffrey Grossus, a contemporary of Bernard. The *Vita Bernardi*, however, is a compilation of many sources and several narrators, stitched together with its inconsistencies unresolved and its Latin unimproved. Geoffrey's autograph manuscript was copied (and probably expanded) by Jean Pignore de Vallea at the order of John II of Chartres, abbot of Tiron (r. 1277–1297). The lives of saints and the foundation stories of monasteries are inspirational genres. Historical facts and institutional memories are combined with miracle stories and literary borrowings from earlier hagiographies. Often failures are ignored or presented as setbacks. The introduction to my translation covers these points in greater detail.

Much of what we know about Tiron's history is derived from the documents compiled as a "cartulary" by Lucien Merlet (1827–1898), the archivist of the département of Eure et Loir. He dated and supplemented the charters in Tiron's twelfth-century manuscript cartulary with other archival materials and rearranged and published them chronologically.[9] The cartulary includes papal bulls, pancartes prepared for the bishop recording gifts made at different times, and charters or letters recording gifts, sales, leases, pawns, exchanges, confirmations thereof, and settlements of disputes. Information about the monks' charitable countergifts in kind to donors' relatives are particularly useful because they indicate such Tironensian specialties. Witnesses for both parties were carefully listed with surnames or place names to avert future disputes. Merlet and Theresa Webber concur that, after the contents list and the papal, episcopal, and comital acts, the manuscript cartulary was organized geographically: possessions near Tiron, in and around Chartres and Châteaudun, privileges of the rulers of England, Normandy, and Scotland, south of the Loire in Anjou and Poitou, acts by the kings of France, possessions in Capetian lands, possessions at Bacqueville in Normandy added in the fifteenth and sixteenth centuries, and finally a copy of the bull of Pope Eugenius III (r. 1145–1153) in 1147 and possessions in Ile-de-France, Maine, and Brittany.[10] Merlet openly acknowledges that the documentary record left by the monks did not include most of the original charters prior to 1428. In that year English troops burned the monastery, including the records in the scriptorium. The monks attempted to reconstitute their archives, but their forged charters added many additional liberties not in the originals.[11] Merlet included some obvious forgeries in the cartulary of Tiron, such as the fifteenth-century version of the foundation charter.[12] The charters Merlet included

---

[9] ADEL, H 1374. Merlet (ed.), *Cartulaire de l'Abbaye de la Sainte-Trinité de Tiron*, 2 vols. Hereafter T1 and T2.

[10] T1: cxiv. Thompson, "The Cartulary of the Monastery of Tiron," 70–72. Thompson provides important correctives for some of the problems created by Merlet's edition. Her critique partly relies on a paleographic analysis of the 325 charters in the cartulary by Theresa Webber, who dates the cartulary as begun in the 1140s and nearly completed in the 1160s.

[11] IS-ADEL, 8:157–58, H 1373 (1611), 1376–77 (1509). Lucien Merlet, "Chartes fausses de l'abbaye de Tiron," *Bibliothèque de l'Ecole des Chartes*, 3rd ser., 5 (1844): 516–27.

[12] T1:3–13, no. 1. The forgery's exemptions caused litigation with the chapter of Chartres 1505–1558, resolved by the chapter's discovery of the authentic charter. Guillaumin, "Thiron, son Abbaye," 31.

as genuine may have undergone some editing subsequent to their date of execution, but they are simple in language, plausible, and reliable enough for my focus on the material aspect of the order.[13]

Local historians have written extensively on Tiron. In his beautifully illustrated history of Tiron Denis Guillemin refers to the historiography of his predecessors and his access to private archives. He lists Arsène Vincent, *Recherches historiques sur le canton de Thiron-Gardais*, a 700-page manuscript, and the manuscript of André Guillaumin's research for his brochure *Thiron, son abbaye, son collège militaire* (1929).[14] In the 1959 article with the same title cited above, Guillaumin describes the *Manuscrit de Tiron* as a long manuscript that is a sort of chronicle begun in 1468, recopied in 1789, and continued and communicated to Arsène Vincent in 1848.[15] In France, the charters of Tiron Abbey and its daughter abbeys and priories are contained in the departmental archives of Eure-et-Loir and other departmental archives in pertinent regions.

In England, the Winchester College Muniments contain local charters and duplicates and certified copies of important Tironensian charters sent to Tiron's alien priories, which were sold to Winchester College in 1391. The Patent Rolls and Close Rolls also contain records of these alien priories and their tribulations during the Hundred Years' War. The Welsh abbey of St. Dogmaels was subject to Canterbury and included in English records. In Scotland, the cartularies of Kelso, Arbroath, and Lindores Abbeys have been published. Secondary regional and archaeological studies are available. Locally, persistent efforts were made in the nineteenth and twentieth centuries to preserve the memory of this lost congregation. Members of the Société Archéologique d'Eure-et-Loir inventoried and discussed the few treasures that survived the sacking and burning of the abbey in 1428 and 1562 and visited and reported on the history of its important priories.

Both chronology and topography are essential to understanding Tiron's expansion. A topographical reorganization of Merlet's edited charters shows the pattern of acquisition of property and assets and the disputes associated with the individual properties. For the purposes at issue here—the geographical range and economic outputs—the data provided by Merlet remain a solid foundation. Merlet was a distinguished archivist and geographer and a recipient of the Legion of Honour.[16] I rely mainly on the "*Dictionnaire topographique*" in appendix for the Latin and French names and the location of the properties. Mapping its abbeys and priories discloses its broad expansion pattern, but

---

[13] Chédeville, *Chartres et ses campagnes*, uses Merlet for his economic study of Chartres and the Perche.

[14] Guillemin, *Thiron, abbaye médiévale*, 119. Guillaumin, *Thiron, son abbaye, son collège militaire, guide*.

[15] Guillaumin, "Thiron, son Abbaye," 23.

[16] Lucien Merlet, *Dictionnaire topographique du département d'Eure-et-Loir, comprenant les noms de lieu anciens et moderne*, 4 vols. (Paris: Imp. 1861), listed in his obituary "Lucien Merlet," *Bibliothèque de l'école des chartes* 60 (1899): 267–80; available online at www.persee.fr/doc/bec_0373-6237_1899_num_60_1_452524. He also organized and published seven volumes of inventories of archives of Eure-et-Loir and organized hospital archives in Chartres and Châteaudun.

mapping its churches, farms, and houses discloses its network and routes. I have used INSEE, GPS, and web searches to assign each property modern geographic coordinates for mapping purposes. Tiron's properties are predominantly located in hamlets, suburbs, and border regions, and mapping them has been likened to pointillism. Once the dots are connected, however, the image of Tiron's expansion pattern emerges, showing that these properties were purposefully acquired to support, unite, and rule an important congregation. Since the extent of Tiron's holdings has never been fully mapped and its extensive economic network has not been documented and understood, this study is pathbreaking.

Bernard of Tiron's experience as a claustral prior and abbot of traditional Benedictine monasteries in Poitou led him to incorporate some of their organizational merits into his reformed congregation. Tiron's growth patterns resembled those of the other new orders, but its revised customs and practices drew many supporters and followers and contributed to the unique profile of the order. The congregation expanded into the equivalent of an international corporation. Tiron was associated with the expansion of trade and commerce and political developments in France and Britain.

This study begins with an overview of Tiron, its place in medieval monasticism, and its distinctiveness, then goes into specifics about the leading abbots and the geography of the expansion in France and the British Isles. It examines the extent to which the Tironensians participated in local communities as educators, healers, horticulturalists, craftsmen and builders, incorporated women, respected the dignity of manual labour, admitted artisans to church and chapter, and supported and profited from shipping and pilgrimages. It concludes with the later history of Tiron's prosperity and upheavals during periods of strong central government and warfare and the legacy of the congregation today. Tiron's distinctive features—royal and aristocratic favour, distances travelled, and products traded—create a more nuanced view of reformed monasticism than the traditional contrast of the congregations of Cluny and Cîteaux.

Chapter 1

THE APPEARANCE OF TIRON WITHIN CHURCH REFORM AND MONASTIC REFORM FROM THE ELEVENTH CENTURY

THE CONGREGATION OF Tiron was an integral part of the religious reformation of the eleventh and twelfth centuries. The sixth-century *Rule of Saint Benedict* (hereinafter the *Rule*)[1] was widely adopted because of its flexibility and balance of prayer and study, manual labour and rest, and Charlemagne (742–814) and his successor Louis the Pious (b. 778, r. 814–840) mandated Benedictine monasticism throughout Europe. The terrifying Viking, Magyar, and Saracen invasions of the ninth and tenth centuries nearly destroyed continental monasticism and separated the Celtic church from the religious developments in Rome. The devastated monasteries were impoverished by heavy wartime taxation, plundered by raiders, and awarded by local rulers to loyal laymen. Lawrence notes that before 900 "regular monastic observance had almost disappeared from western Gaul and England." The monasteries could be restored only when order was restored in the tenth and eleventh centuries. A revival of monasteries under the rule of Saint Benedict of Aniane (747–821) occurred in Aquitaine, Flanders, and Lorraine in the early tenth century.[2] Cluny, founded in 909 by Duke William I the Pious of Aquitaine (875–918), had an unusual charter that protected the monastery from laymen and bishops, ensured independent abbatial elections, and placed the monastery under the protection of the papacy.[3] Cluny became an "empire" of about a thousand monasteries with economic and social ties to their communities and donors.[4] Subordinate only to the pope and centralized under the authority of the abbot, Cluny was an "international" religious order.

By the mid-eleventh century royal leadership was established under Edward the Confessor (r. 1042–1066) and William I "the Conqueror" (r. 1066–1087) in England, Malcolm III "Canmore" (r. 1058–1093) in Scotland, and the Capetians: Robert II (r. 996–1031), Henry I (r. 1031–1060), and Philip I (1060–1108) in France. The reform of the church was also underway, challenging royal and imperial control. Pope Gregory VII (1073–1085) issued decrees against simony and clerical marriage (nicolaitism). He fought for the liberty of the church by forbidding lay investiture: the right of kings and lords to make (or sell) appointments to church offices. He upheld the freedom of the church, *libertas ecclesiae*: the freedom of churchmen to obey canon law and to have no control or interference by lay persons. The reform was carried out in various ways. Church councils were held throughout modern Europe and issued rulings against the

---

1 Benedict of Monte Cassino, *Rule of Saint Benedict*.

2 Lawrence, *Medieval Monasticism*, 73, 76–77.

3 *Testamentum Willelmi Pii*, in PL 133:846, 851.

4 Rosenwein, *To Be the Neighbor of Saint Peter*.

worst abuses. Local magnates divested themselves of church property. Bishoprics and abbacies were filled, by election, with unmarried candidates. These bishops and abbots undertook to reform the clergy in their charge, gradually imposing celibacy on priests and a closer observance of the *Rule* and monastic vows on monks. Many bishops promoted reform by introducing Cluniac monasticism in their dioceses. Toward the end of the century the papacy licensed itinerant preachers to preach against simony and clerical marriage in places where the local clergymen were unreceptive.

Benedictine monasteries were founded or refounded during this reform. The liturgy was expanded in the belief that prayers and masses said by a godly congregation of monks could atone for the sins of the living and the dead and would protect the kinship group, community, and realm against evil powers.[5] Cluny's wealth and patronage resulted in a monastic lifestyle of elaborate liturgies, masses, and prayers for benefactors and the dead, with manual labour performed by lay brothers. Cluny had vast holdings, and its third church, dedicated in 1095 by Pope Urban II (r. 1088–1099), was the largest church in Christendom until the basilica of Saint Peter was built in Rome 1506–1626. While a monk's poverty was supposed to be of the spirit, the Cluniac lifestyle was a generous interpretation of the *Rule*.

Some monastic houses built up enormous endowments, and decadence was always a threat to wealthy communities. In the eleventh and twelfth centuries a new type of hermit attacked the wealth of established monasticism in general and Cluny in particular. Drawn to a more primitive and austere monastic life, these hermits were inspired by the desert fathers of third-century Egypt and withdrew to the forests and islands of Europe, Their image as solitaries is misleading: hermits often lived in communities and with individuals in a teacher–disciple relationship. They sold their wares to the local community to support themselves. Since they were considered to be wise as well as holy, laypersons turned to them for counsel, medical advice, and dispute resolution. Hermits could accumulate money, and their cells and huts were inviolable, so some became involved in primitive banking operations such as money-lending and safe deposits of valuables. Total isolation was not necessarily a feature of hermit life.

The new hermit movement began in the late tenth century with the Italian reformed congregations of Camaldoli (1010) and Vallombrosa (1022), which combined eremitism (hermit life) and cenobitism (community life). The hermit movement spread to France around 1030 with the following of Herluin of Bec (r. ca. 1040–1078), continued with the foundation of La Chaise-Dieu in Auvergne by Saint Robert of Turlande (1001–1067) in 1043, and peaked in 1075–1125. Robert emphasized abandonment of material goods and worldly position, trust in divine Providence, strict abstinence, continual prayer, contemplation, and withdrawal from the world. In the late eleventh century important eremitical foundations were founded and expanded, such as Cîteaux, La Grande Chartreuse, and Tiron. The common goal of these hermit leaders was a return to a stricter observance of the *Rule*, with greater emphasis on manual labour and a simpler liturgy.

---

[5] Lawrence, *Medieval Monasticism*, 64.

There were three generations of reformers in the eleventh century. Bernard of Abbeville (ca. 1050–1116), founder of Tiron (1107–1109), belonged to the third generation together with Robert of Molesme (1028–1111), founder of Cîteaux (1098), Robert of Arbrissel (ca. 1045–1116), founder of Fontevraud (1101), and Vital of Mortain (ca. 1050–1122), founder of Savigny (1112). For some time these hermit preachers preferred an itinerant lifestyle with much local interaction to a settled and isolated way of life. Their world entailed more trade and communication than the world of their early eleventh-century predecessors. Donors supported the new eremitical movement to achieve reform while countering Cluniac claims to independence from overlords and bishops.

In her study of Western European religious communities, Henrietta Leyser notes that the founding and development of the twelfth-century eremitical orders followed a generalized pattern, although individual cases varied. First and foremost was a charismatic leader who fled lay society but accepted companions. Such future hermits who already belonged to a religious community might make an initial attempt to reform it. If dissatisfied, they might escape in secrecy rather than ask permission to leave. When these hermits settled down, they sought foundations in the wastelands outside settlements. Such wastelands were unencumbered by claims but could not sustain a large community, which needed fertile soil and a good water supply. The hermits also needed patrons as they cleared the land and erected their buildings. In hard times they foraged for food and preached to obtain support from often alarmed and hostile neighbours. They did not observe the monastic rule of enclosure and stability of house. Compared to regular Benedictine monasticism, they adopted a lifestyle of simpler liturgies and shortened prayers, more manual labour, coarse clothing, and an austere diet. Sometimes they were admired for their counsel, healing, and mediation skills.[6] Their holy lives and willingness to travel to preach against clerical marriage and simony induced the papacy to license them to travel and preach.

Bernard's foundation in the Perche region fit these criteria. The *Vita Bernardi* shows that his world was a wide one compared with these other hermits. A native of Picardy, he became a reforming Benedictine prior and abbot in Aquitaine and a hermit preacher in Maine, Brittany, and Normandy. He had also travelled to Cluny and Rome to defend the liberty of Saint-Cyprien of Poitiers. His final move was to the diocese of Chartres, where he founded Tiron Abbey. He travelled locally and to the royal court in Normandy and journeyed to Fontevraud and Blois shortly before his death. The contacts he made in his travels became future donors to his diverse early foundations.

Contemporary chroniclers followed Bernard's career.[7] The *Chronicle of Saint-Maixent* (751–1140) is particularly useful, because the writers include the dates of church councils and Easter. The chronicle states that Robert of Arbrissel died on February 25, 1116, and in the same year Bernard died on April 25 and was succeeded

---

[6] Leyser, *Hermits and the New Monasticism*, 20, 38–40. Henry Mayr-Harting, "Functions of a Twelfth-century Recluse," *History* 60 (1975): 337–52.

[7] Beck, *Saint-Bernard de Tiron*, 482–93, and Thompson, *The Monks of Tiron*, 12–19, provide Latin and French texts and citations for these primary sources.

by Tironensian monk Hugh, concurrently with the Fourth Lateran Council at Rome on March 6, 1116.[8] Accordingly, Bernard's death date has been corrected. Later chronicles mention Tiron with Fontevraud, Savigny, and Saint-Sulpice in Brittany. William of Newburgh (1136–1198) wrote of the foundations of the three memorable men, Robert of Arbrissel, Bernard, and Vital, in *Historia Rerum Anglicarum*, 1.15. The *Chronicle* of the Cistercian Alberic of Trois-Fontaines in Châlons-sur-Marne (d. post-1252) describes Vital of Savigny and the founders of Fontevraud, Saint-Sulpice-des-Bois-de-Rennes (Ralph of la Futaye, ca. 1096), and Tiron as four hermits from Aquitaine, an obvious error, s.a. 1110. In his chronicle s.a. 1104 Robert of Auxerre (ca. 1156–1212), a monk of Saint-Marien-d'Auxerre in Burgundy, commended Robert, Ralph, Vital, and Bernard for their asceticism, learning, and piety and situated their foundations in Aquitaine, Brittany, Normandy, and Francia respectively. Bernard and Tiron were mentioned by other contemporary writers. Ivo, bishop of Chartres (ca. 1040–December 23, 1115), notes the consecration of the cemetery at Tiron ca. 1114 in *epistola* 283. William of Malmesbury (ca. 1095/96–ca. 1143) mentions Robert of Arbrissel and Bernard in *De Gestis Regum Anglorum* (1125) describing Tiron at that time as a monastery more celebrated for the piety and number of the monks than for the splendour and extent of its riches. Bernard of Clairvaux (ca. 1090–1153) numbers the Tironensians among the Camaldolense, Vallombrosians, Carthusians, Cluniacs, brethren of Marmoutier, Cistercians, and the brethren of Caen and Savigny in 1131–1132.[9] Orderic Vitalis (1075–1142) states erroneously that Bernard was abbot of the nearby Poitevin abbey of Quinsay.[10] In 1153 in his *Tractatus* Robert of Torigny (ca. 1110–1186) describes Bernard, Robert of Arbrissel, and Vital of Savigny as three associates in religion and names their successors, including Tiron's William of Poitiers (r. 1119–ca. 1150/60).[11] They provide reliable information about Tiron and its founder. Other primary sources involve Bernard of Tiron's cohort group. They include the *vitae* of Robert of Arbrissel by Baudri of Dol and of Vital of Savigny by Stephen of Fougères. Both Bernard and his first abbot, Renaud of Saint-Cyprien of Poitiers (r. November 1073–May 23, 1100), are mentioned in the charters of Saint-Cyprien.[12] The *Chronicle of Melrose* (735–1270) describes the foundation of Tiron and names Ralph and William as the abbots of Selkirk

---

[8] *La Chronique de Saint-Maixent*, ed. Jean Verdon (Paris: Belles Lettres, 1979), 170–74, 180–81, 184–87. It accurately records the death of Abbot Renaud of Saint-Cyprien, Bernard's brief abbacy at Saint-Cyprien in 1100, the November 1100 date of the Council of Poitiers, and the construction of Tiron with one hundred monks in 1107. T1:28–29, no. 14 (Hugh).

[9] Bernard of Clairvaux, *Epistolae*, in *Recueil des historiens des Gaules et de la France*, ed. Brial, 15:556, no. 126.

[10] OV, 8.3.448, 4:328–29. Here and afterwards I provide the book and chapter reference from the *Historia ecclesiastica* of Orderic Vitalis and then the volume and page(s) from the edition by Chibnall.

[11] Robert of Torigny, *Tractatus de immutatione ordinis monachorum*, in *Recueil des historiens des Gaules et de la France*, ed. Bouquet, 14:381–89 at 381–82.

[12] *Cartulaire de l'Abbaye de Saint-Cyprien de Poitiers*, ed. Rédet, 45, no. 43 and 89, no. 123 (Bernard).

who succeeded Bernard.[13] These monastic reformers were associates in life and associated in the memory of contemporaries.

At that time the Perche was a heavily forested region and metallurgical centre, west of the Chartrain wheat fields. Tiron was initially founded in an isolated, swampy forest, and the monks and lay brothers cleared land, created ponds, grew crops, and raised livestock. The impoverished community accepted any income source: monetary gifts, tithes, rents in cash or in kind, moveable property (livestock and human dependants), and immovable property (meadows, vineyards, orchards, houses, mills, market stalls, and ovens). When a famine drove skilled craftsmen to shelter in his remote monastery, Bernard accepted them, organized them in work areas supervised by subpriors, and sold their wares locally and in Chartres. Constance H. Berman notes that this combination of manual labour practices is unlike any other reformed monastic congregation, as welcoming craftsmen into the community was highly unusual.[14]

While many monasteries declined to engage in trade, for Tiron it eventually became a primary focal point, and many of its foundations were acquired to facilitate commercial activities. Bernard's holiness and prophetic gifts made a deep impression on Henry I, king of England and duke of Normandy (r. 1100–1135), and a royal grant of exemption from tolls in Normandy and England was important to Tiron's engagement in trade. Before Bernard's death in 1116, Tiron Abbey established priories north and south of the Loire and alien foundations: the priory of Hamble on the Southampton Water; the future abbey of St. Dogmaels on the Welsh coast; Selkirk Abbey in the Scottish Borders; and the future abbey of Joug-Dieu on the border of Beaujolais south of Burgundy on the Saône near the Rhône. Tiron had local priories and a few others in Normandy and the Beauce, but only limited contact with Ile-de-France.

Tiron's expansion pattern and involvement in trade were exceptional but not unique. A monastery named La Sauve Majeure was founded by 1090 east of Bordeaux, with priories in northern France, Gascony, Spain, and Britain. La Sauve Majeure emulated Cluny but had many features in common with the future congregation of Cîteaux. Charles Higounet used the technique of mapping its foundations to illustrate its expansion. Its monks held serfs, ran markets, built mills, owned townhouses in ports, and protected women.[15] Philip C. Adamo describes the Caulite order, which founded its mother house, Val-des-Choux, in northwest Burgundy in 1193. It expanded into France and further into Scotland, the Netherlands, and possibly Iberia. With land scarce, the Caulites attempted unsuccessfully to live on the abovementioned rents and income sources, but they soon acquired and built up real estate holdings. Like Tiron, the choir monks lived with the lay brothers, whereas the Cistercians lived apart from their manual labourers.[16]

---

13 *Early Sources of Scottish History*, 160, citing the *Chronicle of Melrose*, s.a. 1115.

14 Personal communication with Constance H. Berman, December 15, 2015.

15 *Grand Cartulaire de la Sauve Majeure*, ed. Charles Higounet and Arlette Higounet-Nadal, with Nicole de Peña, 2 vols. (Bordeaux: Fédération Historique du Sud-Ouest, Institut d'Histoire, Université de Bordeaux III, 1996).

16 Adamo, *New Monks in Old Habits*, 3–5, 70–92.

Recent studies document Cistercian engagement in trade in the late twelfth and early thirteenth centuries with clear parallels to the Tironensian engagement in the early twelfth century.[17] The acquisition patterns and trade routes are clearer in mountainous Wales and Scotland, where Celtic abbeys had a broader social and economic role, than they are in lowland France, which was at a later stage of economic development. Specialization in commodities like wheat and wool led to economies of scale through grange agriculture, vertical integration through mills and urban ovens, port properties for exports, and exemptions from taxes and tolls. The Cistercians became more entrepreneurial over the course of the twelfth century but Tiron engaged in trade from its foundation because of its poverty, isolation, and numerous artisans.

The *Vita Bernardi* portrays Bernard as a charismatic spiritual leader, a healer, a clairvoyant, a confessor to the aristocracy and a favourite of bishops. His erudition and abilities shaped the congregation of Tiron, and after his death his personality resonated for a long time. Andreas of Fontevraud wrote in the *Second Life of Robert of Arbrissel* ca. 1120 that Bernard's praises were sung in all the churches of Gaul.[18] Yet he was soon eclipsed by his namesake Bernard of Clairvaux. Despite Tiron's exponential growth in the first half of the twelfth century, it was overtaken by other religious orders, particularly Cîteaux. In like manner, the Cistercians have overtaken the collective historical memory, nearly erasing the memory of the Tironensians. Today Bernard's cult is local, but the order of Tiron encompassed modern France and the British Isles. During the course of the twelfth century Tiron became a centralized international congregation with eight or more dependent abbeys in modern France, four abbeys in Scotland, one abbey in Wales, and over a hundred priories. As such it developed a network of close communication over a large geographical area that would become the Angevin Empire and, later, the core of the French nation. This study has endeavoured to recapture the history, extent, importance, and uniqueness of Tiron and its network.

The congregation of Tiron was not comprehensively served by existing scholarship[19] until Bernard Beck published *Saint-Bernard de Tiron: l'ermite, le moine et le monde* and Kathleen Thompson published *The Monks of Tiron: A Monastic Community and Religious Reform in the Twelfth Century*. Beck provides valuable insights into the holy life of Tiron's founder, maps the abbeys and priories, and includes primary sources with translations. Thompson carefully analyzes the composition of the Latin life of the founder and the manuscript and published versions of the Tironensian cartulary. My English translation of the *Life of Blessed Bernard of Tiron* by Geoffrey Grossus and this study of Tiron's participation in the twelfth-century economy of the Angevin Empire are extensions of my

---

17 Burton and Kerr, *The Cistercians in the Middle Ages*. Also *Monastic Wales: New Approaches*, ed. Burton and Stöber.

18 Andreas of Fontevraud, *Vita Altera* of Robert of Arbrissel, 15, AASS, Feb. 3:0611A: "[...] *Abbas Bernardus bonorum omnium memoria dignus, cuius laus usque hodie per omnes Galliae Ecclesias.*"

19 In addition to the books and articles by André Guillaumin and Denis Guillemin, see Jacques de Bascher, "La 'Vita' de Saint Bernard" and "L'abbaye et l'ordre de Tiron," and Cabanes and Lagrange, *Tiron et Molineuf.*

doctoral dissertation in 2000.[20] I focus on the order of Tiron's rightful place as an important monastic congregation alongside the Cluniac and newer Cistercian foundations.

In comparison with Cluny's initial expansion under Abbot Mayeul (b. ca. 906, r. 954–994), which was concentrated in Burgundy and Provence, and Cîteaux's initial expansion mainly in Burgundy,[21] the earliest Tironensian properties were widely scattered. Bernard consented to establish these distant foundations because of their illustrious royal and noble patrons. These families and kinship groups were motivated by piety but were also funding a start-up group of experts in key crafts and new technologies in rural towns and investing in capital projects such as mills and ovens. To ensure the viability of his new foundations, Bernard astutely obtained land, woodland, and water rights and accepted all income sources for each priory he founded before he sent out monks from his community.[22] Following Cluny's organizational model, Bernard chose a qualified Tironensian monk as prior, relying on him to uphold Tiron's standards while adapting to the particular circumstances of the new location. These far-flung priories were united by their loving memory of Bernard, were headed by his disciples, and often were sponsored by the extensive kinship group of Henry I, king of England.

Bernard's successor William of Poitiers acquired the properties that linked them into a centralized network by the mid-twelfth century. The Tironensians acquired much property purposefully through long-term planning and patient negotiation. Their objectives were to create safe routes for riding and hauling, to encircle towns and supply urban markets, to consolidate and cluster properties for economies of scale in farming, to obtain waterfront property for trading, milling, and stock-raising, to support pilgrims, and to obtain urban and port residences to supervise entrepreneurial and trade activities. Bishops and magnates donated property to create a network that would be useful for their own purposes.

Florian Mazel describes the delimitation of medieval space into religious territories called dioceses ruled by bishops with elected successors and secular territories called counties or fiefs ruled by magnates and transferred by inheritance and warfare. The territories overlapped but were not identical, and lay and religious leaders were entitled to tithes and other feudal dues. Bishops defended their diocesan boundaries by reasserting control over churches under lay ownership, which they transferred to monastic foundations also under their control thereby delimiting their diocesan boundaries. For a bishop the foundation of a new monastery was the establishment of a new *seigneurie*.[23] Tiron was unquestionably in the diocese of Chartres, but it was on the eastern boundary of the county of its patron Rotrou II, count of the Perche (r. 1099–1144), 14 kilometres

---

20 VB in AASS for April 2: Apr. 2:0222C–55A (citations from the online Acta Sanctorum Database with reference to the book and chapter of the text first). VB, trans. Cline, xi.

21 Berman, *The Cistercian Evolution*, 99.

22 Burton and Kerr, *The Cistercians in the Middle Ages*, 160, describe the portfolio of holding and rights a house required for survival and growth, including urban property to facilitate trade. Unlike Tiron, "Early Cistercian legislation prohibited the acquisition of spiritualities (churches and tithes), vils or villeins as well as the rents from mills, ovens and other assets."

23 Mazel, *L'évêque et le territoire*, 256–65.

from his seat at Nogent-le-Rotrou. Tiron Abbey delimited his territory and was an outpost of his authority. His family profited from Tiron's improvements and from the network Tiron developed. Other magnates established Tironensian foundations on land they intended their younger sons to control as priors. Tiron raised and educated those sons as monks before their appointments by Tiron's annual general chapter.

Tiron Abbey was founded a decade after the foundation of Cîteaux in 1098. Both abbeys were located far from population centres and initially supported themselves through agriculture. Both abbeys suffered the famine of 1109–1112 with different outcomes. Cîteaux's membership declined, while Tiron's membership increased because of an influx of displaced persons including craftsmen. Cîteaux revived because of the entry of Bernard of Clairvaux and his relations. His spiritual leadership and that of Stephen Harding (r. 1110–1133, d. 1134) won royal and noble donors. Tiron expanded when Bernard of Tiron suddenly won royal and noble recognition through his spirituality and prophetic gifts ca. 1114. Cîteaux's initial foundations were nearer to the motherhouse. Tiron's patrons established early foundations near and far in modern France and Britain. The Cistercians undercut Tiron by preferring isolation and accepting poorer land while initially rejecting spiritualities and income sources like ovens and mills for which the Tironenisans negotiated. The Tironensians preferred communication and held their own through entrepreneurship. They expanded into hamlets and border regions, sought land near rivers and roads, and turned to non-agricultural income sources: shipping, construction, technology, and trade, including markets and fairs. They accepted income sources from churches and tithes, endowments, and fiscal exemptions. Both congregations brought marginal land into productivity. The Tironensians won patronage by bringing skills and crafts to rural areas whereas the Cistercians were slower to participate in the twelfth-century urban economy. As Bernard of Clairvaux assumed leadership in the 1120s and expanded the number of foundations following the practices of Cîteaux throughout Europe and Britain, his contemporary Abbot William of Tiron created a network linking Tironensian foundations in France and the British Isles. Half a century earlier than Cîteaux, he established centralized rule though annual general chapters and subordinated daughter abbeys to the mother house. As Saint Bernard of Clairvaux eclipsed Blessed Bernard of Tiron, so the Cistercian congregation eclipsed the Tironensian congregation in size and in recognition. Over the course of the twelfth century the Cistercians became more engaged in the urban economy, particularly grange agriculture and the wool trade, but the Tironensians were engaged therein from their foundation. The congregation of Tiron originally flourished and then survived for almost seven centuries alongside Cluny and Cîteaux, incorporating features of both forms of monastic life, but its existence and achievements have not been widely recognized. Its patterns of expansion in its first century contribute significantly to our understanding of the interactions of the reformed Benedictine congregations in Britain and France.

Chapter 2

THE TIRONENSIAN IDENTITY

THE TIRONENSIANS WERE one of the earliest monastic orders to become immersed in the shift from an agricultural economy to an urban economy during the Renaissance of the twelfth century. When Tiron was founded, most monasteries were supported by tithes on the produce of their farms, and their landed endowment shaped their religious identity and their social relations with the community. The established Benedictine monasteries owned the prime real estate and the reformed orders accepted poorer and marginal land. The *locus amoenus* topos in their foundation legends often was a desert they had transformed into a new Eden, although sometimes charters indicate earlier inhabitation and cultivation.[1] Tiron's first foundation at Thiron-Brunelles was truly a desert in an isolated forest on a tract unsuited to growing grain or grapes, staples of monastic life. Nonetheless the forest provided wood for heat and construction, grazing and pannage for livestock, and fur and hides for leather. The stream and ponds provided waterpower, and nearby metallurgy deposits provided iron. The monks built workrooms before they began clearing land for fields. A famine 1109–1112 drove displaced persons to shelter in their community, including skilled agricultural workers and urban craftsmen. Lacking an agricultural base, Tiron produced and marketed artisanal goods as a matter of survival. Refoundation on a farm in Thiron-Gardais improved their food situation, but the artisans were settled members of the community. Most monasteries had a support group of craftsmen, but Tiron had cadres of bakers, smiths, carpenters, masons, and husbandmen. Their collective manpower and expertise led to surpluses that found outlets in Chartres and then through urban trading networks. Their participation in trade was exceptionally early and intrinsic to their identity.

Some indication of Tiron's involvement in trade is contained in the written sources, particularly its financial exemptions, but also in property maps. Riders and carters planned carefully to ensure shelter overnight. A traveller who covered over 15 kilometres would seek shelter instead of returning home the same day. The average day's ride for a monastic official was 25 kilometres out, 29 kilometres home.[2] Tiron adopted spacing for the purposes of centralization similar to the spacing Cîteaux adopted as it expanded and experienced ownership and boundary problems.[3] Tiron's spacing frequently ranged within 10–16 kilometres, a day's journey for walking or carting. The calculations of the location and distances are crucial support for my discovery that much of the congregation

---

[1] Berman, *Medieval Agriculture*, 7, 12.

[2] Vernon, *Travel in the Middle Ages*, 2, 8.

[3] Bouchard, *Holy Entrepreneurs*, 135, citing *Statuta Capitulorum generalium Ordinis Cisterciensis ab anno 1116 ad annum 1786*, ed. J. M. Canivez, 8 vols. (Leuven: Bureau de la Revue d'histoire ecclásiastique, 1933–1941), 1:20, no. 32. The required spacing for Cistercian properties was two to three leagues or 10 to 14 kilometres to avoid disputes.

was connected by a network of properties a day's journey (10–16 kilometres) or ride (25–30 kilometres) apart, most purposefully acquired before 1147.

The Tironensian identity and patterns of development are clearest in their Scottish abbeys of Kelso, Arbroath, Lindores, and Kilwinning. Twelfth-century Scotland had a smaller population and fewer towns than France and was at an earlier stage of development. France's roads covered a terrain with many plains and gently rolling hills; Scotland's roads ran between highlands, islands, and estuaries, so communication routes were clearer. Richard Oram notes that monastic estates were often part of extensive networks established for communication and discipline but were also among "the most highly developed intelligence-gathering systems in the pre-Modern age and brought them into regular communication with the commercial systems of mainland Europe." The monks were agricultural entrepreneurs whose sophisticated, systematic, and productive exploitation of their estates became a model for the Scottish nobility. They became property speculators earning income from their burgh-based properties and contributing to town development. They sold their surpluses, traded, and contributed to the economic development undertaken by David I (b. ca. 1084, Prince of the Cumbrians 1113–1124, by marriage earl of Huntingdon, king of Scotland 1124–1153, hereafter David I).[4]

Alistair Moffat and K. J. Stringer analyze the economic purposes for the properties of Kelso and Lindores.[5] Their founders endowed both abbeys with the property their monks required to travel safely to certain ports and burghs and lodge overnight. Tofts and crofts (townhouses with outbuildings and small gardens), churches with rectories or vicarages, and farms and granges provided food, shelter, and income for travelling monks engaged in trade or other business in towns. Moffat and Stringer find regional, not random, patterns for the abbey's endowments and acquisitions.

When this method is applied to Tiron's abbeys, priories, churches, and significant farms, development patterns emerge in Britain and France that are strikingly similar to those in Scotland. The Scottish abbeys were well endowed at their founding with strategic properties that the French abbeys negotiated to acquire subsequently. Tiron's Scottish connection was formed when William of Poitiers, a Tironensian monk and future abbot of Tiron, travelled north with David I to become abbot of Selkirk ca. 1117–1119. Thus William had personal experience with the endowment of property and income that made Selkirk prosperous from its foundation, and he incorporated features of this Scottish model into Tiron's expansion during his abbacy until 1150/1160. Unlike Selkirk, Tiron was not endowed with strategic properties. Bernard was given a few, and William acquired many more to construct the Tironensian network by the mid-twelfth century.

While initially Tiron's properties may have been randomly acquired through the benevolence of pious donors, my findings show that, when churches and important

---

4 Oram, *David I*, 162.

5 Alistair Moffat analyzes the economic purposes for the properties in the foundation charter of Kelso Abbey, and K. J. Stringer does a similar analysis for Lindores Abbey. See Moffat, *Kelsae, A History of Kelso from Earliest Times*, 11–21, and Stringer, *Earl David of Huntingdon*, 91–103.

farms and properties are mapped with priories and abbeys, and land, water, trade, and pilgrim routes are considered, by the mid-twelfth century the economic rationale underlying the expansion pattern was the creation of a coherent network for trade and communication. Tiron's network of properties was densest in the centre with strands of linear expansion toward major towns and ports. In modern Eure-et-Loir and northern Loir-et-Cher, the region controlled by the count of Blois and Chartres, the community at Tiron consolidated itself at Thiron-Gardais near Nogent-le-Rotrou, established a priory at Chartres and connections in Châteaudun, and acquired closely spaced farms, priories, and churches from the Perche to the Beauce and Blois. From that core Tiron expanded along trade and pilgrimage routes: north on or near the Seine toward Paris, Normandy, and the Channel; west into Brittany and Anjou, and along the Loire to Nantes and the Atlantic; south into Poitou and Beaujolais with an abbey near the Rhône connecting Germany with Marseilles; and east on Seine tributaries into Ile-de-France, Paris, Champagne, and Burgundy. In Britain, Tiron had no holdings in London but many in the diocese of Winchester on the Southampton Water. Tiron expanded along the Channel and Pembrokeshire coasts, the Welsh border, and, ultimately, Ireland. In Scotland Tiron expanded into Scottish Cumbria south of Edinburgh and Glasgow and, after 1178, north on the Firth of Tay and Moray Firth in the directions of Dundee, Aberdeen, and Banff. Tiron's hauled and shipped goods were often exempt from taxes, tolls, and customs in the British Isles, Normandy, and Anjou. Such detailed mapping leads to an appreciation of the economic power of Tiron and its participation in the rise of towns in the twelfth century.

Tiron had other special features, many a legacy of its founder. Bernard's erudition, travels, administrative ability, craftsmanship, healing miracles, and prophetic gifts resonated for a century. He established the Tironensian identity: a simple rule with close supervision, shortened liturgy, veneration of Mary, acceptance of women, inclusion of hermits, expertise in education and medicine, respect for the dignity of labour, skilled craftsmanship, extension of hospitality, exceptional mobility, and engagement in trade. Unlike the older Benedictine congregations with land endowments, Tiron was supported initially by the skills of its monks and lay brethren. Bernard's reputation for holiness won the support of local magnates and bishops and of Louis VI, king of France (b. 1081, r. 1098–1137), Henry I of England, and their kinship groups, which was crucial to Tiron's expansion.

Bernard had been an abbot and claustral prior, and monastic life at Tiron had distinctive features but followed the *Rule*. Discerned from the *Vita Bernardi*, the rule of Tiron emulated the early church. The Egyptian Pachomius (ca. 292–346), formerly a Roman army conscript, founded a desert community supported by trade in Tabennesis on the upper Nile. He organized groups of twenty monks by crafts under priors in houses laid out like army camps and marketed their linen, mats, and baskets in Alexandria.[6] Food was rationed, supplies were inventoried, and the leaders met to balance accounts at Easter and in August. The *Vita Bernardi*'s transgendered citations of *Epistola* 108 "Ad Eustochium" (404 A.D.) by Saint Jerome (b. 340/342, d. 420) indicates familiarity with

---

6 *S. Eusebii Hieronymi Stridonensis Presbyteri Translatio Latina Regulae Sancti Pachomii*, PL 23:0061–99, specifically 0064B–C.

the precepts established by Saint Paula (347–404) for her community in Bethlehem.[7] Tiron's emphasis on crafts and abstinence in food and drink initially resulted from extreme poverty. Bernard reluctantly shortened the schedule of psalms to allow more time for manual labour.[8] As abbot he ate and slept with the monks and refused special treatment. Unlike the Cistercians who maintained class distinctions to the point of lay revolt, Bernard ended his experimentation with the separation of choir monks and lay brethren by ordering the latter's re-inclusion in the liturgy and chapter meetings on his deathbed. The rule of Tiron was simple but enforced by close supervision. Although the usual problems with lay brothers were drinking and violence, the *Vita Bernardi* contains many accounts of thefts. Subpriors monitored the workrooms to enforce the rule of silence except for minimal work-related communication,[9] and undoubtedly they monitored supplies, tools, and marketable goods. Bernard made personal rounds of inspection day and night, circulating without a lamp.[10] Nonetheless he was reluctant to burden his monks with the many regulations and traditions he had enforced as claustral prior in Poitou, and he limited the rules to the essentials, quoting Romans 4:15, "Where there is no law, there is no transgression."[11]

Although the sixteenth-century schedule may not necessarily reflect that of the twelfth century, there are references to Tiron having a rule with an adjustment of the canonical hours to provide for blocks of daylight work time. Guillaumin describes the Tironensian schedule before it began to be ruled by commendatory abbots in 1551. The monks rose at 2 a.m. for the recitation of the office of the Holy Virgin, a short meditation and Matins until 4.30 a.m., and the office of the dead for benefactors, followed by a period of rest or reading until Prime at 5.30 a.m. The abbot or prior gave instructions in chapter at 6.30 a.m. Then the monks began woodwork, sculpture, copying, binding, or gardening until the noon meal, followed by a short prayer, and reading. The monks returned to work at 1 p.m. to work until they chanted None and Vespers before their evening collation. Afterward pious reading in chapter and Compline followed by meditation in church, the monks retired at 8.30 p.m. in summer and at 7.00 p.m. in winter. Guillaumin does not indicate whether or when Tierce and Sext were chanted and a daily mass was celebrated. At that later era the *opus Dei* was consolidated into two periods before sunrise and at sunset.[12] Merlet describes a similarly consolidated schedule for Tiron's school, established in 1630.[13]

---

7 Cline, "*Mutatis Mutandis*: Borrowings from Jerome's Letter to Eustochium and Others."
8 VB, 9.78, AASS, Apr. 2:0240F; VB, trans. Cline, 84.
9 VB, 10.90, AASS, Apr. 2:0244A; VB, trans. Cline, 95.
10 VB, 11.91, AASS, Apr. 2:0244D; VB, trans. Cline, 97.
11 VB, 12.113, AASS, Apr. 2:0249C–D; VB, trans. Cline, 118–19.
12 Guillaumin, "Thiron, son Abbaye," 32. The midday meal consisted of soup, eggs or fish, vegetables, and fruit, without oil or butter on fast days. Guests were served with the monks' fare at the abbot's table. The monks slept fully clothed on a pallet with a straw-filled pillow and coverlet.
13 T1:lxxvii–lxxxii. The students rose around 5.30 a.m. for prayers and instructive reading, heard mass at 7 a.m., began classes at 8 a.m. to 11.30 a.m. with a fifteen-minute break, had their midday

Bernard's personal vision of Mary placed Tiron in the vanguard of thirteenth-century Mariology. Devotion to the Virgin has very ancient roots, but from the year 1000 major churches in Europe began to be dedicated to Mary. Charlemagne gave Chartres Cathedral ca. 876 the relic called the Sancta Camisa, a tunic worn by Mary at Christ's birth, and the town became an important pilgrimage centre for her devotees. The Tironensians believed that the Virgin appeared personally to Bernard at a turning point in his life at Saint-Savin ca. 1097,[14] and he felt lifelong devotion to the Mother of God. When he refounded Tiron Abbey under the protection of the chapter of Chartres and its patroness in 1114, he instituted a special daily mass called La Mère-Dieu that was celebrated with great solemnity for centuries until Tiron Abbey was closed.[15] Tiron may have influenced Bernard of Clairvaux, who held Mary in special devotion, and the Cistercians, who stipulated that all their churches were to be dedicated to Mary. Tiron venerated Mary more than a century before her cult flowered with the construction of the gothic cathedrals of Notre-Dame-de-Paris and Notre-Dame-de-Chartres.

The rule of Tiron appealed to hermits who, as they aged and perceived the benefits of community support, joined the congregation with their disciples and property. Tiron also incorporated hermitages by establishing foundations on sites occupied by holy men in France and Britain. The new foundation acquired both the land and the cult of the local saint and continued to be a place of pilgrimage.[16] East of Le Mans, a hermit gave land to the monks of the abbey of Le Gué-de-Launay ca. 1135.[17] South of the Loire, the abbey of Bois-Aubry, among the eremitical foundations established in Touraine 1110–1120, was originally a cell named Saint-Michel-de-Luzé inhabited by a hermit priest.[18] The abbey of Le Tronchet in Brittany replaced a dwelling for the tenth-century hermit and his disciples.[19] In Northumberland, Kelso Abbey acquired a hermitage named Merchingley in 1168.[20] In Wales, the abbey of St. Dogmaels was built on the site of a sixth-century hermitage.[21] Pyro, the first abbot of Caldey, was a sixth-century hermit who retired to the

---

meal with readings and recreation 11.30 a.m. until 1 p.m., study hall until 2 p.m., classes until 4.15 p.m., a collation until 4.30 p.m., studies until 5.30 p.m., supper and reading until 7 p.m., study and prayer, 8.30 p.m. bedtime. Their monk instructors fitted the *opus Dei* into this schedule.

14 VB, 2:18, AASS, Apr. 2:0227A–B; trans. Cline, 24–25; ibid., 9:78, AASS, Apr. 2:0240F, trans. Cline, 84.

15 T1:xiii.

16 In the Vexin, the hermitage of Saint Adjutor of Vernon (ca. 1170–1131) became the priory of La-Madeleine-sur-Seine, founded before 1131. Other French foundations associated with hermits included the priories of Moussay, Saint-Sulpice-en-Pail, Danguer Guer, and the church of Saint-George-de-Peglait.

17 T1:235–36, no. 207.

18 Gilbert, "Une abbaye tironienne en Touraine," 143. T1:240–41, no. 213 (ca. 1135); ibid., 249–50, no. 221 (1138).

19 Rocher and Trevinal, "Notre-Dame du Tronchet," 299nn2–3.

20 Cowan and Easson, *Medieval Religious Houses: Scotland*.

21 Pritchard, *The History of St. Dogmael's Abbey*, 13.

island with a small community.[22] Kilwinning Abbey was founded on the site of the hermitage of Saint Winning, an eighth-century Irish missionary. The Scottish Célidé lived both as solitaries with disciples and as secular priests with prebends and families living under an abbot. Many were absorbed into Tironensian monasteries, particularly if their female dependants were allowed to reside therein. Lindores Abbey was an early religious settlement of Célidé origin.[23] King William I "the Lion" (r. 1165–1214) gave the church of Abernethy with half its tithes to Arbroath Abbey; the remaining tithes were reserved for the Célidé of Abernethy and their abbot.[24] The king granted Arbroath custody of a great symbol of the Célidé: the Brec Bennoch (holy banner) of Saint Columba (521–597) with the lands of Forglen held by its guardian.[25] The Célidé were sufficiently weakened for the king to entrust a national treasure to the new Tironensian abbey, thereby displacing an old eremitical order by a new one. Tiron's incorporation of marginal religious groups like hermitages regularized their status within Benedictine monasticism.

Acceptance of women was problematic for monks vowed to celibacy, and in practical terms they were considered dependent, demanding, and distracting. Nonetheless, men accepted the responsibility of protecting the weaker sex. During a famine Bernard fed and sheltered families at Tiron, including infants and nursing mothers.[26] He had a good relationship with his overlord Adela, countess of Blois and Chartres (1067/1068–1137), sister of Henry I of England, who offered him land on which to refound his monastery.[27] He had a friend named Mary in Nogent-le-Rotrou, a matron who endeared herself to him by her good works.[28] Many women made an effort to attend Bernard's funeral.[29] The charters of female donors show that they were allowed on the premises to make their donations in the chapter room and to enter the church to place tokens of their gift on the altar. They were associated with the spiritual benefits of Tironensian monasteries and received into confraternity with the monks.[30]

---

22 Howells, *Caldey*, 21.

23 Laing, *Lindores Abbey*, 66–67.

24 Communities of Célidé persisted at St. Andrews and Abernethy, despite repeated efforts throughout the twelfth and thirteenth centuries to absorb them into chapters of regular canons within the reorganized Church of Scotland.

25 The Brec Bennoch, now identified as the Monymusk Reliquary greatly esteemed by the kings of Scotland, was a small house-shaped shrine that purportedly contained a bone of Saint Columba of Iona. *Liber S. Thome de Aberbrothoc*, 1:5, no. 1.

26 VB, 11.92, AASS, Apr. 2: 0244E–F; VB, trans. Cline, 98–99; ibid., 14.130, AASS, Apr. 2: trans. Cline, 132–33.

27 VB, 9.78, AASS, Apr. 2:0240F–41A; VB, trans. Cline, 83–84.

28 VB, 13.117–18, AASS, Apr. 2: 0250A–B; VB, trans. Cline, 121–22.

29 VB, 13:126, AASS, Apr. 2:0251F; VB, trans. Cline, 128–29.

30 Walter Hait, viscount of Mollan/Moulins, made a gift in chapter, in the presence of the abbot and all the monks, who consented to inscribe the viscount and his wife in the Tironensian martyrology after their deaths and to conduct the office for them as for their brothers. T1:217–18, no. 191 (1135).

The Tironensians had a variety of flexible responses to protecting women in religious life. Female houses within the monastery provided a decent life for women with poor alternatives and solved the dilemmas of men with religious vocations and female dependants. Lay women sometimes made arrangements to live in houses under the protection of the monks. Beatrix of Montdidier-Roucy, countess of the Perche (1040–1129), and her daughter Juliana (ca. 1074–ca. 1132) resided in houses at Tiron Abbey instead of the castle of Saint-John in Nogent-le-Rotrou.[31] In 1191, Alix of France (1151–1198), the daughter of Louis VII (b. ca. 1120, r. 1137–1180) and Eleanor of Aquitaine (ca. 1122–1204) and the newly widowed countess of Blois, retired to Tiron Abbey with her four children for a period to recover from her grief.[32] Both men and women were admitted not only as corrodians but with the status of monks (*ad monachatum*).[33] Married couples became Tironensian monks, some of them upon giving their property to the monastery.[34] Hugh of Lièvreville gave himself and all his property to Tiron, and his mother, brother, and sister were admitted to the status of monks.[35] Deathbed clothings were common for men, but Elisenda Pagana, a dying citizen of Le Mans, was veiled and consecrated to Christ by the Tironensian monks.[36] To settle a dispute about the mayorship of Gardais, Tiron's reciprocity included a promise to give a cash gift to one of the mayor's daughters upon her betrothal, to provide for the mayor's wife when she wished to leave the world, and to give her a cell of her own without requiring her to take the veil.[37] To date only two references to young women becoming Tironensian nuns have been found. The *Vita Bernardi* describes Bernard's deathbed clothing of a girl from Nogent-le-Rotrou, who promptly died.[38] The priory of Saint-Barthélemy-du-Vieux-Charencey promised ca. 1135 to pay a donor's daughter a cash gift when she married or, if she preferred, to receive her in religion.[39] It is safe to assume that these families knew that their young daughters

---

31 VB, 9.81, AASS, Apr. 2: 0241D–E; VB, trans. Cline, 86–87.
32 T2:115–16, no. 340 (1195), specifically 115n2.
33 Thompson, "The First Hundred Years," 116–17.
34 T1:57, no. 36 (ca. 1120), "*Girardus Ensaielana at Amelina uxor ejus dederunt se ecclesie Tyronis, quatinus, si vellet, monachi fierent [...]*"; ibid., 1:122–23, no. 101 (ca. 1128), "*Guillelmus faber et uxor ejus Osanna dederunt se et possessionem suam totam et domum suam monachis Tyroni s[...]*"; ibid., 1:165–66, no. 140 (ca. 1130), "*Guillelmus cementarius de Mauritania et Hersendis uxor ejus venerabilis, in conversione sua, monachi enim Tironensis ecclesie fuerunt [...]*"; ibid., 2:45, no. 274 (ca. 1145), "*Herbertus de Ceresvilla et uxor mea Adelina nos nostraque omnia Deo et ecclesie Tyronensi dedimus [...].*"
35 T1:229, no. 201 (ca. 1135). "*Hugo de Levrevilla, propter caritatem quam ei et suis amicis, scilicet matri et fratri et sorori, monachi Tyronenses impenderant, quos ad monachatum susceperant, dedit se suaque omnia predicte ecclesie[...].*"
36 T2:18, no. 246 (ca. 1140), "*Notum sit Elisendam, usitato nomine Paganam, civem Cenomanensem, in extremis vite sue positam, a monachis Tironensibus velatam adque Christo consecratam.*"
37 T2:125, no. 350 (1208).
38 VB, 13.118, AASS, Apr. 2:0250C; VB, trans. Cline, 122–23.
39 T1:239–40, no. 212 (ca. 1135), "*Monachi vero hac de causa cuidam filie sue Hersendi nomine, siquanto maritum acciperet, xxx solidos promiserunt; quod se mallet, ad religionem reciperent.*"

would join an existing group of mature women in residence in separate quarters. Women continued to be admitted in the early thirteenth century.

To date no record has been found of any early Tironensian nunneries.[40] The towns of Lèves and Châteaudun already had nunneries.[41] Recent scholarship has challenged earlier theories that early twelfth-century Premonstratensians and Cistercians were reluctant to found and supervise houses for women. Possibly the women housed and sheltered by the Tironensians were a limited number of dependants and not numerous enough to expand into a separate enclosed female community headed by a prioress or abbess.[42] Therefore, Tiron remained a male congregation but was more welcoming to women than the Cistercians were once reputed to have been.[43] Tiron's acceptance of women in confraternity and in residence as nuns or corrodians was unusual and reflects a transitional period before widespread founding of nunneries with sisters under perpetual vows.

Tiron upheld the dignity of manual labour and craftsmanship but also valued education and learning. Bernard pursued advanced studies throughout his teens and was a scholar of canon law. Seigneurial families sent their sons to be educated at Tiron in the twelfth century. When the Tironensians acquired urban property, eventually they obtained land near the Chartres cathedral school and the schools of Paris, which suggests that they provided higher education for certain scholars. The royal and military school of Tiron was founded ca. 1630, with instruction in fine arts, writing, arithmetic, geography, languages, fencing, dance, and horticulture.[44] The monks of Kelso ran burgh schools in

---

40 An examination of *Les réligieuses en France au XIIIe siècle*, ed. Parisse and Gazeau, "La clôture des moniales," did not indicate any Tironensian nunneries.

41 Chédeville, *Chartres et ses campagnes,* 405n41. T1:218–19, no. 192 (1135).

42 Lawrence, *Medieval Monasticism,* 208–12. See Berman, "Were There Twelfth-Century Cistercian Nuns?", specifically 834, and Yvonne Seale, "Ten Thousand Women."

43 Sally Thompson notes that Cluny and Cîteaux were slow to found nunneries. Eventually, ca. 1055 Abbot Hugh of Cluny founded the Cluniac priory of Marcigny for his female relatives. Thompson observes that the "early Cistercians were remarkable for their hostility to women," in *Women Religious,* 83–84, 94, 113. Tiron's acceptance of women was in line with other contemporary religious orders. Myra Miranda Bom notes that the Knights Hospitallers (1099) included women as benefactors, associates in confraternity, corrodians or pensioners, lay sisters, and fully professed nuns, living first in mixed-sex communities and later, when more numerous, in nunneries, in *Women in the Military Orders of the Crusades,* 8–16, 40, 135–36. Robert of Arbrissel founded the double monastery of Fontevraud in 1115, which was remarkable for its strict observance and for the subordinate position of men. Vital of Savigny founded a nunnery of La Blanche or Abbaye Blanche at Mortain. Gazeau, "La clôture des moniales." The *Vita Bernardi* shows that Bernard of Abbeville's attitude was similar to that of his close associates Robert and Vital, and the Tironensians were accepting of women. While Robert of Arbrissel on his deathbed insisted on continuing Fontevraud as a double monastery headed by an abbess, the Cistercians were reluctant to allow women on their premises. By the mid-thirteenth century, however, nunneries were accepted into the Cistercian order. The Cistercians have been studied so extensively that their antifeminism seems the norm, whereas contemporaries considered them exceptional.

44 Guillaumin, "Thiron, son Abbaye," 34.

the town of Roxburgh and educated the upper classes at their abbey school.[45] A foundation charter of Kelso dated 1147–1152 issued by David I gave Kelso the churches and schools and all their appurtenances in Roxburgh.[46] A privilege issued by Pope Innocent IV (r. 1243–1254) to the abbot of Kelso mentions the schools in Roxburgh as abbey possessions.[47] A charter dated 1219–1225 indicates that Lindores was running an educational establishment sufficient for Gregory, bishop of Brechin (r. 1219–1225), to grant them liberty to plant schools wherever they pleased in the burgh of Dundee.[48] Thus these Tironensian abbeys were considered exceptionally qualified to run schools in important burghs.

By 1126 Tiron had a chancellor and scribes working in a scriptorium where books were copied and charters were drawn up and compiled. Thompson comments on their relatively high standard of education and technical skill, reflected in the quality of the Latin of the sermons and the pirate narrative in the *Vita Bernardi*.[49] Tiron was acquiring property with regional authority and seigneurial rights in border and war-torn regions and on the margins of holdings of older orders. The scribes' drafting skills were essential to creating airtight contracts clarifying rights and boundaries and providing for foreseeable contingencies. The charters were attested to by all male and female parties, buttressed by countergifts, and witnessed by representatives of the donors and of the monks. Although Tiron clearly intended its daughter abbeys to be subordinate to the mother house at an earlier date, the scriptorium created a prototype charter of elevation by 1129.[50] Abbot William obtained full and perpetual liberty for the new abbey of Asnières. Its abbot was to be elected at Tiron and sent therefrom. He owed obedience and precedence to the abbot of Tiron, who might discipline recalcitrant and disobedient monks. Its wording became a prototype for other charters of elevation, such as that of Bois-Aubry.[51] Thompson and Webber have detailed the compilation and copying of Tiron's cartulary ca. 1147–1160s.[52] In Britain Kelso's scriptorium was famous for its calligraphy and illuminations. Arbroath's scriptorium drafted the Scottish declaration of independence in 1320. Education, book production, and record-keeping were important features of Tironensian monasticism.

Tiron's reputation for healing dates back to Bernard, a thaumaturge who healed by touch. Tiron's busy infirmary was a setting for several miracle stories. Tiron had skilled

---

45 *Kelso Liber*, 1:xxxii–xliii (preface).

46 This important border town had several parish churches: St. John the Evangelist in Roxburgh Castle, St. James with St. James Fair, north of the burgh near the Tweed, and the church of the Holy Sepulchre within the burgh. Martin and Oram, "Medieval Roxburgh," 372–74. *Kelso Liber*, 1:5–7, no. 2.

47 *Kelso Liber*, 2:350, no. 460.

48 Laing, *Lindores Abbey*, 470–71 (appendix), no. 9 (15).

49 Thompson, *The Monks of Tiron*, 48–49, 133.

50 T1:131–34, no. 112.

51 T1:249–50, no. 221 (1138).

52 Thompson, "The Cartulary of the Monastery of Tiron," 70–72.

physicians who correctly diagnosed the founder's final communicable illness and prescribed isolation and deep baths. Tiron's physicians also saved the life of Hugh of Blois (d. 1171), the natural son of Thibaut IV, count of Blois and Chartres (b. 1190, r. 1102–1152), subsequently Thibaut II, count of Champagne and Brie (1125–1152), hereafter Thibaut II. Tironensian monks are reputed to have treated sick sailors on seagoing merchant vessels trading in the Loire. Corsept had an oratory and dwelling on an island in the Loire known today as Saint-Nicholas-des-Défunts, the closest island to the Atlantic Ocean. The support given to travellers on Tiron's many riverine and coastal properties may have included medical treatment as well as provisioning.

Like many old and new religious foundations, Tiron supported crusaders and pilgrims to Jerusalem, Rome, and Compostela. Pilgrims and travellers paused at staging posts for food, rest, repairs, and medical treatment. Bernard offered them hospitality and prayers, and Tiron accommodated them by accepting donations, often in coins, a scarce commodity, and providing cash and other valuables to fund such journeys by accepting land and property in pledge.[53] Often this support resulted in a transfer of ownership of the pledged property to Tiron. A few seemingly isolated Tironensian priories were actually on pilgrimage routes to Compostela and thus connected to the Tironensian network.

Tiron also had an outstanding reputation for construction, which was unusual since monastic orders normally employed building crews. Bernard, a scholarly claustral prior, mastered the craft of woodworking and was exposed to ironwork while supporting himself as a hermit. He built a cell for himself at Fontaine-Géhard.[54] At Thiron-Brunelles Bernard's disciples first built huts and a chapel. Tiron was a wooden monastery when Bishop Ivo consecrated it at Easter 1109.[55] When Tiron moved to Thiron-Gardais in 1114, the monks built houses and a dormitory and infirmary, funded by Henry I and Thibaut II. The construction of the Romanesque basilica church began around 1115 and continued during William's tenure. Beatrix, countess of the Perche, and her daughter Juliana contributed to its expenses.[56] Upon Beatrix's death in 1129 Juliana paid for the completion of a considerable part of the workrooms at Tiron.[57] The early charters are witnessed by many carpenters and masons, which was also exceptional.

Abbots Bernard and William sent monks to found priories they were often expected to build, for their woodland rights included lumber for construction.[58] Tironensian monks were given land to build their houses in Val-Saint-Aignan in Châteaudun,

---

[53] T1:17, no. 6 (before 1116); ibid., 1:101–2, no. 82 (ca. 1125); ibid., 1:106–7, no. 86 (ca. 1127); ibid., 2:43–44, no. 272 (ca. 1127); ibid., 2:57–58, no. 289 (ca. 1146); ibid., 2:108, no. 332 (1188).
[54] VB, 5.39, AASS, Apr. 2:0232A; VB, trans. Cline, 46.
[55] VB, 8.69, AASS, Apr. 2:0238F; VB, trans. Cline, 76.
[56] Introduction, T1:cii–cix.
[57] VB, 9.81, AASS, Apr. 2, 0241D–E; VB, trans. Cline, 86–87.
[58] T1:16, no. 5 (ca. 1114). The charter giving lands and fields for Le Méleray ca. 1114 mentions that the land may be used for construction of buildings and a mill, and the gift includes water for a fish pond. T1:20–21, no. 9 (ca. 1115). Cohardon was endowed with woodland rights for construction ca. 1115.

Péronville, Villequoi and Montreuil, Tourny, Les Coutures, and Cohardon.[59] They also brought new land under cultivation around their dwellings.[60] At Tourny near the priory of La Tréhoudière the monks planted a vineyard and an orchard, consistent with their improvements of local gifts of land.[61]

Tiron's outstanding reputation for craftsmanship included the construction of mills, which converted wind and water into mechanical power. Mills provided income, flour, fish, and eels, and energy for other crafts.[62] The local people were required to grind their grain at the mill, and aristocratic and monastic mill owners normally retained a percentage of the flour (multure) as payment for their services.[63] Tiron's new foundations were given multure as an incentive to productivity as well as ownership of existing mills with the requirement to keep them in good repair. Tiron owned many local mills and others in the vicinity of Chartres, Rouen, Paris, and particularly the Beauce.[64]

The Tironensians were also given land on which to build new mills.[65] The new technology of the crown gear and lantern pinion instead of two crown gears engaging at a right angle reduced maintenance and increased productivity.[66] Mill construction was a mutually profitable and cooperative venture for the monks and donors.[67] The

---

59 T1:175-76, no. 152 (1131) (Val-Saint-Aignan); ibid., 1:220-22, no. 193 (1135) (Péronville); ibid., 1:177-78, no. 155 (ca. 1131) (Villequoi and Montreuil); ibid.,1: 211-13, no. 187 (1133-1145) (Tourny); ibid., 1:183-84, no. 160 (1131-1145) (Les Coutures); ibid., 1:20-21, no. 9 (ca. 1115) (Cohardon).

60 T1:168-69, no. 144 (ca. 1130) (Le Raincy) "*terra que tunc inculta erat quando ibi advenerunt*"; ibid, 170, no. 145 (ca. 1130) "*terre que de labore propriarum carrucarum exierit.*"

61 T1:213, no. 187 (1133-1145) "*...dederunt eis frustrum terre juxta domum ipsorum, ubi monachi vineam et virgultum plantaverunt.*"

62 The vertical watermill was more common in northern Europe and replaced the household hand quern for grinding grain. Berman notes that mills were also used for fulling cloth, sawing wood, cutting stone, and running bellows and trip-hammers for forges, in *Medieval Agriculture*, 87. Lucas, "The Role of the Monasteries in the Development of Medieval Milling."

63 La Sauve Majeure was an early example of monastic involvement with milling and mill construction. Its charters ca. 1079-1118 show the acquisition of land on both banks of the millstream, sometimes of land to flood to create a millpond (in exchange for fishing rights and priority at the future mill) or a sluice, mill construction or completion thereof by the monks, and the provision of housing for the miller. *Grand Cartulaire de La Sauve Majeure*, ed. Higounet et al., 1:88, no. 90; 1:90-91, no. 101; 1:97-98, no. 107; 1:116, no. 146; 160-61, nos. 237-38; 1:191, no. 296; 1:219, no. 356; 1:224, no. 366.

64 T1:39-40, no. 22 (ca. 1119); ibid., 1:53-55, no. 33 (ca. 1120); ibid., 2:2-3, no. 228 (ca. 1140) (local); ibid., 1:32-35, no. 18 (ca. 1118); ibid., 1:64-65, no. 45 (1121); ibid., 1:58-59, no. 38 (ca. 1120); ibid., ca. 1135, 1:239-40, no. 212 (1135) (Chartres); ibid., ca. 1145, 2:50-51, no. 281 (ca. 1145); ibid., 2:300 (Rouen); ibid., ca. 1128, 1:119-20, no. 99 (ca. 1128) (Paris); ibid, 1:118-19, no. 98 (ca. 1128) (the Beauce).

65 T1:16, no. 5 (ca. 1114) (midway to Châteaudun), ibid., 1:145, no. 123 (ca. 1130) (Gardais).

66 Brooks, "The 'Vitruvian Mill' in Roman and Medieval Europe," specifically 28.

67 The gifts of Fulk V, count of Anjou (b. ca. 1092, r. 1109-1129, d. 1143), to the priory of Reuzé in Poitou included the mill built by the prior, and the pond and woods. T1:189, no. 165 (ca. 1132).

Tironensians provided the technology for the construction of the mill, millpond, millrace, causeway, and fishponds, and took responsibility for maintenance, renovation, and repairs. The donors provided riverine land, lumber from their woodlands, and a guarantee of monopoly.[68] The monks often stipulated their right to send, remove, or replace the miller to protect their investment in the new technology.[69]

The Beauce was a wheat-growing region where Tiron had numerous granges, and the confluence of the Egvonne, Loir, and Aigre Rivers was well suited to mills.[70] To the south, the priory of Monrion was given a new mill called Moulin-Neuf near Blois, and a confirmation attests that the monks of Tiron built the mill.[71] The monks of the future abbey of Le Gué-de-Launay were given land on both riverbanks to build a mill.[72] Tiron harvested its wheat crops, milled the grain to flour in its own mills, and transported it to towns to meet the demand for bread. The Tironensians also owned ovens, and bakers appear as witnesses to their charters.[73] As with mills, they negotiated woodland rights. With the rise of towns, ovens achieved economies of scale by maximizing the use of a limited supply of firewood and thus required more baking flour than could be produced by hand. That consideration is a factor in the debate about whether mills were built for labour-saving or profiteering purposes.

In Scotland it is widely believed that the monks of Tiron were involved in important local building projects. The Tironensians built magnificent abbatial churches because they had monks and lay brothers with the skills to prepare architectural designs, to do carpentry and masonry, and to craft sculpture, tiles, murals, stained glass, wrought iron, and precious artifacts. Others note of Scottish abbeys in general that building crews came north from Durham for the heavy construction work. In Scotland the Tironensians

---

The monks were given another site to build a mill with income rights, a pond and fishing station, a causeway and its housing, and a mill race. T2:32–33, nos. 264–65 (ca. 1142); ibid., 2:54, no. 285 (ca. 1145).

68 Geoffrey III, viscount of Châteaudun (1080–1143) reached an agreement with the monks of Riboeuf Priory concerning the new mill they had built that the monks and he would share the fish, flour, payments to the miller, grain, income, and the entire profits of the mill. The monks would provide whatever was required for the mill's operation, and the viscount would provide lumber for renovation and repairs. The viscount and monks would have their respective shares of multure. T1:160–61, no. 134 (ca. 1130); also ibid., 1:189, no. 165 (ca. 1132); ibid., 2:32–33, no. 264 (ca. 1142); ibid., 2:91–92, no. 319 (1165); ibid., 1:225, no. 195 (ca. 1135).

69 T1:234–35, no. 206 (ca. 1135); ibid., 2:85–86, no. 312 (1159).

70 T2:106–7, nos. 329 and 330 (ca. 1183); ibid., 2:132–33, no. 356 (1220).

71 T1:231, no. 203 (ca. 1135); ibid., 2:74, no. 300 (ca. 1150).

72 T1:222–23, no. 194 (ca. 1135).

73 Of the twelve dependants Thibaut II, count of Blois-Champagne, gave to Tiron in Chartres, seven were bakers. T1:64–65, no. 45 (1121). Tiron owned or shared ovens in Vaupillon near Nogent-le-Rotrou, T1:224–26, no. 195 (ca. 1135), Chartres, ibid., 1:147–48, no. 126 (ca. 1130), Néron near Dreux, ibid., 1:88–91, no. 71 (ca. 1125), Châteaudun, ibid., 1:129–30, no. 109 (1129), Lésanville near Cloyes-sur-le-Loir, ibid., 1:137–39, no. 117 (ca. 1129), Paris, ibid., 2:131–32, no. 355 (1214); and Chassins in modern Trélou-sur-Marne, Champagne, ibid., 1:130, no. 110 (1129).

displayed exceptional engineering and construction skills in building bridges, consistent with Tiron's emphasis on travel and communication.[74]

Hospitality, a spiritual gift of its founder, was a distinctive feature of Tiron's early period. Bernard delighted in feeding and housing outside guests and the poor, to the point of being considered overly generous. Tiron was a day's journey from Nogent-le-Rotrou and a long day's ride from Chartres, so travellers greatly appreciated its guesthouse. Geoffrey Grossus emphasizes almost defensively that Tiron still had a guesthouse ca. 1147 where all comers were given food and bedding.[75] When William of Poitiers was succeeded by Stephan I (r. ca. 1160–1173) and John I (r. 1173–1178), one of those abbots decided to limit their guests to members of religious congregations. Consequently Tiron had the dubious honour of being satirized in Branch III of the *Roman de Renart*, written ca. 1175. Reynard the fox describes himself as a new member of the monks, actually canons, of the Tironensian order who dine on soft cheeses and fish ("Saint Benedict instructs us never to eat worse than that") and offer lodging only to monks and hermits.[76] The *Roman de Renart* contains some harsh and ribald mockery of the White and Black monks in Branch VII, but only Tiron is singled out for such pointed ridicule. The passage presents the Tironensian monks as enjoying the comfortable uncloistered lifestyle of urban canons and refusing hospitality to laymen, a marked shift from its earlier identity. Tiron's engagement in trade may underlie this decision.

Tiron's increased reluctance to lodge lay travellers and its creation of an unusually dense network of foundations and properties may be related. Although many religious foundations had guesthouses and towns had inns, once the network was established travelling Tironensians could usually lodge on their own property from Normandy to Poitou. The importance Abbot William attached to centralized supervision of daughter abbeys and priories is only one factor. By 1175 the Tironensians had shed their early image of being impoverished but godly monks. They sold produce, livestock, and manufactured goods and collected tithes, proceeds from markets and fairs, and offerings from pilgrims. When they transported their duty-free goods to market, exempt from tolls both locally and in Normandy and Anjou, they must have had resentful lay competitors. Their responsibility for safeguarding merchandise, livestock, cash, valuables, and sensitive correspondence made it desirable to have their own lodgings. Their reluctance to accept hospitality from laymen led to reluctance to extend it to them.

---

74 Thomas de Gordon the younger granted the abbot and monks of Kelso the right to build a stone bridge across the rivulet of Blackburn and to take wood and stone from his wood and Alan's quarry for this purpose, ca. 1180. *Kelso Liber*, 1:93, no. 123. Greenshields, *Annals of the Parish of Lesmahagow*, 5–6, cites "Hamilton Parish" in the "Statistical Account of Scotland," which mentions that the old bridge across the Avon, near Barncluith, was built by the brethren of Lesmahagow. The cartulary of Arbroath mentions a bridge over the [South] Esk at Brechin with land of Drumsleid appropriated for its support in the early thirteenth century. *Liber S. Thome de Aberbrothoc*, 1:xxviii and 1:184, no. 245. Hay, *History of Arbroath*, 57, mentions other bridges built by the abbey.

75 VB, 7:56, AASS, Apr. 2:0235D–F; VB, trans. Cline, 62; ibid., 11:92, AASS, Apr. 2: 0244E–F; VB, trans. Cline, 98–99.

76 *The Romance of Reynard the Fox*, trans. D. D. R. Owen (Oxford: Oxford University Press, 1994), 77, vv. 215–68.

Thompson notes the mobility of the monks of Tiron and explains it by disparaging commentary on wandering hermits, citing Payn Bolotin, "De Falsis Heremitis", although she notes that diplomatic and business travel may be a component.[77] Because of their involvement in trade the Tironensian monks were exceptionally mobile, but mapping shows that they acquired properties for lodging along routes to their houses in markets and ports. Hence they did not wander but travelled as ordered on monastic business, in company and under supervision.

An overview of their network shows that, on the map, roads appear as the most direct routes for transportation and communication. Tiron acquired multiple properties in the vicinity of Nogent-le-Rotrou, along a road north to the paved road between Chartres and Mortagne-au-Perche, along the roads between Chartres and Châteaudun, along a southern road from the farms in the Beauce to the mills and pilgrim staging post of Cloyes-sur-le-Loir, west toward the castle of Mondoubleau, and south toward Vendôme and Blois. Many roads were not paved and often obstructed by mud and washouts. The monks created trails and bridle paths between properties and sometimes widened them to accommodate carts and droving livestock.[78] The old Roman roads were still in use.[79]

On the map, rivers are less visible and non-linear, since naturally they form S-curves and are shaped by the terrain. Their water level varied seasonally with spring freshets and summer droughts. Yet when navigable they facilitated communication by boat and transportation of goods in flat-bottomed barges instead of costlier overland hauling. Rivers were critical to towns, which often grew up around toll stations at important bridges. On the continent Tiron had property near the Seine, the Loire, and the Saône, as well as near many lesser waterways like the Yerre toward Cloyes-sur-le-Loir, indicative of travel and shipping. On the North Sea, the Scottish Tironensian foundations owned property on the Dee toward Aberdeen and on the Tweed toward Berwick-upon-Tweed, and Tiron had property near the mouth of the Humber estuary. Riverine property was highly desirable for religious communities engaged in farming, milling, and stock-raising. Many rivers had roads or towpaths along their banks so land traffic passed through river valleys. Tironensian properties on or near a river or coastline tended to be more widely spaced than on roads. Riverine routes were well travelled in forested regions.

Sea travel was imperilled by bad weather. Medieval seamen preferred to sail within sight of land for navigation and supplies, to shelter in harbours overnight, and to await

---

[77] Thompson, *The Monks of Tiron*, 115–16, 142–43.

[78] Bezant, "Travel and Communication," 137n34 citing Andrew Fleming, "The Making of a Medieval Road: The Monk's Trod Routeway, Mid Wales," *Landscapes* 10, no. 1 (2009): 77–100.

[79] The Roman province of Gallia had paved roads dating back to Marcus Vipsanius Agrippa (64–63 B.C.–12 B.C.), governor of Transalpine Gaul (ca. 39–37 B.C.).

An important north–south road ran from Rouen to Paris, Orléans, Tours, and Poitiers, and another ran from Rouen south to Chartres, Le Mans, and Tours. One important east–west road ran from Orléans west to Blois, Tours, Angers, and Nantes, while another east–west road ran from the Atlantic port of Rochefort to Tours and Lyon. Roads also ran from Angers, Le Mans, and Alençon to Rennes and north to the Channel, and Tironensian abbeys were located nearby. See Barrow, *Roads and Bridges of the Roman Empire*; Vernon, *Travel in the Middle Ages*, 15, 17, 25.

favourable winds for Channel crossings. Although Britain had navigable rivers, most Tironensian properties were coastal and located on virtually all the Bay of Biscay and Channel routes. A route to Wales ran along the northern Cornish coast, crossed the Bristol Channel to Swansea, and proceeded west via Caldey Island, Pill (modern Milford Haven), and around the Pembrokeshire peninsula. Another route ran between Harfleur on the Seine across the Channel to the Isle of Wight and the ports of Hamble and Southampton.[80] The Isle of Wight was a gathering point for ships awaiting favourable winds to cross to France, particularly to the Seine ports.

Tiron's real estate consisted of abbeys, priories, churches, farms and granges, and townhouses. Tithe income, fishing stations, saltworks, mills, and ferries indicate monastic communication, for a representative would have travelled to collect the income. Although consideration is given to the organization of the cartulary, the mapping is based mainly on the properties listed in the papal confirmations. Tiron, like other religious congregations, prepared and paid for papal confirmations of its most important holdings. Tiron obtained papal protection of its properties in 1119 and prepared lists for papal confirmations in 1132, 1147, and 1175.[81] Not all properties were confirmed; other charters show Tironensian monks in residence in towns and farms but not organized into priories.

By the time of the 1147 confirmation, it is clear that the Tironensian churches and priories were not randomly distributed or isolated but purposefully acquired and consolidated. Occasionally they purchased townhouses and waterfront property. In Chartres and Paris, Tiron obtained riverfront property for trade and marketing, established a religious headquarters near the centre of political power, and acquired houses near the centres of learning. Tiron founded and acquired priories on main roads to the south, which were also primary and secondary pilgrimage routes to the shrine of Saint James of Compostela.

By 1147 the congregation of Tiron was under centralized control, with a monarchial organization similar to that of Cluny or Fontevraud. The abbot of Tiron took precedence over abbots of daughter abbeys, who were summoned to a general chapter at Tiron at Pentecost to appoint abbots and priors, enforce discipline, and make decisions.[82] Churches, priories, and abbeys had been acquired and established in and outside towns and along roads and waterways. Monks and lay brothers could shelter after a day's journey. Monastic officials covering longer distances during a day's ride could conduct inspections to follow up on the decisions and disciplinary actions of the general chapters, while familiarizing themselves with desirable properties and their owners. Channels and networks of communication were in place in modern central France extending to the Channel and Atlantic coasts and the British Isles.

---

80 Sean McGrail, "Cross-Channel Seamanship and Navigation in the Late First Millennium B.C.," *Oxford Journal of Archaeology* 2, no. 3 (1983), 299–337 at 309 (Figure 4) and 310 (Table 1).
81 This study relies heavily on three papal confirmations of 1132 (fol. 1v), 1147 (fol. 90r), and 1175 (fol. 58) that were copied into the manuscript cartulary by twelfth-century scribes. In these confirmations the properties are listed by diocese.
82 T1:49–51, specifically 51, no. 30 (1120).

The Tironensians were the opposite of mendicants. They sold high-quality goods below retail price because of their exemptions, travelled on business, negotiated airtight contracts, and paid cash when they could not obtain donations. In Normandy, Maine, Anjou, and the British Isles, produce and merchandise could be carted exempt of tolls along roads to major towns, safely stored overnight in churches and priories a day's journey apart, and sold duty free in urban markets. Tironensian ships sailed along the coasts of Scotland and Northumberland with certain exemptions at ports of call. Channel shipping and communication were possible from Wales and Ireland, the Southampton Water, the Isle of Wight, across the Channel to Normandy, and down the Breton coast to Nantes. The Seine and Loire were waterways for commerce in salt, wine, and grain. The Tironensian trading network preceded the trading zone established throughout the Angevin Empire by Henry II, count of Anjou, duke of Normandy, king of England (b. 1133, r. 1154–1189) during his long and profitable reign. Its French network preceded the nation-building Philip II Augustus (b. 1165, r. 1180–1223) achieved by 1223. In addition to raising the profile of Tiron as a major monastic reform movement, this study endeavours to show how the Tironensian network of trade and communication was established by two remarkable abbots who were well ahead of their times.

Since Tiron was acquiring strategic and valuable properties together with regional authority and seigneurial rights, its expansion process included disputes, conflicting claims with other religious institutions, and occasional local raids by donors in wartime. The bishop and chapter of Chartres were helpful in conflict resolution, and Tiron was fortunate to be able to make cash settlements. A very close local and mutually beneficial working relationship existed between the bishops of Chartres and the abbots of Tiron who did different things in supplying one another with foodstuffs and merchandise and with protection and prayers (see appendix 2, Disputes).

Tironensian abbots had seigneurial authority in France and were statesmen in Scotland. Tiron maintained centralized control over its French foundations, eight of which were raised to abbatial status and acquired subordinate priories of their own. Their attempts to achieve independence of the mother house were quashed by the papacy, but their regional network of expansion became the battlegrounds of the Hundred Years' War (1337–1453) and the Wars of Religion (1562–1598), and their prosperity ended with devastation and depredation. Tiron's English properties were sold by 1414, and Tiron Abbey was mostly burned in 1428. Impoverishment led to decadence, and economic recovery was followed by control by powerful leaders who diverted the wealth to enrich commendatory abbots. Despite efforts at reform, few foundations survived the dissolution of the monasteries in Britain 1536–1541 and in France in 1790.

The congregation of Tiron originally flourished and then survived for almost seven centuries alongside Cluny and Cîteaux, but its existence and achievements have not been widely recognized. From a monastic viewpoint Tiron's strengths were also its weaknesses. In an era when many religious orders lived on their lands, the Tironensians were early participants in the twelfth-century urban economy. The congregation's involvement in trade, education, construction, and politics entailed engagement in the world outside the cloister. Initially such engagement was a matter of survival during famine by supporting refugees and displaced persons. The founder's spiritual renown attracted wealthy and powerful patrons who helped to create a network to support travel and an urban economy. Tiron experienced prosperity and made many contributions to society through improved milling, grange agriculture, horse-breeding and stock-raising, viticulture, and support for pilgrims and travellers on land and sea. Its patterns of expansion in its first century contribute significantly to our understanding of the interactions of the reformed Benedictine congregations in Britain and France. Its abbots' tough pragmatism, negotiating skills, and strategic acquisitions, their management of conflict on borders, their respect for women and craftsmen, and their dedication to excellence in production and education enrich our understanding of reformed monasticism. Their exceptional participation in an international world of trade, communication, and politics was a precursor for subsequent nation- and empire-building.

Chapter 3

BERNARD OF ABBEVILLE AND TIRON'S FOUNDATION

BERNARD OF ABBEVILLE, abbot of Tiron, a reformer who established foundations from Scotland to the Midi, was prominent in the early twelfth century. The most complete account of the personality and career of Tiron's founder is the *Vita Bernardi* by Geoffrey Grossus,[1] written ca. 1147.[2] Despite its inaccuracies and borrowings, Geoffrey Grossus's hagiography shows the strengths and difficulties of community and hermit life, particularly those of a reformed community. It gives the background to the difficulties Tiron faced with the papacy and Cluny. It explains the reasons for the placement of Tiron under the chapter of Chartres. It describes the long-standing support of royal and noble donors and their reverence for Bernard. It emphasizes the centralized structure of Tiron and its authority over its daughter foundations through the general chapter at a time when its Celtic abbeys were challenging that authority. It explains the important position of artisans and their presence in church and chapter. It acknowledges the presence of women in residence on the premises and suggests that some were dependants of the monks as well as of the donors. It deduces a lost monastic rule with simple precepts but close supervision. It defends Tiron's increasing prosperity through the heavenly intervention of its founder. At a time when Tiron was transitioning from love of poverty to

---

[1] Personal communications of December 5, 2006 and February 26, 2013. Constance Brittain Bouchard found no record of Geoffrey Grossus in her study of the Burgundian Grossi family, lords of Uxelles and Brancion, in *Sword, Miter, and Cloister*, 300–303. I am deeply grateful for her contribution. Although Grossus may be an epithet meaning "Big" or "Fat," it may be a family name, for another monk named Walter Grossus appears in the cartulary of Tiron. T1:99, no. 79 (1126) (Geoffrey Grossinus); ibid., 1:120, no. 99 (ca. 1128) and 1:199, no. 179 (ca. 1132) (Walter Grossus). Witnesses named Grossinus are mentioned in *Cartulaire de l'Abbaye de Saint-Père de Chartres*, ed. M. Guérard, Collection des Cartulaires de France, 2 vols. (Paris, 1840), 1:311, no. 59 (Grossinus); 1:336, no. 101 (Grossinus *hospitarius*).

[2] Thompson and I take different approaches to this hagiography. Thompson dates the core of the *vita* 1137–1143 based on the papal legacy of Geoffrey II of Lèves, bishop of Chartres, *Monks*, 11–12. I date it ca. 1147, based on my discovery of the author's two reworkings of the phrase "proponent of justice," first used by Bernard of Clairvaux 1144–1145. See VB, 1:11, AASS, Apr. 2:0225C; VB, trans. Cline, 17n14; ibid., 6:48, AASS, Apr. 2:0233F; VB, trans. Cline, 54–55. Thompson analyzes the *vita* as a retrospective compilation by the copyist Pignore de Vallea 1290–1297, with sections written or amended later than the 1140s, reflecting the poverty, preaching, and ministry to the poor of the thirteenth-century friars, *Monks of Tiron*, 53–61. I contend that the *vita* also reflects the eleventh-century reformers and itinerant preachers who preceded the friars. Since Abbot William of Poitiers and the monks Adelelmus of Saint-Cyprien and Christian, who knew Bernard, were at Tiron (T1:54, no. 33, ca. 1120), and ibid., 2:79, no. 306 (ca. 1150), I consider the *vita* to be the institutional memory and mine it for historical information.

desire for prosperity and from hospitality to exclusivity, the *Vita Bernardi* appeals to the past in an effort to slow the trend. The *Vita Bernardi* supports the canonization of Tiron's founder but also explains the background of its contemporary concerns. Its contextualization within the documentary sources shows a consistent portrait that supports the basic integrity of the hagiography.

The life and times of Bernard of Abbeville, abbot of Tiron, began with his birth in Abbeville in Picardy ca. 1050.[3] His parents were unknown, but perhaps were related to the counts of Ponthieu, seigneurs of Abbeville.[4] They ran a hospice, gave their scholarly son a liberal education in grammar, dialectical reasoning, the literary arts, and scripture, until age nineteen,[5] and were sufficiently aristocratic for him to enter prestigious distant monasteries. Bernard's school is unnamed but was probably the school of the basilica church of Saint-Riquier, northeast of Abbevillle.

Discerning a religious vocation for monastic life, Bernard abandoned his studies and travelled south with companions seeking a strict monastery. He is described as professing at Saint-Cyprien of Poitiers under Abbot Renaud, a famous teacher, scholar, and claustral prior of La Chaise-Dieu in the Auvergne, who had moved with other monks to reform that Poitevin abbey.[6] Since Bernard's other spiritual mentors were

---

[3] Bernard's birthplace: Abbeville, in Picardy, a dependency of the counts of Ponthieu, is confirmed by an anonymous twelfth-century French chronicler, who wrote that Bernard was from Ponthieu, although he knew little about his origins. Geoffroy le Gros, *B. Bernardi, fundatoris et primi abbatis SS Trinitatis de Tironio Vita*, ed. Jean-Baptiste Souchet (Paris: Billaine, 1649; BnF Imprimés 4° LN27 1680). Souchet found this anonymous twelfth-century chronicle in the Bibliothèque de Claude Ménard. Beck dates this chronicle to the 1140s, *Saint-Bernard de Tiron*, 129n12, and 490–91. This birth date is estimated by subtracting at least twenty years from 1073, when Renaud became abbot of Saint-Cyprien and subsequently clothed Bernard as a monk. After a decade, Bernard went to Saint-Savin as claustral prior when Gervais became abbot in 1082.

[4] François César Louandre consideres Bernard's family to have been ancient and noble, allied to the local houses of Montcavrel, Rambures, Monchy, Saint-Blimont, and Bovinet, in *Biographie d'Abbeville*, 2 vols. (Paris, Joubert, 1844–1845), 1:50. *Carmen de Hastingae Proelio* of Bishop Guy of Amiens, ed. and trans. Frank Barlow (Oxford: Clarendon Press, 1999), xlii–xlviii (Boubers family). Genealogical research shows that Anne of Ponthieu (b. ca. 1034), daughter of Hugh II, count of Ponthieu, seigneur of Abbeville (r. ca. 1045–1052), married Godefroy of Montcavrel (ca. 1025–1078). Descendants named Boubers married into the Rambures, Monchy, and Saint-Blimont/Blimond families in the fifteenth and sixteenth centuries. Famille de Boubers © Etienne Pattou: http://racineshistoire.free.fr/LGN/PDF/Boubers1.pdf.

[5] VB, 1.6–7, AASS, Apr. 2:0224D; VB, trans. Cline, 13–14.

[6] William VIII, duke of Aquitaine (ca. 1025–1086), encouraged Durand, abbot of La Chaise-Dieu (r. 1067–1078), to establish foundations in his lands, which Cluny viewed as an incursion. Pierre Roger Gaussin, *Le Rayonnement de la Chaise-Dieu* (Brioude: Watel, 1981), 24. Bascher, "La 'Vita' de Saint Bernard," 439–40n89, cites Dom Chamard, "L'Epitaphe de Raynaud, abbé de Saint-Cyprien," *Bulletin de la Société des Antiquaires de l'Ouest* 14 (1874–1876), 23 and 27. The epitaph dates Abbot Renaud's tenure November 4, 1073–May 23, 1100. VB, 1.9, AASS, Apr. 2, 0224F–25B; VB, trans. Cline, 15. GC, 2:1233–34.

Casadéens,[7] however, he may have professed at La Chaise-Dieu and accompanied Renaud and another monk named Gervais to Saint-Cyprien.

Gervais became abbot of Saint-Savin-sur-Gartempe (r. 1082–1099), an important daughter monastery of Saint-Cyprien located about 50 kilometres east of Poitiers, and insisted on Bernard as his claustral prior. Together they undertook to bring the lukewarm and recalcitrant monks to a closer observance of the *Rule*. The tensions of community life and the realities of monastic reform are portrayed, with Bernard responding to aggravations and invectives with patient firmness punctuated by swiftly fulfilled prophecies of death. Gervais and Bernard fell out, however, and Bernard lost the support of his abbot. Bernard's cloistered life at Saint-Savin concluded with his personal vision of the Virgin, who promised him a life of hardship culminating in Paradise and sainthood.[8] Bernard confided his vision to another monk and left Saint-Savin without authorization.

Bernard lived as a hermit, first locally and then in northern France, until he was recalled to Saint-Cyprien and became prior and abbot. Monasteries were being subordinated to Cluny ostensibly for reform, and Saint-Cyprien's independent status was uncertain.[9] Abbot Renaud had prevailed in church councils ca. 1081, but pressure to subject Saint-Cyprien to Cluny was building up in Rome.[10] When Gervais was killed outside Jerusalem on the First Crusade ca. June 1099, Renaud recalled Bernard to Saint-Cyprien as prior.[11] When Renaud died on May 23, 1100, Bernard was installed as abbot by Peter II, bishop of Poitiers (r. 1087–1115), in a last, desperate attempt to resist the abbey's subordination to Cluny. His installation was a pre-emptive act of defiance directed against Abbot Hugh (b. 1024, r. 1049–1109) and Paschal II (r. 1099–1118).

The *Vita Bernardi* falsely states that at the Council of Poitiers on November 18, 1100 Bernard and Robert of Arbrissel, not the papal legates, excommunicated Philip I, king of France, for his adulterous second union. The fabrication was perhaps intended to encourage royal favour, for the excommunication ensured the succession of his firstborn son Louis VI.[12] Paschal II subordinated Saint-Cyprien to Cluny on November 20, 1100 and issued

---

7 Several reliable sources indicate that Hildebert/Audibert and Garnier of Montmorillon were monks of La Chaise-Dieu, not Saint-Cyprien. See *Vita, Simon, Comes et Monachus Romae* (Saint Simon de Crépy), 1.8–9, AASS, Sept. 8: 0745F–46B, and OV, 4:327–29, 327n3 and 328n1.

8 VB, 2:13–18, AASS, Apr. 2:0225F–27B; VB, trans. Cline, 19–25.

9 Johannes von Walter, *Die Ersten Wanderprediger Frankreichs: Studien zur Geschichte des Mönchtums*, 2 vols. (Leipzig: Dieterich, 1903–1906), 2:4–64, translated into French by J. Cahour in *Bulletin de la Commission Historique et Archéologique de la Mayenne*, 2nd ser., 24 (1908), 385–410 and 25 (1909), 17–44, specifically 23–24, traced the subjection of Saint-Cyprien to Cluny to a letter dated October 28, 1004, from Abbot Abbo of Fleury (d. 1004) to Odilo, abbot of Cluny (ca. 962–1049), suggesting that Cluny enjoyed some right to oversee the abbey. In privileges dated 1058 and 1075, Popes Stephen IX (r. 1057–1058) and Gregory VII granted to Cluny what Cluny's predecessors had at Saint-Cyprien.

10 BC, 16.1, 19.1. *Cartulaire de l'Abbaye de Saint-Cyprien de Poitiers*, ed. Rédet, 43, no. 43.

11 VB, 5.36–43, AASS, Apr. 2:0231B–32F; VB, trans. Cline, 43–50.

12 VB, 6.48, AASS, Apr. 2:0233F; VB, trans. Cline, 54–55.

a brief in 1101 deposing Bernard as abbot. Bernard is inaccurately described as travelling twice to Rome to defend the independence of Saint-Cyprien with successful outcomes because of the justice of his cause.[13] Nonetheless, the description of Bernard's acrimonious second visit is startlingly detailed. When the pope refused to consider the evidence and judge the case, Bernard appealed to the court of Heaven, a variant of a monastic curse. In indignation the pope ordered Bernard to leave his presence.[14] When allowed to resume his defence, Bernard attacked Abbot Hugh for lusting for the powers of an archabbot. Bernard's forceful speech was well preserved, and probably not solely at Tiron.[15]

Bernard's cloistered years were interrupted by periods of hermit life and a preaching tour in Normandy. Bernard first became a disciple of a nearby hermit, Peter of l'Etoile, who founded Fontgombaud in 1091.[16] When Bernard was ordered to return to Saint-Savin, Peter of l'Etoile guided Bernard about 250 kilometres north to the vicinity of Maine and Brittany where Robert of Arbrissel, Vital of Mortain, and Ralph of la Futaye lived as hermits with disciples and subsequently founded monasteries. Entrusted to Vital, Bernard became the disciple of a hermit at Saint-Médard, who taught Bernard woodworking and exposed him to wrought ironwork, the trades by which they supported themselves.[17] When located, Bernard fled offshore to the Chausey Island, supplied by Vital's hermits as the weather permitted, where he was tormented by hallucinations or "phantoms" in his isolation and had a dramatic encounter with pirates.[18] The dynamics and tensions of hermit life, including envy, malice, and over-attachment, parallel those of community life. When Bernard returned to the mainland, he built a cell at Fontaine-Géhard in Maine, where he preached and accrued disciples.

The places where Bernard sought refuge are associated with him today. Saint-Médard is near Saint-Mars-sur-la-Futaie, northeast of Fougères. The Chausey Islands are

---

[13] Reliable sources show that Bernard made a single trip to Rome to appeal his deposition unsuccessfully: BC, 32.2. *Cartulaire de l'Abbaye de Saint-Cyprien de Poitiers,* ed. Rédet, 45–47, no. 43. OV, 8.27, 4:328–29. The last affirmation of Cluny's claim to authority over Saint-Cyprien was a papal privilege issued April 2, 1125 by Honorius II (r. 1124–1130). Another abbot of Saint-Cyprien restored the abbey's liberty subsequently, and Geoffrey Grossus conflated him with Bernard. GC (1873), 2:1235. BC, 42.2.

[14] "Bernard resolutely summoned the pope and all those involved in this matter to an examination at the Last Judgment before a judge who would be undeceived by dark ignorance and uncorrupted by gifts." VB, 7.57, AASS, Apr. 2:0235F; VB, trans. Cline, 63.

[15] VB, 7.58, AASS, Apr. 2:0236A–C; VB, trans. Cline, 64. These confrontations explain Tiron's future disputes with the neighboring Cluniac priory of Saint-Denis-de-Nogent-le-Rotrou and the absence of Tironensian cardinals as late as 1159. Robinson, *The Papacy 1073–1198*, 216–18. Barbara Zenker, "Die Mitglieder des kardinalkollegiums von 1130 bis 1159" (PhD diss., Univ. Würzburg, 1964), indicates no Tironensian cardinals.

[16] VB, 3.19, AASS, Apr. 2:0227C–D; VB, trans. Cline, 26.

[17] VB, 3.21–23, AASS, Apr. 2:0227E–28C; VB, trans. Cline, 28–30.

[18] VB, 4.26–35, AASS, Apr. 2:0228F–30F; VB, trans. Cline, 33–42. In a personal communication of December 1, 2015, Berman comments "The stories of Bernard and the pirates may well be an exemplum that encouraged those monks and brothers to go to sea as they often did."

a granite archipelago lying off the Cotentin peninsula in Mont-Saint-Michel Bay between Jersey and Saint-Malo. The largest island, called Grande Ile or the Chausey Island, is 17 kilometres offshore from Granville. Bernard required permission to live there from the abbey of Mont-Saint-Michel.[19] Fontaine-Géhard, an important centre founded by Saint William Firmat (d. 1095) ca. 1080 for the hermitages of Lower Maine, is located 2 kilometres from Châtillon-sur-Colmont on the edge of the forest of Mayenne.

While Bernard was delaying his deposition, he rejoined Robert of Arbrissel and Vital of Mortain on a tour of Normandy preaching clerical celibacy. Bernard employed contemporary arguments against clerical marriage: church property was alienated to provide dowries for daughters and inheritances for sons; fornication made priests unworthy to approach the sacraments; the marriage vow bound the priest by oath to continued fornication. He encountered violent opposition from married clergy and their wives. Geoffrey Grossus cites Bernard's sermon on the jawbone of an ass, a robust defence of his right as a monk to preach, delivered to a hostile crowd in Coutances.[20] The difficulty of imposing celibacy on the secular clergy and the abuse endured by advocates of clerical reform made a lasting impression.

Possibly Bernard's refusal to break up families seeking refuge at Tiron,[21] the significant number of priests,[22] and the women in residence in Tironensian foundations reflect Bernard's learning from experience about the problems of terminating clerical marriages. Bernard's friend Robert of Arbrissel had prostitute followers, and some were destitute abandoned wives of priests. Bernard may have decided to accept priests as monks and to provide for their dependants. Special emphasis is placed on the outpouring of pious women of high and low degree who flocked to Bernard's funeral, and their grateful presence among the mourners reflects his good relations with them.

Bernard settled in a forest near the castle of Fougères at Chennedet[23] and attracted a larger community of personal disciples. The hermits reluctantly curtailed their daily psalms in order to earn their living, a move toward simpler liturgies and more manual labour. Ralph I, count of Fougères (d. 1124) regretted their occupation of a favourite hunting ground and moved most of them to Savigny near Avranches. Vital and his followers had already occupied part of that forest and overcrowding became

---

[19] Bernard was noted for his hospitality to clerics, pilgrims, and paupers at Saint-Cyprien, and other Tironensian abbots and priors would be supportive of the pilgrimage traffic to Jerusalem, Rome, and Compostela. VB, 6.46, AASS, Apr. 2:0233D; VB, trans. Cline, 53; ibid., 7.56, AASS, Apr. 2:0235D–E; VB, trans. Cline, 62.

[20] VB, 6.50–54, AASS, Apr. 2:0234B–35B; VB, trans. Cline, 56–60.

[21] VB, 11.92, AASS, Apr. 2: 0244E–F; VB, trans. Cline 98–99; ibid., 13.136, AASS, Apr. 2:0253F–54A; VB, trans. Cline, 128–29.

[22] VB, 13.122, AASS, Apr. 2:0251A; VB, trans. Cline, 125–26.

[23] Beck identifies *Quercus-Docta* as Chênedet or Chennedet, in the commune of Landéan, Ille-et-Vilaine, north of Fougères, an ancient Druidic sanctuary, with a chapel named the Hermitage, whose origins are associated with Vital of Savigny, William Firmat of Fontaine-Géhard, and Bernard of Tiron, in *Saint-Bernard de Tiron*, 29n34, 138, 254–58.

a problem.[24] Bernard's search for a place to establish a hermitage for his disciples led him to Tiron.

By 1107 Bernard was the most experienced of his close associates Robert of Arbrissel and Vital of Mortain. He was trained in law, skilled in administration, respected for craftsmanship, and charismatic and controversial in preaching. He had reformed an abbey of lukewarm monks and had experienced hermit life in community and in solitude. He had survived danger and violence. He knew the intrigues of the papal curia first hand and had an abiding enemy in Cluny. As he made plans to establish a permanent foundation for his hermit disciples, he would face additional challenges, but few abbots were better prepared to cope with them.

Around 1107 Bernard sent disciples from Brittany to seek land for a new foundation. Like many Bretons, they gravitated toward the diocese of Chartres, which was ancient, wealthy, and headed by saintly Bishop Ivo. They approached Rotrou II, the crusader count of the Perche, a vassal of Henry I's widowed sister Adela, countess of Blois and Chartres.[25] Rotrou II was related to the Mortagne and Bellême families, and after his return from the First Crusade in 1101 he allied himself by marriage with Henry I in 1104.[26]

Like most of the aristocracy, Rotrou II was a patron of the Cluniac order; the priory of Saint-Denis-de-Nogent-le-Rotrou (1031–1789) was near his castle, and he favoured Cluniac foundations in England. He was a patron of La Trappe, a Cistercian foundation in Mortagne, and of a small Savignac community.[27] Rotrou II first offered the family country house with a farm and an oratory at Arcisses, which his mother Beatrix insisted he withdraw to avoid conflict with Saint-Denis. Instead, he granted Bernard land at Thiron-Brunelles, northeast of Nogent-le-Rotrou, on the boundary of his property. It was remembered as a swampy, forested, brigand-infested valley unsuited for vines or wheat,

---

24 VB, 7.61–62, AASS, Apr. 2:0237A–C; VB, trans. Cline, 67–69.

25 Kimberly A. LoPrete, "Adela of Blois: Familial Alliances and Female Lordship," in *Aristocratic Women in Medieval France*, ed. Theodore Evergates (Philadelphia: University of Pennsylvania Press, 1999), 7–43.

26 Thompson, *Power and Border Lordship*, 54–85, "Chapter 3: Rotrou the Great (1099–1144)." Thompson notes that Rotrou's wife Matilda FitzRoy (d. 1120), a natural daughter of Henry I, brought Rotrou valuable manors in Wiltshire. In 1108 Rotrou II fought in Spain with his first cousin King Alfonso I of Navarre and Aragon (b. 1073/1074, r. 1104–1134). He fought with Henry I against Fulk V, count of Anjou, and was imprisoned until the downfall of Robert of Bellême, lord of Shrewsbury (ca. 1052–post 1130) in November 1112. The king granted Bellême to Rotrou II in 1113. In the shipwreck of the *White Ship* on November 25, 1120, Rotrou II lost his wife and two nephews by his sister Juliana's marriage to Gilbert of L'Aigle (1073–1120). By 1123 Rotrou II was Alfonso I's governour of Tudela, a post he held until the mid-1130s. He married Hawise (b. ca. 1091), daughter of Walter of Salisbury, sheriff of Wiltshire, ca. 1135. Rotrou II returned to the Perche 1135–1144, attending the royal court at Oxford, England, in 1139 and visiting his sister Margaret (1067–1156), the wife of Henry de Beaumont, lord of Le Neubourg (1045–1119), earl of Warwick, lord of Gower. Rotrou II died during the siege of Rouen in 1144.

27 Thompson, *Power and Border Lordship*, 80n114, citing R. H. C. Davis, *King Stephen*, 3rd ed. (London: Longman, 1990), 100.

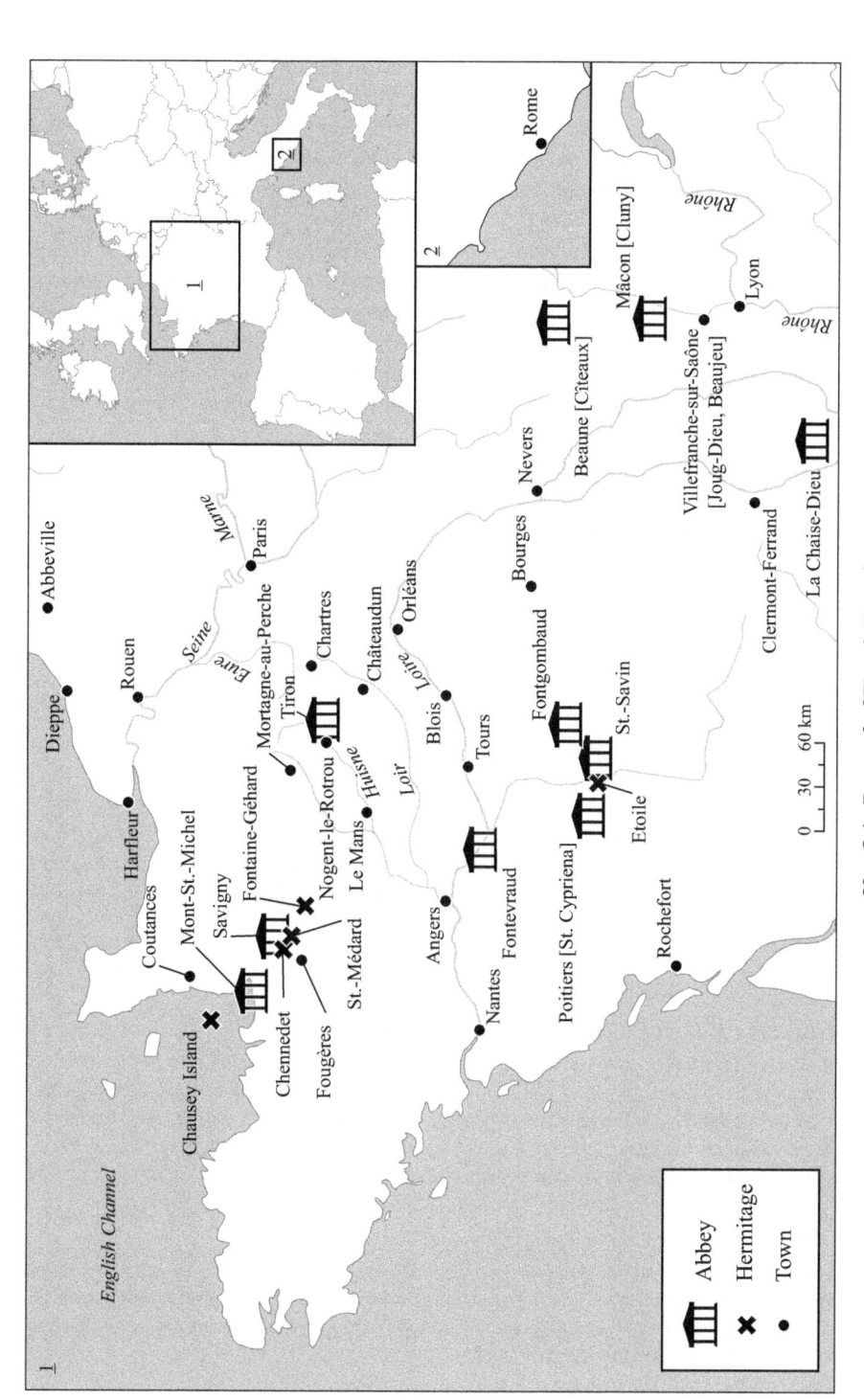

Map 3.1. Bernard of Tiron's Travels

and only suitable for small crops of rye and oats.[28] The monks had to clear land and construct buildings in that isolated and dangerous site. They made a virtue of their extreme poverty and won over the local peasants. The *Vita Bernardi* exhorts the monks not to be ashamed of Bernard's love of poverty or of Tiron's early poverty.[29] Their engagement in trade may have become an issue ca. 1147 or at a later date in response to the thirteenth-century rhetoric of the Franciscans.

Ivo, bishop of Chartres, consecrated Tiron's wooden church and buildings at Easter 1109. That year the region encompassing Chartres and Orléans was ravaged by a feverish sickness and excessive rainfall that ruined the crops and the grape harvest. Three years of famine 1109–1111 brought an influx of unemployed craftsmen, starving peasants, dispossessed families, orphans and wards to Tiron. Whether a monastery should allow crafts and trade was debatable; at Tiron it was a matter of survival.[30] Bernard fed all comers and put the craftsmen to work. Orderic Vitalis describes the famine and listed the artisans as "joiners and blacksmiths, sculptors and goldsmiths, painters and masons, vine-dressers and husbandmen, and skilled artificers of many kinds."[31] William II, count of Nevers (b. pre-1089, r. 1098–1148), sent a heavy gold vase from Burgundy to Bernard, who sold it to buy food for his monks and beggars.[32] Probably Bernard sold the vase in Chartres, but the displaced artisans may have come from more distant towns. Their presence was an incentive to donors to found Tironensian priories so the monks could introduce these crafts locally.

In autumn 1112 a crisis occurred that brought Bernard's spiritual gifts to royal attention.[33] A coalition of leaders of France, Flanders, and Anjou warred with Henry I over his possession of Normandy 1111–1113. Fulk V, count of Anjou, captured Rotrou II and sold him to his cousin Robert of Bellême. In sadistic imprisonment, Rotrou II requested Bernard's prayers for his soul's salvation. Bernard wept, then "filled with prophetic spirit, he admonished the messengers to trust in God's mercy and not to despair in the least of Rotrou's release. He added that this misfortune would be turned into good fortune for Rotrou and into direst misfortune for Robert."[34] In historical fact Robert of

---

28 IS-ADEL, 8:209, H 1952 (1136–1695, specifically 1477). The lack of bread and wine is mentioned in VB, 10.87, AASS, Apr. 2:0243C–D; VB, trans. Cline, 93.

29 VB, 14.134, AASS, Apr. 2:0253E; VB, trans. Cline, 135–36.

30 Sulpicius Severus (ca. 360–ca. 420–425), *Vita Martini*, 10, in PL 20:166C, states that Martin's monks were not allowed to buy or sell anything and no craft was practised there except for the scribes. Bernard did not share an aristocratic prejudice against trade. His parents ran a hospice in Abbeville, an ancient military fortification and commercial centre whose navigable river, markets, and fairs linked Gaul and Italy with the British Isles.

31 OV, 11.38 and 40, 6:166–67 and 172–73 (famine); ibid., 8.27, 4:330–31 (artisans).

32 VB, 8.70, AASS, Apr. 2:0239A–B; VB, trans. Cline, 77–78.

33 Although Henry I's summons precedes Rotrou II's imprisonment in the *Vita Bernardi*, after dating the incidents I concluded that the reversal of fortune in late 1112 induced Rotrou II to bring Bernard to his father-in-law's attention, and royal favour induced the bishop and canons of Chartres to sponsor Tiron's refoundation in early 1114.

34 VB, 9:79–81, AASS, Apr. 2:0241A–E; VB, trans. Cline, 84–87.

Bellême, a vassal of Henry I of England as lord of Shrewsbury, came before the English king as an envoy of the French king. Henry I charged Robert with treason for siding with the rebellious Norman barons on November 3, 1112, put him in chains, and imprisoned him for life. Henry I obtained Rotrou II's release and awarded Bellême to him.

To the medieval mind Bernard's prophetic gift was terrifying, and all concerned wanted to be in favour with the holy man. Henry I requested a personal visit from Bernard, and Louis VI and Fulk V of Anjou heard of the reversal of fortune. All became generous patrons of Tiron Abbey. For Cluny Bernard's sudden prominence must have been intolerable. Saint-Denis claimed the tithes and burial fees of Thiron-Brunelles 1113–1114, forcing Bernard to move out of the parish. At this time the Rotrou family did not counter the claim of their Cluniac foundation, but Rotrou II gave Arcisses in Brunelles to Tiron ca. 1115, and later his mother Beatrix and sister Juliana moved from town to live at Tiron.[35]

Although Adela, countess of Blois and Chartres, offered property and patronage, Bernard refounded his monastery under the protection of the chapter of canons of the cathedral of Chartres. The association with Chartres had attractive features for the new foundation. Although the idea of a corporation was an unfamiliar one at that time, the chapter was a corporate body whose decisions were reached by deliberation and consensus and whose turnover was less abrupt than the death of an overlord and the succession of an heir who might be less supportive. Bernard's refusal of Adela's offer of much better land suggests that he recognized the greater stability offered by the chapter of canons. His foresight contributed to the growth of Tiron.

Lépinois and Merlet describe the responsibilities and financial resources of the chapter of Chartres in the extensive introduction to the *Cartulaire de Notre Dame de Chartres*. The dignitaries of the chapter, seventeen in number, witnessed the foundation charter of Thiron-Gardais on February 3, 1114. Ivo signed as bishop of Chartres, Arnaud as dean (*decanus*), George as precentor (*cantor*), Hugh as subdean (*subdecanus*); other signatories are listed below.[36] The witnesses did not include the chancellor, who was responsible for correspondence and legal instruments, the archives and library, and the schools of Chartres. The number of canon-priests required for the church was thirteen. In addition, the chapter had numerous clerks and other officers. Members of the chapter appear frequently as witnesses to the Tironensian charters. Entitled to income from churches, fairs, tithes, and prebends, they were powerful and wealthy sponsors of Tiron.

The chapter of canons gave a carucate of land from the farm of Blessed Mary with tenants in the nearby hamlet of Gardais, in the provostship of Fontenay-sur-Eure, held

---

35 Lalizel, *Abbaye Royale d'Arcisses*, 134n20, dates the donation ca. 1115.

36 Garin as succentor (*subcantor*). Insgier, Walter, Gauslen, Raimbaud, Landric, and Odo all signed as archdeacons. They occupied the positions of great archdeacon, archdeacon of Dunois, archdeacon of Pinserais, archdeacon of Blois, archdeacon of Dreux, and archdeacon of Vendôme. Geoffrey, Aimeri, Seran, and Hugh signed as provosts (*prepositi*). The great Chartrain provostships at that time were Nogent, Fontenay-sur-Eure, Amilly, and Beauce. CNDC, 1:48n1. Ebrald signed as sacristan or treasurer (*capicerius* or *chevecier*) (ibid., 1:lxxiii–lxxv). Ralph signed as chamberlain (*camerarius*) (T1:2, no. 1 (1114)).

by future bishop Geoffrey II of Lèves at that time. Canon Geoffrey travelled to the farm on an inspection tour of the gift, beginning Tiron's long association with one of the greatest religious leaders and statesmen of the twelfth century. The abbey held the land in freehold but owed obedience to the chapter as well as the bishop.[37] The papal confirmation in 1119, discussed below, confirmed the freehold status by the word *alodio* as well as the canonical jurisdiction of the bishop. Bernard built workrooms on the tract. Although Bishop Ivo criticized the provosts for their rapacity with regard to the produce and livestock in the farms they controlled, the *Vita Bernardi* expresses gratitude for the canons' generosity, patronage, and protection from troublemakers.[38]

By 1114 Bernard was considered a very holy man.[39] David I founded Selkirk Abbey with Tironensian monks. Paschal II was in Chartres at Easter 1114, which seems the likeliest occasion for Bernard's becoming a mitred abbot.[40] Bernard was a confessor and counsellor to the aristocracy and noted for his charity toward the poor. Miracles were attributed to him. His monks had seen showers of roses fall from Heaven when he said mass. He stopped a forest fire that forced his monks to abandon their huts and workrooms and shelter in a recently cleared field. He visited the home of a local knight named Robert of la Motte and restored Robert's fortunes. His presence was instrumental in the recovery of a valuable war horse stolen from Payen of Le Theil-sur-Huisne. He healed a child's eye in Saint-Lubin-des-Cinq-Fonts. He revived a boy crushed by a cart wheel. He had audiences with Henry I and Louis VI and won royal favour that endured for generations.[41]

Ivo, bishop of Chartres, died at the end of December 1115. The Lèves family had extended their status and influence by placing younger sons in ecclesiastical offices, including Geoffrey II and his nephew Gauslen.[42] Through simony they induced the cathedral chapter of canons to elected Geoffrey II to the bishopric without consulting their overlord. Like his uncle Henry I, Thibaut II considered bishops and abbots to be ecclesiastical barons and severely punished all concerned. He sacked the canons' houses, shut

---

37 T1:1–2, no. 1 (1114). In the founding charter Bishop Ivo of Chartres states: "*dono eis predictam terram quietam et immunem a synodo et circada; ab omni etiam consuetudine, ab omni exactione prepetualiter habendam concessimus, salva obedientia que episcopo et capitulo debetur.*"

38 See Grant, "Geoffrey of Lèves, Bishop of Chartres," 47n14, citing GC:8, instr., 314–15, no. 35, and CNDC, 1:119–20, no. 33. VB, 9:77–78, AASS, Apr. 2: 0240E–F; VB, trans. Cline, 83–84.

39 T1:20–21, no. 9 (ca. 1115).

40 Thompson, *The Monks of Tiron*, 106–7. Guillaumin, "Thiron, son Abbaye," 26. Bernard is depicted as a mitred abbot, and his mitre and chasuble were preserved at Tiron until they were pillaged in 1562.

41 VB, 8.75–76, AASS, Apr. 2:0239F–40A; VB, trans. Cline, 80–81 (roses, forest fire); ibid., 10.85, AASS, Apr. 2:0243A; VB, trans. Cline, 91 (Robert of La Motte); ibid., 8.66–68, AASS, Apr. 2:0238C–F; VB, trans. Cline, 73–76 (war horse); ibid., 10.86, AASS, Apr. 2:0243B; VB, trans. Cline, 92 (child's eye); ibid., 10.89, AASS, Apr. 2:0243F–44A; VB, trans. Cline, 94–95 (cart wheel); ibid., 11.96–97, AASS, Apr. 2:0245E–F; VB, trans. Cline, 102–3 (royal favour).

42 Livingstone, *Out of Love for my Kin*, 17–19, 40–41.

them up in their own cloister, and drove Geoffrey II out of town.⁴³ Bernard and Robert of Arbrissel arbitrated the violent dispute and persuaded Thibaut II to accept Geoffrey II, who then travelled to Rome to receive the pallium. Their intervention launched his distinguished career as bishop and papal legate. Upon his return Archdeacon Gauslen and Bishop Geoffrey II founded the Chartrain abbey of Notre-Dame-de-Josaphat in 1118 with Louis VI's approval.⁴⁴ For the next two decades Thibaut II consistently sided with his uncle Henry I, and Bishop Geoffrey II consistently sided with Louis VI, forcing Tiron Abbey to cope with the ensuing tension.

Bernard and Robert were soon forced to intervene again with Thibaut II. In 1116, counselled by William II, count of Nevers, Louis VI refused an act of homage by Henry I's heir William Atheling (1103-1120), backed the claim of William Clito (1102-1128), the son of Robert Curthose (ca. 1054-1134), to the dukedom of Normandy, and supported the rebellious Norman lords.⁴⁵ Although the count of Nevers was a royal ambassador, Thibaut II imprisoned him in Blois for four years. Bernard and Robert of Arbrissel visited William II shortly before the abbots died in February and April 1116 respectively.

A pious death was the culmination of a saintly life, and the *Vita Bernardi* devotes two chapters to Bernard's passing.⁴⁶ Bernard was old, frail, and weary of life. He had groomed potential successors and eagerly anticipated the joys of paradise. Geoffrey Grossus claims to have witnessed Bernard's final illness, and he borrows much suitable language from Jerome's description of the death of Saint Paula.⁴⁷ Bernard collapsed outside church after a hasty exit during the holy office and was isolated by Tiron's physicians in a hut instead of the infirmary. He rejected the baths they had prescribed to treat his inflamed skin. His mind wandered during his suffering, and he described visions to his monks. In lucid moments he preached and summoned the community by rank: priests and monks, adolescent schoolboys, illiterates, for final exhortations. He clothed a young nun from Nogent-le-Rotrou who promptly died.⁴⁸ When Bernard died on April 25, 1116, miraculously monks at the distant priories of Hamble and Joug-Dieu learned instantly of his passing. His funeral was widely attended, and Geoffrey Grossus describes the outpouring of women of every rank from noblewomen to anchorites who came to pay their final respects. Bernard left his monks his body as a relic and his promise to advocate for them in the heavenly court so that their poverty would be relieved.⁴⁹ When the church

---

43 Hollister, *Henry I*, 373. GC, 8:1134C-D.
44 GC, 8:1135A
45 Hallam, *Capetian France*, 117-18.
46 VB, 12-13.105-26, AASS, Apr. 2:0247E-51F; VB, trans. Cline, 111-29.
47 Cline, "*Mutatis Mutandis*: Borrowings from Jerome's Letter to Eustochium and Others," 141-43.
48 In May 2000 John Symington, M.D., an infectious disease specialist in Washington, DC, considered the symptoms. He diagnosed erysipelas, probably caught from the pigs, complicated by streptococcal pneumonia that was communicated to the young woman.
49 VB, 12.107, AASS, Apr. 2: 0248C; VB, trans. Cline, 114 (poverty); ibid., 13.124, AASS, Apr. 2:0251D; VB, trans. Cline, 127 (relic).

was completed, his tomb was placed in a chapel at the angle of the chapter and the north side of the choir.[50]

David I visited Tiron shortly after Bernard's death and took more Tironensian monks to increase the community he had founded at Selkirk. Ralph, the first abbot of Selkirk, was recalled to Tiron as Bernard's successor and was replaced by a Tironensian monk named William of Poitiers. Geoffrey Grossus describes David I's long overland journey "from the north over the borders of many interlying regions," across the Channel through Normandy to Tiron and his equally long and tiring journey back with Abbot William.[51] Ralph died soon after his installation, and William of Poitiers was recalled to Tiron as abbot. A monk named Hugh acted as an interim abbot during this period between 1116 and 1119 when Ralph and William were in transit.[52]

In conclusion, when Bernard of Tiron died in 1116, he had created a poor but well-run reformed Benedictine monastery. Its land was held in freehold but subject to the jurisdiction and under the protection of the bishop and chapter of canons of Chartres. The foundation of its cemetery in 1114 afforded asylum and protection for the abbey tenant farmers.[53] The abbey itself had workers to perform manual labour. Skilled workers and craftsmen dammed the Thironne River to form the west pond for a steady water supply for their forge and workshops. Herds of livestock supplied meat for sale and hides for leatherwork. Upon Bernard's deathbed orders, the lay workers resumed attending the divine office, and they were present in chapter as witnesses to charters. The abbey had priests and physicians. Its school for boys accepted both external students and monastic oblates, some from noble families.[54] Women must have been in residence, because Bernard was permitted to clothe a young local girl as a nun.[55] The abbey had a dependant or serf (*servus*), which was rare in the Perche because so many of the servile class had bettered their fortunes in wartime.[56] Writing from the perspective of Tiron's substantial holdings in 1147, Geoffrey Grossus records Bernard's dying wish that his monks might enjoy greater prosperity.[57]

---

50 Guillaumin, "Thiron, son Abbaye," 26, 39.

51 VB, 11.99, AASS, Apr. 2:0246B–C; VB, trans. Cline, 106–7.

52 Hugh was mentioned as abbot of Tiron in T1:28–29, no. 14 (1117–1119), and *Chronique de Saint-Maixent*, ed. Verdon, 186, 1116. Nonetheless, the mortuary roll of Vital of Savigny circulated after his death in 1122, and the community of Tiron requested prayers only for the deceased Abbots Bernard and Ralph in *Rouleaux des morts du IXe au XVe siècle*, ed. Léopold Delisle (Paris: Renouard, 1866), 323, no. 129. ES, 2:160, cites the *Chronicle of Melrose* s.a. 1115: "Bernard, the first abbot of Tiron, died. He was succeeded by Ralph, the abbot of Selkirk; and William, a Tironian monk, was made abbot of Selkirk."

53 Pierre Duparc, "Le Cimetière Séjour des Vivants (XIe-XIIe Siècle)," *Bulletin philologique et historique (jusqu'à 1610) du Comité des travaux historiques et scientifiques* (1964): 483–504.

54 VB, 8.74, AASS, Apr. 2:0239F; VB, trans. Cline, 80; ibid., 13.122, AASS, Apr. 2:0251A–B; VB, trans. Cline, 125.

55 VB, 9.81, AASS, Apr. 2:0241E; VB, trans. Cline, 87; ibid., 13.117–18, AASS, Apr. 2:0250B–C; VB, trans. Cline, 121–23.

56 VB, 14.142, AASS, Apr. 2:0254E–F; VB, trans. Cline, 140–41. Chédeville, *Chartres et ses campagnes*, 369.

57 VB, 13.125, AASS, Apr. 2:0251E; VB, trans. Cline, 128.

The *Vita Bernardi* largely deserves its reputation as a highly regarded primary source. The later material seems original and accurate. It is a retrospective look at the congregation of Tiron at its zenith, for little expansion occurred in France after the papal confirmation of property in 1147. It was recopied during the reign of John II of Chartres, abbot of Tiron, 1277–1297, a period of prosperity and construction. Tiron had been isolated and rural and had become urban and international; it had special features traceable to its founder, which distinguished it from the Benedictine monasticism of Cluny and Cîteaux; and its rule bridged the divide between community and hermit life. Tiron had been impoverished and hospitable and had become wealthy and more discriminating. Its monks were transitioning from the lifestyle of hermits to that of urban canons. Geoffrey Grossus traces the roots of Tiron's origins, uniqueness, and issues.

It is important to note, however, that Bernard established the distinctive features of Tironensian monasticism, although they were brilliantly developed by the future Abbot William of Poitiers. Reared in Abbeville, Bernard experienced town life and the need for manufactured goods and commodities. His successors rode the wave of twelfth-century developments: the rise and incorporation of towns, international trade and the emergence of the merchant class, the growth of universities, the expansion of male and female monasticism, and devotion to Mary, whereas Bernard anticipated them. Bernard of Abbeville was once venerated throughout modern France and by royalty in France and Britain. He has been eclipsed by his namesake Bernard of Clairvaux, and his associates Robert of Arbrissel and Vital of Savigny are better known. He defined a distinctive congregation with outposts at distant borders, but many of his foundations have been absorbed into the mainstream Benedictine or Cistercian orders. Bernard deserves to be recognized in his own right as an important leader of reformed Benedictine monasticism.

Chapter 4

WILLIAM OF POITIERS AND HIS SUCCESSORS

The foundations established during Bernard of Abbeville's lifetime and shortly after did not follow a pattern of gradual expansion outwards from Tiron Abbey, unlike the early expansion pattern of Cîteaux and Clairvaux. The same famine that flooded Tiron with refugees devastated Cîteaux, until in 1113 the future Bernard of Clairvaux and thirty Burgundian noblemen revived the house. Cîteaux founded its four daughter houses of La Ferté, Pontigny, Morimond, and Clairvaux (pre-1165) within 161 kilometres of the mother house.[1] Clairvaux, with Bernard as abbot, founded two daughter houses: Trois-Fontaines 76 kilometres to the north and Fontenay 77 kilometres to the southwest. In contrast, Tiron's expansion pattern was eccentric and atypical of most monastic reformers: some of the earliest foundations were established on the distant boundaries of the future congregation. Tironensian foundations established during the last two years of Bernard's abbacy, 1114–1116, and shortly afterward to 1119, were in Scotland, Wales, on the Channel coast in England and Normandy, in the Chartrain, the Perche, the Dunois, the Beauce, the Blésois and Anjou in the Loire Valley, and Beaujolais near the Rhône. The pattern is attributed to a surplus of monks at Tiron Abbey and the requests of prominent donors to establish reformed Benedictine foundations of monks who were Bernard's disciples.[2] It is unlikely that Bernard was establishing a network of daughter houses, but he was receiving properties during a wave of enormous celebrity during the last two years of his life. Consequently he needed to groom successors and recruit future leaders.

Donors gave property for spiritual reasons. Bernard was renowned for his holiness of life and the efficacy of his prayers, particularly in healing and in liberating prisoners in fetters. Both Rotrou II, count of the Perche, and the sainted crusader Adjutor of Vernon attributed their release from prison to Bernard's spiritual powers. Many donors sought prayers, confraternity, deathbed clothing, and monastic burial. The Gregorian reform encouraged laymen who owned churches to give them to the local bishop or monastery. Many of Tiron's donors gave for pious reasons, and phrases like "for the remission of sins" and "for the redemption of souls" are used in the early charters.[3] Rotrou II gave land at Thiron-Brunelles to Bernard ca. 1107, in anticipation of his Spanish crusade with his cousin Alfonso I of Navarre and Aragon ca. 1108. He gave the future abbey of Arcisses in Brunelles to Tiron as a priory ca. 1115 before he returned to Spain. Stipulations concerning reciprocity on the part of the Tironensian monks are limited to

---

[1] Berman, *The Cistercian Evolution*, 159.

[2] VB, 10.87, AASS, Apr. 2:0243C; VB, trans. Cline, 92; ibid., 11:95, AASS, Apr. 2:0245E; VB, trans. Cline, 101–2.

[3] T1:17, no. 6 (ca. 1114); ibid., 1:32, nos. 17–18 (ca. 1117).

spiritual benefits, although their countergifts "for charity" confirmed the transactions.[4] Upon Bernard's death additional foundations were given to commemorate him.

Tiron Abbey accepted property for economic reasons. The community began to generate goods and livestock that the local hamlets could not absorb, so the monks sought markets in larger towns. Bernard travelled to Chartres on business "*causam negotii.*"[5] A natural choice because of its size, trade guilds, and pilgrims, Chartres could be approached by the Roman road or along the Eure River. Priories and churches in the vicinity of Chartres could be used to secure goods and livestock from brigands overnight. In war-torn Normandy, a region of otherwise limited expansion, in 1115, Henry I confirmed the previous gift of a wood, church, land, and tithes, comprising the priory of Saint-Blaise-de-Luy (Grémonville) north of Rouen near the Channel.[6] West of the Tironensian foundations in Eure-et-Loir and the Beauce, Tiron began to establish foundations in Anjou, ruled by Fulk V, beginning with the priory of Cohardon ca. 1115 and the priory and future abbey of Asnières in 1118. South of Tiron Abbey, the priory of Saint-Gilles-des-Châtaigniers was endowed in Bernard's memory.[7] Tiron Abbey was given foundations in the Beauce and the Dunois.[8] The gifts of the priory of Yron and the church of Saint-Georges-de-Cloyes suggest that Tiron initially did more business in Cloyes-sur-le-Loir than in nearby Châteaudun.[9] Yron would become the central priory for Tironensian foundations in the Beauce, including Bouche d'Aigre (founded 1114) and Cintry/Saintry (founded 1115). After Bernard's death, Adela, countess of Blois and Chartres, established two priories 1117–1119: Ecoman in the forest of Marchenoir

---

[4] Berman, *The Cistercian Evolution*, 166–75. Bouchard, "Monastic Cartularies: Organizing Eternity." The charters were prepared around the time of a transfer of property or the settlement of a dispute between the monks and laymen. The pancartes were prepared for the bishop and recorded gifts made at various times. The cartulary included papal bulls. The charters recorded gifts, sales, leases, pledges, exchanges, confirmations thereof, and settlements of disputes. A gift was a negotiated transfer of property without a demand for reciprocal performance, frequently made for the donor or a relative becoming a monk, sometimes on his deathbed, or for burial with the monks or for their prayers for his soul and those of his relatives. Male and female donors could make their gifts in chapter and place the evidence thereof on the church altar. The monks' charitable countergifts confirmed the transfer and the spiritual benefits. Countergifts were usually cash, but gifts in kind indicated horses and palfreys, pigs, cows, and white sheep, peas, furs, capes, and boots, and wine. Pledges were often used to raise cash for travel or pilgrimages. Sales, leases, and exchanges consolidated scattered parcels of land into a productive priory or farm. The charters are a record of donors who enjoyed the spiritual and practical benefits of affiliation with Tiron.

[5] VB, 10.88, AASS, Apr. 2:0243E; VB, trans. Cline, 93–94.

[6] T1:27–28, no. 13. Merlet dates the charter ca. 1117, but it is dated "at Rouen on the day on which the barons of Normandy were made the men of the king's son," spring 1115. Farrer, *An Outline Itinerary of King Henry I*, 73. Hollister, *Henry I*, 238n22, citing Achille Luchaire, *Louis VI le gros; annales de sa vie et de son règne* (1081–1137) (Paris: A. Picard, 1890), xxxv–xxxvi.

[7] T1:24–27, no. 12 (ca. 1117).

[8] T1:32–35, no. 18 (ca. 1118).

[9] T1:22–23, no. 10 (ca. 1115) (Yron).

north of Blois and Monrion at Blois on the Loire.[10] They extended Tiron's properties south of Châteaudun to the Loire, with its important river trade involving grain from the Beauce, wine from Anjou, and salt from the islands and marshes near the Atlantic. South of the Loire land and woods were given for Asnières.[11] In southeastern France on the Saône River near the Rhône in the archdiocese of Lyon, the distant abbey of Joug-Dieu was founded because of a vision of Bernard during his lifetime.[12] East of Chartres, the priory of Ablis founded ca. 1115 was a link to Paris, the capital of Ile-de-France. Early Tironensian foundations in strategic areas clearly combine piety and politics.

Tiron was the earliest of the reformed Benedictine congregations to establish foundations in strategic regions of the British Isles. Bernard sent Tironensian monks across the Channel to the dioceses of Winchester and St. Davids and the Scottish Borders. In Britain the priory of Hamble on the Southampton Water was founded ca. 1109 and the priory of Cemaes in Wales (the future abbey of St. Dogmaels) and Selkirk Abbey (forerunner of the future abbey of Kelso) were founded ca. 1114. On the Welsh border, land was given at the market town of Kington.[13] In contrast, the first Cistercian abbey in Britain was Waverley Abbey in Surrey, founded in 1128 from L'Aumône (founded 1121). Hamble was on the Channel and Cemaes/St. Dogmaels was on the Irish Sea, which facilitated communication by water. Selkirk Abbey was connected to the port of Berwick-upon-Tweed on the North Sea. These foundations extended the range of Bernard's foundations by 1119 from Scotland to the Midi.

Like many Cluniac abbots, Bernard negotiated a foundation charter ensuring property and income before sending six to twelve monks to establish a new priory. The land was measured in carucates and arpents. The income sources included tithes, tolls, multure, ovens, coins, vines, and sometimes salt. When the priory of Le Méleray was founded by a gift of lands and fields both at Melleray north of Nogent-le-Rotrou near the Huisne and also at Arrou on the Yerre near roads to Châteaudun and Cloyes-sur-le-Loir,[14] the gift included water rights: a plot on which to construct a mill and a body of water for a fish pond, and woodland rights: an entire wood with entitlement to take dead wood for fuel and living wood for construction, pasturage for livestock, and pannage for pigs.[15] The charter of donation is an early example of the Tironensian prototype of Bernard's minimal requirements for a viable priory. He relied on the prior to maintain Tironensian customs and discipline while adapting to the local situation.

---

10 T1:28–29, no. 14 (1117–1119); ibid., 1:40–41, no. 24 (ca. 1119).

11 T1:35–36, no. 19 (ca. 1118).

12 T1:30–31, no. 16 (1118).

13 T1:29, no. 15 (1117–1126).

14 Merlet distinguishes between Le Méleray (modern Melleray), T1:16, no. 5 (ca. 1114) and ibid., 1:96, no. 77 (ca. 1125) in Margon north of Nogent-le-Rotrou and Les Mellerets in Arrou, ibid., 1:156, no. 130 (ca. 1130), a house (*domus*) in the parish of Saint-Lubin-d'Arrou. The charter for Les Mellerets is copied into the manuscript cartulary as no. 140, and the charters for Le Méleray are grouped together and copied as nos. 309 and 310, so they are different places.

15 T1:16, no. 5 (ca. 1114).

Other foundations did not begin as priories but evolved to that status. A farm might expand to a point where a chapel and other monastic buildings were needed, and a church might acquire adjacent land and become the nucleus of a priory. Sometimes Bernard and his successor William would obtain permission to send monks to dwell in a desirable location, where they erected buildings, planted crops, vines, and copses and otherwise improved the property. Ivo II of Courville (d. ca. 1119) gave land to the Tironensian brothers at Clémas who were dwelling on the Eure close to modern Le Favril near the paved road to Chartres, and the foundation was elevated to priory status.[16] Tironensian houses in Châteaudun and Le Mans were not listed in papal confirmations but were important urban properties. Some town residences attracted local donors and were elevated to priories, whereas in others the Tironensians were allowed to reside but not to recruit and compete with older religious foundations.

There is scholarly debate about the exact number of early foundations. Using Merlet's dating, Beck provides a limited list. To the west, Bernard obtained land and fields at Le Méleray ("Melleray") in Margon north of Nogent-le-Rotrou, and tracts of land and woods at Cohardon southeast of Alençon. To the south, he obtained land and fields in Arrou midway between Tiron and Châteaudun, land in La Forêt northwest of Châteaudun, land at Romainville, land and woods at Montigny-le-Gannelon, and the church of Saint-Georges-de-Cloyes, all in Cloyes-sur-le-Loir, and to the southwest multure in the Atlantic port of Rochefort. To the southeast he obtained land at Cintry/Saintry in the Beauce west of Orléans. To the northeast he obtained the church of Saint-Epaigne and tracts of land at Ablis northeast of Chartres on the road to Paris.[17] Nonetheless the charters of donation do not always mention the intention of founding or expanding a priory. Clearly Tironensian monks were sent to construct the priory of Le Méleray in Margon. The charter for Cohardon includes the church of La Madeleine, other lands, and tithes, providing for the foundation of the priory of Cohardon.[18] Louis VI's gift of land at Saintry was the foundation of the priory of Cintry/Saintry.[19] The charter for the church of Saint-Epaigne and land confirms gifts of other parcels of land and cash from Guy II of Montlhéry, count of Rochefort (1037–1108), comprising the priory of Ablis.[20] Although the properties were given separately, Bernard was assembling them into foundations.

Bernard of Tiron was acclaimed for his holiness throughout Gaul for some years after his death. Notwithstanding, the period after Bernard's death in April 1116 was unsettled with Abbot Hugh's interim rule, Abbot Ralph's recall from Selkirk and death, and Abbot William's recall from Selkirk and accession ca. 1119. English-born Stephen Harding, abbot of Cîteaux, and Bernard, abbot of Clairvaux (founded in June 1115), became prominent leaders of reformed Benedictine monasticism and both were canonized. Bernard of Clairvaux was renowned for his spiritual zeal, political activism,

---

16 T1:32–35, no. 18 (ca. 1118).
17 Beck, *Saint-Bernard de Tiron*, 267–68.
18 T1:20–21, no. 9 (ca. 1115).
19 T1:18, no. 7 (1115).
20 T1:17, no. 6; ibid., 1:19–20, no. 8 (ca. 1115).

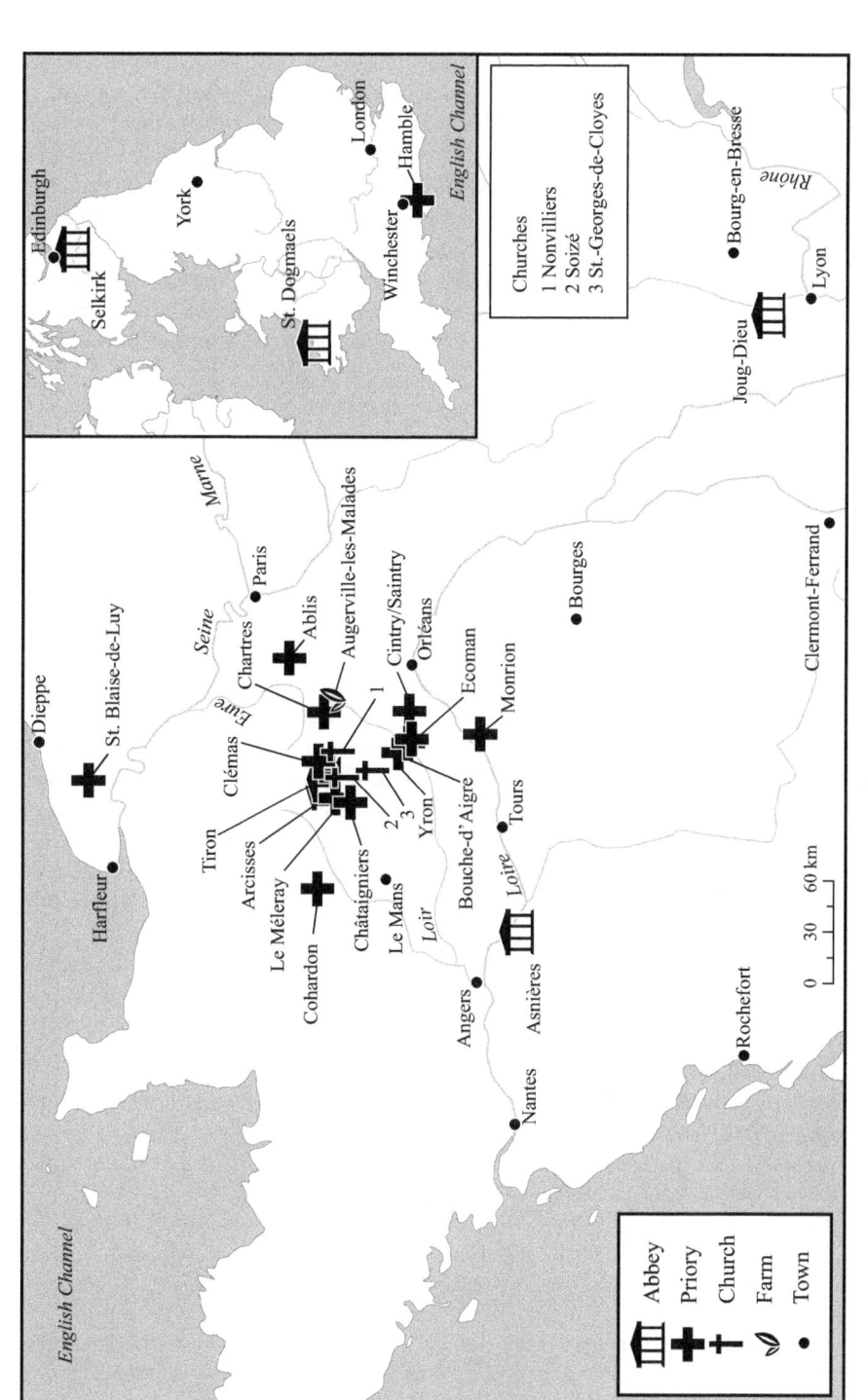

Map 4.1. Congregation of Tiron ca. 1119

and prodigious literary output. Tiron's religious superior Bishop Geoffrey II and its secular overlord Thibaut II became Cistercian patrons. William returned to find them founding the great Cistercian abbey of L'Aumône in 1121, 6 kilometres east of the new Tironensian priory of Ecoman on the road between Châteaudun and Blois.[21] They did not cease to be supportive of Tiron, but L'Aumône's foundation was an early example of the British pattern of founding Cistercian abbeys in the same strategic places in the diocese of Winchester and on the Welsh border where Tironensian priories were located, instead of elevating those priories to abbatial status.[22] Subsequently young Bernard of Clairvaux's growing reputation eclipsed aged Bernard of Tiron's renown for his holiness of life and spiritual gifts, and the expansion of Cîteaux surpassed that of Tiron.

Tiron entered into its period of greatest expansion under William of Poitiers (r. ca. 1119–1160).[23] His extensive network of friends and patrons in France and the British Isles and his astonishing effectiveness as a builder of the Tironensian monastic network of congregations suggest that he was from a distinguished family. He enjoyed the favour of the kings of England, Scotland, and France, the dukes of Normandy, Brittany, and Aquitaine, the counts of Blois and Anjou, and the bishops of Chartres, Paris, Angers, Le Mans, and Poitiers. Described as literate and somewhat religious,[24] he was an outstanding administrator but did not possess the charismatic spirituality of Bernard of Clairvaux, whose public life he did not attempt to emulate.

Although William of Poitiers should be ranked among the prominent abbots of the twelfth century, his identity remains a source of scholarly research and debate. Ten Williams, counts of Poitiers, were dukes of Aquitaine before Eleanor's accession in 1137, which complicates computer searches for this remarkable personage. Thompson notes that as a *vir litteratus*, possibly William taught at the schools in Angers, since Ulger, bishop of Angers (r. 1125–1149), referred to William as "*amicus et dominus suus.*"[25] William was frequently titled "*dominus*" in his charters because of his abbatial rank, which does not preclude his being a teacher. His friendship with the bishop of Angers confirms the high-level contacts he used to further Tiron's expansion.

My working hypothesis is that William was close to a prominent family and possibly the ruling family of Poitiers. William IX, duke of Aquitaine (b. 1071, r. 1086–1127), is

---

21 Grant, "Geoffrey of Lèves, Bishop of Chartres," 51n32, citing GC 8: instr., 419–20, no. 7.

22 Waverley Abbey founded 1128 is east of Basingstoke. Tintern Abbey founded 1131 is on the Wye River on the Welsh border north of the Bristol Channel.

23 Abbot William is last mentioned in T2:67, no. 293, ca. 1147, and ibid., 2:74, no. 299, ca. 1150. His successor Abbot Stephan I is first mentioned in ibid., 2:87, no. 314, ca. 1160.

24 Robert of Torigny, *Tractatus de immutatione ordinis monachorum*, in *Recueil des historiens des Gaules et de la France*, ed. Brial, 14:382. "*Cui successit Willelmus Pictavensis, vir literatus et admodum religiosus.*" Robert describes Vital's successor, Geoffrey of Bayeux, as "*vir admodum literatus et in religione fervens.*"

25 Thompson, *The Monks of Tiron*, 132n31, citing T1:121, no. 100 (ca. 1128). Ulger is thought to have been a pupil of Marbod of Angers (b. 1035), archdeacon and master of the cathedral school of Angers ca. 1076, bishop of Rennes (r. 1096–1123).

mentioned with appreciation in the *Vita Bernardi*.[26] William IX was closely and usually positively involved with Bernard's intimate friend Robert of Arbrissel, who prayed for the duke on his deathbed.[27] Moreover, William IX was often an ally of Henry I, whose prominent relatives included many Tironensian donors. I explored the possibility that William was a kinsman of the ducal family.[28] David I's selection of a kinsman or officer of William IX to be the second abbot of Selkirk might have cemented alliances with William IX after the outbreak of war in 1116, the year when William IX's excommunication for the death of Peter II, bishop of Poitiers, was lifted. Thus William IX had multiple connections with Tiron Abbey.

Notwithstanding, blood kinship with the ducal family would be reflected in the donation patterns of Eleanor of Aquitaine, queen of France (1137–1152) and of England (1154–1189), the daughter of William X (b. 1099, r. 1127–1137) and granddaughter of William IX. As duchess of Aquitaine she would have known her natural kin. Her charters show that she made no gifts to Tironensian abbeys, not even to the one endowed by her aunt. Ferrières's founders included Aimeri V, viscount of Thouars (ca. 1095–1127) and his wife Agnès Maude de Poitiers d'Aquitaine (ca. 1100–1159), sister of William X. Ferrières was southwest of Fontevraud, an abbey that enjoyed Eleanor's patronage. Since Eleanor did make a gift to "Peter Raimond, abbot of Saint-Maixent, described by the queen as her kinsman,"[29] her donation pattern indicates that William was not her kinsman or not one she chose to acknowledge.

Another possibility is that William was close to the ducal household. I am deeply indebted to George T. Beech, Professor Emeritus, Western Michigan University, for communicating a strong possibility for William's identity and Poitevin origins. He wrote "Duke William IX, in a charter of 1104, names as his *prévôt* (provost, an administrative and legal agent) a William, the son of Thibaut, *grammaticus* (grammarian), who was a teacher at the school of the abbey of Saint-Hilaire of Poitiers.[30] This *prévôt* appears in

---

26 VB, 11.98, AASS, Apr. 2:0246A; VB, trans. Cline, 104–6. William IX is named as a benefactor in the wooden pendentives and coats of arms on the ceiling ridge beam of the abbatial church of Tiron for the year 1116, but Tiron's charters show no donations from him. T1:cviii.

27 Andreas, *Vita Altera*, AASS, Feb. 3:0615C.

28 William IX, a troubadour and womanizer, had by one mistress at least four natural children: Raymond of Poitiers; Henry of Poitou, abbot of Saint Jean d'Angély and of Peterborough (r. 1127–1131); Adelaide of Poitiers, wife of Ralph of Faye; and Sibylle of Poitiers, abbess of Saintes (see Wilhelm Karl [von] Isenburg, *Stammtafeln zur Geschichte der europäischen Staaten (Europäische Stammtafeln)*, 2 vols. in 1 (Marburg: Stargardt, 1956–1958), 2:76). He probably had other unacknowledged natural children by other mistresses.

29 Vincent, "Patronage, Politics and Piety in the Charters of Eleanor of Aquitaine," 22, 49n226.

30 Beech cites Emile Lesne, *Histoire de la propriété ecclésiastique en France*, 6 vols. (Lille: Girard/Paris: Champion, 1910–1943), 5:68–79, and Robert Favreau, "Les écoles et la culture à St. Hilaire-le-Grand de Poitiers dès origines au début du 12e siècle," *Cahiers de civilization médiévale* 3 (1960): 473–78. "Then there was a canon of St. Hilaire, William, ca. 1108, whose poem was published in the *MGH, Libelli de Lite imperatorum et Pontificum Saeculis XI et XII conscripti*, vol. 3 (1897), 704." Personal communication from George T. Beech, December 14, 2012.

charters of William IX from about 1103–1114, not thereafter." The date of ca. 1114 for his entrance into Tiron Abbey and his subsequent appointment to replace Ralph as abbot of Selkirk ca. 1117–1119 are consistent with William's religious career. A Poitevin William *prévôt* who had held such high office and had acquired extensive legal and administrative experience seems a strong candidate for Tiron's third abbot.[31]

The ducal and allied families made additional gifts, and Tiron expanded into Poitou and Ile-de-France. Eleanor's marriage to the future Louis VII at Bordeaux in 1137 was attended by his large entourage, including influential patrons of Tiron: Bishop Geoffrey II, papal legate in Aquitaine, Thibaut II, count of Blois-Champagne, William II, count of Nevers, and Rotrou II, count of the Perche.[32] Bishop Geoffrey II and Thibaut II accompanied fifteen-year-old Eleanor from Poitiers to Paris and may have won royal support for Tiron's Poitevin abbot, whose languages included the queen's native Provençal. Thibaut II had transferred much of his patronage to the Cistercians, but he was deeply indebted to Tiron at this time. Thibaut II's natural son Hugh of Blois, a knight, was grievously wounded, probably in 1136,[33] and was transported to Tiron despairing of his life. Tiron's physicians saved him, and he recovered at Tiron and professed there as a monk until he was given abbacies by his extended family.[34] Tiron expanded at the time of the royal marriage: Conan III, duke of Brittany (b. ca. 1095, r. 1112–1148), established the Loire island priory of Corsept; Tiron acquired a fief in Paris, confirmed by the new king; while Bois-Aubry near Tours was elevated to abbatial status.[35] Four priories—Notre-Dame-de-Bréau, Sainte-Radegonde-de-Corbeil, Bouligneau, and Ormoy—were established in the 1140s south of Paris on or near the Seine and the Essonne, linking Paris to the Tironensian granaries in the Beauce. Their foundation suggests some royal support for Tironensian expansion toward the power centre of Paris (see Table 5.5).

Like Tiron's founder, Abbot William was well travelled. Undoubtedly he made acquaintances where he lodged along his route from Poitiers to Tiron. He observed the wheat, wine, and salt trade along the Loire and the importance of Le Mans and Châteaudun. His profession at Tiron grounded him in its interpretation of reformed Benedictine monasticism, with Bernard as his spiritual leader. William was chosen to

---

31 William *prévôt*'s being recorded as the son of a grammarian does not rule out his being an unacknowledged natural son of William IX or another member of the ducal family. As abbot of Saint-Cyprien, Bernard had monks from prominent local families and would have known of William son of Thibaut *grammaticus* or someone like him.

32 *La Chronique de Morigny*, ed. Léon Mirot (Paris: Picard, 1909), 66.

33 War broke out in Normandy in 1135 after the death of Henry I, and the fighting in Exmes came near the Perche in 1136. OV, 6:455–65. Exmes is 92 kilometres northwest of Tiron Abbey.

34 With the support of his uncle, King Stephen I of England (r. 1135–1154), Hugh became abbot of Saint Benet of Hulme in Norfolk, abbot of Saint Peter of Chertsey near London, returned to his half-brothers Henry II, count of Champagne (b. 1127, r. 1151–1181) and Thibaut V, count of Blois (b. 1130, r. 1151–1191), and ended his career as abbot of Lagny west of Paris. Cline, "Abbot Hugh: An Overlooked Brother of Henry I, Count of Champagne," specifically 503n3.

35 T1:244–45, no. 216 (ca. 1137) (Corsept); ibid., 1:247, no. 219 (1138) (Paris); ibid., 1:249–50 (1138) (Bois-Aubry).

replace Ralph as abbot of Selkirk during David I's visit shortly after Bernard's death in 1116. Presumably William and twelve additional monks in David's entourage travelled the royal roads on their overland route from Tiron Abbey.[36] They probably stayed in Rouen and crossed from Dieppe to Southampton, London,[37] and north to David's property in Cambridgeshire and to Selkirk in the Borders.[38] William ruled briefly over the well-endowed abbey with income, properties, and dwellings in the Tweed Valley and its burghs and in Northampton. The contrast with rural impoverished Tiron Abbey and its scattered collection of priories was a stark one.[39] When William was recalled to rule Tiron Abbey within two years, he had the coherent Scottish endowment pattern in mind, and his familiarity with Poitou and the Chartrain had been expanded to include Normandy, eastern England, and southern Scotland.

William's return to Tiron occurred against the background of a war in Normandy. In May–June 1119 Henry I's son William Atheling was married to Matilda of Anjou (ca. 1111–1154), and the Bellême lands were restored to William III Talvas, count of Ponthieu (ca. 1093–1172), Robert of Bellême's son and heir. During the summer of 1119, Henry I burned every stronghold in Normandy and decisively defeated Louis VI at Brémule. A papal council took place at Reims in October 1119, where Pope Callistus II (r. 1119–1124) commanded the warring parties to observe the truce of God. One of Abbot William's first actions was to obtain protection locally and to document the rights and possessions of Tiron at the beginning of his reign, and he obtained a letter of protection from Callistus II at Reims on November 1, 1119. The letter mentions no dependencies, only the mother house in the diocese of Chartres, Holy Saviour of Tiron, and was issued in response to petitions by both William and his bishop, Geoffrey II of Lèves.[40]

Callistus II revived the practice of Gregory VII of not exempting monasteries from the spiritual jurisdiction of their diocesan bishop. This letter of protection containing the phrase "*salva nimirium Carnotensis episcopi canonica reverentia*" was an early example, issued in

---

36 VB, 11.99, AASS, 0246B-C; VB, trans. Cline, 106–7.

37 Farrer, *An Outline Itinerary of King Henry I*, 79, no. 373. A writ was issued addressed to David I, among others, at Westbourne; ibid., 79–80, no. 375. Henry I had left England for Normandy immediately after Easter, and his royal party, including David I, awaited favourable winds at Westbourne east of the Isle of Wight and crossed near Southampton.

38 David I's principality of Cumbria in southern Scotland extended from the western ports of Glasgow and Irvine to the eastern port of Berwick-upon-Tweed, and his marriage to Matilda of Huntingdon (ca. 1074–1130/31) in 1113/1114 made him earl of that region in Cambridgeshire. Oram, *David I*, 62–65 (tables 2 and 5). Ermine Street, the Roman road, ran from London north near Huntingdon, to Lincoln and the mouth of the Humber estuary, into Northumberland which then encompassed York. The Great North Road continued to Berwick-upon-Tweed and the Tweed Valley, near which Selkirk was located.

39 VB, 12.107, AASS, Apr. 2:0248C; VB, trans. Cline, 114 (poverty). Thompson, *The Monks of Tiron*, 170n68, cites the foundation charter of Hambye, GC, 11:241, no. 14, which refers to the poverty of the monks of Tiron ca. 1145.

40 T1:36–37, no. 20.

the first year of his pontificate.[41] The canonical jurisdiction of the bishop referred to his right to inspect a monastery, to ordain priests, to bless any new buildings, and to install a new abbot. Tiron's legal status was complex, and both its foundation charter and its papal letter of protection reflect its actual dependence on the bishop and chapter of Chartres.

The letter of protection specifies that the abbey was located in the diocese of Chartres, states that the abbey held its land in allodial tenure or freehold, and threatens clerics and laymen with excommunication for violating the papal letter protecting the abbey property. Tiron was obtaining protection from Saint-Denis of Nogent-le-Rotrou and possibly from its secular overlord, Thibaut II, who may have attempted to appropriate livestock from the abbey herds for the duration of his conflict with the king of France. Thibaut II also held the Tironensian benefactor William II, count of Nevers, in prison during that time. Abbot William was now the head of a congregation of scattered foundations begun under Bernard, and he would spend his tenure consolidating his holdings.

William was an able administrator and skilled at dealing with the personages of his time. As Bernard came to do, William seems to have appreciated the distinction between voluntary and involuntary poverty. In this regard he was a man of the twelfth century, for contemporary writers including Hildebert of Lavardin, bishop of Le Mans, archbishop of Tours (ca. 1056–1133) and Bruno of La Chartreuse (ca. 1030–1101) opined that to be poor in spirit referred to humility of soul and not economic poverty.[42] While Tiron Abbey shared the reformed objective of a stricter interpretation of the *Rule* and a return to simplicity and manual labour, it did not adopt restrictions on property and income similar to those that were later attributed to the Cistercians. William's interpretation of reform entailed placing the monastery on a sound financial footing, and he began to build Tiron into a well-run and prosperous enterprise.[43] The outcome was a competitive advantage of considerable proportion as the monastery created superior products more cheaply and marketed them more profitably than the local producers and merchants. During his tenure Tiron Abbey underwent a period of reorganization and exponential growth, documented piecemeal in its chronologically organized charters, particularly in the papal confirmations of Tironensian property that William obtained in 1132/1133 and 1147 (see appendix 1, Comparison of the Papal Confirmations).

As he built up holdings, William developed many features of what became the profitable Cistercian model of trade and agriculture, although Tiron had an exceptional emphasis on crafts. The Tironensian monks developed marginal lands and consolidated

---

[41] Robinson, *The Papacy 1073–1198*, 222–31.

[42] Constable, *The Reformation of the Twelfth Century*, 148n105.

[43] Ekelund et al., *Sacred Trust*, 42–54. The authors apply modern economic theory to medieval monasteries as agents of the corporate church. The abbot was likened to an economic entrepreneur whose monastery moved from economic self-sufficiency to generating agricultural surpluses. The result was vertical integration as the monastery assumed control of producing, transporting, and marketing its goods and produce. Exemptions for duties, customs, and tolls increased profits. Greater numbers of lay brothers or *conversi*, who were cheaper than lay workers, not only increased profits further but allowed for more labour per units of land and concomitant experimentation with soils, plants, and breeding stock.

scattered holdings through exchanges, purchases, and gifts. They also obtained water and woodland rights, cleared fields, and planted vineyards. In the Beauce William consolidated Tironensian holdings into granges (*grangiae*) and granaries (*graneas*), and supplemented the monks' efforts with professional lay workers and *servientes*. Constable discusses granges established by the Premonstratensians and later by the Cistercians. They were isolated estates worked by lay brothers which produced food for the mother house. Grange agriculture allowed for the use of more advanced techniques in farming and stock-raising than would be possible on scattered local farms. Planting and harvesting operations and crop rotation could be done more efficiently, and the breeding pool for livestock was larger.[44] Tiron had the grange of Puerthe in 1130 and a granger monk 1133–1145.[45] One version of the 1147 papal confirmation specifically lists thirteen Tironensian granaries (shown with approximate distances from Tiron):

Tiron, <1147, Thiron-Gardais
Lièvreville, ca. 1127–1130, Chartrain, ca. 55 kilometres
Villandon, ca. 1128, Chartrain, ca. 55 kilometres
Augerville-les-Malades, ca. 1118, Chartrain, 57 kilometres
Puerthe, ca. 1130, near Châteaudun, ca. 60 kilometres
Péronville, 1130, near Châteaudun, ca. 60 kilometres
Saintes-Vallées, pre-1147, near Ouzouer-le-Marché, ca. 59 kilometres
Villemafroi, 1126, near Ouzouer-le-Marché, ca. 59 kilometres
Choudri, 1127, near Ouzouer-le-Marché, ca. 59 kilometres
Cintry/Saintry, 1115, Orléanais, ca. 75 kilometres
Gémigny, pre-1147, two granaries, Orléanais, ca. 75 kilometres
Saint-Laurent-des-Coutures, 1131–1145, near Pithiviers, ca. 140 kilometres

The Tironensian granges were preponderantly established ca. 1127–1130 and supplied the mother house and other local towns. Later, Prémontré had twenty-six granges in 1138, and Cîteaux had fifteen granges north of the Beauvaisis between 1140 and 1150.

Whereas Cistercian foundations were often founded on the margin of feudal society and independent of secular authority, regular Benedictine foundations owned parish churches and villages and hamlets administered by mayors and provosts, from which they derived income and over which they exercised authority.[46] Like the Benedictines, the Tironensians owned churches and had seigneurial rights in certain towns. They accepted rents from tenants and occasionally the tenants themselves, usually estate workers. They also owned town houses and ovens, mills to grind their own flour, and multure as exceptionally early as ca. 1114–1118.[47] William derived income from Tiron's

---

44 Berman, *Medieval Agriculture*, 61–66.
45 T1:143, no. 121 (1130); ibid., 1:213, no. 187 (1133–1145).
46 Jean Richard, *Les Ducs de Bourgogne et la formation du duché du XIe au XIVe siècle* (Paris: Belles Lettres, 1954), 76–78.
47 T1:17, no. 6; ibid., 1:32–35, no. 18. Berman, *Medieval Agriculture*, 90–91 on limited acquisition of ovens. Bouchard, *Holy Entrepreneurs*, 115, states that in Paris all orders only acquired rights to

craftsmen and marketed their products in the growing towns. The reformed Benedictine congregation flexibly adopted features of both the Cistercian and Benedictine models in rural and urban settings.

William acquired property and benefits from the wealthy and powerful. He was given and purchased urban real estate in Chartres, Châteaudun, and elsewhere. He obtained safeguards and exemptions from customs and tolls in the domains of Henry I and Waleran II of Meulan (1104–1166), seigneur of Pont Audemer,[48] Fulk V, count of Anjou,[49] and Waleran's brother Robert II de Beaumont (1104–1168), seigneur of Le Neubourg, earl of Leicester.[50] He obtained safeguards from the kings of France,[51] including an exemption from fees and tolls for the priory of Meudon, west of Paris on the Seine.[52] William was effective in encouraging donors and in consolidating his acquisitions and resources.

The community at Tiron Abbey 1119–1147 was central to its expansion. A reconstruction of the administrative and abbatial household based on the witnesses to the charters can only be tentative. The Tironensian witnesses included priests, monks, laypersons, and artisans, who were intermingled even when listed as witnesses for the monks. The congregation was so centralized that Merlet notes the near impossibility of distinguishing the claustral priors of Tiron Abbey from the visiting rural priors,[53] and monks living at priories were often listed as monks of Tiron. Nonetheless, contemporaries concur that the community of Tiron Abbey was a large one; Bernard was able to part with monks sent to found other priories.[54] The considerable number of artisans attending chapter and the visitors from local priories support a heavy orientation toward crafts and close communication between the dependencies and the mother house.

William had a personal entourage of monks and *famuli* or servants who assisted him at home and travelled with him abroad.[55] The monks of Tiron had *famuli* of their own,

---

mills and ovens ca. 1140, followed by the Cistercians late in the twelfth century, and that Bernard of Clairvaux made the monks of Mores sell their mill and would not allow them to obtain income from the work of others, citing in n65, Bernard of Clairvaux, *Opera, Epistolae*, 8:403–4, no. 419.

48 T1:75–77, nos. 54–55 (ca. 1122).
49 T1:63, no. 44 (1120–1129).
50 T1:162–63, no. 137 (for Normandy, ca. 1130).
51 T2:114–15, no. 339 (1994).
52 T1:95, no. 76 (1125–1137). Merlet dates the charter ca. 1125, but the reference to Louis, king of the Franks and duke of the Aquitainians, suggests Louis VII post 1137.
53 T2:28n2, no. 257 (1141).
54 VB, 10:87, AASS, Apr. 2:0243C; VB, trans. Cline, 92n7.
55 Thompson, *The Monks of Tiron*, 143n96, notes William's travels to Tournan, Pithiviers, and Fontenay (respectively T1:198, no. 178 (ca. 1132); ibid. 1:184, no. 160 (1131–1145); ibid. 1:79, no. 58 (1124–1142). In Tournan east of Paris, William was collecting unpaid income to the priory. In Pithiviers on the Essonne William was settling a dispute about cattle in the Cluniac priory, accompanied by his monks Philip, Peter, and Osbert of Coutures. In Fontenay-le-Vicomte on the Essonne southwest of Ormoy he was accepting a gift of tithes, accompanied by his monks Philip, Durand, and Simon.

although occasionally the personal *famuli* of the abbot and other monastery officials were also listed as *famuli* of the monks of Tiron. Ralph was listed as a servant of the guest master (*famulus hospitarii*), which confirms that Tiron had a guesthouse when the *Vita Bernardi* was written.[56] Christian was listed as a *monachorum famulus*.[57] Multiple references to the same person being the servant of the monks or of the abbot suggest a cohesive community centred around William. In 1145 William ruled with Philip of Nonancourt as prior, Stephan as cellarer, and a personal chaplain named Stephan.[58]

The titles *prior* and *prepositus* overlap; both could mean prior, provost, the second in rank to the abbot, and the head of a religious community of clerics, monks, or canons. Tiron Abbey had a cellarer (*cellararius*) and sacristan/treasurer (*camerarius*). The chancellor (*cancellarius*) was Geoffrey Grossinus,[59] with responsibility for the records of the large monastery and the scriptorium and its scribes (*scriptores*).[60] Some of the monks of Tiron who were listed with surnames were from seigneurial families who were Tironensian donors, often of land to found priories; others listed as Tironensian monks may simply be monks of those priories. Clearly persons from the local towns were professing as monks at Tiron. The presence of some members of seigneurial families at Tiron suggests that future rural priors professed and received their training at Tiron Abbey before returning to rule the family endowment.

Some Tironensians held the office of priest (*sacerdos* and *presbiter*) whose presence confirms the *Vita Bernardi*'s account of Bernard's deathbed admonition to "the priests and other ministers of God to serve the altar as if they had made themselves into living hosts."[61] Monks could advance through holy orders to the priesthood, but their presence so early in Bernard's tenure suggests that priests (and perhaps their female dependants) had also entered the community.

Orderic Vitalis wrote of Bernard: "So among the men who hastened to share his life were joiners and blacksmiths, sculptors and goldsmiths, painters and masons, vinedressers and husbandmen and skilled artificers of many kinds."[62] Tiron included its lay brothers or *illiterati*, manual labourers and artisans, not only in the prayers of the *opus Dei*, as Bernard directed on his deathbed in 1116,[63] but in chapter and other formal meetings. The number of lay witnesses to charters and the variety of their occupations are impressive. Domestic service includes cellarers, two pantlers, a steward and a doorkeeper. Cooks and bakers are heavily represented, including a pastry cook and two

---

56 T2:50–51, no. 291 [sic. 281 ca. 1145]. VB, 11.92, AASS, Apr. 2:0244F; VB, trans. Cline, 98–99.
57 T2:79, no. 306 (ca. 1150).
58 T2:38–40, no. 269 (1145).
59 T1:99, no. 79 (1126).
60 T1:45, no. 29 (1119–1141), "*Littere autem iste apud Tyron scripte sunt.*"; ibid., 1:226, no. 195s (ca. 1135), "*...et partem etiam hujus cyrographi reservavit...*". Thompson, "The First Hundred Years," 112–13.
61 VB, 13.122, AASS, Apr. 2:0251A; VB, trans. Cline, 125.
62 OV, 8.27, 4:331.
63 VB, 13.122, AASS, Apr. 2:0251B; VB, trans. Cline, 125–26.

turn-spits. Grain and flour were provided by grangers and millers. Farming professions include sharecroppers (*medietarii*), a carter, and a driver. Wine-related professions include vineyard keepers and a wine retailer. Forestry-related professions include fishers, hunters, foresters, fuellers, a forager or provisioner, and a falconer. Livestock-related professions include butchers, skinners, pelterers, tanners, cobblers, shoemakers, a cordwainer or worker in cordovan leather, a shackler, a harness-maker, and a saddler. The large number of smiths includes a goldsmith and a locksmith. The textile trade includes weavers, a fuller, and a felter. The building profession includes masons and carpenters. Other professions include salt-boilers, ropers, a launderer, and a potter. The business and financial sectors are represented by money-changers, merchants, a mercer, a retailer, and a toll collector. The medical profession includes two physicians and a herbalist. These witnesses confirm the profile of Tiron Abbey and its priories as places engaged in sharecropping (*medietaria/métairie*), forestry, animal husbandry, ironwork, and construction. In medieval monasticism this feature is exceptional and allows for vertical economic integration.

This overview of Tiron Abbey shows why donors and patrons continued to found costlier Tironensian religious houses although Cistercian foundations required lesser outlays. A noble donor visiting Tiron Abbey would have found monks and lay brothers who were skilled in animal husbandry and agriculture, building and construction, markets and money-changing, and crafts and artisanal work. Equipment could have been purchased or repaired, horses treated and shod, loans and pledges arranged, and advice about estate management obtained. Physicians were available for medical treatment and priests for private confessions. The scriptorium provided legal services, with prototypes for airtight contracts providing for multiple contingencies. The abbot had over a thousand-kilometre network of contacts ranging from kings to sharecroppers and could advise on disputes. Tiron Abbey no longer embraced poverty but gave good value for the investment.

Tiron Abbey had some exceptionally distinguished monks. A forged charter dated 1120 claims that Louis VI was cured of an incurable disease by the prayers of Bernard and gave one of his (presumably natural) sons as an oblate to Tiron Abbey.[64] Saint Adjutor of Vernon was an imprisoned crusader who claimed to have been freed from his chains though the intercession of Saint Mary Magdalene and Bernard of Tiron and transported overnight from the Holy Land to his native Vernon. He became a hermit-monk of Tiron Abbey and died there in 1131 in the presence of Abbot William. His life was written up by Hugh of Amiens, archbishop of Rouen (ca. 1085–1164)[65] and ignored by Geoffrey Grossus in the *Vita Bernardi*. John, bishop of Glasgow (r. 1114–1147), was at Tiron during William's tenure. David I of Scotland initially supported his niece,

---

[64] T1:46, 48, no. 30 (1120).

[65] Hugh of Amiens, archbishop of Rouen, *Adiutor, prope Vernonium in Normannia*, AASS, Apr.3:0823F–25D. Adjutor and his brother Matthew (born before 1070) are identified as the sons of John, seigneur of Vernon, and Rosemonde of Blaru. Daniel Power writes, "A full reconstruction of the various Anglo-Norman families called Vernon would require a separate book," in *The Norman Frontier*, 526.

Empress Matilda (1102–1167), who was opposed by the archbishop of York and the bishop of Durham. Under pressure to submit to York, David's former tutor abandoned the bishopric of Glasgow and became a monk at Tiron Abbey 1136–1138 until he was recalled to his see.[66] David I made peace with King Stephen in 1139, and his son Henry (1114–1152) became earl of Northumberland. At the request of Bishop John, David I and Earl Henry granted a Tironensian ship safeguard and exemption from duties as it traded in Scotland and Northumberland.[67] Ties between Tiron and Scotland were close at this time. Residence of such personages at Tiron indicates the abbey's prominence in the mid-twelfth century.

Tiron Abbey was rural and dependent upon the cathedral chapter, so its monks soon established a community and headquarters in the town of Chartres. Tiron Abbey is located in the forests of the Perche and is surrounded by hamlets. The nearest town is Nogent-le-Rotrou, a day's journey away. Tiron's water supply, the Thironne River, is a meandering stream whose flow is temporarily improved by the man-made ponds. The workrooms would have been suited to woodwork, leatherwork, metalwork, and sculpture, but noisy and malodorous trades requiring large amounts of water would have been disruptive to the school, the scriptorium, and the *opus Dei*. Moving such trades to a priory in an urban setting with trade guilds on the Eure River was profitable and ensured greater tranquility at the abbey.

Tiron's secular overlord was Thibaut II and its governing body was the chapter of canons of Chartres Cathedral. The cathedral, bishop's palace, and the canons' cloister were in the town centre, with the comital palace to the south and the church of Saint-Pierre of the Benedictine abbey of Saint-Père-en-Vallée further south. The establishment of a priory in Chartres gave William an urban residence near the religious and political centres.

Bishop Geoffrey II was the brother of Hugh of Lèves, provost of Chartres Cathedral, and of Gauslen, seigneur of Lèves, a town north of Chartres. Lindy Grant describes Bishop Geoffrey II as "a leader of the moderate reformers in the French church," "the most politically adept and thus politically prominent" among them, and "the great conciliator of his time." Grant describes him as "the famous disposer and arranger of secular business," entrusted with the governance of Aquitaine in 1137 upon the accession of Louis VII.[68] Bishop Geoffrey II was a friend and confidant of Popes Callistus II, Honorius II, and Innocent II (r. 1130–1143) and was highly esteemed by Louis VI. He was an active participant in church councils and a fighter of heresy and schism alongside Bernard of Clairvaux. In 1130 he was named papal legate in the provinces of Bourges, Bordeaux, Tours, and Dol-de-Bretagne.[69] He travelled to Milan and to Aquitaine in 1130 to provide critical support for the election of Innocent II. William was backed by his prestigious bishop as Tiron expanded, for Geoffrey II made and confirmed donations

---

66 Oram, *David I*, 152.

67 T1:80–81, no. 60 (1124–1145); ibid., 2:14–15, no. 241 (ca. 1140).

68 Lindy Grant, "Arnulf's Mentor," 173nn3–4, citing the Morigny Chronicle, 70, 68, and 178n25, ibid., 68.

69 GC, 8:1136E; PL 179:0619A, no. 550 (1142).

to Tiron and lent his support in disputes (see Appendix 2, Disputes). His close relationship with Bernard of Clairvaux, the confessor of Thibaut II, provided political balance for his friendship with the rulers of France, with whom the count occasionally warred. His role as Innocent II's papal legate in Aquitaine ca. 1132–1144 reinforced William's ties with the rulers of that region. Whereas Tiron Abbey enjoyed extensive support from the king of England and his relatives early in its founding, Bishop Geoffrey II oriented Tiron toward Paris and furthered better political relations with Ile-de-France because of his support from the French kings.

Bishop Geoffrey II regularly attended important assemblies of bishops. Chartres itself was the site of several episcopal councils during Geoffrey II's reign, and after 1117 Tiron owned houses and real estate in that town. If William attended these councils and events, he would have been exposed to ecclesiastical and secular personages of the highest rank and to the great political and theological issues of his time. Even if William only learned of them secondhand, he had in his immediate superior a wise and skilful adviser as he expanded Tiron's holdings in France, Normandy, and Aquitaine.

Chartres was an important market town with street names that indicate its many trades. Pilgrims and comital troops provided an urban market for produce and crafts. The money-changers ran the mint where local coins, called *chartrains*, had been minted since the ninth century. Tiron's early properties were all on streets that led into the Place des Halles, located southwest of the cathedral and west of the count's castle inside the southwest city gate known today as the Place des Epars, in the market district.[70] In 1121 Thibaut II helped to found or endow several religious foundations, including the priory of Tironensian monks at Chartres. His motives were pious and political. He sincerely grieved the loss of many kin in the 1120 wreck of the *White Ship*. He was also siding with Louis VI in a war that was heating up between the French king and Henry V, king of Germany (b. 1086, r. 1099–1125), in which his uncle Hugh, count of Troyes and Champagne (b. ca. 1074, r. 1093–1125) and he were leading a large army, purportedly of eight thousand men.[71] In a letter dated 1121, Thibaut II granted to the Tironensian priory at Chartres six dependants (*servientes*): a smith, corder, cellarer, baker, vine-dresser, fuller, and another six bakers.[72] The trades named suggests that the Tironensian priory of Chartres was feeding and supplying large numbers of people locally, including, perhaps, Thibaut's army, in addition to pilgrims and townspeople. The fuller suggests that Tiron Abbey was processing its wool clip into textiles; Thibaut II also gave the area around the mill with all its customs. The cellarer may have been responsible for a wine warehouse, as the vine-dresser was responsible for its vines. Other witnesses included Hato the pantler (steward of the bread pantry), Hubert Asinarius/l'Anier, and Lambert

---

70 Chédeville, *Chartres et ses campagnes*, 421, 435.

71 Jean-Baptiste Souchet, *Histoire du diocèse et de la ville de Chartres*, 4 vols. (Chartres: Garnier, 1866–1873), 3:405.

72 T1:64–65, no. 45. CNDC, 1:clxxiii. Merlet notes that the status of serfs or dependants at Chartres in the twelfth century was not exactly servile; they could buy and sell property, testify in court, and were considering forming a commune.

the cellarer. The grant was made in perpetuity and claimed in an inventory.[73] In many of these charters certain witnesses appeared consistently and were either monks or associates of the priory of Chartres.

The witness lists for the Tironensian charters correspond to the family names in the cartulary of Notre-Dame de Chartres and show inclusion of craftsmen with the priory officers. Although many witnesses are listed with occupational surnames, in the Chartrain cartulary those surnames reflect involvement by an ancestor or the witness himself in a trade or craft. Hubert Asinarius, who became prior of Chartres priory, was a member of the family that subsequently produced Roger Asinarius in 1300.[74] Robert and William Aculeus or Aguillon were followers of Stephen-Henry, count of Blois and Chartres, as early as 1100–1101,[75] whereas Dagobert *aculearius*, who witnessed many Tironensian charters related to Chartrain properties, was a maker of pins and needles and a mercer.[76] Other witnesses included Hugh the money-changer (*monetarius*), a cellarer, furriers, a fuller, a locksmith, a launderer,[77] Ralph the goldsmith, Herbert the cutler (*cutellarius*),[78] Hernaud and Gerbert, merchants (*institores*).[79] The distinctions are difficult to discern but suggest that affiliation with the priory of Chartres improved their status. The charters indicate upward mobility for the layman Hubert Asinarius, who became prior, and for the families of the *servientes*. The presence of a large community of Tironensian monks in Chartres does not exclude students and cathedral workers, but the best explanation seems to be that Chartres, with its pilgrims and the comital troops, offered a suitable setting and large market for tradesmen and bakers. A forged charter dated 1179 listed the house that the Tironensian monks had in Chartres, with tracts of land, a meadow, vineyards, mills, and the liberties the monks had in that city.[80] The description of the urban property corresponds to the genuine charters. In all, through gifts and purchases, Tiron built up substantial real-estate holdings within the city wall of Chartres, in addition to vineyards and other properties outside the city.

Tiron purchased a house that became the Hôtel de Tiron ca. 1130, giving William a town residence suitable to his abbatial rank.[81] The headquarters was south of the ecclesiastical centre but close to the cloister of the cathedral canons and the count's castle. By 1132 it had a chapel where charters were witnessed, often in the bishop's presence.[82] By the end of the fourteenth century a beautiful stone cross gave the district the name

---

73 T2:159, no. 377 (ca. 1250).
74 CNDC, 2:385
75 CNDC, 1:107, no. 24.
76 T1:195n4, no. 174 (ca. 1132).
77 T1:147–48, no. 126 (ca. 1130); ibid., 1:190, no. 167 (ca. 1132); ibid., 1: 195, no. 174 (ca. 1132); ibid., 1:228, no. 199 (1135).
78 T2:7, no. 233 (ca. 1140).
79 T2:5, no. 231 (ca. 1140).
80 T2:103–6, specifically 104, no. 328 (1179).
81 T1:147–48, no. 126 (ca. 1130).
82 T1:191, no. 168 (ca. 1132).

of Croix-aux-Moines-de-Tiron.[83] With Waleran II of Meulan to the north engaged in trade with Normandy and England, Tiron became positioned at Chartres to become one of his suppliers and possibly to participate in such trade itself. With a headquarters and a priory, Tiron Abbey had a central urban base for business and communication on major roads and waterways to Normandy, Anjou, the Loire Valley, and Ile-de-France.

William established Tiron's centralized administrative structure and determined its growth patterns. During the course of the twelfth century Tiron expanded its foundation of abbeys and priories in Normandy, Aquitaine, Blois, Anjou, and other regions that now lie within the borders of France. Tiron's expansion in modern France cannot be considered in isolation from the British Isles. During the first part of the twelfth century the abbots were personally acquainted and probably in communication with one another, and their trading patterns crossed the English Channel. Tiron was engaged in agriculture and crafts but also in active marketing of its production. Ultimately the Cistercians also had a vertically integrated enterprise with their sheepfolds in Britain and their sales of finished wool products in the Low Countries and elsewhere. Tiron may have been an economic model for Cîteaux.

The *Rule* stipulates that Benedictine monasteries are to be autonomous and gives the abbot the responsibility of interpreting its provisions by establishing the rules and customs of the house. At the beginning of William's tenure, central administration was impossible. Tiron and its daughter foundations were faced with wars and rebellions in Scotland, Wales, England, Normandy, the Perche, and the Beauce. Thibaut II and Louis VI and VII were involved in local conflicts, with Bernard of Clairvaux and Bishop Geoffrey II acting as respected mediators. The unrest led to requisitioning and pledging property, as did Fulk V of Anjou's journey to Jerusalem in 1128 and the Second Crusade in 1147. The elevation of the most distant foundations to abbeys gave them higher status in hard times. Nevertheless, expansion through wealth and patronage raised the problem of daughter abbeys reverting to the more comfortable lifestyle of the regular Benedictine congregation, particularly if they were controlled by the local aristocracy. The solution was oversight by the mother house. William established himself as an abbot general who ruled over his priors and the abbots of the dependent abbeys of his congregation across political boundaries with the counsel of an annual general chapter.

At the beginning of William's tenure Tiron had two distant abbeys: Selkirk in the Scottish Borders and Joug-Dieu in Beaujolais, and negotiations were under way for the elevation of the priory of Wales to St. Dogmaels Abbey ca. 1120. Early in William's tenure, charters were issued to confirm that David I had founded Selkirk and to list the properties given to the abbeys. Barrow dates the Selkirk charter 1120/1121 or 1123/1124.[84] Three charters confirm the priory of Wales's elevation and the installation of its first Tironensian abbot, Fulchard, in 1121. Henry I issued two confirmations of the perpetual gifts and alms made by Martin FitzMartin (d. 1159) to St. Dogmaels. The first charter,

---

83 Guillemin, *Thiron, abbaye médiévale*, 60.
84 *The Charters of King David I*, ed. G. W. S. Barrow (Woodbridge: Boydell, 1999), 58–59, no. 14. *Kelso Liber*, 1:3–4, no. 1.

issued at Mortain, France, June 1118, does not mention the foundation as an abbey.[85] The second charter, issued at modern Sainte-Gauburge-Sainte-Colombe, southeast of Sées, ca. 1119–1120 to the abbot and entire monastery of Tiron "refers to the abbey (*abbatia*) of Cemais being free and quit (*libra et quieta*) as it was when it was a priory or cell.[86] The third English royal charter was not copied into the cartulary of Tiron, although William was present when it was issued. The royal charter describes how Robert FitzMartin obtained an abbot for St. Dogmaels from William and Tiron Abbey after many entreaties, provided for the abbey's needs to the extent his resources allowed, confirmed the abbey's independence from secular power, and enumerated its extensive properties. Dated September 10 [1121], it was issued when the first abbot Fulchard was enthroned by Bernard, bishop of St. Davids (r. 1115–1148), in the presence of Henry I, Queen Adeliza (ca. 1103–1151), William, and other witnesses who caused their seals to be affixed.[87] Geoffrey Grossus also describes St. Dogmaels as a priory subsequently elevated to an abbey (1121) and Selkirk as a priory elevated to an abbey shortly after Bernard's death in 1116.[88] He emphasizes that the abbot of Tiron chose the abbots of the daughter abbeys of the mother house. Although accurate about France, he may be reacting to moves toward independence by Tiron's British abbeys on the periphery of the Tironensian network.

The fourth Tironensian charter for St. Dogmaels is an acte-notice attaching to a single year the events of several.[89] Merlet notes that the original is on parchment; Thompson describes it as the Cemais chirograph (ADEL, H 1771) in her analysis of its provisions. Several significant passages reflect the situation in Wales. The first passage, taken from the English royal charter of 1121, states that nothing can be established by any secular power, the king, his princes, or his successors. The second passage claims that at Sainte-Gauburge the king, William Atheling, Robert FitzMartin, and the abbot first elected and his monks granted that the abbot and monks of Tiron would determine the future election of the abbots of St. Dogmaels and any subordinate foundations.

---

85 T1:42, no. 26 (ca. 1119). It was witnessed by Ranulf, Chancellor (1107–1123), Geoffrey FitzPain (b. ca. 1081), William Peverel of Dover (ca. 1050–ca. 1115), Hugh IV of Montfort-sur-Risle (ca. 1068–ca. 1147), and William de Roullours/Rollos, lord of Bourne (ca. 1050–ca. 1130), and it bears the king's seal.
86 T1:41–42, no. 25 (ca. 1119). It was witnessed by William "Brito" d'Aubigny (1086–1155), lord of Belvoir, the king's butler, with a confirmation by the king's son William Atheling.
87 *Monasticon Anglicanum*, ed. Dugdale, 4 (1823): 130, no. 2, Charter R (76) 18 Edw. 3^2 m. 13, no. 47. Trans. Pritchard, *The History of St. Dogmael's Abbey*, 46–47.
88 VB, 11.99, AASS, Apr. 2:0246B–C; VB, trans. Cline, 106–7.
89 T1:49–51, no. 31 (1120). It describes St. Dogmaels' elevation to abbatial status and ends with a specific dating clause of 1120 when Louis was king of France and Henry was governour of England. I acknowledge with deep gratitude the contribution of Constance Berman, Professor, Medieval Social, Economic, Religious, and Women's History (France and Italy), University of Iowa. In a personal communication of August 11, 2006, she analyzed no. 31 and concluded that it was an acte-notice, a historical record of Tiron's stipulations for ruling a daughter abbey, backdated to 1120 to show consent by Henry I and his son William Atheling. Her analysis resulted in my noticing its resemblance to the elevation charters of later abbeys.

In fact, the Sainte-Gauburge charter (1119–1120) at Tiron makes no such assertion of Tironensian oversight. The third passage provides for the removal of any abbot improperly and secularly elected and his replacement by the authority of Tiron. The fourth passage prescribes anathema for those who are ambitious or blinded by greed and commit the heretical crime of simony. The fifth passage stipulates that abbots on Tironensian dependencies beyond the seas must attend the annual general chapter at Tiron at Pentecost every three years. Other passages referring to the abbot of Tiron's precedence when he visits,[90] mutual spiritual support, and the requirement of letters of commendation for disobedient brothers seeking to join other religious communities are not unique to Wales. Thompson notes the reference to Tiron's papal confirmation of November 1, 1119, and the charter ends with Bishop Ivo's blessing at the consecration of Tiron's cemetery ca. 1114: "the Lord Jesus Christ, who had been 'made poor when he was rich that he might make us rich in our poverty and cure us in our infirmity.'"[91] The acte-notice is backdated 1120 because it states that the priory of Wales was elevated to abbatial status during William Atheling's lifetime.

It is uncertain whether the Cemais chirograph anticipates or reflects the ongoing problems of the Welsh princes' rebellion against Norman overlords and their desire to profiteer from selling ecclesiastical offices or from installing their kinsmen therein. The *White Ship* sank on November 25, 1120, and the dead included both William Atheling and Richard, earl of Chester, resulting in a rebellion in Powys. In June 1121 Henry I led an expedition against the Welsh, and in September Fulchard travelled to St. Dogmaels with Abbot William and was installed as abbot in the presence of the king, queen, and bishop.[92] This acte-notice may be a response to the princes of Deheubarth seizing control of the abbot's appointment during a period of rebellion against Norman overlordship in late 1120. Other periods of warfare included the war in Wales in 1135 and the pillaging of St. Dogmaels by Welsh princes in 1138.[93] A struggle for the bishopric of St. Davids began in 1198 between Gerald of Wales, archdeacon of Brechin (ca. 1146–ca. 1223), and his illiterate cousin Walter, abbot of St. Dogmaels (r. 1198–1203), both of the ruling house.[94] The election of an illiterate abbot clearly indicates family preferment

---

90 Similar wording is used in the twelfth-century customary of Saint-Victor of Paris: *Consuetudines, Liber ordinis Sancti Victoris Parisiensis*, cap. 6, line 2, "*Quotiens uice abbatis fungitur, ab omnibus ei reuerentia exhibenda est, siue in choro, siue in capitulo, siue refectorio, siue quolibet alio loco, hoc modo.*" The phrase that the *prior major* takes precedence in choir, chapter, and refectory is used by Cluny in the early thirteenth century. *Bibliotheca Cluniacensis*, ed. Martin Marrier (Paris, 1614), 1587: "*Prior Major Cluniacensis in iam dictis quatuor locis, scilicet, Monasterio, Claustro, Capitulo & Refectorio, cum fuerit ibidem, sedeat in loco Prioris, faciatque & exerceat ante omnes ea quae spectant ad Officium Priorum locorum in praefatis quatuor locis.*" www.uni-muenster.de/Fruehmittelalter/Projekte/Cluny/BibliothecaCluniacensis/

91 Thompson, *The Monks of Tiron*, 145–47. T1:36–37, no. 20; ibid., 1:14, no. 2.

92 Farrer, *An Outline Itinerary of King Henry I*, 95. Hollister, *Henry I*, 282.

93 Pritchard, *The History of St. Dogmael's Abbey*, 49.

94 Gerald of Wales, *De Rebus a se Gestis*, 3.4, ed. J. S. Brewer, *Giraldi Cambrensis Opera*, Rolls Series 21, 8 vols. (London: Longman, 1861), 1:94–95.

and not a qualified appointment by the abbot and general chapter of Tiron. If Tiron's approval was sought at all, the decision was to accept the local candidate. An inquisition conducted in 1329 established that the abbey had the right of free election.[95] Clearly St. Dogmaels was outside the sphere of influence and discipline of Tiron and under the control of the ruling house of Deheubarth by the end of the twelfth century.

This acte-notice is an early reference to William's exceptionally centralized rule by an annual general chapter at Tiron to deliberate, impose discipline, and appoint the heads of priories and other foundations. A seasoned traveller, he considered triennial visits appropriate for distant abbeys. Thompson notes that the Cemais chirograph became the template for the elevation of Asnières (1129) and Bois-Aubry (1138), and that the Cistercian houses had independent abbots subject to visitation, whereas Tiron sought to appoint the abbots.[96] Purportedly Cîteaux submitted the *Charter of Charity* and the *Exordium Cistercii*, with a similar provision, to Callistus II for his approval in 1119. Berman establishes a sequence of the manuscripts of Cîteaux's governing charters, proves the 1119 bull a forgery prepared ca. 1170 and backdated, and shows that other manuscripts were prepared ca. 1165–1175 and presented recent innovations as established by earlier generations. In that case Tiron may be an organizational model for Cîteaux.[97]

Good horses were critical to medieval travel and transportation, and Tiron was in a unique position. Rotrou II was lord of Tudela 1123–1135 in the newly conquered Spanish territories, and he also travelled back and forth to England and northern France during that period.[98] His sister Juliana lived near Tiron and acted as regent of the Perche during his absences. He is credited with importing Arab studs from his crusades and expeditions in Spain to cross with "native" draft mares in the Perche, creating the valuable Percheron breed with stamina for hauling and trotting considerable distances. Tiron Abbey obtained and purchased meadowland in the Huisne valley north of Nogent-le-Rotrou, the Percheron breeding centre. Tiron often gave horses as countergifts, and involvement in horse-breeding would have furthered the exceptional mobility of its monks and its involvement in trade.

Several distinctive acquisition patterns emerged from the data provided in subsequent chapters. Clusters of churches and priories were acquired in and around a town, where the priories supplied the town with foodstuffs and livestock and offered lodging for the first leg of a journey. Chains of priories and churches were acquired a day's journey apart between towns, providing overnight lodging along trade routes in war-torn and brigand-infested regions. Carters could not bivouac but needed to reach an enclosure for the night to protect their loads and draft animals. Rural agglomerations of foundations and properties were acquired, spaced so closely that today they share the

---

95 Cowley, *The Monastic Order in South Wales*, 198–99 (chap. 4).
96 Thompson, *The Monks of Tiron*, 148–49. T1:49–51, no. 31 (1120); ibid., 1:131–34, no. 112 (1129); ibid., 1:249–50, no. 221 (1138).
97 Berman, *The Cistercian Evolution*, xii–xv, 59–60, 86–92.
98 Thompson, *Power and Border Lordship*, 71–74.

same postal code, providing economies of scale in grain-growing and animal-husbandry regions. By 1147 most Tironensian foundations in its rural network in modern France were spaced a day's journey or ride apart.

Foundations on navigable rivers were more widely spaced. River travel on flat-bottomed barges was swifter, safer, and cheaper than carts for transporting cargo long distances. Thus Tiron had few foundations between L'Aigle and Pont-Audemer, both on the Risle, and no foundations near Angers, which could be reached via the Huisne and Sarthe by way of Le Mans. The Loire linked Joug-Dieu to the wheat fields of the Beauce, the vineyards of Anjou, and the salt centres at the mouth of the Loire in Brittany, providing a waterway for urban commodity trade. Tiron had important abbeys in the vicinity but few priories near the Loire. The Essonne linked the Beauce to the Seine and Paris.

The expansion of the congregation of Tiron 1119–1147 and subsequently occurred for multiple reasons besides William's administrative skills and strong leadership. The twelfth century itself was an era of transformation and expansion. Favourable climate conditions caused an agricultural surplus that increased population and permitted the rise of towns. The strengthened papacy provided religious leadership and reform. Strong monarchs consolidated independent duchies into kingdoms. Tiron rode this wave and expanded for religious, economic, and political reasons, supported by powerful magnates and their kinship groups.

From the religious viewpoint, the expansion of Tiron reflects the piety of donors and the extension of reformed monasticism supported by bishops. The warring aristocracy had long since concluded that their best chance of salvation lay in obtaining the intercessory prayers of holy religious persons and being buried among them in the monasteries they had founded and endowed. Moreover, as laypersons, they were exhorted to return "unjustly held" income-producing churches and their lands to the religious authorities. Tiron's position was strengthened by other religious leaders, such as the bishop and canons of the cathedral of Chartres, who extended their protection and benefactions to the abbey, and by other bishops, who made gifts and transferred property to the abbey.

From an economic viewpoint, Tiron's expansion was driven by a growing population that required clearing and draining wasteland for cultivation. Livingstone notes that "Early in the twelfth century most of the Chartrain, with the exception of less desirable regions, was either in the process of being cleared or already settled." She observes that, as land grew scarcer, lay and monastic property owners began to use their existing land for sources of income, such as mills, in a cash-based economy.[99] Tiron's donations were not entirely wasteland, but the abbey, with its large community of at least one hundred monks and lay brothers (*illiterati*), had the labour and skills to participate in such projects on land that required significant investments to upgrade it. The development of the monetary economy and urban expansion entailed some breakdown of the traditional village support systems for persons who were economically marginalized. Concurrently, the Perche suffered from exceptional famine and outbreaks of leprosy.[100] Tiron Abbey offered a refuge for the displaced, and the working members of the

---

99 Livingstone, "Kith and Kin," 436–38.

100 Beck, *Saint-Bernard de Tiron*, 226–29.

community supported the monastery by farming, stock-raising, and crafts, to such an extent that the degree of investment in crafts appears to be exceptional and perhaps a particular trademark of Tiron. Moreover, the rise of towns in the twelfth century led to increased demand for wheat, salt, wine, meat, fish, wood, cloth, leather and metal goods, and even luxury goods. As Tiron expanded it became positioned to provide these products to urban centres.

From a political viewpoint, Tiron's expansion was encouraged by royal and noble donors on all sides of a troubled border region, who gave land and income to build priories in strategic areas, sometimes as part of the Normanization process. Henry I, king of England and duke of Normandy; Thibaut II, count of Blois-Champagne; and William IX (d. 1127) and William X (d. 1137), successive counts of Poitiers and dukes of Aquitaine, were donors from one bloc, and Louis VI and Louis VII, successive kings of France, and Fulk V and Geoffrey V (b. 1113, r. 1129–1151), counts of Anjou, were donors from the opposing bloc. Tiron endured requisitioning and strove to maintain its neutrality, but its donors included all the parties involved, and the abbot could encourage negotiations and provide access to a communication network.

The charters support all these religious, economic, and political explanations for Tiron's remarkable growth; their convergence under William's skillful administration led to Tiron's expansion in the first half of the twelfth century. Tiron's acceptance of women, its openness to lay craftsmen, its investment in effective economic and political networks, and its religious authority all help to explain its success. Over the course of the twelfth century the congregation of Tiron continued to be involved in monastic reform, the Normanization of the Celtic fringe of the British Isles, the Scottish independence movement, and mediation and navigation of political tensions on the continent.

The kinship group of Henry I became important Tironensian donors. The *Vita Bernardi* describes Henry I's summons to Bernard of Tiron to visit him in Normandy, where Bernard gave spiritual counsel to the English king and won royal support for the impoverished new abbey. The king's generosity was in character: Henry I extended royal benefactions to Norman Benedictine houses and was supportive of Hildebert, bishop of Le Mans, Ivo, bishop of Chartres, and the monks of Saint-Père at Chartres, through gifts of tithes. Hollister notes that the king gave exceptional support to Cluny including contributions to its basilica church. He had established or encouraged the establishment of foundations of Augustinian canons in England, which preceded the reformed Benedictine Tironensian foundations in the British Isles. He loved hermits very much. He supported Vital of Savigny with gifts and exemptions from tolls,[101] and he extended his patronage to Bernard after their meeting, providing cash income including fifteen marks annually from the Exchequer and building the dormitory to replace their huts.[102] Henry I was a shrewd judge of character, and his meeting with Bernard resulted in high-level patronage of a poor rural hermit community.

The *Vita Bernardi* names Tiron's other major donors besides Henry I—Louis VI, followed by Thibaut II—with their stories and benefactions. The next donors listed,

---

[101] Hollister, *Henry I*, 396–418.
[102] VB, 11.96, AASS, Apr. 2:0245F; VB, trans. Cline, 102–3.

perhaps by rank, are: William [IX or X], duke of Aquitaine; Fulk V, count of Anjou and king of Jerusalem; Robert FitzRoy of Caen, earl of Gloucester (1090/1095–1147), William II, count of Nevers; Guy II of Montlhéry, count of Rochefort, Henry I of Le Neubourg, earl of Warwick (brother of Robert I de Beaumont, count of Meulan, earl of Leicester, ca. 1048–1118), Robert FitzMartin; Guichard III, seigneur of Beaujeu (r. 1102–1137); Geoffrey III, viscount of Châteaudun; Girard II Berlay of Montreuil-Bellay (d. ca. 1155); and Brice of Le Chillou (fl. 1113–1138). The account of the donors ends with the stories of the founding of St. Dogmaels Abbey by Robert FitzMartin and of Selkirk Abbey by David I, Tiron's earliest foundations located in the British Isles.[103] Rotrou II, count of the Perche, is acknowledged earlier.[104] A salient feature of this list of donors is the large number of relatives of Henry I, by blood and by marriage.[105]

Henry I married both his legitimate children by Edith/Matilda of Scotland (ca. 1080–1118) to the children of Fulk V, count of Anjou, his powerful neighbour in Normandy. William Atheling married Matilda of Anjou, an alliance that ended with his drowning in 1120. Empress Matilda (1102–1167) married Geoffrey V, count of Anjou, and she, her son Henry II, and Henry II's son Richard I "the Lionheart" (r. 1189–1199) paid fifteen to twenty marks per year to Tiron Abbey. Henry I's brother-in-law David I founded the Tironensian abbey of Selkirk, later Kelso, and the priory of Lesmahagow. David's grandsons William I "the Lion" and David II, earl of Huntingdon (1152–1219), founded the Tironensian abbeys of Arbroath and Lindores respectively. Henry I's sister Adela, countess of Blois and Chartres, and his nephew Thibaut II were the secular overlords of Tiron and prominent donors. In this way Henry I and his legitimate kinsmen by blood and marriage formed a crucial donor network for Tiron Abbey.

In addition, Henry I had at least twenty-five natural children whom he fathered in the 1080s and 1090s both before his accession and afterwards during his marriage.[106] He married these children into prominent families to establish a calculated network of alliances. The first wife of Rotrou II, count of the Perche, Tiron's earliest benefactor, was Matilda FitzRoy, a natural daughter of Henry I who drowned in the shipwreck of the *White Ship*. Robert, earl of Gloucester, was the oldest son of Henry I and a prominent statesman. In Wales, Robert was lord of Glamorgan, and Henry I de Beaumont, seigneur of Le Neubourg, earl of Warwick, was lord of Gower. As overlords of Robert FitzMartin, lord of Cemaes, they were protectors of St. Dogmaels. Henry I's Welsh mistress Nest, Princess of Deheubarth (ca. 1085–ca. 1136), bore Henry I a son named Henry FitzHenry (ca. 1104–1158). Nest was the daughter of Rhys ap Tewdwr, Prince of Deheubarth (d. 1093), and Gladys of Powys, and the wife of Gerald de Windsor, constable of Pembroke (1070–1136). Her other descendants included both Gerald of Wales and Walter, abbot of St. Dogmaels. The Beaumont-Meulan family had early and multiple connections with

---

103 VB, 11.96–99, AASS, Apr. 2:0245E–46C; VB, trans. Cline, 102–7.
104 VB, 9.81, AASS, Apr. 2:0241D–E; VB, trans. Cline, 86–87.
105 Ruth Harwood Cline, "The Kinship Network of Henry I and the Expansion of the Congregation of Tiron in the Twelfth Century," a research paper presented at 2000 Midwest Conference on British Studies, University of Cincinnati, Ohio, October 27, 2000.
106 Thompson, "Affairs of State."

Henry I and with Tiron, for Henry I de Beaumont and Le Neubourg, earl of Warwick, married Rotrou II's sister Margaret of the Perche. His brother Robert I of Beaumont, count of Meulan, earl of Leicester, married Elisabeth (ca. 1085–ca. 1148), daughter of Hugh the Great, count of Vermandois (1057–1101), the brother of Philip I of France and the uncle of Louis VI. They had twin sons, Waleran II of Meulan and Robert II de Beaumont, and a daughter Isabel of Meulan (b. ca. 1102/1107). The Beaumont twins gave Tiron exemptions from taxes, tolls, and duties as well as other important gifts. When Waleran II of Meulan was imprisoned for rebellion against Henry I (1121–1124), his sister Isabel became the king's mistress, bore him a daughter named Isabel (b. ca. 1120), obtained Waleran II's release, and married Gilbert de Clare, 1st earl of Pembroke (ca. 1100–1148).[107] The union created another royal connection for St. Dogmaels.

Other natural daughters of Henry I had connections with Tiron. Maud FitzRoy (ca. 1091–1128) was the wife of Conan III, duke of Brittany (ca. 1095–1148), the founder of the Loire priories of Corsept and Sept-Faux.[108] Sybilla of Normandy (1092–1122) was the wife of Alexander I, king of Scotland (b. 1078, r. 1107–1124), the brother of David I, founder of Selkirk. Mabel FitzRoy (m. ca. 1110) was the wife of William Gouet III, seigneur of Montmirail (ca. 1120-ca. 1169), who founded the priory of Châtaigniers ca. 1117 in memory of Bernard.[109] Constance FitzRoy (m. ca. 1130) was the wife of Roscelin, viscount of Beaumont-sur-Sarthe (d. 1176). Constance's daughter Ermengarde of Beaumont (ca. 1170–1233/1234) was the wife of William I "the Lion," king of Scotland, the founder of the Tironensian abbey of Arbroath in 1178. This extensive kinship network of Henry I supported Tironensian foundations and expansion in France and the British Isles.

The careers of Bishop Geoffrey II and Abbot William ended ca. 1150. In 1147 Geoffrey II accompanied Bernard of Clairvaux to Toulouse, where Bernard preached against the heretic Henry of Lausanne (d. ca. 1148). Geoffrey II returned to Chartres and died on January 24, 1149.[110] The last Tironensian charter bearing William's name is dated ca. 1150.[111] William died on 6 January of an unspecified year, and he was remembered at Mont-Saint-Michel but not in the obituaries of Chartres. Perhaps he became terminally ill while visiting the daughter abbeys of Le Tronchet or Hambye and was transferred to Mont-Saint-Michel. The next abbot of Tiron appears in a charter dated ca. 1160.[112]

---

[107] Crouch, *The Beaumont Twins*, 12, notes that Ralph I, count of Vermandois (1085–1152), brother of Elizabeth, was a steward at the French court. Ibid., 1–25, 71–79; Beaumont family tree: 16. Waleran II joined an unsuccessful conspiracy and rebellion against Henry I by the Norman magnates 1121–1124. He was sentenced to imprisonment in chains in 1124, removed to Wallingford in 1126, and released and reinstated in 1129. After his rapprochement to Louis VII in 1152, Henry II captured him and deprived him of his Norman lands and castles in 1160. Although his properties were restored to him in 1162, he never enjoyed his brother's prestige and favour at the English court.
[108] T1:185–86, no. 161 (1132). William obtained the gift of the toll at Pont-Rousseau near Nantes from Conan III of Brittany.
[109] T1:24–27, no. 12 (ca. 1117).
[110] GC, 8:1139.
[111] T2:74, no. 299.
[112] T2:87, no. 314.

Abbot William was succeeded by three abbots in eighteen years. Stephan I, William's prior, was a diplomat of Louis VII and obtained privileges from Pope Alexander III (r. 1159–1181). He was succeeded by John I (r. 1173–1178) and Walter (1176/1178–1187). Four more abbots followed: Lambert (1187–1200), Robert I (1200–1201), Hervé (1203–1205), and Geoffrey I (1209–1218).[113] A total of seven abbots in fifty years contrasts with the long-term, energetic leadership that occurred during William's rule of some thirty years at the mother house. The turnover of abbots may be one explanation for Tiron's limited expansion after William. Competition for monastic donations by the rising Cistercian order is another.

In the histories of the twelfth century William of Poitiers has never been evaluated in terms of his own success. Through his brief abbacy of Selkirk he knew the Scottish model whereby rulers founding monasteries expected them to become economic centres as well as religious and educational institutions. Their foundation charters record a generous and diversified initial endowment of townhouses in royal boroughs and strategic properties for trade and communication. On his return to Tiron William began to unite Bernard's far-flung foundations by acquiring farms and churches and negotiating for strategic priories. He developed urban as well as rural foundations, incorporated hermitages, and established foundations on pilgrimage routes and in important pilgrimage centres. During his tenure Tiron joined and probably anticipated Cîteaux as a twelfth-century entrepreneurial system with remarkable economic diversity in its circulation of goods. Tiron embraced the economies of scale and superior products obtained by grange agriculture and selective livestock-breeding. It achieved vertical economic integration by controlling the supply chain for bread, wine, and textiles. It obtained exemptions from taxes and duties and engaged in profitable local and international trade. The Tironensians were monastic pioneers in laying the foundations for economic growth. William skilfully maintained good relations with the local lords and bishops and obtained satisfactory resolutions of disputes. When William's accomplishments are pieced together from disparate sources, it is evident that he was a gifted abbot who has fallen into obscurity. His administrative skills enabled the Tironensian community to survive and expand into a prosperous order. Most of Tiron's expansion in France occurred during his tenure. He forged an exceptionally close network of foundations mainly spaced a day's journey apart along roads and waterways extending from the Channel to the Loire and beyond, a region that later became the Angevin Empire and the nucleus of the French nation. His association with Bishops John and Herbert of Glasgow (r. 1147–1164) and Arnold of St. Andrews (r. 1160–1163), the latter two former Tironensian abbots at Selkirk/Kelso (Herbert r. 1119–1147 and Arnold r. 1147–1160 respectively), laid a strong foundation for the "Auld Alliance" of Scotland and France against England. The next chapters will examine the process by which the network was established, the location of the properties, the agreements and their terms.

---

[113] GC, 4:1264B–C.

Chapter 5

EXPANSION IN FRANCE

WHEN TIRON WAS founded the French nation did not exist. The Capetian kings of the Franks were based in Paris and controlled the limited territory of Ile-de-France and the royal principality (under direct royal rule). To the north, the Seine Valley was controlled in the Vexin by the count of Meulan and therefrom to the Atlantic by the king of England who was also duke of Normandy. In the Loire Valley to the west the territory was controlled by the counts of Blois and Anjou/Maine, and the duke of Brittany, and to the south from Poitou to the Auvergne by the duke of Aquitaine and the seigneur of Beaujeu. To the east, the territory was controlled by the count of Champagne and the duke of Burgundy. Through marriage and warfare over the course of the twelfth- and thirteenth-centuries, these regions were incorporated into the nation of modern France ruled from Paris. Henry II's accession in 1154 brought England, Normandy, Anjou, Aquitaine, and Poitou under Plantagenet rule, and the king won political control of Scotland, Wales, Ireland, and Brittany. These nations and regions comprised a centralized economic region later known as the Angevin trading zone, which Judith Everard and John Gillingham have recently studied. Nonetheless, these French regions and the Angevin Empire were incorporated earlier in the form of the network of foundations established by Abbots Bernard and William of Tiron.

The Tironensians expanded into these regions and participated in their economies. Landed wealth prevailed before the rise of towns, and landholders were expert agronomists acutely aware of the earning potential of their properties. The Tironensian holdings provided wheat, grapes, vegetables, fruit, livestock, fish, saltworks, forest products, and iron, with regional variations. Wheat prevailed in their central core of properties but extended elsewhere into Normandy and Champagne. Normandy and Brittany provided salt, fish and shellfish, dairy products, and cider. Anjou, southern France, and eastern Champagne were noted for wine. Fruits and vegetables flourished in the south but were grown elsewhere too. Depending upon availability, smiths processed metal deposits, masons processed local stone, carpenters processed forest products, and textile workers processed animal hides and wool throughout their holdings. After the rise of towns, people concentrated within walls held markets and fairs to import foodstuffs and products they could not obtain otherwise. The regional trade and marketing patterns are more distinctive than the products in France's mixed economy.

Tiron's central core of properties fell within the diocese of Chartres and the county of Blois. The Perche lies west of the Beauce, an important wheat-growing region extending 74 kilometres from Chartres to Orléans in the modern départements of Loiret and Loir-et-Cher. The axes of Tiron's development followed the local Huisne, Eure, Loir, Sarthe, and Cher Rivers flowing north and south toward the Seine and the Loire. This central region includes the towns of Nogent-le-Rotrou in the Perche and Chartres, Châteaudun, and Blois in the Beauce. The most coherent manner of discerning the development of Tiron is to describe the many foundations clustered in this central region and then to proceed north to Normandy, west to Anjou, Maine, and Brittany, south of the Loire to Poitou and the Rhône, and east to Ile-de-France, Champagne, and Burgundy.

Tiron's expansion depended upon securing patronage. In addition to the kinship network of Henry I, his daughter Empress Matilda, countess of Anjou, his sister Adela, countess of Blois and Chartres, and his nephew Thibaut II, count of Blois and Champagne, together with his natural children, there were regional kinship networks of Tironensian donors. Many of the vassal lords of the count of Blois and Chartres were descended from Thibaut I l'Ancien (ca. 890–943) and Thibaut I "the Trickster" (ca. 910–ca. 977), tenth-century counts of Chartres, and were related to Norman, Angevin, and Aquitainian families across the border. Robert of Bêlleme and Rotrou II, count of the Perche, were cousins. Rotrou II was also more distantly related to the viscounts of Châteaudun and Mortagne. His sisters had married into the L'Aigle and Beaumont-le-Roger families in Lower Normandy. The Gouet family had a matrimonial alliance with the Fréteval family, which was allied by marriage with the viscounts of Châteaudun. The Montigny family had feudal ties with the Courville family, which in turn had Norman connections.[1] They intermarried extensively to improve their holdings. Following the example of their overlord Thibaut II, many of the vassal lords of Blois and Chartres were donors to Tiron and enjoyed the benefits of patronage. Because of these interrelationships, the local families were capable of inspiring their kinsmen and vassals to emulate their generosity in donating tithes, churches, and exemptions and in founding priories, but they were also capable of embroiling Tiron in their disputes.

Tiron's nucleus of properties was centred around the abbey and the nearby town of Nogent-le-Rotrou. On the Huisne, north of Nogent, Tiron had a horse farm, and the abbey also had herds of pigs, cattle, and sheep. Chartres became Tiron's urban headquarters and market, where monks and lay artisans ran ovens and forges, processed leather and wool, and engaged in trade. South of Châteaudun near Yron and Cloyes-sur-le-Loir, Tiron had wheat granges, granaries, mills, and sometimes ovens, supplying flour and bread to urban markets, including Le Mans in Maine. Those regions, in the modern départements of Eure-et-Loir, Loiret, Loir-et-Cher, and Indre-et-Loire, encompassed two abbeys—Tiron and later Arcisses, thirty-one priories, nineteen churches, twelve farms, seven granaries, four houses, and other significant acquisitions.

The expansion process followed several courses. Farms might be acquired and consolidated into granges, sometimes with a chapel. A church might acquire farmland and be elevated to a priory. The early Tironensian confirmations use *ecclesia* for both church and priory, and many priories began as churches and expanded through the acquisition of property and income sources. A priory in a trafficked area might be elevated to an abbey, built in cut stone with a lead roof, tiles, and stained glass, with a dormitory, refectory, chapter, library, scriptorium, and an abbatial church with a treasury of gold and jewels. Priories and abbeys might have houses, mills, ovens, and forges in nearby towns. Build-ups of properties, farms, granges, and granaries reflect economies of scale in

---

1 Livingstone, *Out of Love for my Kin*, 9–26, Genealogical Charts 1–13, 237–45. Chédeville, *Chartres et ses campagnes*, 260–61.

agriculture and sometimes in strategic locations. Churches, with rectories or vicarages, represent both religious obligations and routes of communication, staging posts, and income sources. Priories with six to twelve monks and a prior represent involvement with the local community. Abbeys represent broader regional engagement and are often on roads between important towns or on rivers and seacoasts.

Within the county of Blois-Chartres, the economic centres were Tiron Abbey, its priory of Chartres, and the Beauce. Tiron Abbey had a school and a scriptorium that provided record-keeping and administrative support. Its guesthouse was a staging post for pilgrims and travellers. Its workrooms were used for crafts. Its forests provided wood, pelts, and pannage for pigs, and its orchards provided fruit. It had herds of cattle, sheep, and horses. Its local mills processed cereals. Its priory in Chartres was an urban centre for leather and textile production, forges, ovens, footwear, metalwork, money-changing for merchants and pilgrims, and rental income from townhouses. Its priories and granges in the Beauce supported wheat and grains, milling, and ovens, livestock, and special crops like peas. Tiron marketed to Cloyes-sur-le-Loir and its pilgrim trade and to Le Mans and Châteaudun and communicated with Blois.

The town of Nogent-le-Rotrou, west of Tiron, was on the Huisne in the parish of Brunelles, dominated by the castle of Saint John and the Cluniac priory of Saint-Denis. The counts of the Perche were marcher lords who protected Chartres against incursions from Normandy and Anjou. The generosity of Rotrou II and his family toward Tiron was counterbalanced by the competitiveness of their family priory. Expansion in Nogent was limited: by 1141 Tiron had a townhouse.[2] Tiron's largest nearby holding was the priory and future abbey of Arcisses in Brunelles on the Arcisses River, initially offered to Bernard for his foundation ca. 1107 and then withdrawn. Arcisses was deeply lamented: the *Vita Bernardi* describes Count Rotrou II's country retreat as a fertile land, surrounded on all sides by forests, abundantly watered by springs and brooks, with green meadows and soil suitable for vines and other crops, a chapel, a fishpond, and orchards.[3] Rotrou II gave Arcisses to Tiron, with salt, income, woodland rights, and Arcisses' farm near Luxvillat (Nonvilliers-Grandhoux) with its chapel, pond, mill, and valley land ca. 1115.[4] He confirmed his gift in his plenary court in 1120 (which suggests that a dispute had arisen). The donation included the chapel with its buildings and appurtenances, a sharecropping farm, pasture for oxen in the woods of the Perche and Sela, woodland rights, pasture for other livestock, annual cash income, and tithes on an oven and mills.[5] Tiron was given land in the fief of Tercé near La Gaudaine on the Arcisses, 5 kilometres west of the foundation.[6] Hugh of Crignon relinquished his claims to the nearby mills of Espal to Tiron.[7] Lambert Bigoth gave tracts at La Ferrière and in the fief of la Malaise in the vicinity of Tiron

---

2 T2:26–27, no. 256.
3 VB, 8.64, AASS, Apr. 2:0237F; VB, trans. Cline, 71–72.
4 T1:39–40, no. 22 (1119).
5 T1:53–55, no. 33 (1120).
6 T1:189–90, no. 166 (ca. 1132); ibid., 2:306.
7 T2:2–3, no. 228 (ca. 1140); ibid. 2:273.

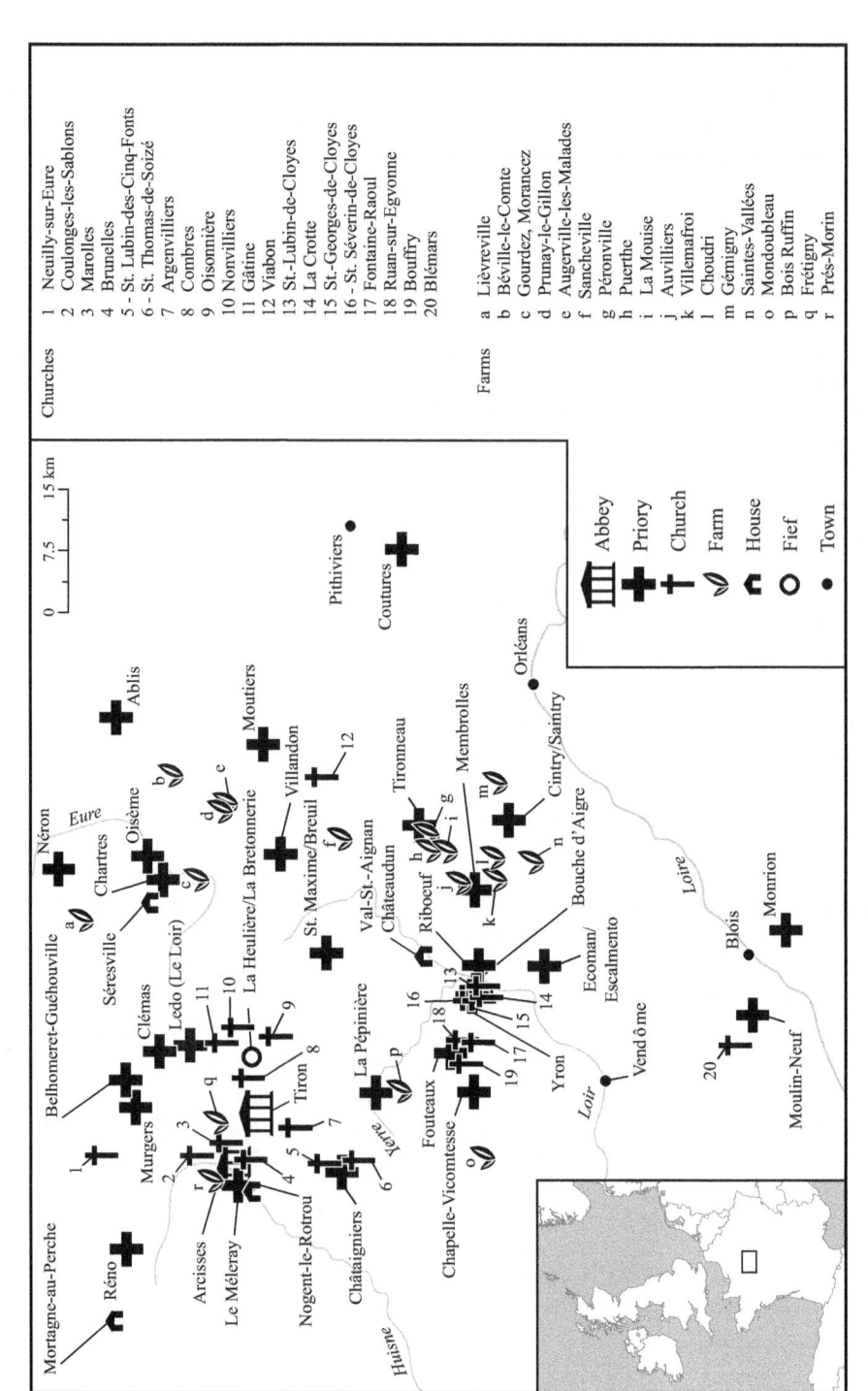

Map 5.1. Chartres-Blois

Churches
1. Neuilly-sur-Eure
2. Coulonges-les-Sablons
3. Marolles
4. Brunelles
5. St. Lubin-des-Cinq-Fonts
6. St. Thomas-de-Soizé
7. Argenvilliers
8. Combres
9. Oisonnière
10. Nonvilliers
11. Gâtine
12. Viabon
13. St. Lubin-de-Cloyes
14. La Crotte
15. St. Georges-de-Cloyes
16. St. Séverin-de-Cloyes
17. Fontaine-Raoul
18. Ruan-sur-Egvonne
19. Bouffry
20. Blémars

Farms
a. Liévreville
b. Béville-le-Comte
c. Gourdez, Morancez
d. Prunay-le-Gillon
e. Augerville-les-Malades
f. Sancheville
g. Péronville
h. Puerthe
i. La Mouise
j. Auvilliers
k. Villemafroi
l. Choudri
m. Gémigny
n. Saintes-Vallées
o. Mondoubleau
p. Bois Ruffin
q. Frétigny
r. Prés-Morin

Table 5.1. Chartres-Blois

Table 5.1a. North of Tiron Abbey
Local near Tiron Abbey and Nogent-le-Rotrou **Tiron**; 1107–1109; Rotrou II, count of Perche (Abbot Bernard) **Arcisses (N.D.+St. Vincent)**; priory/abbey; <1119/1225; Rotrou II, count of Perche (Abbot Bernard); elevation William of Bellême (d. 1226), bishop of Châlons-sur-Marne and count of the Perche **Brunelles (St. Martin)**; church; ca. 1125; Geoffrey II, bishop of Chartres **Nogent-le-Rotrou**; physician's house; 1141; Rotrou II, count of Perche; Arcisses's Nazareth-de-Nogent-le-Rotrou, priory (1411–1790) **Le Méleray**; priory; ca. 1114; Jeremias de Insula or de l'Ile+w. Helvis Sacracerre (Abbot Bernard); hospice <1125 **Prés-Morin**; meadowland on the Huisne; 1120–1150; Hugh de Boigne/Baugny+others **Marolles (St. Vincent)**; church; ca. 1125; Hugues of Rocé *in extremis*/Geoffrey II, bishop of Chartres **Frétigny**; farm, land at Brimont+; Le Pré des Chasseurs at La Richarderie; 1125–1145; Odo du Verger; bourg fair of St. André <1395 Route 1: Tiron Abbey, W 9 km to Arcisses and St.-Martin in Brunelles, W 6 km to Nogent-le-Rotrou, N 2 km to Le Méleray, N 6 km to Prés-Morin *Marolles was 9 km NE of Nogent and 7 km NW of Tiron Abbey, on the east bank of the Cloche River, with Frétigny 4 km NE*
Nogent-le-Rotrou to the paved road between Chartres and Mortagne-au-Perche **Coulonges-les-Sablons (St. Germain)**; church; ca. 1139; Simon of Berlanville/Geoffrey II, bishop of Chartres **Murgers (St. Jean)**; priory; ca. 1133; William of Vaupillon+w. Agnès **Neuilly-sur-Eure**; church; <1147 **Belhomert-Guéhouville**; priory (Arcisses); 1130. Route 2: Nogent-le-Rotrou, NE 12 km to Coulonges-les-Sablons, NE 15 km to Murgers, NW 8 km to Neuilly-sur-Eure on the paved road. Belhomert-Guéhouville is 12 km SE on the Eure *Neuilly-sur-Eure and Belhomert-Guéhouville are both 28 km NE of Nogent-le-Rotrou*
Between Chartres and Mortagne-au-Perche **Clémas (St. Michel)**; priory; 1118; Ivo II of Courville **Réno (La Madeleine)**; priory; <1147; dependency of St.-Victor-de-Réno **Mortagne-au-Perche**; half a house; ca. 1130; William the mason+w. Hersendis+option for other half kinsman Rainerius Chartres, W 18 km to Courville-sur-Eure, W 9 km to Clémas, W 16 km to Murgers, W 8 km to Neuilly-sur-Eure, W 19 km to Réno, W 14 km to Mortagne-au-Perche *Mortagne-au-Perche is 78 km W of Chartres*

(*continued*)

Table 5.1. (Cont.)

5.1b. Tiron Abbey to Chartres

Combres (N.D.); church; <1147
La Heulière-La Bretonnerie; fief; 1276/1277; Robert of Chastelier
Nonvilliers; church; ca. 1119; Rotrou II, count of Perche
Oisonnière; church; <1147
Gâtine (St. Laurent); church; <1147
Ledo/Le Loir (N.D.); priory; ca. 1120; Odo/Eudes de l'Orme
Clémas (St. Michel); priory; < ca. 1118; Ivo II of Courville (also in table 5.1)
Chartres; priory; ca. 1119–1121

Tiron to Chartres: Tiron Abbey, E 7 km to Combres, E 4 km to La Heulière and la Bretonnerie near Happonvilliers, NE 6 km to Nonvilliers (with Oisonnière to the south), N 4 km to St.-Laurent (-de-Gâtine) near Les Corvées-les-Yys, N 6 km to Ledo (Le Loir) in Le Thieulin (with Clémas N 8 km, across the paved road near the Eure), E 11 km on the paved road to Courville-sur-Eure, E 20 km to Chartres

Chartres could also be reached by the Eure River from Clémas

From Chartres to Dreux
Prunay-le-Gillon; farm; <1130; Ivo II of Courville, conf. Renaud son of Hardouin of Andeville
Gourdez, Morancez; farm; 1129; Hugh, viscount of Le Puiset
Séresville; house; ca. 1145; Herbert of Séresville+Adelina; +Le Coin-Houdry land
Oisème (La Madeleine); priory; ca. 1130; Anseau f. Godeschal de Champhol
Lièvreville; farm; ca. 1127–1130; Hugh+Marie of Lièvreville; granary, pilgrimage pledge
Néron (St. Rémy); priory; ca. 1125; André Cholet/Morhier of Nogent

Chartres to Dreux: Chartres, NE 5 km to Oisème, N 12 km to Lièvreville, N 14 km to Néron, N 19 km to Dreux

Table 5.1c. South of Tiron Abbey

Toward Cloyes-sur-le-Loir
Argenvilliers (St. Pierre); church; ca. 1126; Robert+s. Walter of La Motte/ Geoffrey II, bishop of Chartres
St.-Lubin-des-Cinq-Fonts; church; ca. 1128/1132; Robert of La Motte+b. Walter of St.-Lubin/Geoffrey II, bishop of Chartres
Châtaigniers (St. Gilles); priory; ca. 1117; William Gouet+w. Eustachia+children
Soizé (St. Thomas); church; ca. 1117; Gerard La Bazillière+wife+b. Hugh
La Pépinière; priory; <1267; Colin of Le Pré-Méry+w.Amelina
Bois Ruffin; farm; ca. 1130; Jérémie de l'Ile

Tiron Abbey S 7 km to Argenvilliers, SW 10 km to St.-Lubin-des-Cinq-Fonts, S 6 km to Châtaigniers and Soizé; SE 9 km to La Pépinière near La Bazoche-Gouet, SE 13 km along the Yerre to Bois Ruffin near Arrou, SE 15 km to Cloyes-sur-le-Loir

Les Châtaigniers is 20 km SE of Nogent-le-Rotrou and 37 km NW of Cloyes-sur-le-Loir; Arrou is 22 km W of Châteaudun; Cloyes-sur-le-Loir is 12 km SW of Châteaudun

Table 5.1. (Cont.)

From Chartres via Voves to Châteaudun
  Béville-le-Comte; two farms; <1250; Thibaut IV or V, count of Blois; pea crop rights
  Augerville-les-Malades; granary; ca. 1118; Ivo II of Courville
  Moutiers; priory; <1179
  Viabon (St. Médard); church; <1175–1176
  Villandon; priory and granary; ca. 1128; William of Queux+w. Agnès
  Sancheville; farm; 1141; Robert of Blainville
  St.-Maxime/Breuil; priory; ca. 1140; Abbey of Bonneval
  Val-St.-Aignan Châteaudun; house, 1131; Algarda w. Ansold Fitz Godeschal; vines
Chartres, SE 23 km to Voves, SW 38 km to Châteaudun

Béville-le-Comte is a mid-point 24 km E of Chartres and 24 km SW of Ablis. Voves cluster of foundations: Augerville-les-Malades is 14 km SE of Chartres and 11 km N of Voves; Moutiers is 13 km NE of Voves; Viabon is 9 km SE of Voves; Villandon near Montainville is 8 km W of Voves; and Sancheville is 11 km SW of Voves. Sancheville is 20 km E of St.-Maxime/le Breuil-St.-Mesme near the town of Trizay-lès-Bonneval 19 km N of Châteaudun

Table 5.1d. South of Châteaudun

Southeast of Châteaudun
  Péronville; granary on the Conie; 1130; Hubert+s. Peter of Péronville; white sheep, peas
  Tironneau; priory; <1263; on the Conie
  Puerthe; farm; ca. 1130; Gosbert+b. Guiard Trobel of Châteaudun+Peter of Péronville+others
  La Mouise; farm; 1126; Peter Leroy
  Auvilliers; farm; 1127; Girard le Diable, seigneur of Plessis-Maillé
  Villemafroi; granary; 1133; Albert of Cherville; some land owned by St.-Gilles-des-Châtaigniers
  Membrolles; priory; ca. 1129; Helgodus of Membrolles+Pagan of Frouville
  Choudri; granary; 1127; Girard le Diable, seigneur of Plessis-Maillé
  Saintes-Vallées; granary; <1147; Robert b. Geoffrey of Ouzouer
  Cintry/Saintry (St. Georges); priory+granary; 1115; Louis VI (Abbot Bernard)
  Gémigny; granary; <1147; Odo of Gémigny
Péronville (with Tironneau NE 1 km), W 3 km to Puerthe, SW 11 km via La Mouise and Auvilliers, to Villemafroi and Membrolles, SE 6 km to Choudri near Prénouvellon, S 7 km to Saintes-Vallées near Ouzouer-le-Marché; SE 10 km to Cintry/Saintry; E 9 km to Gémigny

The port of Meung-sur-Loire is 18 km SE of Ouzouer-le-Marché. Orléans is 18 km upriver, and Blois is 45 km downriver

(*continued*)

Table 5.1. (Cont.)

Southwest of Châteaudun
    Bouche d'Aigre (Sts. Jean+Paul); priory; ca. 1114; Reginald Percehaie, seigneur of Romainville, a vassal of Agnès of Montigny (Abbot Bernard); fishing rights St.-Calais 1190
    Riboeuf (N.D.); priory; ca. 1128; Reginald/Renaud of Espiez+w. Ada; old and new mills
    St.-Georges-de-Cloyes; church; ca. 1114; Reginald Percehaie (Abbot Bernard), pilgrimage
    St.-Lubin-de-Cloyes; church; <1142–1145; pilgrimage
    St.-Séverin-de-Cloyes; church; <1142–1145; pilgrimage
    La Crotte; church; 1131; Geoffrey III, viscount of Châteaudun
    Yron (N.D.); priory; 1115; Agnès of Montigny+Odo (Abbot Bernard); pilgrimage
    Fouteaux (St. Nicolas); priory; ca. 1125; Guérin sans Barbe; land+woods at Vallis-Manselli
    Bouffry; church; ca. 1131; Aimery, seigneur of Bouffry and b. Hugh; land at Château-Bouffry and on the Grenne River+**Montluiser/Mons-Lusellus (St. Silvestre)**; priory; ca. 1140; Hugh of Poncé-sur-le-Loir (not mapped)
    Ruan-sur-Egvonne; church; 1133; Geoffrey II, bishop of Chartres; deserted church
    Fontaine-Raoul; church; 1133; Geoffrey IV, viscount of Châteaudun
    Plains/ Chapelle-Vicomtesse; priory; <1147
    Mondoubleau; land of Fosse-Robert by castle; ca. 1133; Geoffrey III, viscount of Châteaudun+Helvisa (see Map 5.3)
Membrolles, W 15 km to Riboeuf in Romilly-sur-Aigre and Bouche d'Aigre, W 4 km to Cloyes-sur-le-Loir, with the churches on the east bank and La Crotte and Yron on the west bank
Yron, NW 13 km to a cluster of properties near Les Fouteaux: Bouffry, Montluiser, and Ruan-sur-Egvonne
Yron to Mondoubleau: Yron, W 10 km to Fontaine-Raoul, W 8 km to la Chapelle-Vicomtesse, W 12 km to Mondoubleau
Châtaigniers south of Tiron is 24 km NW of Mondoubleau

South to Blois
    Ecoman/Escalmento (St. André); priory; Ecoman 1117–1119, Escalmento <1516; Adela+Thibaut IV of Blois-Chartres
    Blémars (St. Georges); church; <1147; Renaud+Sibyl of Château-Renault
    Moulin-Neuf (Sts. Marie+Pierre); priory; ca. 1121; Geoffrey de Bourreau; new mill
    Monrion (St. Eutrope/N.D.); priory; ca. 1119; Adela, countess of Blois+Chartres; new mill
Châteaudun, S 58 km to Blois. Route 1: Châteaudun, S 11 km to Romilly-sur-Aigre, S 12 km to Ecoman and Escalmento, S 36 km to Blois. Route 2: Châteaudun, SW 12 km to Cloyes-sur-le-Loir, S 14 km downriver to Fréteval and 19 km to Vendôme, S 26 km to Blémars, E 9 km to Moulin-Neuf, E 13 km to Blois, S 8 km across the Loire to Monrion

East of Orléans   **Coutures (St. Laurent)**; priory; 1131–1145; Adam, kin of Dreux Brochart de la Varenne Cintry/Saintry and Gémigny, E 25 km to Orléans, NE 35 km to Les Coutures, NE 28 km to Augerville-la-Rivière, N along the Essonne to the Seine and Paris

Abbey.[8] The donations reflect the increasing importance of Arcisses as an agricultural centre in a strategic location. Arcisses was raised to abbatial status in 1225 through the efforts of William of Bellême (d. 1226), bishop of Châlons-sur-Marne (modern Châlons-en-Champagne) and count of the Perche. The abbey was to be built and ceded together with its lands, woods, mills, wheat fields, vines, ponds, meadows, pastures, income and other possessions.[9] Its form of tenure was free alms, meaning that the property was a gift to God in exchange for prayers, had no secular overlord, and was under the jurisdiction of ecclesiastical courts. Eventually Arcisses had two dependent priories: Nazareth-de-Nogent-le-Rotrou (1411–1790) and Belhomert-Guéhouville (1130–1791) northeast of Nogent-le-Rotrou and southwest of Châteauneuf-en-Thymerais, a mid-point between the two towns[10] (see Map 5.6, Tiron and Daughter Abbeys' Dependent Priories).

The Huisne Valley is the centre of the region between Mortagne-au-Perche and La Ferté-Bernard, and it is celebrated today for the Percheron horse. The priory of Le Méleray was founded ca. 1114 by a gift of lands and fields north of Nogent-le-Rotrou near the Huisne. Between 1120 and 1150 Tiron Abbey steadily accrued meadows at Le Méleray[11] and Prés-Morin, which suggests that the monks were breeding horses and expanding their herds, probably in cooperation with the comital family.[12] Twelfth-century farming methods were changing from oxen- to horse-drawn plows, making horse-breeding even more profitable. Tiron encouraged gifts but sometimes had to purchase waterfront property.[13] Other acquisitions expanded Prés-Morin to 26 arpents or 45.76 acres.[14] Arcisses and nearby foundations became the centre of horse-breeding and livestock-raising in the meadows of the Huisne Valley.

North of the Huisne Valley a paved road ran between Chartres and Mortagne-au-Perche. The Tironensians frequently travelled from Arcisses and Tiron Abbeys to their headquarters in Chartres. From Arcisses they acquired properties on the road from Nogent-le-Rotrou to the paved road and along it to communicate with those important towns:[15] churches

---

8 T2:80–81, no. 307 (ca. 1142); ibid., 2:275, 284. Merlet situates La Ferrière near Brunelles and la Malaise near Soizé.

9 T2:134–36, no. 358 (1225).

10 Lalizel, *Abbaye Royale d'Arcissses*, 134.

11 T1:14–16, nos. 3 and 5 (ca. 1114); ibid., 2:44, no. 273 (ca. 1145).

12 Guillemin, *Thiron, abbaye médiévale*, 44, states that the Tironensian monks wrote the first treatises on curing horses, without giving a source for this assertion.

13 A gift listed under Arcisses was one arpent of meadowland in Prés-Morin (at or adjacent to *Prata Comitis*, the count's meadow), together with census income, given by Hugh of Boigne/Baugny and his family ca. 1120. Hugh consented to a vassal's sale of land on the Huisne and received a countergift of a horse. T1:55–56, nos. 34–35 (ca. 1120). Hugh exchanged two arpents of meadow at Prés-Morin for three in Condé-sur-Huisne ca. 1125, enabling the monks to consolidate their holdings. In 1130 Hugh's wife Osanna and son Odo sold Tiron meadow near the river. T1:142, no. 120 (1130).

14 CNDC, 1:ccxliii. 1 arpent in the Perche equalled 71 *ares*, 33 *centiares* 20; 1 arpent equals 7133.2 square metres or 1.76 acres; 26 arpents = 45.76 acres.

15 T1:39–40, no. 22 (ca. 1119). Power, *The Norman Frontier*, 339. Chédeville, *Chartres et ses campagnes*, 279.

in Brunelles, Coulonges-les-Sablons, and Marolles, the farm of Frétigny, and the priory of Murgers. The castle of Courville near Chartres was strategically important in border warfare. Rotrou II's vassal Ivo II of Courville-sur-Eure established Tironensian priories on his lands midway between Nogent-le-Rotrou and Chartres, including the priory of Clémas, north of the paved road.[16] The church of Neuilly-sur-Eure and the priory of Réno extended the chain of properties west to Mortagne-au-Perche.

(See Table 5.1b.) From Tiron Abbey the Tironensians acquired properties on the road east to the churches of Combres and Nonvilliers[17] (with Oisonnière to the south), then north to Saint-Laurent-de-Gâtine, and on to the priory of Ledo (Le Loir), south of the paved road. The acquisition pattern suggests that the route through a forested region was not diagonal but ran east, turned north midway along a north–south chain of properties, and continued east to Chartres. That chain of properties was 27–34 kilometres from Nogent-le-Rotrou and from Chartres, logical places for a rider to break the journey, and their close spacing suggests hauling or driving livestock.

Tiron's initial expansion in Chartres was for trade. Tiron owned at least two houses in the marketplace, which it exchanged for a smith's house with a forge on the rue de la Clouterie.[18] The nucleus of the priory of Chartres was Thibaut II's gift in 1121 of twelve dependants preponderantly in the baking and wine trades, together with a smith, roper, and fuller.[19] The monk Dom Alcherius, son of Aalon, purchased a butcher's house in Chartres, probably with a downstairs slaughterhouse and stall on the rue des Bouchers.[20] The Tironensians limited their protein sources to fish and dairy products, and the local markets for their meat and wares must have been saturated.

In Chartres Tiron Abbey acquired considerable real estate.[21] Tiron was given four houses by a money-changer,[22] a smith, and two other citizens.[23] Geoffrey the

---

16 Ivo II of Courville also gave income from a mill and an oven at Courville, a pond and sluicegate, woodland rights and meadows. T1:32–35, no. 18 (ca. 1118).

17 T1:39–40, no. 22 (ca. 1119) (Nonvilliers). Chédeville, *Chartres et ses campagnes*, 279. La Heulière-la Bretonnerie was nearby; T2:191–92, no. 397.

18 T1:44, no. 28 (1119–36). Then the rue aux Fèvres, the street was the centre of the corporation of blacksmiths, coppersmiths, armourers, nail-makers, farriers, locksmiths, and ironmongers. Guillois, *Histoire des rues de Chartres*, 70–71.

19 T1:64–65, no. 45.

20 T1:73–74, nos. 52–53 (ca. 1122). Guillois, *Histoire des rues de Chartres*, 94–95.

21 Burton and Kerr, *The Cistercians in the Middle Ages*, 182–83, describe the Cistercians acquiring urban real estate, obtaining exemptions from taxes and tolls, selling both agricultural surplus and market-oriented products, and establishing contacts with the townspeople who witnessed their charters as early as the mid-twelfth century. Tiron was much earlier, doing business in Chartres before 1116 and establishing a priory and acquiring houses, shops, and rental properties during the 1120s.

22 T1:122–23, no. 101 (ca. 1128). The money-changer's house may have been on the rue du Petit Change near the rue des Bouchers and the southwest gate (modern Place des Epars), where money-changers with their tables had accommodated international travellers since the eleventh century; the rue des Changes near the comital palace is another possibility. Guillois, *Histoire des rues de Chartres*, 9, 96.

23 T1:122–23, no. 101 (ca. 1128). William and the community leased Orioz's house to Hugh of Vendôme and his wife Erembourg, for their lifetimes, probably at a low rent, specifying that the

money-changer witnessed the foundation charter of the Tironensian priory of La-Madeleine-d'Oisème, and Geoffrey and Hugh, money-changers, witnessed alongside the *praepositus*, which suggests Tironensian association with that important trade.[24] Tiron was given an oven and purchased the house that became the Hôtel de Tiron ca. 1130.[25] The buyer for the monks was Adelard le Roux, a member of an important Chartrain burgher family.[26] The property was located in the modern rue de Bois-Merrain (barrel staves), near the southwest city gate. Other properties may have been located in east Chartres downriver on the Eure where tanners, leatherworkers, and fullers plied their trades. The only clue to the location of another house is that it was witnessed by Gobertus (*coriarius*), a shoemaker or tanner.[27] The witnesses to the gift of another house include a weaver in the Chartrain textile trade where cloth was woven, fulled, and dyed.[28]

In addition to its townhouse and chapel, oven, and forge, after a decade the Tironensian properties in Chartres included residential homes, including one near a prominent monastery, a tract in the Breton district, and property to the north. Tiron was given houses, one on the rue Saint-Pierre, southeast of the comital palace near the Benedictine abbey of Saint-Père-en-Vallée.[29] Possibly the novices and secular students at Tiron completed their advanced studies at the schools of Chartres, and this house was a convenient residence. Anseau Berbel restored to Tiron the tract of la Bretonnerie, near the cathedral cloister.[30] These residences provided rental income but also economical housing to reward donors. These acquisitions show monastic urban development early in the twelfth century.

Tiron acquired land in hamlets near Chartres: Porte-Drouaise (the north city gate to Dreux), an unknown Grosselle, Prunay-le-Gillon, Gourdez near Morancez on the Eure, Séresville and Le Coin-Houdry. Two priories, Oisème and Néron, and a farm, Lièvreville, were acquired on the road to Dreux, 32 kilometres to the north. The fortress of Dreux was part of the royal domain, ruled by Louis VII's brother Robert I, count of Dreux (ca. 1123–1188).[31] From Chartres Tiron's expansion proceeded east toward Paris and north of Dreux into Normandy, which will be discussed subsequently.

---

house was to revert to Tiron upon their deaths; T2:29, no. 258 (ca. 1141). Bartholomew of Vendôme had approved a gift to Tiron of lands and woods at Bouffry, and the lifetime lease of a house in Chartres to relatives may have been an act of reciprocity. T2:1–2, no. 227 (ca. 1140).

24 T1:149, no. 127 (ca. 1130); ibid., 195, no. 174 (ca. 1132); ibid., 2:43, no. 271 (ca. 1145).

25 T1:147–48, no. 126 (ca. 1130).

26 CNDC, 1:134, no. 43. Adelard le Roux witnessed a donation by Thibaut II in 1128.

27 T1:251, no. 222 (ca. 1138).

28 T2:6, no. 232 (ca. 1140).

29 T1:194–95, no. 174 (ca. 1132); ibid., 2:6, no. 232 (ca. 1140).

30 T1:182–83, no. 159 (1131–1141). Chédeville, *Chartres et ses campagnes*, 100–3, mentions the Breton masters at Chartres and the concentration of Bretons in the district around the rue de la Bretonnerie.

31 Power, *The Norman Frontier*, 93–94.

(See Table 5.1c.) Tiron expanded south of Chartres into the Dunois near Châteaudun and the Beauce. In this region Tiron had at least eight southern priories that were directly dependent upon it in the thirteenth century. The priory of Châtaigniers was closest to Tiron Abbey, with the nearby churches of Argenvilliers, Saint-Lubin-des-Cinq-Fonts, and Soizé. Further south were Yron, Fouteaux, Plains/Chapelle-Vicomtesse, Bouche d'Aigre, Riboeuf, Tironneau, and Ecoman. They extend south of Nogent-le-Rotrou and Tiron Abbey, mainly run east near the Egvonne and Grenne Rivers toward Cloyes-sur-le-Loir and continue south of Châteaudun along the Aigre River, with Tironneau further east of Châteaudun near Péronville on the Conie River, a distance of about 72 kilometres. They are part of the concentration of priories, granges, and churches in the Beauce[32] (see Map 5.6). Two Tironensian abbeys across the western border of Blois, Le Gué-de-Launay and La Pelice in the diocese of Le Mans south of Tiron Abbey, will be discussed subsequently with west France but drew wealth from the Beauce.

The Beauce is known as the breadbasket of France for its grain production. The charters of Tironensian granaries in this region[33] record exchanges of property to build up contiguous fields for more efficient sowing and harvesting with a shift from sharecropping toward granges run by lay brothers. They refer to the settlement of many disputes about property, both real estate and food and livestock, in a region with contentious leaders. They also show Tiron's multiple countergifts to any relations and overlords who might contest their investment in this profitable real estate. The negotiating skills of the Tironensians are evident. The Beauce was torn by local unrest 1135–1136 and 1145–1146, and Tiron profited by increasing its holdings.

Several routes can be discerned to the cluster of wheat farms northwest of Orléans. A western route runs from Nogent-le-Rotrou and Tiron Abbey southeast to Cloyes-sur-le-Loir into the Dunois and the Beauce. The priory of Châtaigniers and nearby churches were near Authon-du-Perche. The Yerre flows between the forest of Bois Ruffin and the towns of Arrou and Courtalain. Tiron owned property and a dwelling (Les Mellerets) near Bois Ruffin.[34] Midway between Châtaigniers and Arrou, Tiron established the priory of La Pépinière in the vicinity of La Bazoche-Gouet on the Yerre. Tiron Abbey purchased lands and meadows between the priory land and Châtaigniers, for thirty-six livres and other benefits.[35] Together with Le Méleray, Tiron was given land at Arrou to the southeast near the Yerre on the route to Cloyes-sur-le-Loir and Châteaudun. That same year Tiron was given land in the vicinity of Montigny-le-Gannelon between Arrou and Cloyes.[36]

In northern Beauce Tiron owned two farms at Béville-le-Comte midway between Chartres and Saint-Epaigne-d'Ablis. An eastern route runs southeast from Chartres and Voves to Châteaudun. Five properties encircled Voves: a granary at Augerville-les-Malades,

---

32 IS-ADEL, 8:195, H 1772 (1263).
33 T2:61, no. 291.
34 T1:155–57, no. 130 (ca. 1130); ibid., 172–73, no. 149 (1130–1145).
35 T2:184, no. 391 (1267).
36 T1:14–16, nos. 3 and 5 (ca. 1114).

the priory of Moutiers, the church of Viabon, the priory and granary of Villandon, and property at Sancheville. Augerville-aux-Malades, or Augerville-les-Malades, was formerly owned by the leper house of Grand-Beaulieu.[37] Villandon, on the road to Orléans, was one of the wealthiest Tironensian priories.[38] North of Châteaudun a priory called Saint-Maxime/le Breuil-Saint-Mesme is near a Compostela pilgrimage route. These properties facilitated travel and communication to Châteaudun on the Loir.

Châteaudun was dominated by its imposing castle. The Hôtel-Dieu and the Augustinian abbey of La Madeleine were built into the ramparts of the south city wall. The Templars owned a large leper house called the Boissière near Châteaudun. The town also had a school for advanced studies and a mint.[39] The ties between Tiron and Châteaudun began when William Gouet II, lord of Montmirail (ca. 1072–1117) gave Châtaigniers two sharecropping farms near Châteaudun, in Bishop Geoffrey II's presence.[40] Geoffrey III, viscount of Châteaudun, gave the Tiron Abbey tithes he was owed there on the *tonlieu*, toll, fodder, his own coins, and salt.[41] Blanche of Membrolles gave a quarter of an oven and her townhouse.[42] In 1131 Viscount Geoffrey III confirmed a gift of a tract at Le-Val-Saint-Aignan, a suburb of Châteaudun on the east bank of the Loir, for the Tironensian monks to build dwellings, together with a tract of Gorth, the future property of the church of La Crotte.[43] Its substantial holdings ca. 1128 included land at an unidentified Mons Simphorianus, a mill on the River Aigre, meadows, vines and a garden.[44] Saint-Aignan was not a priory but a *dominium* or estate with liberties and vines.[45] Tiron owned other vines in the vicinity of Châteaudun and compiled a list of their locations and rents.[46] Hugh of Montluiser (ca. 1120–1180), son of Geoffrey III, confirmed all his father's gifts to Tiron Abbey, when Geoffrey III was in the prison of Ursio of Fréteval (ca. 1107–1143/46), also a Tironensian benefactor. They included land, fields, woods, bodies of water, and mills, as well as income and the right to collect all the customs in the city of Châteaudun every tenth week.[47] Tiron was a substantial presence in that town.

---

37 T2:290.

38 T1:117–18, no. 97 (ca. 1128); ibid., 1:118n1; ibid., 135–36, no. 115 (ca. 1129); ibid., 1:152–54, nos. 128 and 128 bis (ca. 1130); ibid., 1:192–93, nos. 170–71 (ca. 1132); ibid,1:227–29, nos. 197–98 (ca. 1135); ibid., 1:251–52, no. 223 (ca. 1138); ibid., 2:10, no. 236 (ca. 1140); ibid., 45–47, nos. 275–76 (ca. 1145).

39 Thompson, *Power and Border Lordship*, 33.

40 T1:24–27, no. 12 (ca. 1117). His son William Gouet III added a third contiguous sharecropping farm after his father's death.

41 T1:37–38, no. 21 (1119).

42 T1:129–30, no. 109; ibid., 1:136–37, no. 116 (1129).

43 T1:175–76, nos. 152–53.

44 T1:118, no. 98; ibid., 1:175–76, no. 152 (ca. 1128).

45 T2:104, no. 328 (1179).

46 Reginald/Renaud of Epieds, lord of Lanneray, gave the monks vines in Châteaudun. T1:181, no. 158 (ca. 1131); ibid., 1:177, no. 154 (ca. 1131); ibid., 1:181, no. 158 (ca. 1131); ibid., 2:12, no. 239 (ca. 1140); ibid., 2:47, no. 277 (ca. 1145) (list).

47 T1:242–43, no. 215 (1136–1137). Livingstone, *Out of Love for my Kin*, 76–77.

Tiron's southern axis of development branched out at Châteaudun east, south, and west toward the Loire, mirroring its northern axis of development, which branched out at Evreux to the Seine and the English Channel. To the east were wheat farms and granaries, to the south were mills and a market in the vicinity of Cloyes-sur-le-Loir, and to the west was a chain of foundations for trade via Mondoubleau to Le Mans. This agglomeration of priories, foundations, farms, and granaries extending from Cloyes-sur-le-Loir to Péronville is a day's journey from the town. The pattern suggests that wheat and grain crops were ground at the mills in Bouche d'Aigre and Romily-sur-Aigre and the flour marketed with other foodstuffs to the townspeople and pilgrims in Cloyes-sur-le-Loir, Châteaudun, and Le Mans. The Tironensians obtained property through gifts of cash and wheat and consolidated holdings by complicated land exchanges and pledges to support pilgrimages. Their countergifts of white sheep, pigs, and peas reflected Tiron's advances in agriculture and stock-raising.[48] In this region the Tironensians provided for contingencies.

(See Table 5.1d.) In the Beauce, southeast of Châteaudun, Tiron established a denser agglomeration of farms and priories between Péronville and Puerthe near the Conie (a tributary of the Loir) south to Prénouvellon, Cintry/Saintry, and Gémigny, a distance of about 20 kilometres. Membrolles, Tironneau, and Cintry/Saintry attained the status of priories amid other important farms and granaries, including Choudri, Auvilliers, and La Mouise. Peter of Péronville (fl. ca. 1130–1164) was an important donor, but property was obtained from many other local families, and the magnates Ursio of Fréteval and Geoffrey III, viscount of Châteaudun, confirmed many donations. The Beauce was torn by local unrest 1135–1136 and 1145–1146, and Tiron profited by increasing its holdings.

Saint-Georges-de-Cintry/Saintry was established ca. 1115 in Epieds-en-Beauce and the diocese of Orléans.[49] Tiron Abbey took pride in its royal patrons, and the donor Louis VI was mentioned with deep gratitude in the *Vita Bernardi*.[50] The king's gift was land at Cintry/Saintry and the wood of Melleray for housing and firewood, the nucleus of the priory. Cintry/Saintry and the granary of Gémigny are the southeastern terminus of this concentration of foundations in the Chartrain, Dunois, and Beauce. Those southern towns were a short distance from the market town of Ouzouer-le-Marché, a day's journey from the port of Meung-sur-Loire, between Orléans and Blois.

---

48 T1:236–37, no. 208 (ca. 1135) (white sheep, peas).

49 T1:18, no. 7 (1115); ibid., 1:233n2, no. 205 (ca. 1135) (Cintry/Saintry). Merlet uncertainly situated Cintry/Saintry near Epieds-en-Beauce, ibid., 2:268. My provisional situation of the priory at nearby Saintry is confirmed by the *Bulletin de la Société Archéologique de l'Orléanais* 12 (1853): 323–25 at 324 (meeting of March 11, 1853). At that time a sheepfold of Saint George's farm had sculpture fragments indicating that it was formerly the priory's chapel. "*La ferme de Saint-Georges était autrefois un prieuré du même nom, situé sur le territoire de la paroisse d'Epieds*, Appiaria villa, *au hameau de Saintry*, Sintriacum. *Ce prieuré dépendait de l'abbaye de Tiron, dans le Perche. Dans une bergerie de la ferme de Saint-Georges se voient encore des fragments de sculptures annonçant que cette bergerie était autrefois la chapelle du prieuré*," available online at https://books.google.com/books?id=jAdKAAAAcAAJ.

50 VB, 11.97, AASS, Apr. 2:0245F; VB, trans. Cline, 103–4.

Southwest of Châteaudun the road from Membrolles ran a day's journey west to Romilly-sur-Aigre and Bouche d'Aigre, and further west along the Aigre to Cloyes-sur-le-Loir, a town a day's journey southwest of Châteaudun. A cluster of properties was acquired at the confluence of the Egvonne, Aigre, and Loir Rivers: the priories of Saints-Jean and Paul of Bouche d'Aigre and Notre-Dame-de-Riboeuf, three churches in Cloyes-sur-le-Loir and one in La Crotte, and the priory of Notre-Dame-d'Yron. Another cluster formed near the Egvonne River northwest of Yron. The counts of Blois gave Bouche d'Aigre the right of high justice (jurisdiction over capital offences).[51] The priory of Fouteaux with the churches of La Chapelle-Vicomtesse and Fontaine-Raoul, had holdings northwest near the churches of Bouffry and Ruan-sur-Egvonne and the priory of Montluiser/Mons-Lusellus. The chain of properties continues west along the road to Mondoubleau (see Map 5.3, West France).

By the 1140s in Cloyes-sur-le-Loir the churches of Saint-Georges, Saint-Lubin, and Saint-Séverin and the priory of Yron gave Tiron a near-monopoly at that pilgrim staging post. By the sixteenth century Yron had become an important source of income second to the Paris rents.[52] In the seventeenth century Yron's income sources included sharecropping farms, the Cloyes churches, and several mills, including the large mills of Châteaudun.[53] Montluiser had more distant donors and holdings, including a dwelling in the castle of Montigny-le-Gannelon north of Cloyes, a sluice-gate on the Loir, and land and woods at Bouffry.[54] Merlet uncertainly placed Montluiser near Bouffry; it is thought to have disappeared or merged with Yron or Montigny.[55]

The castle of Mondoubleau, northwest of Vendôme, was on the Grenne River and the road running south from Nogent-le-Rotrou to Tours. The ruling family was related to the comital families of Vendôme and Châteaudun and the seigneurial family of Fréteval, and family members witnessed donations to Tiron.[56] Mondoubleau (see Map 5.3) and Bouffry were the western terminus of a chain of priories and churches southwest of Châteaudun, which continued west to Le Mans in Maine. These towns were only a day's ride southeast of Châtaigniers near Soizé south of Tiron Abbey and Nogent-le-Rotrou.

Tiron acquired property on two routes south from Châteaudun to Blois. One route ran south via the priories at Romilly-sur-Aigre and Ecoman (and pre-1516 Escalmento). Another route followed the Loir southwest to Cloyes-sur-le-Loir, south downriver to

---

51 IS-ADEL, 8:198, H 1806 (1690–1730).

52 IS-ADEL, 8:168, H 1438 (1573). "*Sommaire des cens, rentes en deniers, grains, moissons et autres appartenant à l'abbaye de Tiron (revenue en deniers) 2231 liv. 10 s; plus 187 chapons et 235 poules; plus le revenue d'Yron fournant la somme de 16 à 1800 livres plus le revenu des cens et rentes de la ville de Paris montant à 5000 livres.*"

53 IS-ADEL 8:202, H 1862 (1665).

54 T2:38–40, no. 269 (1145). T1:97–98, no. 78 (1125–1131), ibid., 1:103–4, no. 84 (1126–1131). T2:1–2, no. 227 (ca. 1140).

55 T2:287.

56 Livingstone, *Out of Love for my Kin*, 61–65, 156–58, 243. T1:37–38, no. 21 (1119); ibid., 1:87–88, no. 69 (ca. 1125); ibid., 1:174–75, no. 151 (1131); ibid., 1:179–80, no. 157 (ca. 1131).

Fréteval and Vendôme, south by land to the church of Blémars and the priory of Moulin-Neuf on the Cisse River, near the Loire, east to Blois. The priory of Monrion was south of Blois and the Loire. Milling was important: Moulin-Neuf did included a new mill (Molineuf), and Monrion acquired a new mill on Le Beuvron River ca. 1135, built by the monks.[57] From Blémars the road ran 43 kilometres southwest to the Loire crossing point at Tours, and 52 kilometres southwest to the Tironensian abbey of Bois-Aubry, a considerable distance unbroken by properties, implying little overland travel.

At least one new priory was founded to the east between Cintry/Saintry and Orléans and Paris after 1130. The expansion went from Cintry/Saintry and Gémigny, east to Orléans, and northeast to the priory and granary of Coutures near Mareau-au-Bois, southwest of Pithiviers. The Cluniac priory of Saint-Pierre-de-Pithiviers was on the Oeuf, a tributary of the Essonne, which flows by Augerville-la-Rivière near Puiseaux, and continues northeast to the Seine upriver of Paris. Merlet believes that Augerville-la-Rivière, with a Latin name *Ogerivilla* identical to that of Augerville-les-Malades southeast of Chartres, was another Tironensian priory.[58]

The density of this centre of the Tironensian network from Dreux to Blois and from Nogent-le-Rotrou to Cintry/Saintry and the Loiret is noteworthy. Multiple interconnecting routes crisscross the Perche and the Chartrain, indicating frequent local interaction and communication. Yet longer trade and pilgrimage routes can be discerned. There are two major north–south routes: one from Mortagne-au-Perche through Nogent-le-Rotrou, Soizé, Mondoubleau, to Vendôme, and another along the Compostela route from Dreux through Chartres to Châteaudun and Blois on the Loire. The east–west route from Péronville through Cloyes-sur-le-Loir to Mondoubleau continues west to Le Mans and east to Paris.

In an overview of France, Tironensian expansion continued along roads to the north in Normandy, to the west in Anjou and Brittany, to the south in Poitou, and to the east in the vicinity of Paris. Although Tiron's supporter Bishop Geoffrey II was papal legate to the provinces of Bourges, Bordeaux, Tours, Dol-en-Bretagne, and Aquitaine, these regions were outside the spheres of influence of the interrrelated families of the lands of the Loire, and Tiron won donors by its reputation and merits.

Four regional groups were on the periphery of this central core of Tiron's properties. To the north was Normandy, whose overlords were the kings of England, until Geoffrey V, count of Anjou, conquered the duchy in 1144. To the west, the counts of Anjou (who controlled Maine) and the dukes of Brittany, whose lands extended south to the Loire Valley, were generous Tironensian benefactors. To the south, William X, duke of Aquitaine, encouraged expansion south of the Loire in Poitou, and Joug-Dieu and a few priories were far to the southeast. To the east, in the realm of Louis VI and

---

57 T1:231, no. 203 (ca. 1140). Ibid., 2:74, no. 300 (ca. 1150). "*In qua area postea monachi Tironis molendinum fecerunt.*"

58 T1:158–59n3 (ca. 1130); ibid., 2:290. Although a chapel and church of Saint-Pierre-et-Saint-Paul founded during the eleventh and twelfth centuries exist west of Augerville-la-Rivière, the prevailing scholarly opinion is that *Ogerivilla* refers only to the Chartrain farm.

VII, foundations were established around Paris and at the confluence of the Seine and the Essonne. Tiron successfully obtained support from the Anglo-Norman and Capetian blocs. Little Tironensian expansion occurred further east into Champagne.

The rise of towns and the merchant class created demand for grain, wine, dried fish, salt, wool cloth, leather and hides, ceramics, wax, lead, tin, building materials, horses, and other merchandise. These goods were carted or shipped from producing regions to urban markets. Exchanges of grain, wine, salt, and wool predominated. Scotland produced superior wool and Ireland superior hides, wool, fish, and horses, and both regions preferred French wine to their local beverages.[59] The Seine, Loire, and Garonne were the major river routes by which wine was transported to the Channel and Atlantic ports and on to the British Isles, and their coastal regions had many salt centres. Flat-bottomed barges and cogs were used for river and sea transport in the second half of the twelfth century.[60] The dangers of pirates and shipwrecks were real, but so were the profits.

When the foundations and properties in the 1147 and 1176/1177 confirmations are mapped, axes of development emerge from the core of local Tironensian establishments. In the Vexin, northeast of Evreux, Tiron extended its network along the Eure and the Seine northwest of Paris. In Normandy, at Rouen (where the Eure joined the Seine), it continued north to Dieppe, a sailing point for pilgrimages to Compostela. Another northwest axis followed the Risle from L'Aigle past Le Neubourg to the Seine ports of Pont Audemer and Harfleur. Another northwest axis proceeded from Evreux to Bernay, Lisieux, and the port of Caen. In Lower Normandy, a northwest axis proceeded from Nogent-le-Rotrou to Mortagne-au-Perche, Alençon and Sées, and turned southwest into Maine and northern Brittany. A southern axis proceeded from Alençon to Le Mans and Angers to the Loire River, then turned west toward southern Brittany and the Atlantic. Further south, three important abbeys were established south of the Loire. Then the axis extended south into Poitou and Aquitaine and far southeast to the abbey of Joug-Dieu on the Saône River near the Rhône. To the east, a cluster of priories and churches formed around Paris and extended east into Champagne and southeast into Burgundy. These foundations were connected to the central core of local properties by the road from Chartres to Rambouillet and by the Essonne River from the Beauce to Fontainebleau.

Tiron's northern expansion from Dreux into the Vexin and Normandy occurred in the Seine Valley toward the Channel ports. Cross-Channel trade in this region was dominated by the comparative advantage of British wool and French wine. The wine trade was concentrated in Rouen, through which the Seine flowed to Harfleur, but Dieppe 55 kilometres due north of Rouen was the major port and shipping point to Southampton. Normandy specialized in butter, cheese, fruit, cider, wine, wheat, flax, livestock including horses, fish, and salt. Ship-building was an important industry. The Seine connected this region with Paris, with a tremendous demand for flour, meat, fish, and other foodstuffs, wine and cider, salt and spices, wood and charcoal, cloth, luxury goods, and building materials. The rulers of Normandy and the Vexin also supported trade and profited from

---

59 Everard, "Le duché de Bretagne," 197–98.
60 Gillingham, *The Angevin Empire*, 43–44.

numerous taxes and tolls. Despite political tensions, the French kings maintained considerable influence in the entire Seine Valley, for the flow of trade between Paris and the Atlantic was paramount.

At that time, Normandy and the Vexin were war zones. Henry I, king of England and duke of Normandy, dealt with rebellious Norman barons until his death in 1135. By 1120 he allied his legitimate son William Atheling with Matilda, daughter of Fulk V, count of Anjou, who controlled much of western France, and his natural daughter Maud/Matilda FitzRoy with Conan III, duke of Brittany, who controlled the northwestern coastline. In June 1120 Louis VI granted Normandy to William Atheling, whose drowning in November 1120 destabilized the succession to the English throne and the Norman dukedom. In 1123 Fulk V briefly allied his daughter Sybil (ca. 1112–1165) with William Clito, son of Henry I's older brother Robert Curthose, who claimed Normandy until his death in 1128. Louis VI supported the Norman rebellions. In 1128 Henry I allied his legitimate daughter, the widowed Empress Matilda, with Fulk's son Geoffrey V, count of Anjou. The unhappy union produced three sons, and Henry I repeatedly made his barons swear to support Empress Matilda as his successor. The king's sudden death on December 1, 1135 precipitated a crisis over the succession, and his sister's son Stephen seized the English throne. Stephen's son Eustace IV, count of Boulogne (ca. 1129–1153), was designated his successor in 1136[61] and was invested with Normandy in 1137. Stephen's vacillating rule engendered support for Empress Matilda, who crossed to England in 1139, precipitating a decade of civil war. Empress Matilda's oldest son Henry became duke of Normandy and count of Anjou upon his father's death in 1151, married Eleanor of Aquitaine in 1152, and was acknowledged Stephen's successor in 1153. Henry II's accession in 1154 restored English control over Normandy.

In Normandy, Rotrou II, count of the Perche, had multiple connections. Henry I was his father-in-law. His sister Juliana married Gilbert of L'Aigle, lord of a strategically important castle and town near the Perche border in southern Normandy, inherited by their son Richer II. His sister Margaret married Henry I de Beaumont, seigneur of Le Neubourg and earl of Warwick.[62] When Robert I de Beaumont, count of Meulan, earl of Leicester, died ca. 1118, Henry I divided his lands, approximately by the English Channel, between Robert's twin older sons: Waleran II and Robert II, both Tironensian donors. Waleran II became count of Meulan and obtained the honours of Pont Audemer, Beaumont-le-Roger, and Brionne in Normandy. His position in the Vexin required him to balance the demands of the French and English kings and the duke of Normandy.[63] Robert II obtained the earldom of Leicester and considerable property in England as well as the castle of Le Neubourg in Normandy.[64] The Beaumont twins' maternal uncle, Ralph I, count of Vermandois (1085–1152), was a steward at the French court.

---

61 Hollister, *Henry I*, 274–78, 292–95, 313–14, 466–67, 477–79, 482.
62 Thompson, *The Monks of Tiron*, 114.
63 T1:76–77, nos. 55–56 (ca. 1122).
64 His son Geoffrey de Beaumont (b. ca. 1146) confirmed his gifts to Tiron in 1202. T1:82–83, nos. 62–63 (ca. 1125); ibid., 2:117–18, no. 342 (1202).

Tiron's northern expansion followed the Eure from Dreux to Evreux and then branched out toward the Seine and the English Channel. Around 1137 Evreux was held by Waleran II during the minorities of Counts Amaury II (r. 1137–1140) and Simon (r. 1140–ca. 1146).[65] Waleran II's holdings included Pont-Audemer, a major port on the Risle inland below Harfleur, and the county of Meulan in the Vexin.[66] Crouch notes that, in addition to collecting duties on goods entering towns and tolls on the Seine river traffic at Meulan, a bridging point, Waleran II was trading directly, employing agents in Southampton, a main entry point for the wine trade between England and France, and in Pont-Audemer and Ile-de-France. A herring fleet became established at Pont-Audemer 1106–1130, and Waleran II made grants of salted or smoked herring to inland religious houses, including Tiron ca. 1122.[67] Leather and cloth were also important industries.[68] Prayers for the brothers of Holy Saviour of Tiron were included in a pre-fourteenth-century necrology of the priory of Saint-Nicaise-de-Meulan.[69] The entry supports Tironensian contacts with that town. In addition to his English lands, Waleran II's twin brother Robert II, earl of Leicester, through his marriage to Amice of Montfort-Gael (ca. 1106–1168) in 1121, held the honours of Breteuil-sur-Iton, northeast of L'Aigle and Pacy-sur-Eure, southwest of Vernon and east of Evreux. Hugh IV of Montfort-sur-Risle, husband of Waleran II's and Robert II's sister Adelina de Beaumont (b. ca. 1098), witnessed the confirmation of Robert FitzMartin's donation in Wales ca. 1119.[70] The Beaumont and Meulan families and their associates were long-time benefactors of Tiron Abbey.[71]

An important reason for Tiron's northern expansion is that ca. 1122 Abbot William obtained an exemption from tolls and customs for Tiron's goods throughout the domains of Henry I and Waleran II of Meulan.[72] Waleran II's connections and benefactions to Tiron Abbey can be explained by religious enthusiasm for a new monastic order in the vicinity of his domains.[73] Significantly, Waleran II's exemption specified leather straps and footwear as well as other products, so Tiron's priory at Chartres may have been

---

65 Power, *The Norman Frontier*, 65.

66 Crouch, *The Beaumont Twins*, 9–12.

67 T1:77, no. 56 (ca. 1122). Tiron had 7000 herrings in Lent in Pont-Audemer, 2000 from Robert II, 2000 from Waleran II, and 3000, or 1000 plus 30 solidi, from the family of a local butcher. Ibid., 2:158–59, 164, no. 377 (ca. 1250).

68 Crouch, *The Beaumont Twins*, 185–89.

69 *Obituaires de la Province de Sens*, ed. Auguste Molinier and Auguste Lognon. Recueil des historiens de France, Obituaires, 4 vols. in 5 (Paris: Klincksieck, 1902–1923), 2:240B. "*Commemoratio fratrum defunctorum Sancti Remigii Remensis et Sancti Salvatoris Tironis*", citing *Recueil des chartes de Saint-Nicaise de Meulan, prieuré de l'Ordre de Bec*, ed. Emile Houth (Paris: Champion, 1924), 196.

70 Robert II, earl of Leicester, received a tract of land from Tiron Abbey and gave the monks wheat at Frétigny annually. Robert II's son Geoffrey de Beaumont confirmed his father's donation to the monks of Tiron of woodland in the forest of Brimont. T1:42, no. 26 (ca. 1119). Crouch, *The Beaumont Twins*, 16.

71 T2:117–18, no. 362 (1202).

72 T1:75–77, nos. 54–55 (ca. 1122).

73 Waleran II was so pious that he employed four chaplains at one time, and he gave gifts to many religious foundations. His concern for lepers led him to found a priory-hospital of Saint Gilles at

one of his suppliers.[74] Robert II, earl of Leicester, exempted the monks from all tolls and customs in his Norman domains and accorded them his firm peace, or protection.[75] The exemptions at Pacy-sur-Eure would have increased the profits of trade on the Eure from Dreux to the south and between the Seine and Evreux. During the reign of David I, Abbot William obtained one exemption from fees annually for one ship of Kelso Abbey engaged in fishing and trade in Scotland and Northumberland, based in Perth on the Firth of Tay.[76] Possibly Abbot William not only supplied but emulated the trade with England from which Waleran II profited. The pattern of exemptions suggests that Tiron Abbey was engaged in trade in Normandy and the British Isles,[77] through mutually beneficial religious and economic connections.

The route across the Seine is east of Evreux. The northern route from Dreux, Evreux, to Dieppe via Rouen also shows properties between Dieppe and Yvetôt. The western route from Evreux and Lisieux leads to Caen. In Normandy Tiron had no abbeys, thirteen priories, thirteen churches, and only one farm. The pattern suggests the importance of communication and trade to the Seine and Channel ports.

From Dreux on the road north toward Evreux, five foundations—Vert-en-Drouais, Heudreville, Saint-Germain-sur-Avre, Boissy-sur-Damville, and Chavigny-Bailleuil—ran a day's journey west along the Avre River, a tributary of the Eure, near Nonancourt, a town on the road west to L'Aigle. The Eure connected Dreux to tax-exempt trade in Pacy-sur-Eure, a day's ride north, with Vernon a day's journey northeast on the Seine. The Iton River connected Damville to tax-exempt trade in Breteuil-sur-Iton, a day's journey west. From Breteuil-sur-Iton the road ran a day's ride southwest to L'Aigle on the Risle, much of it along the Iton River.

Heudreville-sur-Eure was an early riverine priory listed in the 1132/1133 papal confirmation. William of Glos, seneschal of the house of Breteuil, and all the clergy and burghers of L'Aigle offered a cash inducement to be permitted to enter into confraternity with Tiron Abbey, to have their living and dead commemorated in the monks' prayers on Ash Wednesday, and to receive letters from the abbey and an annual visit from a Tironensian monk.[78] The request suggests a close association between Tiron Abbey and the border town ruled by Rotrou's nephew Richer II.[79] Then the road ran a day's ride north to Evreux. Northeast of Evreux, the Eure and the Seine are 12 kilometres apart.

Pont-Audemer ca. 1135 in the little-known order of Grand-Beaulieu-lès-Chartres whose prior was Ralph Cantel, a monk of Tiron. Crouch, *The Beaumont Twins*, 199n19.

74 T1:76–77, no. 56 (ca. 1122).

75 T1:162–63, no. 137 (ca. 1130).

76 T1: 80–81, no. 60 (1124–1145); ibid., 2:159, no. 377 (ca. 1250). *Kelso Liber*, 2:310–11, nos. 397–98.

77 T2:104, no. 328 (1179). A forged papal confirmation by Alexander III to the incorrectly named Abbot William includes a spurious right to free transit through all the ports of England and Normandy belonging to the king of England.

78 T1:91, no. 72 (ca. 1125).

79 Richer II or his son and namesake granted Tiron 2000 herrings annually at L'Aigle. T2:164, no. 377 (ca. 1250).

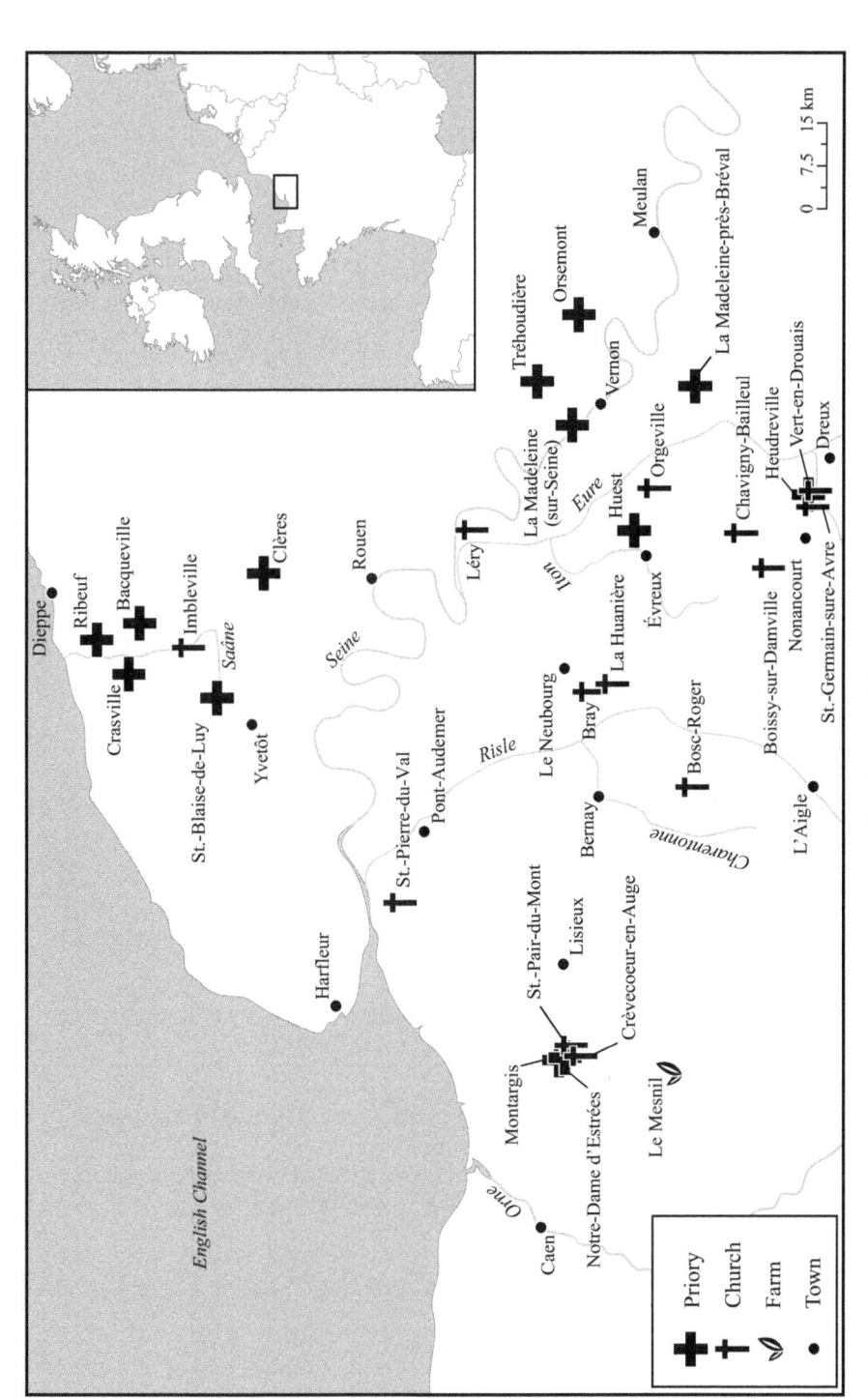

Map 5.2. North France

94 EXPANSION IN FRANCE

Table 5.2. North France

Dreux to Evreux
Vert-en-Drouais (St. Pierre); church; <1147
Heudreville (St. Martin); priory; <1132
St.-Germain-sur-Avre; church; <1147
Boissy-sur-Damville (St. Martin); church; <1147
Chavigny-Bailleul (St. Laumer); church; <1147
Dreux to Evreux: Dreux, NW 8 km to Vert-en-Drouais, NW 1 km to Heudreville, W 3 km to St.-Germain-sur-Avre, NW 16 km via Nonancourt to Boissy-sur-Damville, NE 9 km to Chavigny-Bailleuil, N 19 km to Evreux
Nonancourt is 31 km S of Evreux
To L'Aigle: Damville, W 17 km to Breteuil-sur-Iton, SW 5 km to L'Aigle
Evreux to the Seine Valley
Huest (St. Cécile); priory; <1147
Orgeville; church; <1516
La-Madeleine-près-Bréval; priory; ca. 1130; William of St.-Chéron
La-Madeleine (sur-Seine); priory; <1131; St. Adjutor of Vernon; hermitage
Tréhoudière (N.D.); priory; 1133–1145; Matthew of Vernon
Orsemont (St. Jean); priory; <1147
Evreux, NE 6 km to Huest, E 11 km to Orgeville, E 6 km across the Eure at Pacy-sur-Eure (with La-Madeleine-près-Bréval) 16 km SE of Pacy-sur-Eure and 20 km S of Vernon, NE 20 km across the Seine to La-Madeleine-sur-Seine at Pressagny l'Orgueilleux, SE 6 km to Vernon
Tréhoudière is 14 km NE of Vernon, and Orsemont is 18 km E of Vernon
Evreux to Dieppe
Léry; church; <1516
Clères (St. Silvestre); priory; ca. 1140; Gillebert (de l'Ile)
Bacqueville (-en-Caux) (N.D.+St. Pierre); priory; ca. 1133; William Martel, English royal steward
Imbleville (Wimbelevilla) (St. Jean-B.); church; 1133; Hugh III of Amiens, archbishop of Rouen
Ribeuf (St. Laurent); priory; <1147
Evreux, N 32 km to Léry, N 24 km to Rouen, N 16 km to Clères, N 31 km to Bacqueville-en-Caux, N 10 km to Ribeuf, NE 15 km to Dieppe
Dieppe to Yvetot
Crasville (-la-Roquefort) (St. Martin); priory; ca. 1126; Robert of Crasville
St.-Blaise-de-Luy; priory; ca. 1117; Adam of Grémonville
Northern route: Dieppe, SW 15 km to Ribeuf, SW 11 km to Crasville-la-Rocquefort, SW 18 km to St.-Blaise-de-Luy (Grémonville), S 9 km to Yvetot

Table 5.2. (Cont.)

Southern route: Dieppe, SW 15 km to Ribeuf, S 10 km to Bacqueville-en-Caux, S 11 km to Imbleville, SW 11 km to St.-Blaise-de-Luy (Grémonville), S 9 km to Yvetot *St.-Wandrille or Fontenelle, founded 649 on the Seine near Caudebec-en-Caux (modern commune of St.-Wandrille-Rançon) is 22 km S of St.-Blaise-de-Luy (Grémonville) and 15 km S of Yvetot*
Evreux to Le Neubourg and the Channel ports of Pont-Audemer (on the Risle) and Harfleur (on the Seine)   **Bosc-Roger (St. Jean)**; church; <1147; fair confirmed by Henry I *Bosc-Roger is 39 km W of Evreux, 23 km N of L'Aigle, 20 km S of the town of Bernay on the Charentonne, 9 km E of the Charentonne and 11 km W of the Risle*

La Huanière; church; <1147
    Bray; church; <1147
    N.D./St.-Pierre-du-Val; church; 1147
Evreux, NW 23 km to La Huanière, N 6 km to Bray, N 6 km to Le Neubourg. From Bray, the route continued NW 41 km down the Risle to Pont-Audemer, NW 15 km to St.-Pierre-du-Val, and NW 11 km to Harfleur

Evreux to Caen
  Montargis (St. Antonin); priory; <1147; Hugh of Crèvecoeur +s. William
  Notre-Dame d'Estrées; priory; <1147; Hugh of Crèvecoeur
  St.-Pair-du-Mont; church; <1147
  Crèvecoeur-en-Auge; church; <1147; Hugh of Crèvecoeur+s. William
  Le Mesnil; farm; <1147; Alexander of Nouères
Evreux, NW 23 km to La Huanière, N 6 km to Bray, W 23 km to Bernay (on the Charentonne), W 29 km to Lisieux, W 14 km to Montargis, Estrées, St.-Pair-du-Mont and Crèvecoeur-en-Auge (clustered within 6 km), W 14 km to Le Mesnil, NW 25 km to Caen

One axis of expansion was toward and across the Seine. The route from Evreux ran northeast to the priory of Huest, east to the church of Orgeville, east across the Eure at Pacy-sur-Eure, and northeast across the Seine. The priory of La-Madeleine-sur-Seine was founded before 1131 by Saint Adjutor of Vernon and is an example of the incorporation of a hermitage into an eremitical congregation. Vernon was situated in the western French Vexin, 78 kilometres northwest of Paris. In terms of trade, the priory's location was Tiron's link northeast of Evreux to the Seine traffic between Paris and the port of Harfleur. The lords of Vernon charged tolls on the water route for trade between Paris and the Channel and were closely governed by the French kings. The priory of La-Madeleine-près-Bréval between the Eure and the Seine was a day's ride from Dreux,

Pacy-sur-Eure, and Vernon. East of Vernon and the Seine were two priories. Saint Adjutor's brother Matthew of Vernon established La Tréhoudière in Tourny. The gift was confirmed by Hugh III of Amiens, archbishop of Rouen (r. 1129–1164), and the donations included a mill and an annual gift of nuts, an important regional crop.[80] Orsemont was also in the Seine Valley.

Another axis of expansion ran from Evreux via Rouen, 123 kilometres north to the port of Dieppe.[81] The priory of Clères was founded ca. 1140.[82] The Saâne River connected two priories with the Channel. Bacqueville-en-Caux was founded and richly endowed in 1133 by William Martel, the English royal steward 1130–1153.[83] Archbishop Hugh III confirmed his gifts and granted three churches, preserving the rights of other religious orders.[84] The priory of Ribeuf was near the port of Quiberville, east of the Dun River's outlet at Saint-Aubin-sur-Mer.

Two routes ran southwest from Dieppe indicating considerable traffic between that port and the priory of Saint-Blaise-de-Luy (Grémonville). The priory of Crasville-la-Rocquefort was a day's journey from the coast near the town of Fontaine-le-Dun on the Dun River.[85] The location of Crasville and Ribeuf, a day's journey apart near small Channel ports not far from the major port of Dieppe, mirrored the location of the English priory of Hamble on the Channel near the major port of Southampton. The priory of Saint-Blaise-de-Luy (Grémonville) was founded ca. 1115–1117, midway between Dieppe and Rouen. Its strategic importance is evident in its confirmation by Henry I, William I Bonne Ame, archbishop of Rouen (r. 1071–1119), and Henry Hastings, count of Eu (r. 1096–1140), as well as by donor Adam of Grémonville. The high-ranking witnesses were Robert Bloet, bishop of Lincoln (r. 1093–1123), Robert I of Beaumont, count of Meulan and earl of Leicester, William of Warenne, 2nd earl of Surrey (d. 1138), William of Tancarville (1072–1129), chamberlain of Normandy and England, and Stephen, count of Aumale (1070–1127), the son of Odo/Eudes II, count of Troyes, Meaux, and Aumale and of Adelaide of Normandy, the sister of William the Conqueror.[86]

---

80 T1:213, no. 187 (1133–1145), n1, mentions the special nut market in Vernon and the widespread use of nut oil at this time; ibid., 1:214, no. 188 (1133–1145); ibid., 1:241–42, no. 214 (ca. 1135).

81 By 1516 Tiron had acquired the church of Léry near Pont-de-l'Arche at the confluence of the Eure and the Seine, downriver of Rouen.

82 T2:17, no. 245 (ca. 1140). The endowment included multure, income from William Martel's rents in Normandy and census income in England, tithes on crops from many local families, foodstuffs in Bacqueville, and wine in Rouen to celebrate masses.

83 Hollister, *Henry I*, 362.

84 T1:203–5, no. 183 (1133). The church of Imbleville is south of Bacqueville-en-Caux. William Martel's confirmation added a share of the chantry of Saint-Pierre, together with land and income in Ouville-la Rivière slightly north of Saint-Laurent-de-Ribeuf, and in Raslonde. T1:216–17, no. 190 (1134).

85 The priory was given the church of Crasville and its appurtenances, tithes of all its mills, and land and pasture at Crasville and Rocquefort. T1:102–3, no. 83 (ca. 1126). Archbishop Hugh IV's confirmation specified the tithes of two mills in the fief of Galeran of Rocquefort. T1:193–94, no. 172 (ca. 1132).

86 T1:27–28, specifically 28nn1–4, no. 13 (ca. 1117; spring 1115). Hollister, *Henry I*, 221, notes these members of the king's inner circle of advisers.

Saint-Blaise-de-Luy is north of the eleventh-century fief of Yvetot, a day's journey north of the Seine. The southern terminus of this route southwest of Dieppe is probably the ancient and illustrious Benedictine abbey of Saint-Wandrille or Fontenelle, founded on the Seine in 649 near Caudebec-en-Caux. The abbey is mentioned in Tiron's foundation charter for Bacqueville-en-Caux, conceding its appurtenances except for the portion of the monks of Saint-Wandrille.[87] The exemption would have brought the monks in contact over mutual concerns.

Another axis of expansion ran from Evreux to the Risle north of L'Aigle, Le Neubourg and the Channel port of Pont-Audemer, controlled by Waleran II of Meulan and his family. Tiron had gifts of income and herrings and exemptions from the tonlieu and tolls and was in confraternity with the towns.[88] By 1250 Tiron claimed both the church of Bosc-Roger and its fair, a much earlier gift of Henry [I], king of the English.[89] La Huanière and Bray are near the confluence of the Risle and Charentonne Rivers. From Bray, the route continued northwest down the Risle to Pont-Audemer, to the church at Saint-Pierre-du-Val near the coast and northwest to Harfleur.

Another axis of expansion ran 121 kilometres from Evreux northwest through the towns of Bernay (on the Charentonne) and Lisieux to the port of Caen on the Orne. A day's journey west of Lisieux, Tiron owned a cluster of properties. Montargis was a priory founded by the Crèvecoeur family on the promontory of Montargis, protected by ditches and an embankment. Notre-Dame-d'Estrées was across the road to the south, grouped with the church of Crèvecoeur-en-Auge. By 1179 the church of Saint-Pair-du-Mont was established between Notre-Dame-d'Estrées and Crèvecoeur-en-Auge, with property at Le Mesnil to the south. Caen was another day's ride to the west.[90]

Tiron's Norman foundations provided inland land trade and communication routes between Evreux and the major ports of Dieppe, Pont-Audemer, and Caen. They extended Tiron's network to the Seine and along a considerable expanse of Channel coastline, a significant duty-free region for marketing and shipping its production from Chartres. They also provided routes for supplying Chartres with coastal products like fish and salt and imports like wool and minerals, maximizing profits from fixed transport costs.

In west France Tiron's expansion into Lower Normandy, Maine, and Anjou (north of the Loire) with access to the Atlantic in northern and southern Brittany was far more significant than its expansion into Normandy. Brittany was on important Channel, Atlantic, and Loire shipping routes, and strategically it extended to Poitou. Conan III ruled Brittany 1112–1148 and was eventually succeeded by his granddaughter Constance of Penthièvre (r. 1166–1201) whose husbands included Henry II's son Geoffrey (r. 1181–1186). The dukes of Brittany controlled two major trading areas around the old and new capitals of Rennes and Nantes. Rennes was the site of the ducal mint; Nantes was a city and port. The dukes owned Guérande with its salt marshes, an

---

87 T1:203–5, specifically 204, no. 183 (1133).
88 T2:165, no. 377 (ca. 1250).
89 T2:159, no. 377 (ca. 1250).
90 T2:70–71, no. 297 (1149); ibid., 2:75–76, no. 302 (ca. 1150), n1; ibid., 2:104, no. 328 (1179).

important saltworks today, together with castellanies and forests in the Loire Valley.[91] The coastal regions provided fish, shellfish, and salt; the inland areas were suited for fruit and cereal production and livestock; the forested regions provided lumber, nuts, and pannage. Fulk V, count of Anjou, married Eremburge (ca. 1096–ca. 1126), the daughter and heiress of Helias, count of Maine (r. 1091–1110), and ruled Maine 1110–1129, when it passed with Anjou to his son Geoffrey V and subsequently to his grandson Henry II, king of England. Anjou supported many crops but was a major wine region. The port of Nantes was central to the Atlantic–Loire trade; Angers, the Plantegenet seat, had access to the Loire via the Maine River. Tironensian foundations participated in this economy but also supported shipping by acting as staging posts for repairs, reprovisioning, medical treatment, and burials. It is noteworthy, however, that Tiron's expansion was mainly north of Rennes and northeast of Angers, and did not extend to the north bank of the Loire in this region.

Tiron obtained a safeguard and exemption from tolls and customs throughout the lands of the Angevin rulers.[92] Their strong support resulted in expansion west and south of the Tironensian core in Eure-et-Loir and the Beauce. Tiron eventually had five abbeys in this region: Hambye in Lower Normandy, Le Tronchet and Saint-Méen in Brittany, and Le Gué-de-Launay and La Pelice on the Angevin border southwest of Tiron Abbey. The sixth Angevin abbey of Ferrières will be described with the nearby Poitevin abbey of Asnières and Bois-Aubry in the Touraine, together with other properties south of the Loire. Tiron also founded and acquired fifteen priories, twenty churches, and two farms in this region, as well as a house with vines in Le Mans. The pattern represented the heaviest local and regional community involvement, significant communication, and substantial agricultural activity including vineyards. As in Normandy, Tiron's expansion in Maine and Anjou was supported by the kinship network of Henry I.

The towns of Mortagne-au-Perche and Mondoubleau were the northwestern and southwestern terminations of the concentration of priories in the vicinity of Tiron Abbey and Chartres. Mortagne-au-Perche is in modern Lower Normandy on the border of Maine on the road running between Alençon and Dreux. Between Mortagne-au-Perche and Dreux, much of the route followed the Avre River. The Tironensian foundations were mainly a day's ride apart along this route, from Dreux northwest to the aforementioned cluster of the priory of Saint-Martin-d'Heudreville in Mesnil-sur-l'Estrée[93] and the church of Saint-Pierre-de-Vert-en-Drouais on the north and south banks of the Avre and Saint-Germain-sur-Avre, west to the town of Nonancourt. The route to Mortagne-au-Perche ran southwest a long day's ride (or boat ride) along the Avre to the priory of Saint-Barthélemy-du-Vieux-Charencey and the church of Saint-Maurice-lès-Charencey (with the church of La Bourgonnière a day's journey to the east), another day's journey to the town of Tourouvre, and another day's journey to Mortagne-au-Perche. Power

---

91 Everard, "Le duché de Bretagne," 21–23.

92 T1:63, no. 44 (1120–1129).

93 Thompson, *The Monks of Tiron*, 230, corrects Merlet's situation of this priory in Heudreville-sur-Eure. T2:279.

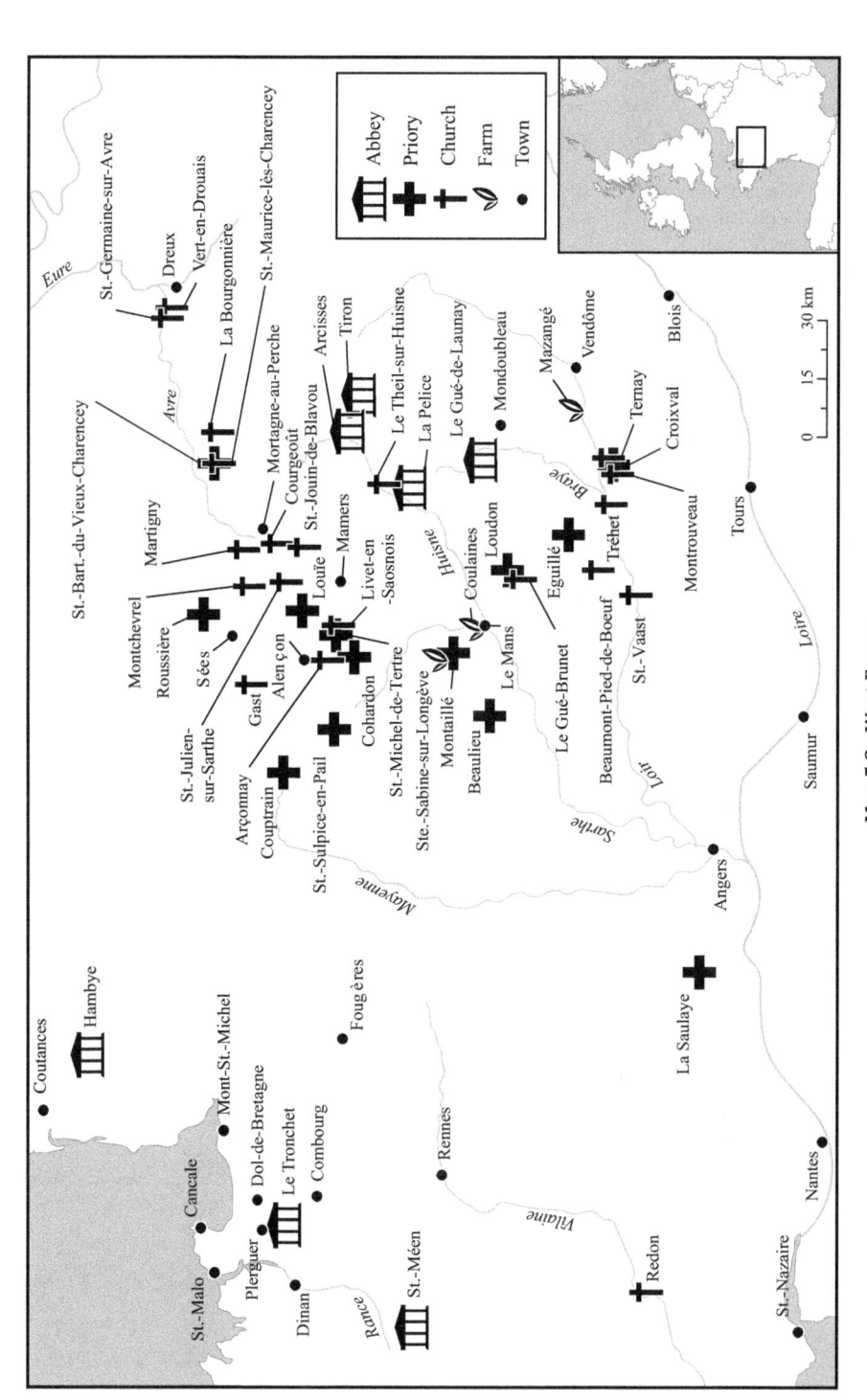

Map 5.3. West France

Table 5.3. West France

Dreux to Mortagne-au-Perche **St.-Bart-du-Vieux-Charencey**; priory; ca. 1130; Stephen of Gardais+uncle Girard s. of Fulbert; **St.-Maurice-lès-Charencey**; church; ca. 1135; merged with St.-Barthélemy-du-Vieux-Charencey **La Bourgonnière**; church; <1147 Dreux, W 17 km to Nonancourt, SW 37 km along the Avre to Charencey (with La Bourgonnière E 10 km), SW 11 km to Tourouvre, SW 12 km to Mortagne-au-Perche *Mortagne-au-Perche is 35 km NW of Nogent-le-Rotrou and 39 km NE of Alençon*
Mortagne-au-Perche to Sées **Martigny (St. Germain)**; church; <1147 **Montchevrel (St. Pierre)**; church; <1147 **Roussière (St. Léonard)**; priory; <1147 **Gast (St. Pierre)**; church; <1147 **Trahant or Tréhiant**; church; <1147 (not mapped) Mortagne-au-Perche, NW 12 km to Martigny, W 11 km to Montchevrel, W 14 km to Sées *La-Roussière is 11 km NE of Sées. Le Gast is near Tanville 15 km SW of Sées*
Mortagne-au-Perche to Alençon **Courgeoût (St. Laumer)**; church; <1147; Pagan of Courgeôut **St-Jouin-de-Blavou**; church; <1147; William of Blavou, uncle Naimerus **St-Julien-sur-Sarthe**; church; 1145 **Louïe (St. Pierre)**; priory; ca. 1128 Mortagne-au-Perche SW 6 km to Courgeoût, St.-Jouin-de-Blavou and St.-Julien-sur-Sarthe, SW 10 km to St-Pierre-de-Louïe, W 14 km to Alençon
West of Alençon in Mayenne, Lower Normandy, and Brittany **St.-Sulpice-en-Pail**; priory; ca. 1140; Hugh of St.-Aubin-du-Désert; hermitage **Couptrain (St. Maurice)**; priory; <1147 **Hambye (N.D.)**; abbey; ca. 1145; William Painel, seigneur of Hambye; independent order by 1181 (daughter abbeys and priories not mapped) **Le Tronchet (N.D.)**; abbey; 1133–1147; Alan FitzJordan, seneschal of Dol; hermitage **St. Méen**; ca. 600 by St. Méen; abbey; <1516 *St.-Sulpice-en-Pail is 20 km W of Alençon, and Couptrain is 27 km NW of Alençon. Hambye is 81 km SW of Caen. Le Tronchet is 11 km SW of Dol-de-Bretagne, 12 km SE of Châteauneuf-d'Ille-et-Vilaine, 26 km SE of St.-Malo, 37 km SW of Mont-St.-Michel, and 50 km N of Rennes. St.-Méen is 43 km W of Rennes and 60 km S of St.-Malo*

Table 5.3. (Cont.)

Alençon to Le Mans **Arçonnay (St. Pierre)**; church; <1175–1176 **Livet-en-Saosnois**; church; 1147; Walter Hait, viscount of Mollan/Moulins **St-Michel-du-Tertre**; priory; 1128; Gervais of Le Verzet+mother Breta **Cohardon (La Madeleine/St. Jean)**; priory; ca. 1115; William of Champfleur **Chérancé**; tithes; <1175–1176 **Ste-Sabine-sur-Longève**; farm; 1128 Haois of Montfaucon **Montaillé (La Madeleine)**; priory; 1121; Alberic, seigneur of La Milesse **Coulaines, Le Mans**; vines; ca. 1140; Elisenda/Pagana, citizen of Le Mans house; 1179 **Beaulieu (La Madeleine)**; priory; <1128; Fulk of Montfaucon Alençon, S 4 km to Arçonnay, SE 12 km to Livet-en-Saosnois and St.-Michel-du-Tertre, SW 6 km to Cohardon, SE 11 km to Chérancé, S 9 km to Beaumont-sur-Sarthe, S 12 km to Sainte-Sabine-sur-Longève and Montaillé, S 19 km to Le Mans *Beaulieu is 22 km W of Le Mans*
Alençon via Mamers, approaches **Le Theil-sur-Huisne (N.D.)**; church; <1147; Pagan of Le Theil **La Pelice**; abbey; <1187; Bernard III, seigneur of La Ferté; given to Tiron in 1205 by Hamelin, bishop of Le Mans and Bernard IV, seigneur of La Ferté **Le Gué-de-Launay (St. Laurent)**; priory/abbey; ca. 1132/1150; William of Souday+m. Mathea *Mamers is SE 25 km of Alençon. Mortagne-au-Perche is NE 26 km of Mamers, and Mondoubleau is SE 64 km of Mamers* Northern route: Mortagne-au-Perche, SW 11 km to Blavou, SW 15 km to Mamers Southern route: Mondoubleau, NW 13 km to Le Gué-de-Launay, NW 22 km to La Pelice, N 10 km to Le Theil-sur-Huisne, NW 30 km to Mamers Mamers to Alençon. Mamers, W 13 km to Livet-en-Saosnois, NW 12 km to St.-Paterne, NW 3 km to Alençon *Livet-en-Saosnois is 10 km S of St-Pierre-de-Louïe. Les Mées-en-Saosnois is 7 km S of Livet-en-Saosnois*
Le Mans toward Vendôme and St.-Vaast **Coulaines**; vines; ca. 1140; Elisenda/Pagana, citizen of Le Mans **Loudon (St. Michel)**; priory; <1175–1176 **Le Gué-Brunet**; hamlet and church; <1147 **Eguillé (N.D.)**; priory; <1132 **Tréhet**; church; <1147 **Croixval (La Madeleine)**; priory; ca. 1125; Hubert Salva-Granum+wife Elisabeth, conf. Payen Hélinand

(continued)

102 EXPANSION IN FRANCE

Table 5.3. (Cont.)

Montrouveau; church, <1147 **Ternay (St. Pierre)**; church; <1175–1176 **Mazangé**; farm; 1131; Hubert Tortus of Mondoubleau; mill and field **Beaumont-Pied-du-Boeuf (St.-Pierre)**; church; <1147 **St.-Vaast**; church; <1147 Coulaines, Le Mans, SE 16 km to Le Gué-Brunet and Loudon near Parigné-l'Evêque, SE 15 km to Eguillé. Eguillé SE 9 km to Tréhet, E 10 km to the cluster of Croixval, Montrouveau, Ternay, NE 16 km to Mazangé and E 11 km to Vendôme. Eguillé SW 5 km to Beaumont-Pied-de-Boeuf, S 15 km to St.-Vaast *These properties are 40 km N of Tours and 32 km W of Vendôme. Le Mans is connected to the Loire via the Sarthe and Maine Rivers. St.-Vaast on the Loir is 61 km NW of Saumur*
La Saulaye; priory; <1147 **Redon (St. Nicolas)**; church; <1175–1176 *St.-Vaast in Vaas on the Loir is 15 km S of Beaumont-Pied-du-Boeuf, 42 km S of Le Mans, and 61 km NW of Saumur. La Saulaye is 40 km W of Angers, 15 km N of the Loire, and 6 km SE of Candé. Redon is 51 km N of the port of St.-Nazaire and 65 km SW of Rennes*
Note: One route runs from Dreux via Mortagne-au-Perche southwest to Alençon and Sées and south to Le Mans, with properties further south near the Loir between Le Mans and Vendôme. The Sarthe rises north of Alençon and converges with the Huisne at Le Mans (northeast of Angers). The eastern Loir and western Mayenne converge with the Sarthe north of Angers flowing south to its confluence with the Loire. The Braye is a tributary of the Loir. The abbeys of St.-Laurent-du-Gué-de-Launay (on the Braye) and La Pelice (on the Huisne) are on the north–south route from the Loir properties toward Nogent-le-Rotrou. The abbeys are indicated without their dependencies (see Map 5.6).

notes that the Corbonnais district around Mortagne-au-Perche was in the diocese of Sées but never under Norman rule, and the Bellêmois to the north was only nominally under Norman lordship.[94] One axis of expansion ran from Mortagne-au-Perche a day's ride northwest to Sées and Alençon. The road from Mortagne-au-Perche to Sées runs a day's ride northwest via the churches of Martigny and Montchevrel. The priory of Roussière and the church of Gast were northeast and southwest of Sées. Thompson lists an unknown church called Trahant or Tréhiant in the diocese of Sées.[95] All were founded or acquired before 1147.

---

94 Power, *The Norman Frontier*, 116.
95 Thompson, *The Monks of Tiron*, 242. T2:65, no. 292; ibid., 2:100, no. 326.

Alençon is a day's ride southwest of Mortagne-au-Perche and south of Sées. The route ran from Mortagne-au-Perche to the churches of Courgeoût, Saint-Jouin-de-Blavou, and Saint-Julien-sur-Sarthe, the priory of Louïe, and Alençon. Courgeoût was given by Pagan of Courgeoût, who made a donation of meadow on the Yerre 1130–1147.[96] Louïe was listed in the papal confirmation of 1132/1133. The cluster of the churches and priories southeast of Alençon will be described subsequently.

West of Alençon Tiron expanded into Mayenne, Lower Normandy, and northern Brittany, where many overlords and donors held property on both sides of the Channel. The lords of Mayenne and Fougères controlled this border region.[97] Coutances, Fougères, and the abbey of Mont-Saint-Michel had associations with Bernard of Tiron during his hermit retreats. No Tironensian foundations were confirmed there until 1133–1147 when the priories of Saint-Sulpice-en-Pail and Couptrain, later Saint-Maurice-de-René, were established west and northwest of Alençon. Saint-Sulpice was in the forest of Pail on the road to Mayenne and Fontaine-Géhard, the site of Bernard's hermit retreat. The charter traced its history as a parish deserted by its priest and farmers and frequented only by hermits. Hugh of Saint-Aubin-du-Désert gave it to Bernard ca. 1116 so the church could be restored, then placed the priory under the jurisdiction of the bishop of Le Mans. Despite vicissitudes with the heirs of the overlords, the priory was confirmed as Tironensian ca. 1140.[98] The Breton abbeys of Notre-Dame-du-Tronchet, and Saint-Méen were distant from Alençon and widely spaced. They extended the Tironensian network to an outer boundary of the Angevin trading zone as Brittany came under the control of Henry II.

The Tironensian confirmations and charters do not mention the foundation of the abbey of Hambye in Lower Normandy, northeast of Avranches and southeast of Coutances. William Painel, seigneur of Hambye, founded the abbey shortly before his death ca. 1145 at the advice of Algar, bishop of Coutances (r. 1132–1151). The licence specifies that Hambye was of the order of Tiron. The first abbot was Fulk, who came with twelve companions, probably from the Perche.[99] Hambye was an independent order by 1181, and its widely spaced property included at least six daughter abbeys and five priories.[100]

Near the coast of northern Brittany, the abbey of Notre-Dame-du-Tronchet became a Tironensian foundation at the end of Abbot William's reign. Although distant from the core of Tironensian foundations, Le Tronchet was located in a strategic border region favourable to trade. The abbey was near the crossroads of the roads between Dinan and Dol-de-Bretagne and between Rennes and Saint-Malo. The salt centre of Cancale was a day's ride to the north. The abbey received support from the archdiocese of Dol and

---

96 T1:172–73, no. 149 (1130–1145), ibid., 2:86, no. 313 (1159–1170).
97 Power, *The Norman Frontier*, 218.
98 T2:23–26, no. 254, specifically 23.
99 Beck, *Saint-Bernard de Tiron*, 278n31. GC,11, Instrumenta: 241, nos. 14–15.
100 Beck lists the daughter abbeys but could not identify Osnon or the English abbeys of Mula and Olnon. Beck, *Saint-Bernard de Tiron*, 277–79. Two abbeys were founded on the northern Breton

from the rulers of England and France. Around 1168 to 1173 Henry II granted the abbey a three-day fair.[101] Le Tronchet entered into a company of prayers with the abbeys of Saint-Melaine-de-Rennes and coastal Saint-Jacut-de-la-Mer.[102]

Le Tronchet's location by the forest of Mesnil near Châteauneuf-en-Bretagne and Saint-Malo on the Channel was in the domain of Ralph I, count of Fougères, Bernard's benefactor in his hermit days. The hermit Walter, son of Main, miraculously cured of leprosy by Barthélemy, abbot of Marmoutier, lived with disciples at Le Tronchet between 1063 and 1084.[103] Alan FitzJordan, seneschal of Dol and lord of Tuxford, Nottinghamshire, founded a church at Le Tronchet 1133–1147,[104] and turned the foundation over to Hugh le Roux, archbishop of Dol (r. ca. 1154–1160), who placed it under Abbot Stephan I of Tiron ca. 1160.[105] Alan FitzJordan gave Le Tronchet property in England, including churches on the Great North Road and Ermine Street.[106] Geoffrey, dean of Dol and precentor, his brother Gervais, William of Dinan, and William of Epiniac, all canons of the chapter of the cathedral of Saint-Samson of Dol, granted the church of Plerguer to the priory of Notre-Dame du Tronchet.[107] Brébel states that Le Tronchet owned property in Saint-Pierre-de-Plesguen, Miniac-Morvan, Pleudihen, Plouer, Dinan, and particularly in Plerguer, which included sharecropping farms, mills and millponds, acres of woods with rights, and vines in Lauriers. Abbot John I (r. 1228–1246) extended the abbey's possessions along the Rance into Dinan. Its holdings, mainly in Dol and its enclaves, included nine priories, thirteen bailiwicks, some in Dinan, Plouer, and Pleurtuit, and sizeable tithes in many parishes in Dol, Châteauneuf, Saint-Suliac and the diocese of Saint-Malo.[108]

---

coast: Sainte-Marie-de-Longues-sur-Mer (1168) and Notre-Dame-du-Pré-de-Valmont (1169). In 1248 Hambye acquired Notre-Dame de Lanthenac (founded 1149), inland near La Chèze southeast of Loudeac and a considerable distance south of the Bay of Saint-Brieuc. The sixth abbey, St. Mary and St. Peter of Humberston, was in Lincolnshire at the mouth of the Humber estuary of the North Sea. These abbeys are a long distance from Hambye. Hambye had five priories: one near Coutances, one near its Bayeux abbey, and three over 130 kilometres southeast at or near Le Merlerault in the diocese of Sées, also the name of the local horse breed. Saint-Laurent-des-Près in Quettreville-sur-Sienne was a mid-point between Hambye and Coutances. Saint-Nicolas-de-Buron was near Thury-Harcourt, Cavaldos, northwest of Caen and southwest of Bayeux. Le Merlerault was west of L'Aigle with La Madeleine-de-La Génevraie nearby to the southeast. Notre-Dame-des-Houlettes near Les Moûtiers-Hubert, north of Le Merlerault. Beck mentions that the order had other unidentified priories among its extensive holdings. (Not mapped.)

101 Everard, *Brittany and the Angevins*, 64n145, citing BnF MSS fr. 22319, 238 and 22325, 621.
102 Brébel, *Essai historique sur Pleudihen*, 301.
103 Rocher and Trevinal, "Notre-Dame du Tronchet," 299n2.
104 GC, 14: 1074–77.
105 T2:87, no. 314; ibid., 2:90, no. 317. Pope Alexander III confirmed that Alan had given the church and land to Abbot Stephan I of Tiron in 1164–1172.
106 T2:90, no. 317 (1164–1172). Tuxford and Warsop in Nottinghamshire, Sharrington in Norfolk, and Broughton, Lincolnshire, on Ermine Street south of the Humber. (Not mapped.)
107 T2:87, no. 314 (ca. 1160).
108 Rocher and Trevinal, "Notre-Dame du Tronchet," 300.

Ultimately Le Tronchet had nine priories (see Map 5.6).[109] To the north were the priories of Saint-Lunaire-de-La Barre and Saint-Petreuc in Plerguer, Notre-Dame-de-Lillemer north of Plerguer, and Saint-Nicolas-du-Vieux-Castel in Saint-Coulomb north of Lillemer near the coast. Saint-Nicolas-du-Vieux-Castel linked Le Tronchet to the Channel west of the port of Cancale and east of the port of Saint-Malo. Saint-Pierre-et-Saint-Paul in Roz-Landrieux north of Le Tronchet was on the western outskirts of Dol-de-Bretagne. To the northwest of Le Tronchet, Saint-Colomban-de-la-Mare-Ferron in Miniac-Morvan was on the road connecting Combourg with the Rance basin between Dinan and the ports of Dinard and Saint-Malo. Saint-Lunaire-de-l'Hostellerie in Pleudihen-sur-Rance was west of Miniac-Morvan near the Rance basin. To the southeast of Le Tronchet, Saint-Denis-de-La-Roche-Montbourcher in Cuguen was northeast of Combourg, and Saint-Julien-de-la-Chattière in Tremblay was midway between Combourg and Fougères and midway between Rennes and Mont-Saint-Michel. The priories in those towns linked Le Tronchet to those routes. With the exception of Saint-Denis-de-La-Roche-Montbourcher in Cuguen to the east, these priories were situated between the Rance to the west and Combourg and Dol-de-Bretagne.

Saint-Méen, first called Gaël, was founded ca. 600 by that sixth-century saint with the permission of Hoël III, king of Brittany (d. ca. 612), at an important crossroads of Roman roads from Rennes and Saint-Malo. It was destroyed twice, by the Vikings and Normans, and was restored and protected twice, by Charlemagne and in 1008 by the dukes of Brittany.[110] The town of Gaël is southwest of Saint-Méen-le-Grand, and the abbey's church and later priory of Le Crouais was to the northeast (see Map 5.6). Danguern Guer south of the abbey was built on the site of a hermitage abandoned by Saint Malo in 541. Saint-Méen-du-Cellier was in Le Cellier on the Loire northeast of the port of Nantes, a long distance southeast of the abbey. The Breton abbey of Saint-Méen was first recorded among the Tironensian dependencies in 1516.[111]

South of Alençon, other Tironensian properties were acquired toward Le Mans. Power notes that the lords of Beaumont-sur-Sarthe, who controlled the road between Alençon and Le Mans, were "amongst the greatest magnates in Maine."[112] The Sarthe flows south from Alençon to the towns of Chérancé, where Tiron had tithes, and Beaumont-sur-Sarthe. The Tironensian foundations were near the Sarthe and were spaced from Alençon southeast to a cluster of properties: the churches of Arçonnay and Livet-en-Saosnois with vines and a weir or fishing station, together with the nearby priory of Saint-Michel-du-Tertre and, to the south, the priory of Cohardon.[113] Further south Tiron had the farm of Sainte-Sabine-sur-Longève and the priory of Montaillé near its confluence with the Huisne north of Le Mans, the capital of the county of Maine. Montaillé's

---

109 Brébel, *Essai historique sur Pleudihen*, 304.
110 Tresvaux, *L'Eglise de Bretagne*, 431–37 (chap. 5), available online at https://books.google.com/books?id=Ze0DAAAAQAAJ.
111 T2:235, no. 419.
112 Power, *The Norman Frontier*, 220.
113 T1:20–21, no. 9 (ca. 1115).

founder Alberic, seigneur of La Milesse, whose son was a new monk, gave all the land and men of Montaillé, near the castle of Saint-Calais, which he had received from Louis VI, and the fief and men of Aunay in Tucé.[114] In Coulaines, Le Mans, Tiron was given vines in town, and later had a house surrounded by vines in that town.[115] Le Mans is connected to the Loire via the Sarthe and Maine Rivers. The priory of La Madeleine-de-Beaulieu was founded west of Le Mans by 1128. No Tironensian expansion occurred west of Beaulieu.

Mondoubleau as the western terminus of Tiron's Beauce properties was discussed previously with Tiron's properties in the diocese of Chartres. Another important route from Tiron to Mondoubleau ran mainly through the diocese of Le Mans. The church of Le-Theil-sur-Huisne southwest of Arcisses in the diocese of Sées[116] and two abbeys in the diocese of Le Mans north of Mondoubleau—La Pelice and Le Gué-de-Launay— connected the Tiron-Nogent-le-Rotrou region and the Beauce with Le Mans. They were on the border of Blois and respectively 37 and 52 kilometres southwest of Tiron Abbey. Their presence suggests that this route was a significant link to the priories, farms, and granaries in the Beauce.

La Pelice, in the diocese of Le Mans near Cherreau in la Ferté-Bernard, was founded by 1187 as a Benedictine abbey and given to Tiron in 1205.[117] Ultimately La Pelice established four dependent priories on the road between La Ferté-Bernard and Mamers: Saint-Nicolas-du-Hallais in Bellou-le-Trichard; Sainte-Madeleine-de-Guémançais in Rouperroux-le-Coquet; and Saint-Vu or -Leu and Saint-Gilles-de-Contres in Saint-Rémy-des-Monts southeast of Mamers.[118] Another priory, Saint-Blaise-des-Vignes, was located in Sainte-Croix, at that time an eastern suburb of Le Mans, southwest of La Pelice (see Map 5.6). Clearly La Pelice traded with Mamers and Alençon was represented in Le Mans.

The future abbey of Saint-Laurent-du-Gué-de-Launay, a priory listed in the 1132/1133 confirmation, was located east of Vibraye on the Braye. The initial foundation was on the more isolated land of Insula-Goscelini. Rotrou II of Nogent, seigneur of Montfort, Malestable and Vibraye, and his family gave land on the Braye for construction of a mill and a fishing station. Hugh Amicus-Bonus of Valennes gave land to his hermit brother, Thibaut Amicus-Bonus, who gave the site to the monks.[119] William of Fâtines, their advocate, gave his entire tithe in the fief of Vibraye and was buried in their cloister.[120] Le Gué-de-Launay exchanged land in Vibraye for land at Le-Gué-du-Perray, on the Braye, thereby acquiring more riverine property.[121] It was transferred before 1208 to Vibraye on the right bank of the Braye.

---

114 T1:65–67, no. 46 (1121).
115 T2:18, no. 146 (ca. 1140); ibid., 2:104, no. 328 (1179). Merlet considers it an interesting forgery (ibid., 2:106n1).
116 T1:62, no. 42. n2 (1120–1128).
117 T2:120–21, no. 345 (1205), specifically 121n1. GC, 14:498–501.
118 Naud, *Guide des archives de la Sarthe*, 131–32, G 769–72 (1160). Beck, *Saint-Bernard de Tiron*, 272.
119 T1:223, no. 194 (1135); ibid., 235–36, no. 207 (ca. 1135).
120 T2:4–5, no. 230 (ca. 1140).
121 T2:72–74, no. 299 (ca. 1150).

Although the number is disputed, Le Gué-de-Launay probably had at least six dependent priories:[122] Saint-Antoine to the north in the nearby Montmirail; Saint-Sauveur to the northwest in the nearby Vibraye; Montcollain or Montcolin to the northwest in Saint-Georges-du-Rosay between La Ferté-Bernard and Bonnétable; La-Madeleine-de-Rossay to the west in Changé close to and southeast of Le Mans; and Saint-Jean-de-Grandry due south in Fontaine-les-Coteaux, formerly Fontaine-en-Beauce, north of Montoire-sur-le-Loir[123] (see Map 5.6). Another priory was Saint-Antoine in Thorigné-sur-Dué west of Le-Gué-de-Launay midway between the abbey and Le Mans. Le Gué-de-Launay was raised to abbatial status ca. 1150 and confirmed as a Tironensian abbey 1165–1173.[124]

These two abbeys with nine dependent priories mainly between Alençon, Mamers, Le Mans, and Mondoubleau show a concentration of Tironensian activity in the Huisne and Sarthe valleys west of Tiron Abbey's dependent priories in the Beauce and Loir Valley. The Tironensian foundations were spaced from Mondoubleau, northwest to Le Gué-de-Launay, west to its dependent priories of Saint-Antoine in Thorigné-sur-Dué and La-Madeleine-de-Rossay in Changé, west to Le Mans. There are no other Tironensian foundations southwest of Le Mans on the Sarthe, which flows south to its confluence with the Loir north of Angers, into the Loire.

Tironensian foundations were established southeast of Le Mans in the direction of Vendôme via the Loir. The priory of Loudon and the hamlet and church of Le Gué-Brunet were near Parigné-l'Evêque, with the priory of Eguillé further southeast in Pruillé-l'Eguillé. Toward Vendôme were the church of Tréhet, the cluster of the priory of Croixval and the churches of Montrouveau and Ternay, and the mill and field at Mazangé. Southwest of Eguillé were the churches of Beaumont-Pied-du-Boeuf and Saint-Vaast. This cluster of churches and priories near the Loir was a day's ride west of Vendôme and southwest of Mondoubleau.

Croixval was established ca. 1125 by combined gifts and negotiated purchases of land and fields, a day's ride from Tours and Vendôme.[125] The mill at Mazangé was near the confluence of the Boulon and Loir Rivers. The property consisted of the mill, land owned by the cathedral chapter of Chartres, and a field. Hubert Tortus of Mondoubleau, a knight, gave the mill, field, and his tract of land in free and perpetual alms in the chapter of Tiron Abbey, a gift that was disputed subsequently.[126] Again, Tiron was expanding into a desirable location.

---

122 Naud, *Guide des archives de la Sarthe*, 128–29. Paul Piolin includes another priory: Saint-Antoine in Thorigné-sur-Dué west of Le Gué-de-Launay midway between the abbey and Le Mans, in *Histoire de l'Eglise du Mans*, 6 vols. (Paris: Lanier, 1851–1863), 4:74–75.

123 T1:114, no. 92 (1128); ibid., 1:196–97n2, no. 176 (ca. 1128/1132). Merlet dates the founding of Grandry to 1128, on land given by Erembourg of Launay, whose son Arnulf was a new monk.

124 T2:92–93, no. 320 (1165–1173).

125 T1:93–94, no. 74 (ca. 1125); ibid., 1:166–67, no. 141 (ca. 1130); ibid., 1:237–38, no. 209 (ca. 1135).

126 T1:174–75, no. 151 (1131).

A monastery official travelling from Le Mans to the abbey of Asnières in Cizay-la-Madeleine, crossing the Loire at Saumur, faced a long ride of 106 kilometres. He could have broken his journey at Saint-Vaast in Vaas, but the distance is considerable. The church of Saint-Vaast in Vaas on the Loir was on a Roman road from Le Mans to Tours.[127] By water, Saumur is 162 kilometres downriver of Meung-sur-Loire in the Beauce, a more feasable journey of about four days between the Tironensian foundations in the Loire Valley. Tiron Abbey and Saint-Florent-de-Saumur were in confraternity, and Tiron elected John III abbot (r. 1354–1383), formerly an abbot of that monastery, indicating closer connections than the map suggests.[128] Another approach was travelling by water from Le Mans down the Sarthe to its confluence with the Mayenne River, which flows through Angers into the Loire, depending upon the navigability of the rivers.

On the north bank of the Loire, Tiron had no properties around Angers and only the priory of La Saulaye southeast of Candé before 1147. Between 1147 and 1175–1176 the church of Redon on the Vilaine was acquired north of the port of Saint-Nazaire and southwest of Rennes, a day's ride from the coast. The Vilaine was a waterway for transporting salt and wine between Rennes and the Atlantic.[129] Tiron's expansion west of Angers proceeded 89 kilometres to Nantes and on to Saint-Nazaire and the Atlantic, but the important properties were concentrated on the south bank, in the Loire Valley and beyond. These foundations became outlets for southern trade from Poitou.

South France was mainly ruled by the dukes of Brittany and Aquitaine and the counts of Anjou. There were two areas of expansion in this region: one around Tours and Poitiers feeding into the Loire Valley, and one on the Saône downriver of Cîteaux and Cluny near Mâcon and Lyon on the Rhône. The Saône and the Rhône linked the Low Countries with the Mediterranean. Poitou was noted for wheat and cereals, wine (later distilled into cognac), livestock, and coastal salt, fish and shellfish, particularly oysters. Georges Duby describes the economy of the region around Mâcon, which lies north of Tiron's southern abbey of Joug-Dieu. Mâcon was at the crossroads of the eastern markets of Sens and Langres and the Champagne fairs and the Mediterranean pilgrimages to Rome, the Holy Land, and Compostela, and trade with Italy, Spain, and Byzantium. Chalon-sur-Saône, north of Mâcon, held great fairs, but travellers from the north continued to Mâcon and disembarked to take land routes toward the Loire, the Alps, and the Pyranees. The abbey of Cluny was located 23 kilometres northwest of Mâcon and was an important pilgrimage centre. Cluny introduced considerable coin for the religious who collected duties, tolls, and alms, and obtained scarce currency to purchase spices, luxury items, salt, ironwork, and fine fabrics. Burghers concerned that God did not love merchants gave generously to religious foundations. The lords exploited the Jews and built new churches with the cash. Regional coinages and the development of exchange rates were features of this region.[130]

---

127 Barrow, *Roads and Bridges of the Roman Empire*, 45.
128 T2:177–78, no. 386 (1263).
129 Everard, "Le duché de Bretagne," 196.
130 Duby, *La société aux XIe et XIIe siècles dans la region mâconnaise*, 332–34, 348–57.

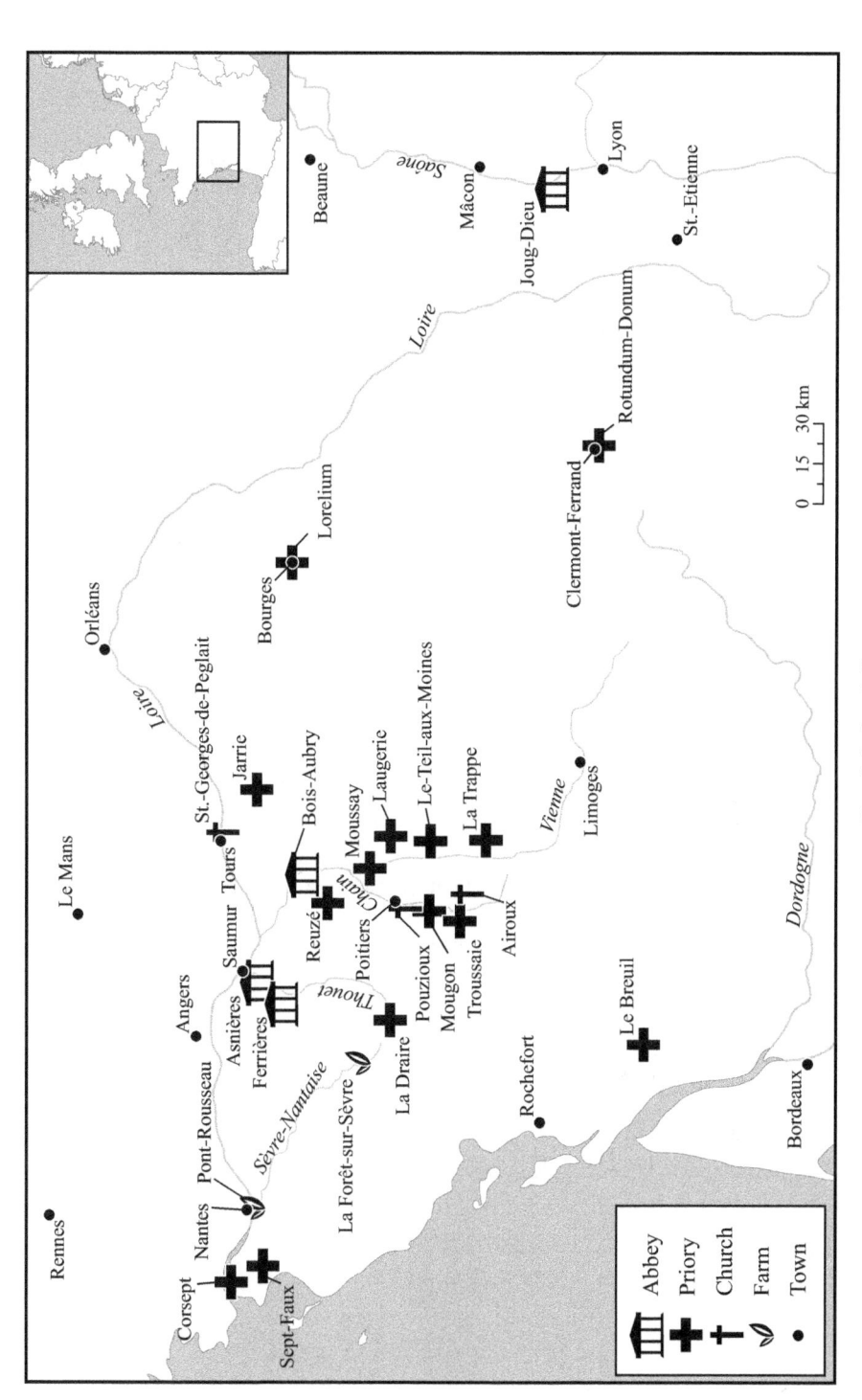

Map 5.4. South France

Table 5.4. South France

South of the Loire
  Jarrie (St.-Jean-B.); priory; <1147
  St.-Georges-de-Peglait; church; ca. 1160; Robert of Roche-Corbon to d. Sibyl and h. Renaud of Château-Renault; hermitage; exchanged for land in St.-Avertin near Tours
  Bois-Aubry (St. Michel); priory/abbey; ca. 1118/1138; Brice of Le Chillou; hermitage
  Asnières (N.D.); priory/abbey; ca. 1118/1129; Girard II Berlay of Montreuil-Bellay
  Ferrières (St. Léonard); priory/abbey; ca. 1130/1184; Geoffrey of Doué-la-Fontaine/Aimeri, viscount of Thouars
  Pont-Rousseau; fishing station and toll to Nantes; 1132; Conan III, duke of Brittany +m. Ermengarde
  Sept-Faux (St. Blaise); priory; 1132; Conan III, duke of Brittany
  Corsept (St. Nicolas); priory; ca. 1137; Conan III, duke of Brittany
Jarrie, NW 32 km to Peglait in St.-Avertin S of Tours, W 53 km to Bois-Aubry, W 62 km to Asnières, SW 16 km to Ferrières, W 111 km to Nantes and Pont-Rousseau, W 32 km to Sept-Faux, N 20 km to Corsept, W 17 km to the Atlantic port of St.-Nazaire
Asnières and Ferrières are respectively 14 km and 27 km SW of Saumur. Bois-Aubry is 52 km S of Tours by land and 58 km SE of Saumur via the Loire and Vienne Rivers

Poitou-Charentes
  La Draire; priory; <1147
  Reuzé (La Madeleine); priory; <1132; Fulk V, count of Anjou
La Draire is 62 km S Ferrières, 9 km W of Parthenay, and 60 km W of Poitiers. Reuzé is 14 km S of Richelieu, and 20 km NW of Châtellerault
  Moussay; priory; ca. 1132; hermitage
  Laugerie; priory; <1147
  Le Teil-aux-Moines (N.D.-de-Sainte-Croix); priory; ca. 1120; Ama+s. Reginald+Seibrand of La-Forêt-sur-Sèvre
  La Forêt-sur-Sèvre; farm; ca. 1120; Ama of La-Forêt-sur-Sèvre
  Pouzioux; church; <1147
  Mougon; priory; <1147
  Troussaie (St. Radegonde); priory; <1147
  Airoux; church; <1147
  La Trappe; priory; <1147
Bois-Aubry, S 23 km to Reuzé, SE 29 km to Moussay (south of Châtellerault), SE 23 km to Laugerie, S 21 km to Le Teil-aux-Moines
Le Teil-aux-Moines is 12 km S of Chauvigny, and SW 18 km SW of St.-Savin-sur-Gartempe
Moussay, S 32 km to Pouzioux-La Jarrie, S 16 km to Mougon, S 18 km to Troussaie, SE 15 km to Airoux, SE 36 km to La Trappe (near Montmorillon)

Table 5.4. (Cont.)

Southern France
 Le Breuil; priory; <1147
 Le Breuil is 6 km S of Pons and 27 km S of Saintes, on the Seugne River, a tributary of the Charente River, 60 km SE of the port of Rochefort
 Lorelium Bourges; priory; <1147
 Rotundum-Donum Clermont-Ferrand; priory; <1147
 Joug-Dieu (N.D.) Lyon; abbey; 1115; Guichard III of Beaujeu
 Bourges was on a Roman road between Nevers and Tours, and Clermont-Ferrand was on a Roman road from Lyon and Joug-Dieu, which ran W via Saintes to Rochefort

---

Bernard had been abbot of Saint-Cyprien of Poitiers and had travelled to Cluny before continuing to Rome so he was familiar with the region and its languages and rulers. Two foundations were established near the time of his death. In south France Tiron had four abbeys, fourteen priories, three churches, and one farm, a presence similar to its holdings in west France but with fewer churches.

The first area of expansion ran east to west toward the Atlantic on the south bank of the Loire and developed to the south into Poitou with priories near the Loire's tributaries. Tiron had three abbeys, one church, and three priories near the south bank of the Loire. Bois-Aubry was southeast of Tours between the Bourouse and Veude tributaries of the Vienne River. Asnières and Ferrières were southeast of Saumur near the Thouet River, a tributary of the Loire flowing north from its source through Parthenay, Thouars, and Montreuil-Bellay to Saumur. The Thouet Valley was a secondary pilgrimage route from Brittany and Normandy to Compostela. These abbeys' access to the Atlantic was furthered by priories established near the Loire port of Saint-Nazaire near Nantes, Brittany. The presence of three abbeys and other foundations on the south bank of the Loire near its confluence with the Vienne River in the vicinity of Fontevraud Abbey indicates the importance of the Loire trade to the Atlantic and into Poitou.

Note: One route runs north–south between Tours and Poitiers. Another route runs east–west between Tours and Nantes along the Loire.

The easternmost Tironensian foundations south of the Loire were the priory of Jarrie in Chédigny southeast of Tours, and the church of Saint-Georges-de-Peglait with its hermits at Saint-Avertin near Tours.[131] Three abbeys were in the southern Loire Valley: Bois-Aubry, midway between Tours and Poitiers; and Asnières and Ferrières in the Thouet valley south of Saumur, near Montreuil-Bellay west of Fontevraud.

Saint-Michel-de-Bois-Aubry was located southeast of Luzé near the Vienne Valley. Thought to be one of a number of foundations of hermit origin established in Touraine

---

[131] T2:88, no. 315 (ca. 1160).

1110–1120,[132] Bois-Aubry was originally a cell inhabited by a hermit priest. Merlet dates the donation charter, witnessed by the hermit and his disciples, ca. 1135.[133] Allegedly hermit Robert thought his dwelling at Luzé well-sited for an abbey and won the support of the knight Brice of Le Chillou, a vassal of the viscount of Thouars.[134] Probably ca. 1135 Brice gave Tiron land with a promise to increase the donation upon the priory's elevation to abbatial status (in 1138). The property included a mill, vineyard, gardens, arable land, woodland rights excluding Brice's enclosure and oak trees, and pasturage for livestock.[135] The monks of Bois-Aubry were assisted by the nearby Benedictine abbey of Notre-Dame-de-Noyers, founded in 1031 near Nouâtre northeast across the Vienne. The first abbot, Clement, entered into association with Gilles, abbot of Noyers, after 1149. The chapters maintained a relationship of spiritual fraternity and, in 1150, reached an agreement on prayers and funeral rites.[136] Again, Tiron was moving into an area with existing religious foundations. Bois-Aubry had at least three dependencies: the priory of Saint-Blaise-en-Gaudrée, the chapel of Montgauger/Montgorger, and the priory of Saint-Jacques-de-la Bruère/de-la-Lande, founded before 1147 (see Map 5.6). The priory of Jarrie was 53 kilometres northeast of Bois-Aubry and 37 kilometres southeast of Tours.

Notre-Dame-d'Asnières was an early priory founded ca. 1118 after Bernard's death south of the Loire near the Thouet Valley on neglected land originally given to the monks of Saint-Nicolas d'Angers.[137] Around 1128 Ulger, bishop of Angers, requested Abbot William to allow its elevation to the status of a daughter abbey of Tiron. Under Louis VII, the founder Girard II Berlay of Montreuil-Bellay, became the king's seneschal in Poitou. On a tributary of the Loire a day's journey southwest of Saumur, it became a prosperous abbey noted for its murals. By the fifteenth century Asnières had acquired the dependent priories of Saint-Martin-de-Fosse-Bellay in Cizay-la-Madeleine and La Grézillé[138] (see Map 5.6).

The abbey of Saint-Léonard-de-Ferrières a day's journey southwest of Asnières was located near Bouillé-Loretz in the diocese of Poitiers, on the site of the modern Château de Ferrières.[139] The abbey was on a plateau with springs near the forest of Brignon, equidistant from Doué-la-Fontaine and Thouars and midway between Angers and Poitiers. The abbey is near the Argenton, a tributary of the Thouet. Ferrières was allegedly founded in the time of Louis the Pious; the letters of Servat Loup, abbot of Ferrières (842–862), have survived. The Tironensian foundation was established before 1127 by

---

132 Gilbert, "Une abbaye tironienne en Touraine," 8, 143, 164n7, 165n16.
133 T1:240nn1–2, no. 213 (ca. 1135); ibid., 1:249n1, no. 221 (1138).
134 VB, 11.98, AASS, Apr. 2:0246A; VB, trans. Cline, 105.
135 T1:240–41, no. 213, specifically 241; ibid., 1:249–50, no. 221.
136 GC, 14:306–7. Gilbert, "Une abbaye tironienne en Touraine," 142–43.
137 T1:35–36, no. 19 (ca. 1118).
138 *Inventaire sommaire des archives départementales antérieurs à 1790: Maine-et-Loire. Archives ecclésiastiques, série H*, ed. Celestin Port (Angers: Lachèse, 1898), H 189, H 1381.
139 Château de Ferrières: www.chateau-fort-manoir-chateau.eu/chateaux-deux-sevres-chateau-bouille-chateau-de-ferrieres.html

Geoffrey, seigneur of Doué-la-Fontaine, and Aimeri V, viscount of Thouars. Aimeri's wife Agnès Maude of Aquitaine (1100–1147) was the daughter of William IX of Aquitaine. Geoffrey of Doué-la-Fontaine gave all his own land and income from the men of his fief ca. 1130. The mill of Tueboeuf yielded grain and eels. Aimeri V and Agnès gave the Tironensian monks vines and other property at Ferrières before 1127 and settled a dispute.[140] Ferrières was expanded by other gifts and census income.[141] At an unspecified time, Ferrières had exemption from duties and tolls in the towns of Saumur, Thouars, Montreuil-Bellay, and Doué-la-Fontaine, together with fishing rights and a two-wheeled mill at Sault, suitable for grain. Its obligation to send salt to the military government of Saumur indicates involvement in the salt trade. The abbey also had fishing rights on the Argenton River and a mill.[142] Ferrières was raised to abbatial status in 1184.[143] Its three dependent priories were west of the abbey (see Map 5.6). Two southern priories were founded a day's journey from Bressuire: Saint-Marc-de-Primart in Saint-Clémentin and Saint-Clémentin-de-la-Tisonnière in Noirterre. Saint-Sauveur-de-la Guichardière in Saint-Hilaire-du-Bois was near modern Vihiers.[144]

On the roads from Nantes west to the Atlantic ports of Saint-Nazaire and Pornic, Tiron acquired three properties on the south bank of the Loire. Conan III, duke of Brittany, and his mother Ermengarde confirmed that they gave Tiron the toll and Pont-Rousseau's causeway to Nantes and provided income, protection, wood, and a plot of land for the priory of Corsept upon its foundation ca. 1137.[145] To the south, Conan III gave Tiron and the priory of Sept-Faux the toll and fishing station at Pont-Rousseau, requesting the monks' prayers for his trip to Vézelay in Champagne in support of Count Thibaut II.[146] Garsire I, lord of Rais (later Retz) (ca. 1093–1153) and his brother and son confirmed Tiron's ownership of Sept-Faux.[147] Gauslen of Corsept and Ralph of La Guerche expanded Corsept's holdings to include the island of Saint-Nicolas-en-Loire with an oratory, land to the priest Martin, and, off-island, land and a meadow, a fish pond, and a share of salt.[148] Corsept is the first Loire island inland of the Atlantic, and the monks provided a staging post for ocean-going vessels in need of repairs, supplies, medical treatment for their sick, and burial for their dead, before their cargos were transported to the port of Nantes. The island is also called Saint-Nicolas-des-Défunts because of the mortality rate. The location of Sept-Faux and Corsept near two salt

---

140 T1:170–72, nos. 146–48 (ca. 1130).
141 T2:21, no. 250 (ca. 1140); ibid., 2:53–54, no. 284 (ca. 1140).
142 Sauzé de L'houmeau, *L'Abbaye de Saint Léonard de Ferrières*, 11–26.
143 T1:170–71, specifically 171n1, no. 146 (ca. 1132).
144 Sauzé de L'houmeau, *L'Abbaye de Saint Léonard de Ferrières*, 44.
145 T1:244–45, specifically 244, no. 216 (ca. 1137).
146 T1:185–86, specifically 185n1, no. 161 (1132).
147 T2:55, no. 286 (ca. 1145).
148 T2:34–35, no. 266 (ca. 1142). www.ouest-france.fr/pays-de-la-loire/nantes-44000/lhistoire-inouie-de-la-derniere-ile-de-loire-avant-locean-1374503

centres, Guérande and Ile de Noirmoutier, suggests trade in grain and salt between the abbeys and the Atlantic coast. The acquisition of the island priory as a staging post is a similar pattern to that of Tiron's foundation of priories on Caldey and the Isle of Wight in the English Channel.

After 1130, Tiron's expansion proceeded south of the Loire into Poitou during the reign of William X, duke of Aquitaine, and his daughter Eleanor. Bishop Geoffrey II accompanied Bernard of Clairvaux to Aquitaine in 1135 and deterred William X from schism.[149] Tironensian properties in Poitou increased during this period. Bishop Geoffrey II was papal legate in Aquitaine and may have encouraged the establishment of Tironensian foundations, and Abbot William's languages included Provençal. Some of these foundations owned distant land.

Tiron had one abbey—Joug-Dieu, eleven priories, two churches, and one property in Poitou and Beaujolais. This pattern indicates regional and local involvement, little communication, and almost no isolated farming. South of Ferrières and west of Poitiers, the priory of La Draire was near Azay-sur-Thouet west of Parthenay and linked to Ferrières and Asnières by the Thouet River. In Poitou, within 107 kilometres north–south, with Poitiers midway, Bois-Aubry, Moussay, Laugerie, Le-Teil-aux-Moines, and La Trappe were on the Vienne, and Poitiers, Pouzioux, Mougon, Troussaie, and Airoux were on the Clain. The abbey of Joug-Dieu (Lyon) and the priories of Rotundum-Donum (Clermont-Ferrand), Le Breuil (Saintes), and Lorelium (Bourges) were distant from the development in Poitou.

In Poitou, the priory of Reuzé was founded by Fulk V, count of Anjou, south of Richelieu and northwest of Châtellerault. Geoffrey V, count of Anjou, confirmed his father's gifts, including land, water, and building rights for mills.[150] Reuzé received income and property from local families, together with another mill site.[151] South of Châtellerault is the confluence of the Clain, which flows through Poitiers, and the Vienne, which flows to the east through the town of Chauvigny. The priory of Moussay between the two rivers was associated with a hermit community holding a share in two mills[152] and thereby participating in the local economy.

The priory of Le-Teil-aux-Moines, also Grand-Teil, was founded ca. 1120 by the La Forêt-sur-Sèvre family south of Chauvigny, and southwest of Saint-Savin-sur-Gartempe. Le-Teil-aux-Moines had distant property. La Forêt-sur-Sèvre southwest of Bressuire is on the Sèvre-Nantaise River, a tributary of the Loire, which rises at Secondigny close to the source of the Thouet River and runs 95 kilometres northwest from La Forêt-sur-Sèvre to the Loire at Nantes. Bressuire was on the secondary pilgrimage route from Angers to Parthenay and the nearby priory of La Draire. Ama of La Forêt-sur-Sèvre gave Tiron lands near Cerizay and Bressuire over 81 kilometres west of Châtellerault and

---

149 GC, 8:1137E.
150 T1:189, no. 165 (ca. 1132).
151 T2:22–23, no. 253 (ca. 1140); ibid., 2:32–33, nos. 264–65 (ca. 1142); ibid., 2:54, no. 285 (ca. 1145).
152 T1:199–200, no. 180 (ca. 1132); ibid., 2:20–21, no. 249 (ca. 1140).

123 kilometres northwest of the priory. Upon her death, Ama's son Reginald increased the gifts, including land between two roads at Le Teil-aux-Moines, vineyards, and the right to sell bread at one of the fairs in La Forêt-sur-Sèvre.[153] The priory's holdings were expanded near La Forêt-sur-Sèvre, Chauvigny, and Montmorillon.[154] It was unusual for a Tironensian priory to have extensive holdings concentrated in two widely separated areas, but the configuration reflects the pattern of the donors' holdings.

The remaining southern foundations were widely scattered. Le Breuil, a priory near Fléac-sur-Seugne, was south of Pons, a town southeast of Rochefort, which was the stronghold of lords who were adversaries of the king of France. Pons was also on the secondary pilgrimage route from Thouars to Parthenay south to Niort and Pons, and Le Breuil may have benefitted from the Compostela pilgrim trade. The Ile d'Oléron offshore from Rochefort is a salt centre, and the town of Brouage just south of Rochefort was a salt-trading site. Tiron had income from multure in Rochefort and may have purchased and shipped salt inland. Le Breuil was founded north of Bordeaux.[155] The priories of Lorelium in the archdiocese of Bourges and Rotundum-Donum in the diocese of Clermont-Ferrand were founded before 1147. Bourges, near a road between Tours and Nevers, cutting across the Loire's loop north toward Orléans, was on the Vézelay pilgrimage route. Clermont-Ferrand, on a Roman road from Lyon and Joug-Dieu running west via Saintes to Rochefort, was on the Le-Puy-en-Velay route. Merlet could not situate these priories, but the Tironensian settlement pattern suggests that they were near these roads.

Another important area of expansion was east in the Mâconnais and Saône Valley. The abbey of Notre-Dame-du-Joug-Dieu was founded in southeastern France on the Saône River near the Rhône in the archdiocese of Lyon ca. 1115 by Guichard III, seigneur of Beaujeu, whose wife Lucienne was the daughter of Guy II of Montlhéry, count of Rochefort (1037–1108), an ally of Thibaut II mentioned as a donor in the *Vita Bernardi*.[156] Joug-Dieu was associated with two miracle stories involving Bernard: the donor's vision of the abbot plowing a field with six men instead of oxen, from which fruits came forth,[157] and another of locks of his beard, which the monks soaked in water to make a healing lotion, emitting a fragrant odour at the time of his death.[158] The date on the forged charter is June 28, 1118, but presumably the priory was established ca. 1115 during Bernard's lifetime.[159] Guichard III went to Bernard and established six monks there, with himself and his successors as its defenders.

---

153 T1:60–61, no. 40 (ca. 1120).

154 T1:62–63, nos. 42–43 (1120–1128); ibid., 1:123–24, nos. 102–5 (1128–1140); ibid., 2:21–22, nos. 250–51 (ca. 1140). The monks made countergifts of a horse, cash, grain, boots, and a cow.

155 T2:32, no. 263 (ca. 1142).

156 VB, 11.98, AASS, Apr. 2:0246A; VB, trans. Cline, 104–6. Bouchard, *Sword, Miter, and Cloister*, 292.

157 T1:30–31, no. 16, specifically 31n1 (1118). Merlet noted that this charter was a forgery but the only one about Joug-Dieu in the Tironensian cartulary.

158 VB, 13.125. AASS, Apr. 2: 0251E; VB, trans. Cline, 128.

159 The first abbot or superior, Gaucerius, was allegedly installed by Bernard of Tiron but died a Cistercian or Cluniac monk on December 11 in an unspecified year. The second abbot, Englebert,

116   EXPANSION IN FRANCE

The fortress of Beaujeu, bordering the dioceses of Mâcon, Lyon, and Autun, dominated the road from Switzerland and the Danube to the Atlantic Ocean. The seigneurs of Beaujeu established their capital at Beaujeu in the tenth century, came to rule the region of Beaujolais extending from the Loire to the Saône, and were relatively autonomous by the end of the eleventh century. Beaujeu was isolated from the highway and trade route running along the Saône from Lyon to Chalon-sur-Saône on their eastern border. Their southern border was threatened by the castle at Anse owned by their opponents the archbishops of Lyon. The domain of Joug-Dieu on the Saône River north of Anse at Arnas is described as one of the most beautiful and fertile tracts in the province, but the priory so piously founded was the first step in the establishment of a trade and defence system. In disputed regions where castle-building was prohibited, a monastery was a different kind of fortress that controlled space without arousing antagonism. Joug-Dieu was near an east–west Roman road running 64 kilometres between the Saône and the Loire port of Roanne. Therefrom, the Loire was navigable and ran through Nevers, Orléans, and Blois, so Joug-Dieu is not as isolated from Tiron as it appears to be on the map.

Joug-Dieu was not listed in the 1132/1133 confirmation, but it was elevated to abbatial status in 1138 at the request of Peter I, archbishop of Lyon (d. 1139), and of Humbert III of Beaujeu (1110–1175), Guichard's son. With Joug-Dieu at the northern end of the Morgon river valley, downriver Humbert III fortified a hamlet around a toll tower on the Saône opposite Anse in 1140, giving privileges to the new capital that were reflected in its name of Villefranche-sur-Saône. The toll tower was at the crossroads of two major highways. One, running north–south, linked Lyon to Langres via Anse, and the other, running west–east from Roanne on the Loire, connected with the Saône.[160] The lords of Beaujeu extended the defence system in the twelfth century by the foundation of the Augustinian abbey at Belleville north of Villefranche. Lyon itself was the hub of the network of Roman roads in Gaul extending to the Atlantic, the North Sea, the Rhine, and Marseille. Joug-Dieu was listed in the 1147 papal confirmations of Tironensian properties.[161]

Joug-Dieu was associated with the abbey of Notre-Dame-de-Belleville a day's journey upriver to the north. Joug-Dieu had at least two dependent priories in the vicinity of Bourg-en-Bresse: Seillon, in the town of Bourg-en-Bresse, and Montmerle-du-Val-Saint-Etienne near Saint-Julien-sur-Reyssouze (see Map 5.6). The abbey of Cîteaux is located 134 kilometres north of Joug-Dieu but only 11 kilometres from the Saône, so the river was a route of communication with the Cluniacs and the Cistercians.

In east France the cluster of foundations in and around Paris is the last part of Tiron's network in Eure-et-Loir and the Beauce. Paris, the seat of the Capetian kings, was an administrative, commercial, and religious centre. In addition to its royally supported

---

a disciple of Bernard of Tiron, died April 2 in an unspecified year. Joug-Dieu and its abbots are described in differing accounts in GC, 4:281 and 8:1272.
160 Joseph Balloffet, *Histoire de Villefranche, Capitale du Beaujolais* (Villefranche: Guillermet, 1932; repr. Marseille: Lafitte, 1980), 3–10, 130.
161 T2:65, no. 292 (1147).

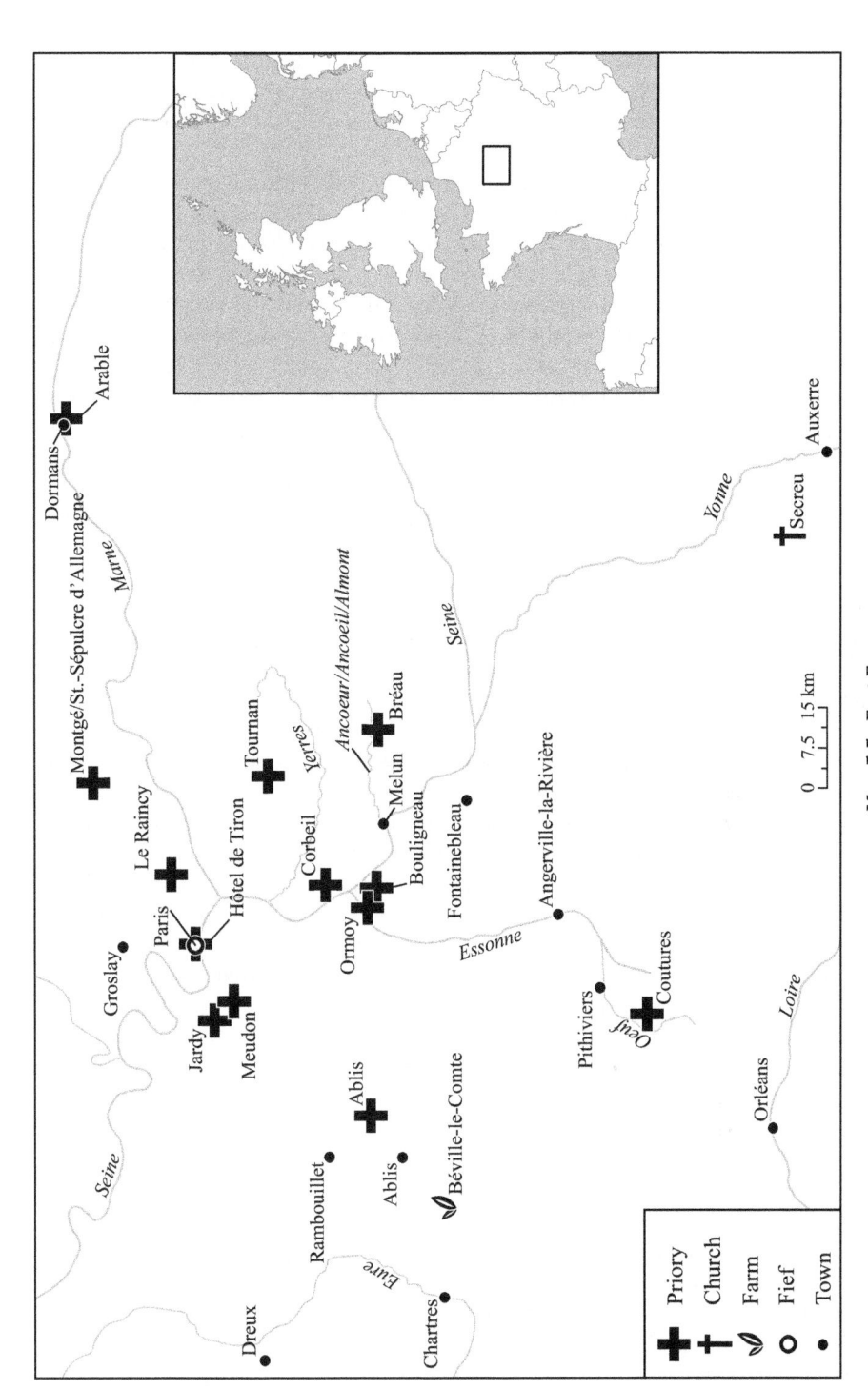

Map 5.5. East France

merchants, fairs, markets, and ports, the nearby town of Lagny hosted one of the four annual Champagne fairs linking cloth production in the Low Countries with dyeing and export in Italy. Tiron had limited expansion in Ile-de-France and almost none in Champagne and Burgundy.

Tiron expanded east toward Ile-de-France through episcopal and royal favour. Bishop Geoffrey II, a steadfast royal supporter, and two bishops of Paris, Girbert (r. 1116–1123) and Stephen of Senlis (r. 1123–1142), were instrumental. The patronage of Louis VI was extremely important, and his support and that of his grandson Philip II Augustus was communicated through forged charters. Instead of exempting Tiron from customs and tolls, the earlier charter places Tiron under special royal legal protection in spiritual and temporal matters throughout the realm, including civil and criminal cases.[162] In another Philip II Augustus referred to Tiron as being under the special protection of his predecessors.[163] Therefore, a close relationship with these Capetian monarchs was abbey lore.

In eastern France river travel with flat-bottomed barges was used extensively to transport goods. Properties could be spaced more widely because the boat afforded shelter overnight. Between 1119 and 1147 Tiron expanded its holdings in the vicinity of Paris, mainly near the navigable Seine River, which makes sweeping curves to the north and south. Paris was upriver of Tiron's priories in Vernon and downriver of the Seine's confluence with three tributaries with additional priories: the Essonne from the Beauce, the Marne from Champagne, and the Yonne from Auxerre. By the end of the twelfth century Tiron owned several quays in Paris. The pattern of expansion was twelve priories and one unknown church, which suggests involvement in trade.

Tiron's expansion east toward Ile-de-France began during Bernard's lifetime with the foundation of the priory of Ablis east of Chartres by Geoffrey of Presle, who gave the church, waterfront property, and a wood. Other donors gave and sold the monks additional land near Ablis and Rambouillet. Guy II, count of Rochefort, gave the Tironensian monks annual toll income at Ablis and exemption from a toll for their harvest.[164] Ablis was expanded ca. 1120–1140.[165] The priory was a link to Paris and a staging post on a pilgrimage route to Compostela.

The road from Chartres east to Paris via Rambouillet was well travelled, but the distance was a long haul for carts. The properties at Béville-le-Comte and the priories of Ablis and Jardy in Marnes-la-Coquette (with the priory of Meudon to the southeast) broke the trip. Bishop Girbert gave Jardy to Tiron in 1120. The priory was located in woods and farmland owned jointly by the bishop of Paris and Hugh of Chaumont, the

---

162 T1:46–48, no. 30 (1120).

163 T2:114–15, no. 339 (1194). Thompson, "The First Hundred Years," 115n99, comments "Merlet accepts the act as genuine, but Berger and Delaborde, editors of the acts of Philip Augustus regard it with suspicion," citing *Recueil des actes de Philippe Auguste, roi de France*, ed. É. Berger et al., 6 vols. (Paris: Impr. Nationale, 1916–2005), 1, no. 468.

164 T1:19–20, no. 8 (ca. 1115).

165 T1:57, no. 36 (ca. 1120); ibid., 2:10–11, no. 237 (ca. 1140).

Table 5.5. East France

Central and East France
Ablis (St. Epaigne); priory; ca. 1115; Geoffrey of Presle
Jardy (La Madeleine); priory; 1120; Girbert, bishop of Paris
Meudon; priory; ca. 1125
Chartres, E 24 to Béville-le-Comte, NE 25 km to Ablis, NE 49 km to Jardy in Marnes-la-Coquette with Meudon SE 6 km, NE 11 km to Paris
Bouligneau; priory; <1147
Corbeil (St. Radegonde)/Tigery; priory; 1124–1142; Payen Biseuil
Ormoy; priory; <1147
Melun, W downriver 14 km to Bouligneau near St.-Fargeau, NW downriver 14 km to St.-Radegonde-de-Corbeil or Tigery near Corbeil-Essonnes, with Ormoy on the Essonne near its confluence with the Seine 11 km SW of St.-Radegonde-de-Corbeil or Tigery
Paris is 32 km N of St.-Radegonde-de-Corbeil and this cluster of priories
Hôtel de Tiron; priory, fief; 1138; Anselme de Groslay, conf. Louis VII
Le Raincy (St. Blaise/N.D.); priory; ca. 1130; Baldwin of Villeflix
Montgé/St.-Sépulchre-d'Allemagne; priory; ca. 1145; Ralph of Bolerio, dau. Alice of Forfry, and Peter Maleit
Arable (N.D.); priory; ca. 1125; André of Baudement, seneschal of Champagne
Tournan (St. Ouen); priory; ca. 1128; Manassès of Tournan
Bréau (N.D.); priory; ca. 1140; Dodouin de Bombon
Arable, W 78 km to St.-Sépulcre d'Allemagne, SW 28 km to Le Raincy, SW 16 km to Paris
St.-Ouen (de-Tournan) is 46 km S of St.-Sepulchre d'Allemagne and 19 km S of the Marne
St.-Ouen (de-Tournan), S 26 km to Bréau
Secreu; church; ca. 1140; Tescelin, son Daimbert+Amica, Fulk of Tallouan+others
Secreu is near the Yonne, which flows through Auxerre into the Seine SE of Fontainebleau
Note: The routes run along the Essonne, Marne, and Yonne Rivers, tributaries of the Seine upriver of Paris

king's constable, and was in the fief of the Abbey of Saint-Germain-des-Prés.[166] Louis VII granted the priory of Meudon exemption from tolls and other exactions,[167] which suggests involvement in trade and shipping on the Seine.

The Tironensians had a riverine route from the Beauce to Paris, via Meung-sur-Loire, Orléans, northeast to Saint-Laurent-des-Coutures near Mareau-au-Bois along the

---

166 T1:51–53, no. 32 (1120).
167 T1:95, no. 76 (ca. 1125/post 1137).

Oeuf River, and down the Essonne to the Seine. Tiron had three priories a day's journey apart near the confluence of the Seine and the Essonne northwest of Melun: Bouligneau, Corbeil or Tigery, and Ormoy.[168] The cluster was a day's ride south of Paris.

Tiron's expansion into downtown Paris mirrored its earlier expansion into Chartres, with a headquarters near the political and religious centres, and property in the commercial and educational centres. Ralph V. Turner describes Paris at the beginning of the reign of Louis VII and Eleanor of Aquitaine in summer 1137. The royal palace and ancient Merovingian cathedral were on the Ile de la Cité. On the Right Bank near the Grand Pont (modern Pont au Change, for the money-lenders, jewellers, and goldsmiths) was a settlement of tradespeople surrounded by a wooden stockade. On the Left Bank, accessed by the Petit Pont, were the religious houses of Sainte-Geneviève, Saint-Victor, and Saint-Germain-des-Prés, together with the schools in the Latin Quarter.[169] Maartin Ultee's study of Saint-Germain-des-Prés presents the religious foundation as a powerful corporation and describes its holdings, financial transactions, and sources of revenue.[170] Paris had been an important trading centre since it came under Roman control as Lutetia in 52 B.C. The Capetian kings supported the river merchants, and the monasteries held large fairs. In 1138, with royal approval, Tiron acquired a fief on the Right Bank east of the commercial centre.

The acquisition must have required high-level contacts and considerable negotiation and inducement. The wars between Thibaut II and Louis VI resulted in Tiron owning many properties leading to the Seine and its ports in the Vexin and Normandy but none in Paris. The accession of pious seventeen-year-old Louis VII offered the possibility of better relations. Upon William X's death in 1137, Thibaut II and Bishop Geoffrey II escorted the ducal heiress, Eleanor, to her July marriage, and Louis VII and Eleanor ascended the French throne on August 1, 1137. Thibaut II was a long-standing patron of Tiron, where his natural son Hugh was living. Another patron, Waleran II of Meulan, had political and feudal alliances that extended to the Montmorency fortress of Marly west of Paris. Waleran's vassal Matthew I of Montmorency became the new king's constable.[171] The new reign was a propitious time for Tiron to acquire Parisian property, and in 1138 Tiron acquired the fief through a gift of land from Anselme, seigneur of Groslay, confirmed by Louis VII as fiefholder.[172] Groslay is a town north of Paris near Montmorency. Although no other evidence has been found of a Groslay connection, Tiron's acquisition of their seigneuriel fief suggests that Abbot William enjoyed considerable noble and royal favour.

---

168 When Corbeil/Tigery was founded, the donor, Pagan Biseuil (1124–1142), gave tithe income and other benefits in the church of Saint-Remy-de-Fontenay-le-Vicomte upriver on the Essonne, and Bishop Stephen confirmed the donation. T1:79–80, nos. 58–59 (1124–1142).

169 Ralph V. Turner, *Eleanor of Aquitaine: Queen of France, Queen of England* (New Haven: Yale University Press, 2009), 50.

170 Ultee, *The Abbey of St. Germain des Prés in the Seventeenth Century*, 63–88, 102–3.

171 Crouch, *The Beaumont Twins*, 60, 64.

172 T1:247, no. 219 (1138). Charles Lefeuve, *Groslay* (Fontainebleau: Bourges, 1866), 13, mentions the seigneurs Odon de Groslay 1108, and Anselme de Groslay, available online at https://books.google.nl/books?id=jRNOBC-OH7IC.

Tiron's fief was in the modern Marais at the intersection of the rue Saint-Antoine and the rue Tiron. The Hôtel de Tiron was established by 1677, and the watercolour floor plan of 1721 shows a large courtyard, four smaller courtyards, a chapel, large reception rooms, and a seigneurial tower. In 1194 Philip II Augustus issued letters of protection for Tiron, conferring on it the prestigious status of a royal abbey.[173] The defeat of John I, king of England (r. 1199–1216) at Bouvines in 1214 secured Normandy for the French crown, and Tiron also reoriented itself away from Normandy toward Paris.

Tiron expanded its holdings by acquiring houses on the rue Tiron and the rue du Roi-de-Sicile in the modern 75004 arrondissement of central Paris in 1236.[174] The Tironensian properties were located by 1772 in arrondissement 75004 on the rue Saint-Antoine, rue Vieille-du-Temple, rue du Roi-de-Sicile, rue Cloche-Perce, rue Tiron, rue des Nonains d'Hyères, rue de Jouy, quai des Ormes (modern quai des Célestins), rue de la Mortellerie (modern rue de l'Hôtel de Ville), rue des Barres, rue du Figuier, rue des Fauconniers, rue Percée (modern rue du Prévôt),[175] quai de la place aux Veaux (modern quai de Gesvres and quai de l'Hôtel de Ville). The residents in Tiron's fief were under Tiron's jurisdiction and paid census income.[176] These streets extend north of the Hôtel de Tiron and southeast toward the old port aux Pavés on the modern quai des Célestins.

A forged confirmation by Pope Alexander III of the property and privileges of the abbey, dated August 23, 1179, mentions Tironensian land in the Place de Grève,[177] now the Place de l'Hôtel-de-Ville, the major market of Paris. The port de Grève was the most important port in Paris, where wood, wheat, wine, and hay were unloaded and marketed.[178] The location suggests Tiron's involvement in Parisian trade. The property is near the modern quai de l'Hôtel-de-Ville on the Right Bank of the Seine north of the Ile de la Cité and Notre-Dame.

Due south, across the Ile-de-la-Cité, Tiron had property on the Left Bank in modern arrondissement 75005. The port Saint-Bernard at the confluence of the Seine and the Bièvre was the centre of the Parisian wine trade. Now the quai de la Tournelle, the site is located east of the rue Saint-Jacques at a site where the Seine flows between the Ile-de-la-Cité and the Ile-Saint-Louis.[179] Tiron had property on rue des Chantiers south of the quai.[180] Tiron owned a property in the fief of the Chardonnet between the church

---

173 Guillemin, *Thiron, abbaye médiévale*, 59. T2:114–15, no. 339 (1994).
174 T2:145–46, no. 367 (1236).
175 Hillairet, *Dictionnaire historique des rues de Paris*, 2:303.
176 IS-ADEL, 8:189, H 1689 (1722?), 1692 (1677?), 1693 (1680?). Guillemin, *Thiron, abbaye médiévale*, 58–59, cites Archives nationales, Z I J 1028 (Plans et élévations de l'hôtel de Tiron à Paris, procès-verbal de visite et état des reparations et des reconstructions à faire aux maisons, fermes, et autres domains dépendants de l'abbaye de Thiron, 1760).
177 T2:103–6, no. 328 (1179).
178 Félix Lazare and Louis Lazare, *Dictionnaire administrative et historique des rues et des monuments de Paris*, 2 vols. (Paris: Lazare 1844–1849), 1:322–24, available online at http://gallica.bnf.fr/ark:/12148/bpt6k200946t/f328.image.r=
179 Hillairet, *Dictionnaire historique des rues de Paris*, 2:385.
180 IS-ADEL 8:189, H 1693 (1680?).

of Saint-Nicolas-du-Chardonnet and the Seine near the corner of the modern rue des Bernardins. The church was named for its location in a thorny wasteland, due south of the cathedral of Notre-Dame and slightly east of the rue Saint-Jacques, a pilgrimage route to Compostela. Tiron Abbey won a dispute with Henry the Fleming for an unauthorized house and walls he built on their land.[181] The location suggests involvement in the wine trade as well as higher education.

The schools of Notre-Dame-de-Paris and the abbeys of Saint-Victor, and Sainte-Geneviève on the Left Bank of the Seine were the nucleus of the University of Paris. Geoffrey I, abbot of Tiron, reached an agreement with the abbey and chapter of Notre-Dame-de-Paris concerning a tract outside the city wall in the Paris Valley, planted in vines, and a tract within the walls.[182] An agreement was reached between Tiron Abbey and the Royal Abbey and School of Saint-Victor-de-Paris with regard to quitrent owed by the monks of Saint-Victor at their gate within the walls of Paris (Porte Saint-Victor). The Tironensians waived the quitrent in exchange for nine deniers of census income on three-quarters of a tract of land on the Seine bank near the church of Saint-Nicolas-du-Chardonnet.[183] The agreement was made at the nearby new church. Tiron Abbey reached an agreement with Renaud Mignon de Corbeil, bishop of Paris (r. 1250–1268) for land at Chardonnet on the Seine and quitrent owed to Saint-Victor.[184] In a necrology of the Abbey of Sainte-Geneviève-de-Paris dated 1275–1285, probably 1284, the brothers of the monastery of Tiron were commemorated on June 1, indicating confraternity.[185] Tiron was involved with the religious institutions of the Latin Quarter in business and other areas.

Thus Tiron expanded its holdings in Paris over the ensuing centuries, concentrating them on the Right and Left Banks opposite the Ile-Saint-Louis, extending into the Latin Quarter. The acquisition of quays suggests involvement in trade. The expansion toward the Latin Quarter, together with the connection with Saint-Victor, suggests that Tironensians were pursuing advanced studies. Abbot Léonet Grimault (r. 1453–1498) was exempted from tolls and other duties while studying at the University of Paris 1459–1462.[186] As such, the later expansion in Paris resembles the earlier move into Chartres. Although trade and education may explain these expanded Tironensian holdings in urban centres, ultimately the income from real estate was most profitable.

East of Paris to Champagne, the properties were a day's journey north of the Marne and more widely spaced. The riverine route ran west from Arable in Dormans, Champagne, to Montgé/Saint-Sépulcre d'Allemagne in Montgé-en-Goële to Le Raincy and Paris. The priory of Tournan was 46 kilometres south of Saint-Sepulchre d'Allemagne and a day's journey south of the Marne. Its river, La Marsange, flowed into the Yerres, a

---

[181] T2:172–73, no. 383 (January 1259/1260).
[182] T2:131, no. 355 (1214).
[183] T2:147–48, no. 369 (1239).
[184] T2:175–77, no. 385 (1260).
[185] *Obituaires de la Province de Sens*, ed. Auguste Molinier and Auguste Lognon. Recueil des historiens de France, Obituaires, 4 vols. in 5 (Paris: Klincksieck, 1902–1923), 1.1:501.
[186] IS-ADEL 8:167, H 1428 (1438–1462).

tributary of the Seine, at Villeneuve-Saint-Georges. From Tournan the route ran south to the priory of Bréau, on the Ancoeur/Ancoeuil/Almont River, which passes through Vaux-le-Vicomte to its confluence with the Seine at Melun. Thus these priories mainly encircled Paris on the east and connected by water with the southern priories on the Seine downriver of Melun.

On the Marne, Arable was the only Tironensian priory in Champagne, west of Epernay. The founder André of Baudement, seneschal of Champagne (1111–1133),[187] gave the Tironensian monks census income at Barzy-sur-Marne and Passy-sur-Marne, towns a day's journey west of Dormans.[188] Other donors confirmed their gifts, including the oven of Chassins in the neighbouring town, land with nut trees, and meadows at the source of the Arable, and tithe income.[189] Thibaut II's son Hugh was prior of Arable, the only Tironensian foundation in Champagne.[190] South of the Marne, Tournan was founded through the agency of Bishop Stephen. Manassès of Tournan-en-Brie and his wife Beatrix, together with other lesser donors, gave the priory two mills with adjacent land, fields, and cash gifts, including income from Tournan-en-Brie.[191] The priory's holdings were expanded by gifts of land confirmed by countergifts of wheat and oats, a cape, a pig, furs, and income. Lesser donors forgave produce owed by the monks. A confirmation of gifts of land in nearby Villemigeon ca. 1135 names an additional donor: Gislebert, formerly a butler of the king, and his family.[192]

East of Paris and Melun in the diocese of Sens, the priory of Bréau was founded by Dodouin of Bombon, a new monk, who, with other families, granted the church, lands, and income.[193] Further south, the Yonne flows northwest through Auxerre, Migennes, Joigny, Villeneuve-sur-Yonne, to its confluence with the Seine at Montereau-Fault-Yonne southeast of Fontainebleau. Thompson identifies and locates a church Merlet did not list in his topographical index: Secreu, listed with Bréau in the papal confirmations, in the vicinity of Aillant-sur-Tholon south of Joigny, given to Tiron ca. 1140. The fiefholder was Renaud of Champvallon, and the donation was witnessed by Renaud, count of Joigny. This church extended Tiron's foundations east of Paris into Burgundy.[194]

This overview of Tiron's expansion patterns in modern France reflects the thirty years of Abbot William's patient negotiation and purposeful acquisitions to transform Bernard's rural abbey and scattered foundations into a centralized congregation and a network for trade and communication. Much expansion was achieved by acquisitions of

---

[187] Evergates, *The Aristocracy in the County of Champagne*, 9, 216.
[188] T1:92, no. 73 (ca. 1125).
[189] T1:130, no. 110 (1129); ibid., 2:19–20, no. 248 (ca. 1140).
[190] T2:83–84, no. 310 (1156).
[191] T1:119–20, no. 99 (ca. 1128).
[192] T1:167–68, no. 142 (ca. 1132); ibid., 1:198–99, nos. 178–79 (ca. 1132); ibid., 1:239, no. 211 (ca. 1135).
[193] T2:32, no. 263 (ca. 1142); ibid., 2:51, no. 283 (ca. 1145).
[194] Thompson, *The Monks of Tiron*, 240. T2:264, *Campovallum*, no. 248 [sic, Merlet's error] 247. T2:18–19, no. 247 (ca. 1140); ibid., 2:64, no. 292 (1147); ibid., 2:99, no. 326 (1175–1176).

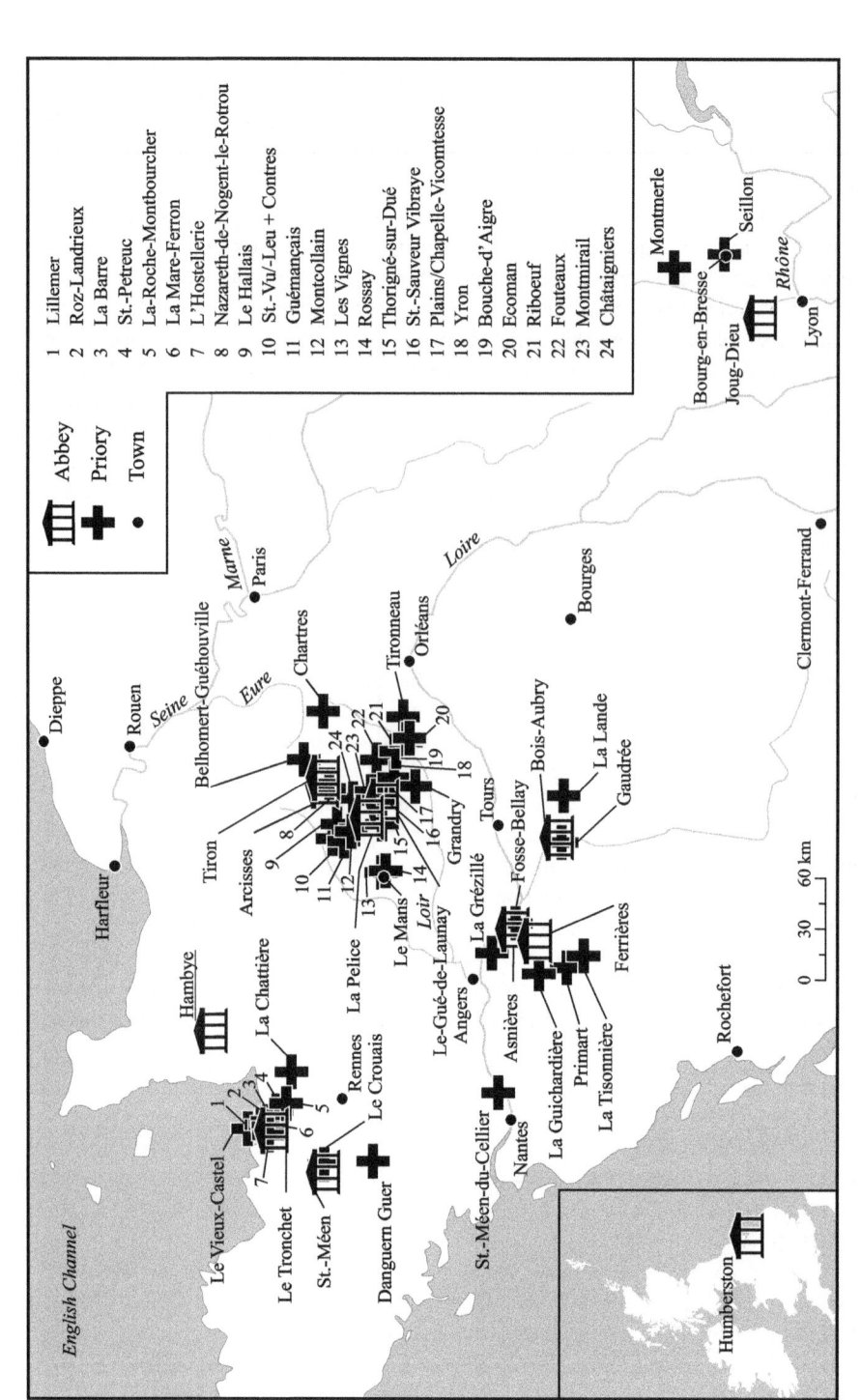

Map 5.6. Tiron and Daughter Abbeys' Dependent Priories

small properties in hamlets or episcopal donations of churches formerly in lay ownership. Many priories began by acceptance of younger sons as monks together with their family property. Many priories and abbeys began by the acquisition of hermitages in strategic areas together with their patrons. Tiron's network coexisted with the networks formed by other religious foundations for their own purposes and was shaped and sometimes limited by competition from older foundations and new ones following the rule of Cîteaux. William created his own administrative model of centralized rule by the annual general chapter at Tiron, which appointed religious leaders, discussed strategy, and imposed discipline. He created his own business model of exemptions, vertical economic integration, airtight contracts, meticulous record-keeping, and skilful dispute mediation. After his early travels from Poitou to Scotland, he continued to travel to negotiate important foundations: to Wales early in his tenure, to Pithiviers and the Paris area, and at the end of his life to Normandy where his death was commemorated at Mont-Saint-Michel. He persuaded diverse donors from Brittany to Beaujolais to support Tiron's expansion and retained generations of royal, noble, and episcopal donors first won by the saintliness of Tiron's founder. His accomplishments were not unique but they were remarkable and well ahead of their times for reformed Benedictine monastic congregations. Under his leadership, rural Tiron Abbey, with its impoverished but godly monks, expanded into a prosperous international congregation that endured for eight centuries within the emerging French nation.

Chapter 6

EXPANSION IN THE BRITISH ISLES

A DETAILED ANALYSIS of the establishment and growth of Tiron's English priories and its foundations in Wales and Scotland on the Celtic periphery of the Tironensian network shows that the French and British foundations followed strikingly different patterns of development during the course of the twelfth century. The French foundations expanded steadily during the first half of the century, whereas the alien priories established in England ca. 1115–1150 remained small cells. In Wales and Scotland two Tironensian foundations were elevated to abbeys, but in England other congregations, particularly the Cistercians, expanded more rapidly. The lack of growth of the Tironensian establishments is significant against the larger overall background of generous English religious endowment. In England, the first wave of eremitism involved the monks of Evesham who left their monastery 1073/1074 and went to Jarrow, Wearmouth, Whitby, and finally Durham. A second wave occurred in the early twelfth century[1] and included Tiron's small, mainly coastal priories near Southampton and on the Isle of Wight. Their foundation occurred concurrently with the elevation of St. Dogmaels in Wales to abbatial status ca. 1121 and contrasts sharply with it. Henry of Blois (1101–1171), bishop of Winchester (ca. 1129) and abbot of Glastonbury (1126), was the brother of Tiron's patron Thibaut II, count of Blois-Champagne. Although many of these Tironensian priories and cells were in his diocese, he did not encourage their growth. His other brother, King Stephen, favoured the congregation of Savigny, which was located in his French possessions. Tiron's connection to Count Thibaut II may have made potential English donors reluctant to take sides by supporting Tironensian foundations during the civil wars (ca. 1138–1152). Moreover, the congregation of Cîteaux had emerged as an alternative reformed order. The English nobility favoured the Cistercians, whose abbeys were less costly to found while remaining a source of political and financial influence for their patrons. Thibaut II's son Henry II, count of Champagne, was also generous to the Cistercian order.

Another factor may be the personality and political connections of the abbot. The English background of Stephen Harding was probably not significant, since he was considered a member of the Norman ruling class. The influence of Bernard of Clairvaux, a prestigious international personage and renowned churchman, was far more important. Although Abbot William of Tiron was an excellent administrator, he was not a public figure or acclaimed for his spirituality. Bishop Geoffrey II's close ties to the king of France and his own close ties to Scotland may not have encouraged English royal favour. Henry I gave William strong support for superiority over St. Dogmaels in Wales in 1121 but was less enthusiastic about extending his authority in England.

Accordingly there was a consistent pattern of the English nobility founding Cistercian abbeys in the same regions where Tiron's priories were located instead of expanding

---

1 Leyser, *Hermits and the New Monasticism*, 29–37.

Tiron's priories into abbeys. Cistercian Beaulieu and Netley were situated near Hamble priory below Southampton. Cistercian Waverley, near Andwell priory in Surrey, was settled in 1129 from L'Aumône, followed by Rievaulx in 1132 and Fountains in 1135. St. Cross, Isle of Wight remained a priory, while Savigny founded Quarr nearby in 1132 and the abbey became Cistercian after Savigny merged with Cîteaux. Cistercian Forde was founded in 1136 in Dorset, east of Tiron's church of Bradford Peverell. On the Welsh border, L'Aumône also founded Tintern in Monmouthshire, Wales in 1131 and Cistercian Dore was founded in 1147 in Herefordshire, south of Tiron's church of Kington and Titley priory. These coastal and border regions were strategic and desirable.

In Wales and Scotland Tironensian expansion was not as eclipsed by the Cistercian order. The princes of Deheubarth did become patrons of the Cistercian abbeys of Whitland, founded in 1140, and Strata Florida, founded in 1164. Nonetheless St. Dogmaels Abbey was well endowed and enjoyed the patronage of the ruling house, whose members considered it family property. St. Dogmaels remained self-sufficient and gradually acquired properties and founded priories in Pembrokeshire and Ireland. Pill Priory was the nucleus of the port of Milford Haven. With generous bequests from the Scottish kings and nobility, Tironensian foundations flourished alongside the Cistercian and other foundations in Scotland and played important roles in the history of Scottish independence.

The large Scottish abbeys of Kelso, Arbroath, Kilwinning, and Lindores and the priory of Lesmahagow were founded over the course of the twelfth century. The border abbey of Kelso (formerly Selkirk) became an educational centre, a diplomatic meeting place, and a market outlet for wool and other commodities, with a ship trading in the North Sea. The northern coastal abbey of Arbroath between Dundee and Aberdeen ran a market, a regality court (a court with territorial jurisdiction of a royal nature formerly conferred by the sovereign), and a harbour that connected the region with England, Denmark, and Flanders. The Declaration of Arbroath affirming Scottish independence was drawn up there in 1320. The abbey of Lindores on the Firth of Tay, noted for its orchards, was a midpoint between the ports of Perth and Dundee. The abbey of Kilwinning was near the Firth of Clyde, Glasgow, and the Isle of Arran. In Scotland Tironensian abbeys were majestic and richly endowed, but they gave good value for the investment to their donors and the community.

The group that founded Selkirk in 1113–1114 seems to have retained connections for life. David I; John, bishop of Glasgow; Herbert, abbot of Selkirk/Kelso (1119–1147) and bishop of Glasgow (1147–1164); and Arnold (abbot of Kelso 1147–1160, bishop of St. Andrews 1160–1163), appear together as witnesses to many charters. Their connection to Abbot William would have been reinforced if the abbots of Kelso had attended the Tironensian general chapter every three years. At present, however, no evidence has been found to confirm or disprove their attendance. Pirates added to the natural dangers of rough weather in the North Sea and the Channel, and the civil war between King Stephen and Empress Matilda 1135–1153 was a period of anarchy endangering overland travel. In peacetime, however, a summer visit to Tiron and nearby Chartres might have been a pleasant and instructive experience for an abbot in a northern border region. David I's decision in 1128 to move the Selkirk community from its rural setting to Kelso, across the Tweed from his court in the market town of Roxburgh, was probably discussed and approved at Tiron. The papal confirmation of 1132 affirmed that Kelso and St. Dogmaels were subordinate to Tiron. John, bishop of Glasgow, under pressure from the Roman curia to yield obedience to York, transferred his allegiance to the anti-pope Anacletus II (r. 1130–1138) and, feeling out of favour, became a monk at Tiron in 1136 or 1137 until he was recalled to his see by the papal legate in 1138.[2] Bishop John might have departed gracefully by accompanying Abbot Herbert to the general chapter; his profession suggests ongoing connections. Abbot William had died by 1160 and Abbot Herbert died in 1164, almost fifty years after their association at Selkirk. Subsequently St. Dogmaels and Kelso distanced themselves from Tiron while retaining loosened connections.

In South Britain, despite its navigable rivers, Tironensian properties were mainly coastal and concentrated between the Southampton Water and Basingstoke in Hampshire and along the coast of Pembrokeshire. There were none in the vicinity of London and the Thames basin and very few near the Humber estuary.

In England, Henry I was instrumental in founding three Tironensian priories in the diocese of Winchester and a church and priory on the Welsh border, all ca. 1120, when he was subduing Normandy and Wales and warring with France. Although Henry I deposed his older brother Robert Curthose and became duke of Normandy in 1106, Robert's son William Clito was a rival claimant, and the Norman lords were always ready to rebel. In subsequent periods of war between England and France, alien priories of all orders were widely regarded as centres of espionage whose cover for communications and financial transactions was sheltering wayfarers and alms-giving. They were repeatedly seized by the crown and ultimately dissolved and sold.[3] The modest annual cash payment to Tiron of fifteen to twenty marks from the English Exchequer granted by Henry I and his descendants through Edward III (r. 1327–1377) suggests Tiron's early participation in an English intelligence network.[4]

Mainly the Tironensian priories farmed and furthered travel and communication. Gillingham notes that medieval ships sailing from London for the continent were unfit to survive storms at sea, and their crews were unwilling to risk their lives, vessels, and cargoes. They preferred to hug the coast and seek havens awaiting favourable winds, and they needed constant revictualing. From London they rounded the coast of Kent to Southampton or Portsmouth and waited there or near the Isle of Wight for suitable conditions for crossing to France. Hamble-le-Rice, north of the Isle of Wight, is the first port a ship would reach in the Southampton Water. At a rise on the Hamble River, in later centuries it became an important shipyard where vessels were built and repaired. Other vessels continued down the English coast to Cornwall before crossing,[5] and the Tironensian properties near Weymouth and Torquay were near this route. St. Dogmaels'

---

2 Oram, *David I*, cites Richard of Hexham, *De Gestis Regis Stephani*, 152n32, and 153.
3 New, "History of the Alien Priories in England," 45–83, specifically 74.
4 T1:43, no. 27 (1119–1126). WCM, 2:430, no. 10682 (1362).
5 Gillingham, *The Angevin Empire*, 119–20, 124.

coastal location near Cardigan and its coastal properties at Pill near modern Milford Haven and on Caldey Island facilitated shipping in the Bristol Channel. The Tironensians probably provisioned the vessels, but they had exemptions to engage in other trade in the middle of an important shipping route from London to the continent.

In England Tiron had six priories, eleven churches, fifteen farms, and eight houses, of which five were on the Isle of Wight. St. Andrew of Hamble, founded 1109 by William Giffard, bishop of Winchester (r. 1100–1128), was Tiron's earliest alien priory.[6] Orderic records that on November 25, 1120, two Tironensian monks, probably headed for Hamble, sailed for England with Henry I and escaped shipwreck on the *White Ship*.[7] The priory of St. Swithun at Winchester paid the monks of Hamble a weekly corrody of bread and beer and an annual corrody of pelisses, shoes, and boots, and a charter provides specific information about the small community.[8] Emma, the wife of Roger Alys, gave the monks of Hamble land and a meadow they possessed at Auditon (probably Allington), free and quit from any secular customs. The monks—Geoffrey the prior, Robert Rufus his kinsman, Aimeri the priest, Archembaud, and Ruallenus, subsequently a monk[9]— prevailed upon the owner to give them a clear title to the land they were working. Ascelina, wife of Guimund, gave Hamble the house and land pertaining to it, a gift from her brother Roaudus, and confirmed all his gifts to the monks upon entering religion.[10] The priory expanded to having a prior's house and garden, a dovecote (a privilege of the nobility), over ninety acres of land and woods, and tenants.

The Hamble charters include a confirmation by Henry (II) of an annual grant by Henry I to the monks of Tiron of fifteen silver marks for footwear for the monks. They also include a grant by Henry II to the monks of Tiron of freedom from toll, passage, pontage, and every custom throughout England and Normandy for all the dominical possessions of the monks, probably a copy of a similar exemption for the monks of Tiron.[11] Thus Tiron Abbey in France had an annual income in England, which could be sent to Tiron, paid to Hamble priory, or allocated at the abbot's discretion.[12] Together with exemption from tolls and customs, the English royal family was subsidizing Tiron's early involvement in trade.

These early charters indicate that the monks of Hamble were acquiring property up the Southampton Water in the town of Southampton and the nearby manor of Allington.[13] In Hampshire, the monks had tithes from their land at St. Peter's Waltham

---

[6] T1:201–3, no. 182 (1132/1133). WCM, 2:422, no. 10624a (1133).

[7] OV, 12.26, 6:296–97.

[8] WCM, 2:428, nos. 10668 (1326) and 10669 (1337).

[9] T1:232, no. 204 (ca. 1135).

[10] T2:31, no. 262 (ca. 1142). VCH Hampshire, 2:221.

[11] WCM, 2:422, nos. 10625 (1155–1162) and 10626 (n.d.). T1:75, no. 54 (ca. 1122).

[12] Hamble's income was valued at £18 14s 8d in 1294. VCH Hampshire, 2:223n4. It was valued at £13 6s when sold in 1391. VCH Hampshire, 2:223n4 and 225n9, citing Arthur Frances Leach, *A History of Winchester College* (New York: Duckworth, 1899), 145.

[13] WCM, 2:427, no. 10661A (n.d.). See WCM, 2:421–56, nos. 10624–26852 for Hamble's properties, including Hamble Manor Farm.

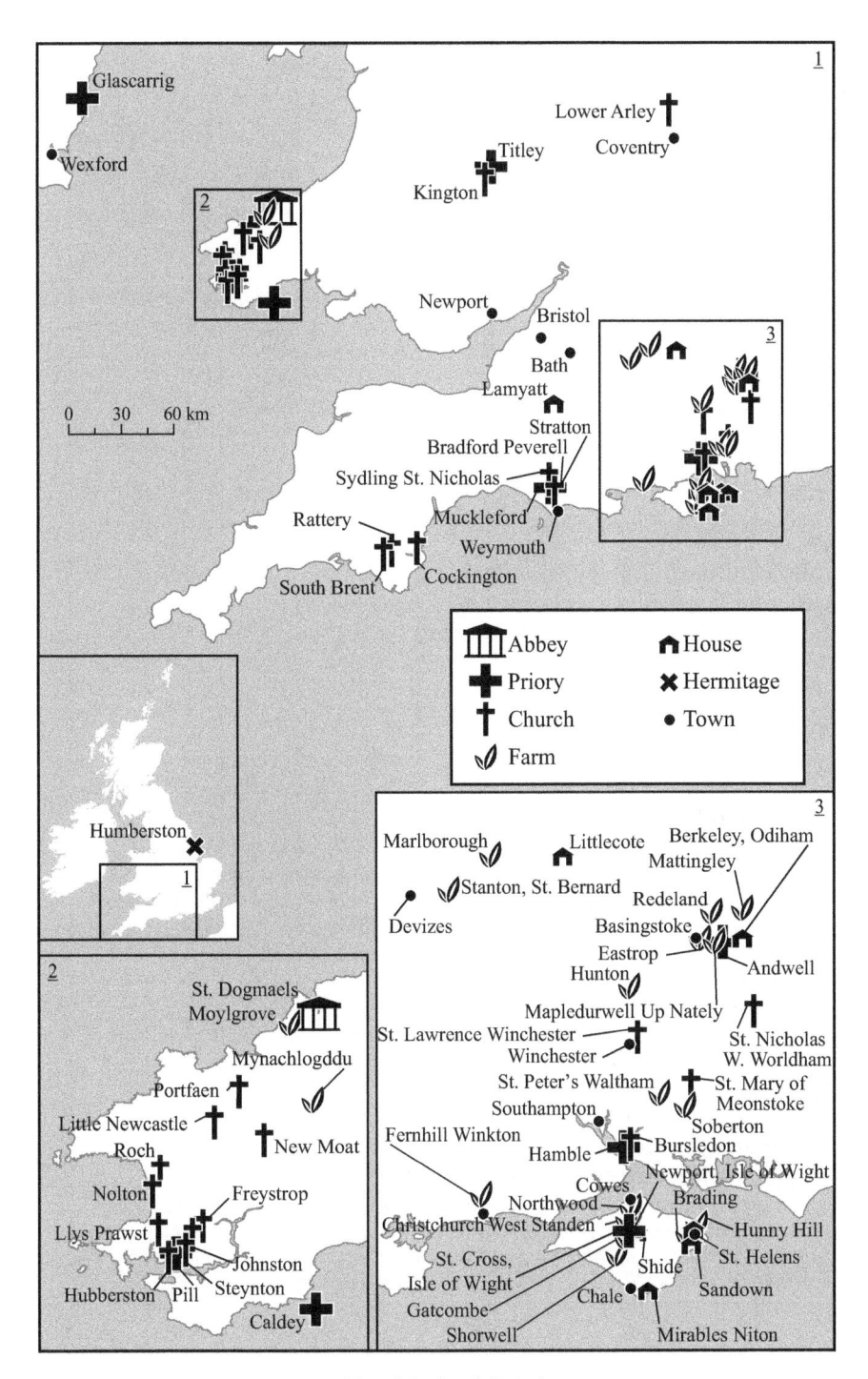

Map 6.1. South Britain

Table 6.1. South Britain

England: Hamble Priory
Hamble (St. Andrew); priory, 1109–1116; William Giffard, b. of Winchester (Abbot Bernard)
St. Peter's Waltham; tithes; 1153–1171; Henry of Blois, b. of Winchester
Bursledon; church; 1153–1171; Henry of Blois, b. of Winchester
St. Mary of Meonstoke; church; <1194
Soberton; farm; <1194
St. Nicholas W. Worldham; church; twelfth century; Richard de Anesy+Isabella
St. Lawrence Winchester; church; <1147
Hunton; farm; twelfth century; Herbert s. of Herbert+Lucy
Redeland; farm; twelfth century; Herbert s. of Herbert+s. Peter
Hamble, N 6 km to Bursledon, W 10 km to Southampton
Bursledon, N 13 km to Bishops Waltham with Meonstoke and Soberton E 9 km in the Meon Valley
Meonstoke, N 9 km to West Worldham and NW 23 km to Basingstoke
Winchester is 31 km N of Hamble-le-Rice. Hamble is 10 km N of Cowes on the Isle of Wight
Lamyatt; house by a pear tree; twelfth century; Baldwin of Columbars
Littlecote; house; twelfth century; Robert s. of Heldebert
Stanton, St. Bernard; farm; twelfth century; Herbert s. of Herbert+Lucy
The Lamyatt Somerset property was 112 km W of Hamble, and the other Wiltshire properties were 102 km NW of Hamble
England: Andwell, Humberston and Titley Priories
Andwell (St. Mary+St. John the Baptist); priory, ca. 1120; Adam I de Port
Eastrop (Worting, Basingstoke); farm; ca. 1141; Empress Matilda
Mapledurwell Up Nately/Newnham; church; <1131–1133; Adam I de Port
Mattingley; farm in the royal demesne; <1131–1133; Adam I de Port
Berkeley, Odiham; house; <1150–1161; Sibilla Daubeny w. Roger de Port
Andwell is 34 km NE of Winchester and 73 km W of London. Mapledurwell, Andwell, Scures, and Newnham are 5–6 km E of Basingstoke. Berkeley is 12 km E of Basingstoke, and 6 km SE of Andwell. Mattingley is 14 km NE of Basingstoke and 8 km NE of Andwell. Berkeley and Odiham are 56 km W of London
Fernhill Winkton; farm; <1189; Henry de Port
Fernhill is near Winkton, 3 km N of the port of Christchurch, 85 km SW of Andwell
Stratton; church; 1154–1189; Roger de Port+wife Sibilla Daubeny
Bradford Peverell; church; 1117–1126; Sibilla Daubeny w. Roger de Port
Muckleford; priory; 1154–1189; Sibilla Daubeny+sons Adam III and Henry de Port; church of Tiron
Sydling St. Nicholas; church; confirmed 1150–1161; Adam III de Port
The port of Weymouth is 103 km W of Hamble-le-Rice and 141 km W of Andwell. Dorchester is 13 km N of Weymouth. Stratton, Bradford Peverell, and Muckleford lie along a 3 km stretch of the Dorchester Road to Weymouth and are 5 km NW of Dorchester. Sydling St. Nicholas is 8 km NW of Bradford Peverell

EXPANSION IN THE BRITISH ISLES 133

Table 6.1. (Cont.)

Lower Arley; church; confirmed 1188–1198; Adam I de Port+son Roger **Humberston**; cell of Andwell **Kington**; church; 1117–1126, ?1121–1122; Adam I de Port **Titley (St. Mary or St. Peter)**; priory; <1147 *Lower Arley is 15 km N of Coventry. Kington is 29 km NW of Hereford, 177 km NW of Andwell and 225 km N of Bradford Peverell. Titley is located 5 km N of Kington. Leominster is 19 km E of Titley and 22 km E of Kington*

England: St. Cross Priory, Isle of Wight
  St. Cross, Isle of Wight; priory; ca. 1120; Robert Colaws
  Northwood, Gurnard; house; Robert Colaws
  Hunny Hill; farm; <1135; Baldwin de Redvers, earl of Exeter+lord of the Isle of Wight; north Newport
  Newport, Isle of Wight; houses, pier, Laford Mill; <1135; Robert Colaws+Great Balhill (Seaclose); house; 1337; Robert, prior of St. Cross
  Shide; farm; <1135; Robert Colaws
  West Standen; farm; <1135; Robert Colaws; Newport hill
  Gatcombe; farm
  Shorwell; farm
  Mirablesland Niton; farm; <1426
  Brading; Kern farm; <1699
  St. Helens; house
  Sandown; house
The Medina River runs 7 km N to the port of Cowes. Northwood is 5 km N of Newport. Hunny Hill is 1 km NW of Newport. Great Balhill (modern Seaclose) is in NE Newport and Shide is 2 km SE of Newport. West Standen is 2 km S of Newport. Gatcombe is 4 km S of West Standen and 10 km NE of the port of Chale. From Cridmore Farm in Carisbrooke, Shorwell is 9 km SW and 7 km N of Chale. Mirablesland in Niton is 4 km E of Chale. Kern Farm in Brading is 13 km E of St. Cross. From Brading St. Cross had property in two eastern ports: St. Helens 4 km NW of Bembridge Harbour and Sandown 3 km SW of Bembridge Harbour

Wales: St. Dogmaels Abbey
  Cockington; church; ca. 1120; Robert FitzMartin
  Rattery; church and manor; ca. 1120; Robert FitzMartin
  South Brent; church; ca. 1120, <1159; Robert FitzMartin
Torquay is 121 km by land W of Weymouth. Cockington is 5 km W of Torquay, Rattery is 20 km W of Torquay, and East Brent, near modern South Brent, is 6 km SW of Rattery
  St. Dogmaels; priory/abbey; ca. 1114/1121; Robert FitzMartin
  Mynachlogddu; farm; 19 km S of Cardigan
  Caldey (St. Mary/St. Illtud); priory; 1131; Geva de Burci, mother of Robert FitzMartin
  Moylgrove; farm; ca. 1120; Matilda Peverel, wife of FitzMartin
  Llys Prawst/Newton; church; 1115–1148
  Pill (St. Mary+St. Budoc); priory; ca. 1180–1190; Adam de Roche
  Hubberston (St. David); thirteenth century, Pill church
  Steynton (St. Peter); Pill church

(*continued*)

Table 6.1. (Cont.)

> **Johnston (St. Peter)**; Pill church
> **Freystrop (St. Justinian)**; Pill church
> **Little Newcastle (St. Peter)**; Pill church
>
> *Hubberston and Pill, Steynton, Johnston, and Freystrop are on the road to Haverfordwest Castle, the lowest fordable point on the Western Cleddau. The NE route runs to Little Newcastle, coastal Fishguard, and St. Dogmaels*
>
> Hubberston, N 4 km to Steynton, N 3 km to Johnston, NE 3 km to Freystrop, N 6 km to Haverfordwest, N 19 km to Little Newcastle, N 13 km to Fishguard, NE 32 km to St. Dogmaels
>
> **Nolton (St. Madoc)**; Pill church
> **Roch**; Pill church
> **Pontfaen**; Pill church
> **New Moat (St. Nicholas)**; Pill church
>
> Haverfordwest, NW 12 km to Nolton or NW 11 km to Roch (coastal)
>
> *St. Dogmaels is 28 km NE of Pontfaen. Pontfaen and New Moat are on a route between Fishguard and St. Dogmaels SE to coastal Tenby and the crossing to Caldey Island*
>
> Fishguard, SE 12 km to Pontfaen, SE 14 km New Moat, S 33 km to Tenby, S 4 km to Caldey Island

Ireland
> **Glascarrig (St. Mary)**; priory; 1192; Condons, Roches, De Burgos, Barrys, Carrins
> *Glascarrig is in Courtown Harbour, Wexford*

(modern Bishop's Waltham) at the head of the Hamble River and at nearby Bursledon close to Southampton, where they built a chapel.[14] They also owned land and tithes at the church of St. Mary of Meonstoke on the River Meon and at Flexland and Huntborne in the parish of Soberton.[15] Their chapel of St. Nicholas of West Worldham[16] was south of Basingstoke and their church of St. Lawrence was in downtown Winchester.[17] They owned sheep pasture in Hunton, Winchester,[18] and a property called Hambleland at Redeland, possibly Chineham Redlands, Basingstoke.[19] Far to the west Hamble owned a house at Lamyatt, Somerset, between Weymouth and Bristol.[20] Hamble had property and income in Wiltshire, east of Bristol: the village of Littlecote, probably modern Littlecote House, in the parishes of Ramsbury and Chilton Foliat.[21] Hamble had land in Stanton

---

[14] WCM, 2:423, no. 10629 (1153–1171).
[15] WCM, 2:423, no. 10631 (1194).
[16] WCM, 2:424, no. 10639a (n.d.).
[17] T2:60–67, nos. 291–92 (1147); ibid., 2:201, no. 326 (1175–1176).
[18] WCM, 2:423–24, no. 10635 (twelfth century).
[19] WCM, 2:423, no. 10632 (twelfth century).
[20] WCM, 2:424, no. 10636a, b (twelfth century).
[21] WCM, 2:423, no. 10633 (twelfth century).

St. Bernard,[22] east of Devizes, and alms from the nearby market town of Marlborough to the northeast on the Old Bath Road between Bath and London.[23] Hamble's loose connections to Wales, Bristol, and London are evident.

The priory of St. Mary or St. John the Baptist of Andwell (also Mapledurwell) was established ca. 1120 by Adam I de Port, steward of the household of Henry I, northeast of Winchester on the North Downs between Basingstoke and Hertfordbridge, Hampshire.[24] Andwell housed about six monks[25] and was a family foundation of several generations of the Port family. Hubert de Port, the father of Adam I, owned Mapledurwell east of Basingstoke in 1086.[26] Adam I de Port, lord of Mapledurwell at the beginning of the twelfth century, attested charters primarily in England, until 1130.[27] Adam I originally gave the Tironensian monks land in a valley called "Arga" and in Mapledurwell, which he exchanged for land in Up Nately, which Henry I had given him from the royal demesne.[28] Adam I also gave the monks a manse, adjacent demesne pasture and exemption from multure, and pannage. At Woodstock, Henry I confirmed Adam I's gifts in Nately and Mapledurwell, specifying that the monks' land in the royal demesne was further north in Mattingley.[29] Adam's son Roger de Port gave the monks of Andwell the mill before their gate. The witnesses include Walter of St. Davids (*Sanctus-Manevue* or *Menevia*), a Welsh connection. Another charter with the same witnesses stipulated that Roger also gave the miller of Andwell, together with the property's tithes.[30] Roger entered into fraternity with the monks and granted them land in Winchester above the brook ca. 1150, which they later exchanged for land alongside the spring of Andwell and a house in Berkeley, Odiham.[31] Empress Matilda's grant of land at Eastrop in Basingstoke ca. 1141 was listed in the confirmation of Theobald, archbishop of Canterbury (r. 1139–1161) as a grant by King Stephen 1150–1161.[32] The donation reflected continued support by the English royal family. Andwell accrued lands, tenants, a mill, a dovecote, and livestock.[33]

---

22 WCM, 2:423, no. 10634 (twelfth century); ibid., 2:424, no. 10641 (twelfth century).

23 T2:66, no. 292 (1147); ibid., 2:101, no. 326 (1175–1176); ibid., 2:285 (town in the diocese of Salisbury). Thompson, *The Monks of Tiron*, 244 identifies *Melleberga* as Marlborough SNB, near Wiltshire, Salisbury; see WCM, 3:1416 for other variants.

24 T1:60, no. 39 (ca. 1120). Hollister, *Henry I*, 361, 365.

25 Knowles, *The Religious Orders in England*, 1:106.

26 Mapledurwell included the parishes of Mapledurwell, Newnham, and Up Nately and the extraparochial district of Andwell. Together with Nately Scures, they form a cluster of small towns east of Basingstoke; Berkeley in Odiham and Mattingley are further northeast of Basingstoke.

27 VCH Hampshire, 4:149. Farrer, *An Outline Itinerary of King Henry I*, 132, no. 615 (1130).

28 WCM, 2:95, no. 2788 (Henry I).

29 WCM, 2:95, no. 2789 (1115–1148). Farrer, *An Outline Itinerary of King Henry I*, 141, no. 664A (ca. 1131–1133). The witnesses included Bernard, bishop of St. Davids, John of Bayeux (d. ca. 1131), Robert FitzRoy of Caen, earl of Gloucester, and Robert FitzMartin.

30 T1:60, no. 39 (ca. 1120). WCM, 2:96, nos. 2793 (?Henry II) and 2794 (Hugh, prior).

31 WCM, 2:95–96, nos. 2791 (ca. 1150) and 2792 (Henry II).

32 WCM, 2:95–96, nos. 2785 (1150–?1161) and 2797 (?1141).

33 Andwell was valued in 1294 at £26 12s and in 1391 at £10 10s. VCH Hampshire, 2:223–25.

The Port family owned property in the coastal region, and Andwell also acquired property at considerable distances near the Channel ports of Christchurch and Weymouth, and in Coventry[34] and Lincolnshire, where Andwell had a coastal cell named Humberston at the mouth of the Humber estuary.[35] This cell linked Andwell with Ermine Street and the North Sea trade. Subsequently the abbey of St. Mary and St. Peter of Humberston would be founded as a Tironensian start-up, like Hambye, and would become independent of the congregation of Tiron.[36] David I and Henry, earl of Huntingdon, granted one Tironensian ship safeguard and exemption from duties once a year as it traded in Scotland and Northumberland.[37] Another distant grant by Adam I de Port included land and the church of Kington and Beverton (perhaps nearby Barton Manor),[38] Herefordshire. Kington is a market town on Offa's Dike at the Welsh border. The abbot of Tiron was entitled to the advowson.[39] The priory of St. Peter of Titley, north of Kington, appears in the papal confirmations of 1147, 1175–1176, and 1179.[40] Probably Titley was founded to receive revenue from the properties on the Welsh border. Thus Andwell's properties extended east on the road to London, west along the Channel Coast near the ports of Christchurch and Weymouth, and north to the Welsh border, Coventry, and the Humber estuary and the North Sea.

The priory of St. Cross was particularly important because of the strategic position of the Isle of Wight in the Solent south of the Southampton Water. Like Hamble, the Isle of Wight was a landing point for invaders and smugglers and a natural centre for seaborne communication with the Hampshire and Dorsetshire properties and St. Dogmaels' Pembrokeshire and Irish foundations. Richard de Redvers (ca. 1045–1107) was seigneur of Vernon, a member of the English branch of that French family. A member of the inner council of Henry I, Richard was granted the lordship of Carisbrooke comprising most of the Isle of Wight. Richard's son Baldwin de Redvers (ca. 1095–1155), earl of Exeter, considered King Stephen to be a usurper and mounted opposition to him in various ways, including engaging in piracy from his castle on the Isle of Wight. Ultimately he made peace with

---

34 Near Christchurch: Fernhill, WCM, 2:96, no. 2796 (Henry II). Near Weymouth and Dorchester: Stratton, WCM, 2:96, no. 2798 (Henry II); ibid., 2:95, no. 2785 (1150–?1161); Bradford Peverell, T1:29, no. 15 (1117–1126); WCM, 2:208, nos. 4269 (n.d.), 4270a–b (Henry II), 4271 (1142–1165). Muckleford, WCM, 2:208, no. 4270 (Henry II), and Sydling St. Nicholas, WCM 2:95, no. 2785. Near Coventry: Lower Arley. WCM, 2:210, nos. 4286–88 (n.d.). The abbot of Tiron had the right of presentment or advowson.

35 Knowles, *The Religious Orders in England*, 2:214, 237, 247, and 3:64–65.

36 A. E. Kirkby, A. R. Tailby, *The Abbey of St. Mary & St. Peter, Humberston, Lincolnshire* (New Waltham: Waltham Toll Bar School, 1974). "House of Benedictine monks of the Order of Tiron," *A History of the County of Lincolnshire*, ed. William Page, VCH (London: Constable, 1906), 2:133–34.

37 T1:80–81, no. 60 (1124–1145); ibid., 2:14–15, no. 241 (ca. 1140).

38 T1:29, no. 15 (1117–1126); ibid., 2:267. WCM, 2:95, no. 2785 (1150–?1161). WCM, 3:956, no. 18945 (1671), "Kington, Old Kington, Barton [in Kington]."

39 WCM, 2:209, no. 4280b (1293); WCM, 3:952, no. 18930 (1293).

40 T2:60, no. 291; ibid., 2: 66, no. 292 (1147); ibid., 2:101, no. 326 (1175–1176); ibid., 2:104, no. 328. Farrer, *An Outline Itinerary of King Henry I*, 95, no. 433 (1121–1122).

Stephen and received the title of earl of Devon. Baldwin was buried at Quarr Abbey, which he had founded.[41]

St. Cross, Isle of Wight was founded by Robert Colaws ca. 1120 on his patrimonial estate on the north side of modern Newport near the head of the Medina estuary flowing to the Channel at Cowes, protected by Carisbrooke Castle.[42] The Winchester College Muniments contain an early confirmation of the foundation charter of St. Cross, Isle of Wight, but no other twelfth-century records. The confirmation was issued by Baldwin de Redvers ca. 1132–1136, with signatories similar to those of the foundation charter of Quarr Abbey dated 1131–1132.[43] One witness to this confirmation and grant was Gervase, abbot of the island, the first abbot of Quarr (r. 1140–1150). Baldwin de Redvers made additional grants, including his demesne land of Shide, Laford Mill, and Standen in Newport, property at Gurnard, Northwood near Cowes, and land at Hunny Hill with grazing rights in his moorlands.[44]

Tiron's first papal confirmation does not list St. Cross.[45] The priory's chapel was dedicated by Henry, bishop of Winchester, around 1140 in honour of the Holy Cross and is frequently confused with the mainland hospice of St. Cross outside Winchester. Subsequently St. Cross was listed in Tiron's papal confirmations.[46]

The priory expanded during and after the twelfth century. In modern downtown Newport, St. Cross owned many houses and gardens in Crocker Street (where its name is commemorated in St. Cross Lane) and High Street,[47] four shops in the Market Place,[48] and a house on St. Cross Pier.[49] Its milling and stock-raising are reflected in the taxation of 1291. St. Cross owned property on both banks of the Medina River running north to the port of Cowes. On the west bank St. Cross owned property in Northwood; on the east bank, it owned a croft called Great Balhill, now Newport's Sea Close, and by 1396 houses and crofts in Shide in East Cowes.[50] St. Cross owned property to the south in West Standen, Gatcombe, and Shorwell, a day's ride from port of Chale, and a house

---

41 Hollister, *Henry I*, 344. Hockey, *Quarr Abbey and its Lands*, 2–5 and 267.

42 *Monasticon Anglicanum*, ed. Dugdale, 6.2:1047. Knowles and Hadcock, *Medieval Religious Houses: England and Wales*, 106–7.

43 Hockey, *Quarr Abbey and its Lands*, 6. WCM, 3:839, no. 17213 (?Temp. Henry I).

44 Hockey, *Insula Vecta*, 46–48.

45 T1:201–3, no. 182 (1132/1133) and WCM, 2:422, no. 10624a (1133).

46 T2:60–63, specifically 60, no. 291; ibid., 2:63–67, specifically 66, no. 292 (1147); ibid., 2:98–102, specifically 101, no. 326 (1175–1176).

47 Crocker Street: WCM, 3:840, no. 17222 (1413); High Street: ibid., no. 17227 (1509).

48 Market Place: WCM, 3:839, no. 17214 (1361); ibid., 3:853–54, nos. 28681A–84 (1394–1638).

49 St. Cross Pier: WCM, 3:853, nos. 28667–75 (nineteenth century).

50 Norwood: WCM, 3:848, nos. 17456–57 (1804, 1852). Great Balhill: WCM, 3:839, no. 17215 (1337); ibid., 3:846, no. 17294 (ca. 1597–1616); ibid., 3:849, no. 28588 (1426); ibid., 3:849–50, no. 28595 (1593); ibid., 3:851, no. 28626 (1838). Shide: WCM, 3:840, no. 17226 (1455); ibid., 3:849–50, no. 28595 (1593); ibid., 3:851, no. 28626 (1838); ibid., 851–52, nos. 28631–39 (nineteenth century).

called Mirablesland[51] near coastal Niton east of Chale. St. Cross owned Cridmore Farm in Carisbrooke, Kern Farm in the parish of Brading to the east, and houses and property in two eastern ports: in St. Helens near Bembridge Harbour and Sandown.[52] Thus St. Cross was connected to the ports on the routes of transit between Southampton and Portsmouth and Harfleur and Caen.

As in England, Tironensian expansion in Wales was surpassed by that of the Cistercian order. Whether Tiron was perceived as Anglo-Norman or French in England and Wales is uncertain, but the lack of development suggests that the order was too French for the English and too Anglo-Norman for the Welsh. Notwithstanding, St. Dogmaels Abbey had three priories (one in Ireland), twelve churches, and two farms, so Tiron was an important presence in Pembrokeshire.

The priory of Wales, the future abbey of St. Dogmaels, was established ca. 1114–1115 by Robert FitzMartin, the son of Martin des Tours (d. ca. 1189–1196), a Norman knight who crossed the English Channel with William the Conqueror. William I established the earldoms of Chester, Hereford, and Shrewsbury on the Welsh marches, from which the Normans invaded Wales upon his death in 1087. Norman lords invaded southern Wales in 1093 upon the death of Rhys ap Tewdwr, prince of Deheubarth, establishing the major lordships of Cardigan, Pembroke, Brecon, and Glamorgan. Martin des Tours conquered Cemaes and built a castle at Nevern before his death.[53] He married Geva de Burci (b. ca. 1070), daughter and heiress of a land-holding baron in Somerset. The Normans replaced the *clas* organization of groups of churches affiliated with a monastery by a parochial organization of four bishoprics: Bangor, St. Davids, Llandaff, and St. Asaph. They controlled the dioceses by installing Norman bishops who swore obedience to Canterbury and upheld Benedictine monasticism.

Martin's son, Robert FitzMartin, also a benefactor of Savigny, established the "Priory of Wales" (St. Dogmaels) to replace the *clas* of Llandudoch in the diocese of St. Davids, protected by Cardigan Castle.[54] The foundation date coincided with the invasion of Wales in 1114 by Henry I, meant to stabilize the situation created by the Welsh princes' challenges to the strong Norman lordships. Henry I forced the election of the queen's Norman chaplain and chancellor Bernard to the bishopric of St. Davids and installed him after he professed obedience to Canterbury. In 1116 Henry I invested Henry I de Beaumont and Le Neubourg, earl of Warwick, with the lordship of Gower, a peninsula

---

[51] West Standen, Gatcombe, and Shorwell: WCM, 3:842, no. 17250 (n.d.). Mirablesland: WCM, 3:841, no. 17236 (1426).

[52] Cridmore Farm: WCM, 3:855–56, nos. 28728–32 (nineteenth century). Brading: WCM, 3:849, no. 17469 (ca. 1731). Hockey provides an overview of St. Cross's holdings in *Insula Vecta*, 46–48. St. Cross was to pay Tiron Abbey fifty marks per year from income from agriculture, rents, one and one-half mills of the original two given by Robert Colaws, a meadow and profits from cows and pigs. In 1295 its possessions included a horse, cattle, and pigs. In 1391 it was assessed at £10 3s 8d. and at its sale £5, VCH, Hampshire, 2:225nn3 and 9.

[53] Pritchard, *The History of St. Dogmael's Abbey*, 24–27, 60–61.

[54] Pritchard, *The History of St. Dogmael's Abbey*, 54–61.

extending into Carmarthen Bay east of Caldey Island, where Henry built Swansea Castle. Henry I's natural son Robert FitzRoy of Caen, earl of Gloucester, was also lord of Glamorgan, Wales, with its seat at Cardiff Castle.[55] Probably because of their Welsh connections, Earls Henry and Robert were listed as benefactors in the *Vita Bernardi*.[56] Thus the foundation of St. Dogmaels, strongly encouraged by Henry I, whose patronage of Tiron was a decisive factor in Robert's choice of order, was part of the Norman conquest of south Wales.

Robert FitzMartin was responsible for much of the landed endowment. St. Dogmaels held a large block of territory in the north of the lordship of Cemaes. Robert gave the ancient church of St. Dogmaels on the *clas* of Llandudoch with the adjacent lands, land for the new abbey, tracts by streams and on the Teifi estuary, and land to the south and in the Preseli range near the source of the East Cleddau River in Mynachlogddu south of Cardigan. His mother Geva gave Caldey Island in the Channel offshore from Tenby, and his wife, Matilda/Maud Peverel, gave Moylgrove on the coast. Robert also gave English property in south Devon: the manor of Rattery near Totnes with all its customs and three churches in Cockington, Rattery, and South Brent.

The elevation of St. Dogmaels occurred when Henry I invaded Wales in summer 1121. The king was making another attempt to stabilize the conflict between Norman marcher barons penetrating into *pura Wallia* and the Welsh efforts to deter them through battle. Abbot William also travelled to Wales and joined the king for the installation of Fulchard, the first abbot of St. Dogmaels, chosen by him and the chapter of Tiron. On that occasion a royal charter was issued, dated September 10, 1121 and witnessed by Henry I, given in William's presence, and bearing the seals of Henry I, Queen Adeliza, Bernard, bishop of St. Davids, and Robert FitzMartin, among others. The charter confirms the abbey property, with a detailed description of its boundaries between Cardigan and St. Dogmaels due south to Tenby (the departure point for Caldey Island), a distance of 52 kilometres. This royal charter is not in the Tironensian cartulary.[57]

When Henry I's firm control ended in 1135, civil war broke out in the British Isles. In Wales, Gruffydd ap Rhys ap Tewdwr (ca. 1081–1137) led a revolt against the marcher lords in Deheubarth. During this same period ca. 1138 Wales became consolidated into three kingdoms: Gwynedd, Deheubarth, and Powys, geographically divided by the Cambrian Mountains, dense forests, and marshes. The Welsh princes availed themselves of the anarchy and strengthened their position. St. Dogmaels was vulnerable because of its isolated coastal location and was pillaged for fifteen shiploads of valuable booty by four Welsh princes in 1138 after their failure to capture Cardigan Castle. A subsequent charter refers to "the honourable manner of life and hospitality of the aforesaid monks and no less to the poverty of the said monastery." The monks suffered during the

---

55 Hollister, *Henry I*, 236, 241–42.
56 VB, 11.98, AASS, Apr. 2:0246A; VB, trans. Cline, 104–6.
57 Pritchard, *The History of St. Dogmael's Abbey*, 27–28 and 45. *Monasticon Anglicanum*, ed. Dugdale, 4:130, no. 2. Farrer, *An Outline Itinerary of King Henry I*, 95–96, no. 435 (1121–1122).

war in Wales.[58] Subsequently St. Dogmaels prospered: its imposing buildings included an important library and the twelfth-century Y Felin water mill is believed to have been built by the monks. It established three coastal priories and was confirmed as a Tironensian abbey as late as 1516.[59]

Roscoe Howells describes the priory of St. Mary of Caldey as constructed on an earlier establishment and fortified with battlemented towers. A watch tower was built on the top of a cliff overlooking Priory Bay. The records mention ships calling at Caldey. The priory was built to house a dozen monks, and the local families were its lay congregation.[60] Together with the priors of Hamble, St. Cross, Andwell, and Titley, the religious of Caldey were in procurial relationships with the abbot of Tiron, acting as his legal representatives.

Around 1180–1190 Adam de la Roche (b. ca. 1160) founded another Tironensian priory dedicated to Saints Mary and Budoc at modern Lower Priory at the head of Hubberston Pill, a tidal inlet west of the modern port of Milford Haven, near Castle Pill and the manor of Pill. The community had about five monks.[61] The priory owned the churches of New Moat, Steynton, Roch, Little Newcastle, Johnston, Hubberston, Nolton, Freystrop, and Pontfaen. Pill and Hubberston, Steynton, Johnston, and Freystrop are on the road to Haverfordwest Castle, the lowest fordable point on the Western Cleddau. The route northeast runs to Little Newcastle, coastal Fishguard, and St. Dogmaels. During Bernard's episcopate St. Dogmaels acquired the land and church of Llys Prawst or Newton near St. Bride's Bay in Pembrokeshire. Nolton and Roch are northwest of Haverfordwest near the coast.[62] Pontfaen and New Moat are on a southeastern route between Fishguard and St. Dogmaels to Tenby and the crossing to Caldey Island. Pill's lands, over 1300 acres in the cantref of Roose or Rhos, were mainly acquired in the thirteenth century.

In 1192, the Roche family founded a priory of St. Dogmaels: St. Mary of Glascarrig, across St. George's Channel in Courtown Harbour, Wexford, Ireland.[63] They granted lands, woods, meadows, pastures, with a mill in their special lands of Consinquilos and Trahir, with the long marsh, fisheries, and salvage rights for wrecks in the Barony of Ballaghkeen.[64] Glascarrig and its churches and parishes mainly extended between Cork and Dublin with concentrations near Wexford and the market town of Gorey. It extended Tiron's chain of British coastal foundations and provided a centre for shipping between Ireland and the

---

58 Pritchard, *The History of St. Dogmael's Abbey*, 49–52.

59 T2:235, no. 419.

60 Howells, *Caldey*, 30–35.

61 Ludlow, "Pill Priory, 1996–1999," 41–80, esp. 47n29 (churches).

62 In the 1291 valuation the temporalities of Pill were assessed at £21 4s. 10d. St. Dogmaels and Pill had important income from these churches at the dissolution in 1536. Cowley, *The Monastic Order in South Wales*, 20, 63–64.

63 Pritchard, *The History of St. Dogmael's Abbey*, 159.

64 The charters of St. Dogmaels are in *Monasticon Anglicanum*, ed. Dugdale, 4:129–33. Pritchard, *The History of St. Dogmael's Abbey*, publishes charters of St. Dogmaels (41–55), Pill (123–38), and Glascarrig (159–67).

French and English coastal properties. It grew to be a wealthy priory and flourished until the Reformation.[65]

St. Dogmaels with its strategic priories of Caldey and Pill was a presence in the Pembrokeshire peninsula. With the abbey near Cardigan Castle on the River Teifi, Glascarrig across St. George's Channel, and Pill and Caldey Island on the Bristol Channel, the Welsh Tironensian foundations were well situated at the border of the Angevin trading zone for Atlantic trade north to Scotland and Norway and to western England. The spacing of these Tironensian properties suggests coastal shipping from St. Dogmaels via Caldey Island east to Torquay and on toward St. Cross, Hamble, and Southampton.

Tiron's earliest foundation in Scotland began concurrently with the priory of Wales, but its Scottish abbeys expanded to the point of becoming a separate order with nominal and procurial ties to the mother house. In the Borders, David I established Selkirk Abbey ca. 1113–1114, when he became earl of Huntingdon by marriage and claimed his inheritance in Strathclyde or Cumbria. Twelve monks from Tiron were sent under Abbot Ralph to the newly restored diocese of Glasgow headed by Bishop John, David's tutor.[66] The foundation was located in the vicinity of the Lindean church northwest of Selkirk on the Ettrick Water, a tributary of the River Tweed. David I gave the monks all his land at Selkirk with forest, pasture, and water rights. Selkirk Abbey was richly endowed with properties extending east of the abbey north to the Tweed, northeast along the Tweed Valley to the port of Berwick-upon-Tweed, and far south near Northampton. The dwellings in the burghs of Roxburgh and Berwick-upon-Tweed and in the town of Northampton provided both income and lodging for the monks of Selkirk.

David I became king of Scots in 1124 and, around 1128, moved the monks from Selkirk a day's ride east to Kelso, at the confluence of the Rivers Tweed and Teviot, near the royal court and the important market town of Roxburgh upriver of the port of Berwick-upon-Tweed. The transfer removed the monks from the diocese of Glasgow to the diocese of St. Andrews. Kelso was a frontier town of the kingdom, offering hospitality to English and Scottish sovereigns and a place for negotiating truces and treaties. Martin and Oram note, "The king was clearly concentrating resources at the heart of the Tweed Basin."[67]

Kelso Abbey, also Our Lady of Roxburgh, with its dependencies of Lesmahagow, Fogo, and Merchingley, must be considered in the broader context of David I's religious foundations. Oram notes that David I's mother Queen Margaret (ca. 1045–1093) brought the Benedictines to Dunfermline in 1073, and his older brother Alexander I introduced the Augustinian order at Scone 1114x1122. David I extended his patronage of the Benedictines to the Tironensians, Augustinians, and Cistercians. Before his accession David I established Selkirk Abbey in 1114 and the Augustinian Jedburgh Priory in 1118 (elevated 1147). In 1128, concurrently with Kelso, David I established Augustinian

---

65 Gwynn and Hadcock, *Medieval Religious Houses: Ireland*, 112–13 (chap. 6). Glascarrig's possessions in 1559 amounted to £16 14s. 0d.
66 ES, 2:163, citing the *Chronicle of Melrose*, 66, ca. 1119 (Ralph).
67 Martin and Oram, "Medieval Roxburgh," 377.

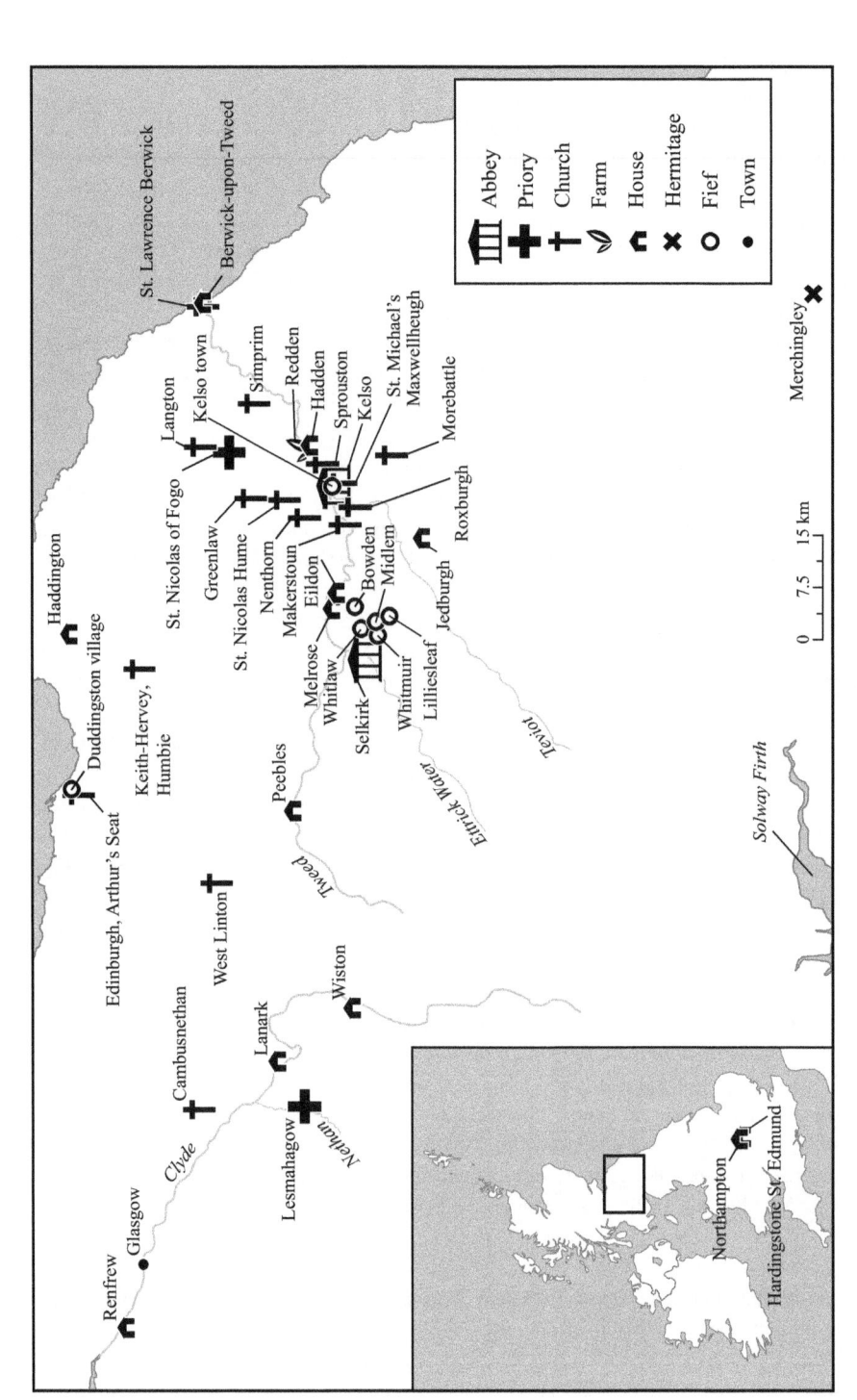

Map 6.2. Kelso Abbey

Table 6.2. Kelso Abbey

Local and to Berwick-upon-Tweed
Kelso (N.D. de Roxburgh); abbey; 1128; David I
Kelso town; 1128; David I
Nenthorn+St. Mary's; farm and church
St. Michael's Maxwellheugh; church; <1159; Herbert of Maxwellheugh
Roxburgh; two houses, three churches, schools, multure; 1114–1128; David I; Selkirk
Greenlaw; church with Lambden chapel; <1165; Cospatrick III, earl of Dunbar
Sprouston; church and quarry; 1114–1128; David I
Redden; farm; 1128; David I
St. Nicholas Hume; church; <1165; Cospatrick III, earl of Dunbar
Hadden; house; <1165; Walde
Makerstoun; church; <1165; Walter Corbet
Morebattle (Mow); church; <1165; Uchtred of Mow
Jedburgh; house; <1165; William I
North of Kelso: Greenlaw N 13 km; Sprouston, 5 km; Hume, 10 km; Hadden, NW 8 km. Southwest of Kelso: Roxburgh, 7 km; Makerstoun, 8 km; Jedburgh, 18 km; and Morebattle, SE 12 km
Simprim; church; <1165; Hye+son Peter
Fogo (St. Nicolas); priory; <1165; Cospatrick III, earl of Dunbar
Langton; church; <1165; Roger of Eu
St. Lawrence Berwick; land+church; <1159; Robert FitzWilliam
Berwick-upon-Tweed; two houses; 1114–1128; David I, Selkirk; Walkelin son of Ernebald
Berwick-upon-Tweed is 37 km NE of Kelso. Simprim and Fogo are 19 km NE of Kelso and 11 km apart. Langton (modern Gavinton) is 5 km N of Fogo
Kelso Abbey to Glasgow and Renfrew
Bowden; town; 1114; David I; Selkirk
Midlem; town; 1114; David I; Selkirk
Lilliesleaf; town; 1128; David I; Selkirk
Whitlaw; town; 1128; David I; Selkirk
Whitmuir; town; <1165; William I; Selkirk
Selkirk; abbey; 1114; David I, John, bishop of Glasgow (Abbot Bernard)
Eildon; house; 1114; David I; Selkirk (Abbot Bernard)
Melrose; house; 1114; David I, Selkirk (Abbot Bernard)
Peebles; house; <1165; William I
Lanark; house; <1165; William I
Wiston; house; <1165;
Lesmahagow; priory; 1144; David I+John, bishop of Glasgow
Cambusnethan; church; <1165; William Finemund
Renfrew; house+ship; <1165; William I
Kelso, W 18–21 km to Midlem, Bowden and Lilliesleaf, W 6–8 km to Selkirk, NW 34 km to Peebles, W 44 km to Lanark (with Wiston S 20 km)
Route 1: Lanark, SW 11 km to Lesmahagow, NW 38 km to Glasgow
Route 2: Lanark, NW 16 km to Cambusnethan near Wishaw, NW 30 km to Glasgow, W 11 km to Renfrew on the Clyde

(continued)

Table 6.2. (Cont.)

Kelso Abbey to Edinburgh 　**West Linton**; church; <1165; Richard Cumin 　**Edinburgh**; house 　**Edinburgh, Arthur's Seat**; pilgrimage site; 1128; David I; dispute with Alwin, abbot of Holyrood 　**Duddingston village (Trauerlen)**; town 　**Haddington**; house<1165; William I 　**Keith-Hervey, Humbie**; church; <1165; William I Route 1: Kelso, NW 61 km to Peebles, NW 22 km to West Linton, NE 27 km to Edinburgh Route 2: Kelso Abbey, NW 40 km to Humbie, NW 21 km to Edinburgh, or Humbie, NE 11 km to Haddington, W 28 km to Edinburgh
England 　**Merchingley**; Northumberland; church; 1168 　**Hardingstone St. Edmund Northampton**; house; 1114; David I; Selkirk 　**Northampton**; house; 1114; David I; Selkirk

Holyrood Abbey outside Edinburgh.[68] At that time the Tironensians represented a more austere form of reformed monasticism. In 1132 Cistercians from Clairvaux established their first abbey in northern England, Rievaulx in Yorkshire, and won David I's patronage for even greater austerity and spirituality. David I resolved to establish the Cistercians between Selkirk and Kelso at Melrose in the Tweed Valley.

A new religious foundation acquired both the land and the cult of its location, often supplanting or absorbing an earlier religious community while remaining a pilgrimage site to venerate a Celtic saint. Although David I gave Selkirk part of Melrose, he withheld the site of the old monastery of Melrose, where Saint Cuthbert (ca. 634–687) was venerated. In 1136 David I granted the monks of Saint Cuthbert the church of St. Mary in Berwick in exchange for the church of Melrose and their rights and property there. David I then brought Cistercian monks from Rievaulx to represent the cult of St. Cuthbert in Scotland and settled them on formerly Tironensian land at Melrose. Oram notes that the site of the new Melrose Abbey "was in the heart of a concentration of important royal estates in one of the most densely populated and intensively exploited zones of the Southern Uplands." David I was careful to delineate the boundaries to avoid any dispute between the two houses.[69] Thus two reformed Benedictine orders coexisted in Scotland under royal patronage.

By that time the Tironensians were well established and richly endowed at Kelso near the royal court. Kelso's land was excellent, with loam by the rivers for early abundant crops. Black cattle and sheep were reared in the hills to the north. In the northwest, the soil was red clay. The Sprouston quarry, a short distance from town, produced light

---

[68] Oram, *David I*, 145, 159–65.
[69] Oram, *David I*, 163.

blue freestone. By the end of the twelfth century Roxburgh was an international trading centre, particularly for wool from the Border abbeys and estates. St. James' Fair, held in late July and early August, drew foreign merchants who subsequently shipped the goods for which they had transacted in Roxburgh to the port of Berwick-upon-Tweed. Nearby Kelso Abbey prospered from the expansion of Roxburgh and its involvement in continental trade. David I gave Kelso responsibility for the churches and schools of Roxburgh.[70] Moving from a rural to an urban setting to facilitate trade is a recurrent aspect of Tironensian monasticism. The move to Kelso parallels Tiron's establishment of a priory and headquarters in Chartres with its important market in the 1120s, and its headquarters in Paris in 1138 with properties near the market and quays. Kelso's holdings extended east to Berwick-upon-Tweed, north to Edinburgh, and west to Glasgow.

The scope of the property of Kelso Abbey after 1147 is evident from two confirmations issued by Malcolm IV in 1159 and William I "the Lion" ca. 1165–1166.[71] Kelso's holdings included two abbeys, two priories, seventeen churches, two farms, and sixteen houses. The abbey owned the church of the Virgin Mary and the village of Kelso, with land extending to Nenthorn in the Mers, and the local church of St. Michael's Maxwellheugh. Kelso owned the following property and privileges in the vicinity of the abbey. In Greenlaw it owned the church with Lambden Chapel. In Roxburgh, the abbey had tax income, all the churches and schools, and two and one-half tofts, multure, and a share of the fishing station.[72] In the parish of Sprouston, Kelso owned land with dwellings, pasture, and the church with its lands, together with Redden, with land and water rights, pastures, and moors for peat. They had land in an unknown Presterbridge, Roxburgh, granted by the king in exchange for the monks' holding of land at the church of St. Lawrence of Berwick-upon-Tweed. The abbey owned the church of St. Nicholas of Hume with land and a field in the nearby village. The monks had land and a toft and croft in Hadden to the northwest. Kelso was given two churches with land to the south: Makerstoun and Morebattle, as well as one toft in Jedburgh to the southwest.[73] Along the roads to Berwick-upon-Tweed, Kelso was given two churches midway: Simprim, and Fogo, which became a dependent priory of Kelso between 1253 and 1297.[74] Kelso retained Selkirk's holdings, including the church of St. Lawrence.[75]

Kelso was given property along roads leading to its priory of Lesmagahow and on to Glasgow and Renfrew on the Firth of Clyde, a distance of 149 kilometres. To the west Kelso retained its Selkirk property: Bowden, Midlem, and Lilliesleaf, Whitlaw, Whitmuir, and

---

70 Roxburgh had several churches: St. John the Evangelist in Roxburgh Castle, St. James with St. James Fair, north of the burgh near the Tweed, and the church of the Holy Sepulchre within the burgh. Martin and Oram, "Medieval Roxburgh," 372–78. *Kelso Liber*, 1:5–7, no. 2.

71 *Acts of Malcolm IV*, 1:192–94, no. 131 (1159). *Acts of William I*, 166–68, no. 63 (ca. 1165–1166).

72 *Kelso Liber*, 2:350, no. 460.

73 *Acts of William I*, 167.

74 Cowan and Easson, *Medieval Religious Houses: Scotland*, 67.

75 *Kelso Liber*, 2:350, no. 460.

Selkirk itself with its church and land and water rights. On the road to Glasgow, Selkirk had single tofts in Peebles and Lanark. Kelso had one toft in Wiston south of Lanark, the priory of Lesmahagow southwest of Lanark, and the church of Cambusnethan northwest of Lanark. Cambusnethan and Lesmahagow were southern approaches to Glasgow. Renfrew is west of Glasgow, and in that port town Kelso had a toft and a ship free from all customs duties.[76] The distances were feasible for lodgings for business trips to Glasgow.

Toward Edinburgh, Kelso owned the church of West Linton northwest of its toft in Peebles, with Edinburgh a day's ride further northeast. David I repaid a loan from Kelso with a gift of choice property in Edinburgh: the village of Duddingston, easements in Cameron, and the pilgrimage site of Arthur's Seat. Kelso also owned a toft in Haddington east of Edinburgh midway between that city and the port of Dunbar. Southwest of Haddington Kelso owned the church of Keith (Keith-Hervey) in the parish of Humbie. Kelso's expansion into Edinburgh contrasts sharply with Tiron's absence in London.

Kelso Abbey itself was an economic centre, but around 1290 Kelso had several granges, where lay brothers and tenants raised oats, barley, and wheat, pastured large flocks of sheep and smaller herds of cattle and horses, kept swine and oxen for plowing, brewed ale, and used carts to haul peat. Kelso also owned at least one vessel and engaged in trade and fishing.[77] In a document that Francesco Balducci Pegolotti (fl. 1290–1347) incorporated into his book entitled *La practica della Mercatura*, Kelso is listed as a thirteenth- to fourteenth-century supplier of wool to Flanders.[78] Thus Kelso was engaged in commerce and international trade.

David I and John, bishop of Glasgow, founded the priory of St. Machutus of Lesmahagow in 1144 on the River Nethan a day's ride southeast of Glasgow.[79] Perhaps they extended Kelso's holdings westward because of the refuge given at Tiron to Bishop John in 1136 or 1137. The deed of Pope Innocent IV confirmed the rights of the church and cell of Lesmahagow,[80] and King Alexander II (r. 1214–1249) granted letters of protection to the priory in 1222 and 1230.[81] Lesmahagow was a large parish with extensive possessions.

In England, the road between western Carlisle and eastern Newcastle-upon-Tyne runs 90 kilometres between the coasts. Merchingley in Northumberland, occupied by two monks of Kelso, was granted by Walter de Bolbec in 1168.[82] The hermitage, which has disappeared, was situated in the parish of Slaley near the March burn, 40 kilometres

---

[76] Tiron had one ship free of cain from Henry, son of the king of Scotland, which could call anywhere freely. T2:159, no. 377 (ca. 1250). An earlier version specified "once a year," ibid., 1:80–81, no. 60 (1124–1145).

[77] T1: 80–81, no. 60 (1124–1145).

[78] Cunningham, *The Growth of English Industry and Commerce during the Early and Middle Ages*, 60 (appendix D).

[79] *Kelso Liber*, 1:9, no. 8.

[80] *Kelso Liber*, 2:350–54, no. 460.

[81] *Kelso Liber*, 1:150–51, no. 182 (1222); ibid., 1:151–52, no. 184 (1230).

[82] Cowan and Easson, *Medieval Religious Houses: Scotland*, 71.

west of Newcastle-upon-Tyne.[83] In the English East Midlands, Kelso had income from and connections with the manor of Hardingstone St. Edmund and the town of Northampton. Their oversight extended Kelso's influence far south of the Borders.

During the twelfth century Kelso became a separate congregation with nominal and procurial ties to Tiron. Kelso was released from all subjection and any exactions by Robert of Scone, bishop of St. Andrews (r. 1123/1124–1159) in 1147.[84] Thompson describes the annoyance at St. Andrews and Canterbury about the abbot of Kelso's ambition in 1157.[85] Kelso's liberty was asserted ca. 1160, with the accession of Abbot Stephan I of Tiron.[86] With the death of Herbert, bishop of Glasgow, in 1164, personal ties between Tiron and Kelso were broken. Abbots John and Osbert (r. 1180–1203) sought to obtain the status of *filia specialis* of the Roman Church for Kelso, making it independent of Tiron Abbey. Pope Alexander III issued a bull dated 1165 to Abbot John in Rome, describing Kelso as a *filia specialis* of the papacy but ambivalently omitting the customary phrases *jus et jurisdictio* and *nullo mediante*.[87] Thompson describes the ensuing litigation that resulted in Alexander III's confirmation of Kelso's subordination to Tiron in a bull dated April 22, probably 1173.[88] Stephan I's authority was confirmed, and the Tironensian abbeys of Kelso, St. Dogmaels, Le Gué-de-Launay, Le Tronchet, Bois-Aubry, Asnières, and Joug-Dieu were to obey the *Rule* and Stephan's institutions. In 1176 John, abbot of Kelso, was involved in a dispute over subjection with the abbot of Tiron, concerning which one was greater.[89] In 1182 Lucius III (b. ca. 1100, r. 1181–1185) confirmed the rights and liberties of Kelso and clarified any ambiguity about its Roman liberty fostered in 1165.[90] The high annual cash payment suggests that this unambiguous bull established Kelso's Roman

---

83 *Kelso Liber,* 1:219–22, nos. 264–67.

84 *Kelso Liber,* 2:339, no. 443.

85 Thompson, *The Monks of Tiron,* 174n89, citing *The Letters of John of Salisbury,* vol. 1, *The Early Letters (1153–61),* ed. and trans. W. J. Miller and H. E. Butler, rev. C. N. L. Brooke (Edinburgh: Nelson, 1955), 78.

86 *Kelso Liber,* 2:337, no. 439.

87 *Kelso Liber,* 2:359–60, no. 467.

88 Thompson, *The Monks of Tiron,* 174–76.

89 ES, 2:263, citing the *Chronicle of Melrose,* 80, s.a. 1165; ibid., *Chronicle of Melrose,* 88, s.a. 1176.

90 In one bull, Lucius III stated: "[…] *specialem nos oportet curam inpendere que ad iurisdictionem beati Petri et nostram noscuntur nullo mediante spectare*" *Kelso Liber,* 2:359, no. 466. In another bull issued the same day, Lucius III stated that Kelso had been "*specialiter beati Petri iuris existit, ad exemplar sancte recordationis Innocentii, Adriani, et Alexandri Romanorum pontificum* [Innocent II, Hadrian IV (r. 1154–1159) and Alexander III]." Kelso's immunities from the bishops of Glasgow and St. Andrews were confirmed, and it was granted immunity from excommunication by any bishop or archbishop or papal legate. *Scotia Pontificia, Papal Letters to Scotland before the Pontificate of Innocent III,* ed. Robert Somerville (Oxford: Clarendon Press, 1982), 106–10, no. 114. MSS A=Edinburgh, SRO, Ch 7/3; MSS B, Edinburgh NLS, Adv. 29.4.2 (vol. 5), fols. 44r–49r. Kelso's annual payment for direct subjection to the papacy was one ounce of gold or one silver mark. Robinson, *The Papacy 1073–1198,* 270, notes that the average payment of the great majority of monasteries, according to the *Liber Censuum,* was two golden *marabotini*; one ounce of gold equalled seven *marabotini*.

liberty retroactively. The *filia specialis* bull, issued by Celestine III (r. 1191–1198) on March 13, 1192, removed the Scottish church from submission to York and Canterbury and placed it in immediate subjection to the Holy See.[91]

Thus Kelso's independence from Tiron was confirmed repeatedly in the thirteenth century.[92] Notwithstanding, the business relationship persisted and was reflected in charters that seem contradictory. In 1233, the monks of Kelso were described as proctors of the monks of Holy Trinity of Tiron.[93] Tiron regularly designated the priors of Andwell, St. Cross, Isle of Wight, and Titley as its proctors in England.[94] St. Dogmaels issued a bond for a one-year loan from Tiron, in 1292, repayable on the Isle of Wight (St. Cross).[95] The abbot of Arcisses was designated proctor general in England in 1362.[96]

Thus Tiron's relationship with its British abbeys and alien priories entailed nominal assertions of superiority to formalize mutually profitable business dealings. A sealed copy of Alexander III's important bull affirming Tiron's superiority over Kelso and other daughter abbeys was prepared 1217–1234, certified by the bishop of Chartres and the abbots of four Chartrain monasteries, and sent to England.[97] Abbot Stephan II (r. 1255–1273) purportedly obtained letters from Alexander IV (r. 1254–1261) in 1255 affirming him as the head of the abbeys of Kelso, St. Dogmaels, and Tiron's French abbeys.[98] Tiron claimed to be owed oaths of submission by its abbots in France and in the British Isles 1479–1558, long after the sale of the alien priories (1391) and during the dissolution 1536–1541, and summoned them to attend the Tironensian general chapter under threat of excommunication as late as 1537–1548.[99] Kelso asserted its independence but acted as Tiron's proctor in Scottish trade, and Tiron asserted its authority over Kelso to validate its representation.

David I's son Earl Henry predeceased his father by one year and was buried at Kelso. David I ensured the succession for his grandson, Malcolm IV (d. 1165). The succession passed to Malcolm's brother William I "the Lion," who ruled until 1214. These grandsons

---

91 R. K. Hannay, "The Date of the *Filia Specialis* Bull," *Scottish Historical Review* 23 (April 1926): 171–77.
92 *Kelso Liber*, 2:357–58, no. 464 (1119–1216); ibid., 328–29, no. 428 (1201); ibid., 2:308, no. 393 (1224).
93 *Kelso Liber*, 2:310–11, no. 398.
94 WCM, 2:427, no. 10663 (1266); ibid., 2:107, no. 2874 (1315); ibid., 2:209, no. 4280a (1327) (Andwell). WCM, 2:107, no. 2873 (1297) (St. Cross). WCM, 2:209, no. 4280a (1327) (Titley).
95 WCM, 2:427, no. 10664 (1292) (St. Cross).
96 WCM, 2:430, no. 10682; ibid., 2:209, no. 4278; ibid., 2:432, no. 19703 (1362) (Arcisses).
97 T2: 92–93, no. 320. WCM, 2:95, no. 2784. "(1159–1181, June 22) 'Anagnie'. Certified copy of Bull of Pope Alexander III to Abbot and brethren of Monastery of Tiron confirming possessions of certain abbacies [named] in France and institution of abbots. Certifiers: Walter, Bp of Chartres (r. 1217–1234), Guy (I, d. 1231), Abbot of St Peter's (Saint-Père) Chartres, Guarinus (Guérin) (1225), Abbot of St John de Valleia (Saint-Jean-en-Vallée), Guarinus (Guérin), Abbot of St Mary (Notre-Dame) de Josaphat (1215), Peter, Abbot of St Karaunus (St Chéron) (1235), Chartres. Seal."
98 GC, 8:1264. The wording is identical to the certified copy in WCM, 2:95, no. 2784 (1217–1234).
99 T2:234–37, no. 419 (1516). IS-ADEL, 6:163–66, specifically 165, H 1424 (1531–1548).

of David I continued the pious work of erecting and endowing monasteries. The abbots of Kelso furthered new Tironensian monasteries in northern Scotland to the point of being referred to as the heads of the "Congregation of Kelso."

In 1174 William I rashly invaded England while Henry II was dealing with an attack on Normandy by Louis VII. Upon his return, Henry II did public penance at the tomb of Archbishop Thomas Becket (ca. 1120–1170) in Canterbury and learned next day that the Scottish king had been captured in Yorkshire. Under the terms of the Treaty of Falaise of December 1175, William I acknowledged Henry II's lordship over himself and his lands and surrendered five Scottish castles to English control. English garrisons were stationed in Berwick, Roxburgh, and Edinburgh Castles until December 1189, when the treaty's terms were abrogated by the Quitclaim of Canterbury.[100] The English occupation gave William I an incentive to extend the active exploitation of the royal demesne to the north of the Firths of Forth and Tay. The abbeys of Arbroath and Lindores are in the shires of Angus and Fife on the east coast of Scotland northeast and south of Dundee on the Firth of Tay and southwest of Aberdeen. The nearest towns are Dundee and Perth, where Tiron had a ship during Abbot William's reign. The port of Aberdeen became the important new centre for the Scottish royal courts. Accordingly the northern abbeys of Arbroath and Lindores acquired strategic holdings northwest of Aberdeen and south of Moray Firth, which favoured trade and communication with Aberdeen.

Arbroath's properties were heavily concentrated between Dundee and Aberdeen, with an east–west river route along the Dee and coastal properties along Moray Firth toward Inverness. Arbroath had a church on the east–west route between Newcastle-upon-Tyne and Carlisle.

William I founded the abbey of Arbroath in 1178 and dedicated it to Thomas Becket, whom he had known and admired as a boy at Henry II's court. William's political need to expand to the north was combined with his devout wish to honour and placate the saint because of the coincidence of Henry II's penance at Canterbury and William's capture.[101] To this end he chose to found a Tironensian abbey, perhaps feeling that an austere Cistercian foundation would be less pleasing to the former Lord Chancellor. Built of red sandstone by the monks of Kelso but not subject to that abbey,[102] Arbroath was situated on the North Sea northeast of the Firth of Tay in the fishing port by that name. Founded "rich," it was a "hermit" abbey writ large. As a hermit Bernard of Tiron sold his crafts, travelled extensively, and settled disputes. The abbot of Arbroath was responsible for a large market, a harbour that accommodated both local and continental trade, and a regality court with civil and criminal jurisdiction granted solely by the king. In addition to its lighthouse window, the "O" of Arbroath, the abbey maintained a pier in the harbour and placed a bell buoy on a dangerous submerged reef called Bell Rock. The abbey was deeply engaged in maritime trade.

---

[100] Owen, *William the Lion*, 55.
[101] Owen, *William the Lion*, 19, 53, 79.
[102] *Liber S. Thome de Aberbrothoc*, 1:8, no. 2. "*monachos nostros illi ad edificandum locum illum accomodavimus.*" Cowan and Easson, *Medieval Religious Houses: Scotland*, 58.

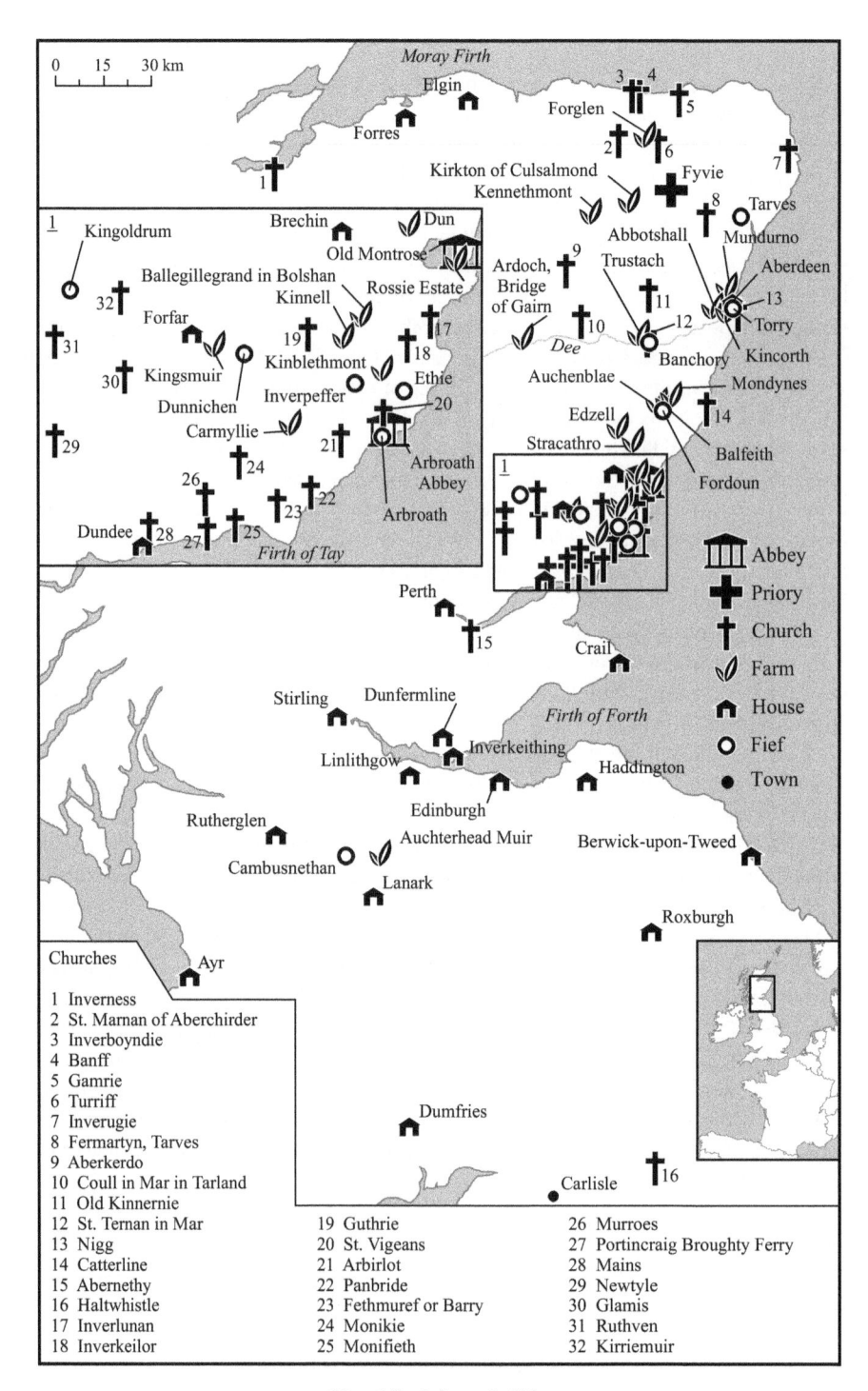

Map 6.3. Arbroath Abbey

Churches
1. Inverness
2. St. Marnan of Aberchirder
3. Inverboyndie
4. Banff
5. Gamrie
6. Turriff
7. Inverugie
8. Fermartyn, Tarves
9. Aberkerdo
10. Coull in Mar in Tarland
11. Old Kinnernie
12. St. Ternan in Mar
13. Nigg
14. Catterline
15. Abernethy
16. Haltwhistle
17. Inverlunan
18. Inverkeilor
19. Guthrie
20. St. Vigeans
21. Arbirlot
22. Panbride
23. Fethmuref or Barry
24. Monikie
25. Monifieth
26. Murroes
27. Portincraig Broughty Ferry
28. Mains
29. Newtyle
30. Glamis
31. Ruthven
32. Kirriemuir

Table 6.3. Arbroath Abbey

Royal Burghs **Arbroath**; house; 1178; William I **Berwick-upon-Tweed**; house; 1178; William I **Edinburgh**; house; 1178; William I **Roxburgh**; house; 1178; William I **Haddington**; house; 1178; William I **Linlithgow**; house; 1178; William I **Stirling**; house; 1178; William I **Rutherglen**; house; 1178; William I **Lanark**; house; 1178; William I **Inverkeithing**; house; 1178; William I **Dunfermline**; house; 1178; William I **Crail**; house; 1178; William I **Perth**; house+fishing station; 1178; William I **Elgin**; house; 1178; William I **Ayr**; house; 1178; William I **Dumfries**; house; 1178; William I **Old Montrose**; abbey, house; 1178; William I **Aberdeen**; house; 1178; William I **Torry**; fief; 1178; William I **Forfar**; house; 1178; William I **Dundee**; house; 1178; William I
Arbroath Abbey to Dundee **Arbroath (St. Thomas)**; abbey; 1178; William I **Inverpeffer**; fief; <1213; William I **Panbride**; church; <1213; William I **Fethmuref or Barry**; church; <1213; William I+William Cumin (b. 1163), Sheriff of Forfar (1195–1211), Justiciar of Scotland (1205–1233) **Monifieth**; church Célidé; <1213; Gilchrist, earl of Angus **Portincraig Broughty Ferry**; church+fishing station; <1213; Gilchrist, earl of Angus Coastal route: Arbroath, SW 11 km to Panbride via Inverpeffer (modern East Haven Airport); W 35 km to Fethmuref or Barry; SW 5 km to Monifieth; SW 4 km to Portincraig, and the fishing station at Broughty Ferry; W 8 km to Dundee **Arbirlot**; church; <1213; Roger, bishop of St. Andrews **Carmyllie**; farm **Monikie**; church; <1213; William I **Murroes**; church; <1213; Gilchrist, earl of Angus **Mains**; church; <1213; Gilchrist, earl of Angus Inland route: Arbroath, W 5 km to Arbirlot, W 8 km to Carmyllie, SW 8 km to Monikie near Barry, SW 13 km to the church of Murroes, SW 8 km to Mains (Stradechty Comitis), S 3 km to Dundee **Abernethy**; church; <1213; William I *Perth is 37 km W of Dundee. Abernethy is 36 km SW of Dundee and 15 km SW of Perth*

(*continued*)

Table 6.3. (Cont.)

Arbroath Abbey to Forfar 　**St. Vigeans**; church 　**Kinblethmont**; farm 　**Kinnell**; farm 　**Ballegillegrand in Bolshan**; farm; <1213; Donald, abbot of Brechin 　**Guthrie**; church; <1213; William I 　**Dunnichen**; town; 1178; William I 　**Kingsmuir**; farm 　**Forfar**; two houses; <1213; Hugh, chancellor of William I, Andrew, bishop of Caithness Arbroath, N 3 km to St. Vigeans and Adinaglas, N 7 km to Kinblethmont, N 7 km to Kinnell, NE 3 km to Ballegillegrand in Bolshan, W 5 km to Guthrie, W 8 km to Dunnichen, W 3 km to Kingsmuir, W 3 km to Forfar *Forfar is 24 km NW of Arbroath* 　**Kirriemuir**; church; William I and Gilchrist, earl of Angus 　**Kingoldrum**; fief and church; 1178; William I 　**Glamis**; church; 1178; William I 　**Ruthven**; church; <1213; Robert of London 　**Newtyle**; church; 1178; William I *Kirriemuir is 11 km NW of Forfar and Kingoldrum is 7 km NW of Kirriemuir. Glamis is 10 km SW of Forfar. Ruthven is 12 km SW of Kirriemuir and 13 km W of Glamis. Newtyle is 11 km SE of Ruthven, 15 km SW of Glamis, and 17 km NW of the church of Mains, 13 km N of Dundee* Kirriemuir to Dundee: Kirriemuir, S 9 km to Glamis, S 8 km to Mains, S 3 km to Dundee 　**Perth; fishing station at "Stok"**; 1213; William I 　**Carse in Stirling**; saltwork; 1178; William I 　**Auchterhead Muir**; farm <1213; Thomas Thancard
Arbroath Abbey to Montrose and Aberdeen 　**Ethie**; town; <1213; Willliam I 　**Inverkeilor**; church; Walter de Berkeley (ca. 1136–ca. 1190), lord of Inverkeilor, chamberlain of William I 　**Inverlunan**; church; <1213; William I 　**Old Montrose+North Esk fishing station** near Montrose; 1178; William I Arbroath, N 3 km to St. Vigeans, N 7 km to Kinblethmont, N 7 km to Ethie village and the church and lands in Inverkeilor, N 5 km to the church and lands in Inverlunan, N 8 km to the house and the abbey of St. Mary of Old Montrose *Montrose is 21 km N of Arbroath*
West of Montrose 　**Dun+Hedderwick**; saltwork and farm; <1213; William I 　**Brechin**; house and farm; <1213; Turpin, bishop of Brechin 　**Stracathro**; farm; <1213; Turpin, bishop of Brechin 　**Rossie Estate**; farm; <1213; Hugh Malherbe 　**Edzell**; farm; <1213; John Abbe (son of Malise), abbot of Brechin (floruit 1210 x 1223) *Brechin is 23 km N of Arbroath and 12 km N of Bolshan. Dun is 9 km E of Brechin and 7 km W of Montrose. Stracathro is 8 km NE of Brechin and 4 km SE of Edzell*

Table 6.3. (Cont.)

Montrose to Stonehaven and Aberdeen
   Fordoun; fief
   Auchenblae; farm
   Mondynes; farm; <1213; William I+Philip de Melville, Justicitar of Scotland 1241–1244+wife Eve, Walter son of Sibald ca. 1200, and Richard de Freville (b. ca. 1182)+wife Eve
   Balfeith; farm; <1213; Humphrey de Berkeley (1167–ca. 1225)
   Catterline; church; <1213; William I+**Glaskeler** in Catterline; farm; <1213; John de Montfort+**Rath** in Catterline; farm; <1213; William FitzBernard
   Nigg; church; fief of **Torry**, Aberdeen <1213; William I
   Kincorth; ferry-boat (farm symbol); Aberdeen; William I
   Abbotshall; farm; Aberdeen
   Mundurno; farm; Aberdeen; <1213; Roger de St. Michael
Montrose, N 23 km to Fordoun, Mondynes, and Balfeith and land on the Bervie, E 17 km to Glaskeler in Catterline, N 10 km to Stonehaven, NE 29 km to Aberdeen

West of Stonehaven and Aberdeen
   Banchory; fief +church; 1178; William I
   St. Ternan in Mar; church; William I
   Ardoch, Bridge of Gairn; farm
   Trustach; farm+wood; <1213; Thomas de Lundyn, the Durward
   Aberkerdo; church; Gilchrist, earl of Mar
   Coull in Mar in Tarland; church; <1213; William I
Banchory is 27 km NW of Stonehaven and 32 km SW of Aberdeen. Trustach was 14 km W of Banchory and 5 km S of Kincardine O'Neil
Aberkerdo near Kildrummy is 46 km NW of Banchory and 23 km N of Tarland

Aberdeen inland to Kennethmont and Culsalmond
   Old Kinnernie (St. Mary's); church; 1204 x 1211; Thomas de Lundyn, the Durward
   Kennethmont; farm
   Kirkton of Culsalmond; farm; <1213; David, earl of Huntingdon; brother of William I
Aberdeen, W 25 km to the church of Old Kinnernie NW of Echt, NW 35 km to Kennethmont, NE 18 km to Culsalmond
Old Kinnernie NW of Echt is 20 km N of Banchory and 24 km W of Aberdeen. The distance from Aberdeen NW to Kennethmont is 54 km

North of Aberdeen to Moray Firth
   Tarves; church+fief; <1213; William I
   Fyvie; priory; ca. 1178, Willliam I; 1285, Reginald le Cheyne+**St. Mary+All Saints**, priory church; 1179; William I, Fergus, earl of Buchan+**St. Peter**, parish church, Fyvie; 1179; William I, Fergus, earl of Buchan
   Turriff; church;<1213; Marjorie, countess of Buchan
   Forglen; land with Brecbennoch (Molymusk reliquary); <1213; William I
   St. Marnan of Aberchirder; church; <1213; William I
   Inverboyndie; church; <1213; William I
   Banff; church; <1213; William I
   Gamrie; church; <1213; William I
   Forres; house

(continued)

154   EXPANSION IN THE BRITISH ISLES

Table 6.3. (Cont.)

Inverness; church; <1213; William I **Inverugie**; church; <1213; Ralph Namus (le Neym) Aberdeen, N 8 km to Mundurno, NW 21 km to Tarves, NW 15 km to Fyvie, N 15 km to Turriff (with Forglen and Aberdicher respectively W 7 km and 13 km) *Tarves and Fyvie are respectively 28 km and 40 km N of Aberdeen. Forglen is 21 km N of Fyvie* From Turriff, Forglen, and Aberdicher, N respectively 21 km, 18 km, and 17 km to Inverboyndie, E to Banff and Gamrie respectively 2 km and 15 km *The port of Banff on Moray Firth is 73 km NW of Aberdeen. The church of Inverness is 117 km W of Banff. Inverugie is 55 km N of Aberdeen and 5 km NW of Peterhead*
South of Glasgow **Cambusnethan**; fief; William I *Cambusnethan is 7 km W of Auchterhead Muir*
England **Haltwhistle** in Tynedale, Northumberland; church; 1178; William I Carlisle to Newcastle-upon-Tyne: Carlisle, E 36 km to Haltwhistle (Arbroath), E 35 km to Merchingly (Kelso) near Slaley, E 35 km to Newcastle-upon-Tyne

Arbroath was well endowed by the king and the leading local families at its foundation.[103] William I's natural son Robert of London (d. 1227), Gilchrist, earl of Angus (d. after 1207), Fergus, earl of Buchan (d. ca. 1214), Gilchrist, earl of Mar (ca. 1139–ca. 1228), Roger de Beaumont, bishop of St. Andrews (r. 1189–1202), Turpin, bishop of Brechin (r. 1178–1198), and Donald, abbot of Brechin (late twelfth century) appear as donors on the first confirmation charter, dated 1211–1214. The abbey enjoyed royal and episcopal patronage and noble and local support. William I and his earls and bishops founded Arbroath with a network of properties concentrated on three major routes to the ports of Dundee, Aberdeen, and Banff, together with holdings in and near other burghs. Arbroath's holdings included two abbeys, one priory, thirty-eight churches, and twenty-seven houses. William I gave Arbroath houses in all the royal burghs. These houses are preponderantly in coastal burghs and most are near Edinburgh and Glasgow, with the exceptions of those in Elgin far north on Moray Firth and in Dumfries far south near Solway Firth. Arbroath owned two burghs: Arbroath with its regality, and Torry in Aberdeen.[104] These urban properties ensured private townhouses for travelling monastery officials. Even within the Tironensian congregation, the abbeys of Lindores and Arbroath often had separate houses in the same burghs. Moreover, these properties facilitated ports of call from Inverness to Berwick-upon-Tweed.

---

[103] Hay, *History of Arbroath*, 44–46, summarizes the properties of Arbroath, most given at its founding.

[104] *Liber S. Thome de Aberbrothoc*, 1:xxvi (preface) and 1:3–8, no. 1.

The densest concentration extended from Arbroath 27 kilometres southwest to Dundee on the Firth of Tay, where a coastal and an inland chain of properties may be discerned. The coastal properties ran from Arbroath a day's journey southwest via William I's gift of the barony of Inverpeffer to the churches of Panbride and Fethmuref or Barry, with considerable holdings in the parish of Barry given by William Comyn (b. 1163), Sheriff of Forfar (1195–1211), Justiciar of Scotland (1205–1233) to land, a house, and a church in Monifieth, owned by the Célidé, to land and the hospital at Portincraig, and the fishing station at Broughty Ferry at the mouth of the Firth of Tay, west to Arbroath's house in Dundee. Gilchrist, earl of Angus, gave Monifieth, Portincraig, and Broughty Ferry. The inland properties ran from Arbroath west to the church of Arbirlot, given by Roger, bishop of St. Andrews, and to land at Carmyllie, southwest to the churches of Monikie near Barry, Murroes, and Mains (Stradechty Comitis) in north Dundee. Gilchrist, earl of Angus, gave Murroes and Mains. The close spacing suggests transporting building materials for the new abbey.

The burgh of Forfar was a day's ride northwest of Arbroath. The properties ran north from Arbroath to the parish of St. Vigeans and on to land at Kinblethmont and Kinnell. The route continued to land at Ballegillegrand in Bolshan, then west to the church of Guthrie, the village and church of Dunnichen, land at Kingsmuir, and Forfar. William I ensured that Arbroath had two houses in Forfar, one from Hugh his chancellor, and another from Andrew, bishop of Caithness. Northwest of Forfar William I and Gilchrist, earl of Angus, gave Arbroath the land and church of Kirriemuir and the barony of Kingoldrum. Southwest of Forfar Arbroath was given the church of Glamis and the churches of Ruthven and Newtyle west and southwest of Glamis respectively. Robert of London gave Ruthven. Dundee was a day's ride south of Kirrimuir via Glamis.

The port of Perth is on the west coast of the Firth of Tay, and Arbroath had a house, a fishing station at "Stok," and the church of Abernethy in Strathern. Lindores Abbey would be founded subsequently east of Abernethy with a much smaller but similar network of properties. Arbroath's southern holdings will be discussed subsequently.

Montrose, a coastal burgh, was a day's ride north of Arbroath. The properties ran from Arbroath north to St. Vigeans, Kinblethmont, Ethie village, and the church and lands in Inverkeilor and Inverlunan in Lunan, to the house and abbey of St. Mary of Old Montrose. Arbroath had the right to a ferry-boat at Montrose. William I gave Arbroath the lands of Hedderwick and the nearby saltwork at Dun. Arbroath had a house in Brechin, and Turpin, bishop of Brechin, gave land at Stracathro. In Edzell John Abbe, son of Malise of Brechin [fl. 1210x1223] gave a wood. Hugh Malherbe II gave Arbroath land from his Rossie Estate in the Melrose basin on the South Esk River.

Toward Aberdeen, the region north of Montrose and Brechin is called the Mearns, and Arbroath was given both churches and farmland in this rich agricultural region. The road north of Montrose crosses the North Esk, where William I gave Arbroath a fishing station, and proceeds north to the fortresses and port of Stonehaven. William I gave considerable property in the parish of Fordoun and Auchenblae to the northwest, called the barony of Newlands, including Mondynes on the Bervie River flowing into the North Sea at Inverbervie. Arbroath had land at Balfeith and land, a cove, and a church and farm (Glaskeler) in Catterline on the coast south of Stonehaven. Further north, the roads converge at the port of Stonehaven, the only route north to Aberdeen at the foot of the Hill of Trusta.

During the reign of William I, Stonehaven, sometimes called Stonehive, was the centre of local administration for the Mearns. The port had a toll booth at the harbour and two fortresses: Dunnottar Castle 3 kilometres south, on a rocky headland overlooking the land and sea routes, and Cowrie Castle, with Cowrie Bridge to the north. Portlethen Moss, an acidic bog with a ridge along which a road ran, is north of Stonehaven. From Cowrie Bridge, a trackway in raised stone called Causey Mounth, a drovers' road, was constructed in the twelfth century and connected the fortresses at Stonehaven with Aberdeen.

The Dee flows into the North Sea at Aberdeen, where Arbroath had considerable property: coastal land, the church of Nigg in the barony of Torry, the right to a ferry-boat on the Dee at Kincorth in southern Aberdeen, land at Abbotshall in Cults southwest of the burgh, and land at Mundurno on the Don River in northern Aberdeen. Upriver on the Dee the abbey owned the barony of Banchory, the church of St. Ternan in Mar, the wood of Trustach south of Kincardine O'Neil, and the farm of Ardoch, Bridge of Gairn. Arbroath had two churches northwest of Banchory: Aberkerdo near Kildrummy Castle given by Gilchrist, earl of Mar, and Coull in Mar in Tarland. West of Aberdeen and north of its Dee valley properties Thomas de Lundyn, the Durward, gave Arbroath the church of Old Kinnernie 1204x1211 northwest of Echt. Further north it had land in Kennethmont, an important market town, and in Kirkton of Culsalmond.

Further north, in Aberdeenshire and Banffshire, Arbroath's royal gifts were concentrated in the baronies of Tarves and Fyvie, where the abbey owned three churches and a mill. In Tarves, William I gave the church of Fernmartyn. William I gave the churches of Banff and St. Peter of Fyvie with Peter's Well in the foundation charter of 1178. William I built a castle at Fyvie the following year. Various accounts attribute the founding of Fyvie priory to William I and Fergus, earl of Buchan, in 1179, or to Reginald le Cheyne in 1285. The priory church was named for Saint Mary and All Saints.[105] Fyvie is on the River Ythan flowing into the North Sea north of Aberdeen, and the priory provided a base midway between Aberdeen and Banff. Arbroath owned a church in Turriff and, to the west, land in Forglen near the Deveron River and the church of St. Marnan of Aberchirder. Roads north from Turriff, Forglen, and Aberchirder converged at Banff on Moray Firth. Arbroath had church land and fishing rights in Inverboyndie west of Banff on the north coast, together with the right to a boat in nearby St. Brandon's Haven and coastal churches in Banff and Gamrie to the east. West of Banff, Arbroath had houses in the burghs of Elgin and Forres. Arbroath also had the church, and fishing rights payable in herrings, in Inverness to the west. North of Aberdeen and northwest of Peterhead, Ralph le Neym (fl. 1159–1200) gave the church of Inverugie on the east coast at the mouth of the River Ugie. Thus Arbroath's properties extended 161 kilometres to the north, with valuable river property on the Bervie and Dee and coastal property on Moray Firth and the North Sea.

---

105 *Liber S. Thome de Aberbrothoc*, 1:5, no. 1. Cowan and Easson, *Medieval Religious Houses: Scotland*, 67.

Townhouses provided residences for Arbroath's officials in strategic areas. Arbroath had houses on the southeastern border in the port of Berwick-upon-Tweed and the market town of Roxburgh and on the southwestern border in Dumfries. On the southern bank of the Firth of Forth, Arbroath had houses in Haddington, Edinburgh and its village of Duddingston (see Map 6.2), and Linlithgow, in Stirling northwest of Edinburgh at the crossing point of the River Forth (together with Carse, a saltwork), and on the northern bank in Inverkeithing, Dunfermline, and the port of Crail. In the vicinity of Glasgow, Arbroath had a house in Lanark and Rutherglen, as well as the western port of Ayr. Given the presence of Henry II's military occupation, William I gave little land to the south. In Lanarkshire the king gave Arbroath a barony of land in the parish of Cambusnethan near Wishaw southeast of Glasgow. The abbey had land between Auchter Water and South Calder Water, now Auchterhead Muir, in the vicinity of Cambusnethan.

In England, the ports of Carlisle and Newcastle-upon-Tyne are 94 kilometres apart. Both Kelso and Arbroath owned property at midpoints between the coasts. Kelso's hermitage of Merchingley near Slaley has been discussed. Arbroath had the church of Haltwhistle in Tynedale, Northumberland. An official could have ridden the distance between Carlisle and Newcastle-upon-Tyne in three days, lodging at the church of Hartwhistle and the hermitage of Merchingley.

The charter of confirmation of 1214 indicates that Arbroath enjoyed the tithes and patronage of twenty-four parish churches, a toft of land in every one of the royal burghs, lands, fisheries, ferries, saltworks throughout Scotland, and the town and region of Arbroath itself. The abbey had the right to establish a burgh in Arbroath whose burgesses would be exempt from tolls throughout Scotland, to hold a Saturday market, and to build a harbour to which cargoes would be admitted duty-free except for the abbot's customs. The earls of Angus and other subjects added lands, fisheries, ferries, and churches.[106] John, king of England, granted a charter to the abbots, monks, and citizens of Arbroath ca. 1204, allowing them to sell their proper goods and buy them for their own proper uses, as they please, throughout his whole territories, unhindered by all public burdens or any other custom, except for the liberties of the city of London.[107] Arbroath was heavily involved in trade and, although far from Tiron, had negotiated for Britain the same exemptions Tiron had obtained in England and western France.

Lindores Abbey, west of Arbroath on the south bank of the Firth of Tay, was founded between 1178 and 1191 by David, earl of Huntingdon, the grandson of David I and brother of Malcolm IV and William I.[108] The foundation charter states Lindores was founded to the honour of God, Saint Mary, Saint Andrew, and All Saints, and for the weal of the souls

---

[106] *Liber S. Thome de Aberbrothoc*, 1:3–8, no. 1.
[107] M. A. Pollock, *Scotland, England and France After the Loss of Normandy, 1204–1296: 'Auld Amitie'* (Woodbridge: Boydell, 2015), 15n36, citing *Calendar of Documents Relating to Scotland 1108–1509*, ed. Joseph Bain, 5 vols. (Edinburgh: General Register House, 1881–1888 and 1986), 1:65, no. 398.
[108] In 1178–1182 William I conferred the earldom of Lennox, Garioch, Lindores, and Dundee on his brother David. See further Dowden's edition of the *Chartulary of the Abbey of Lindores 1195–1479*: Lindores Cart., 1–2, no. 1.

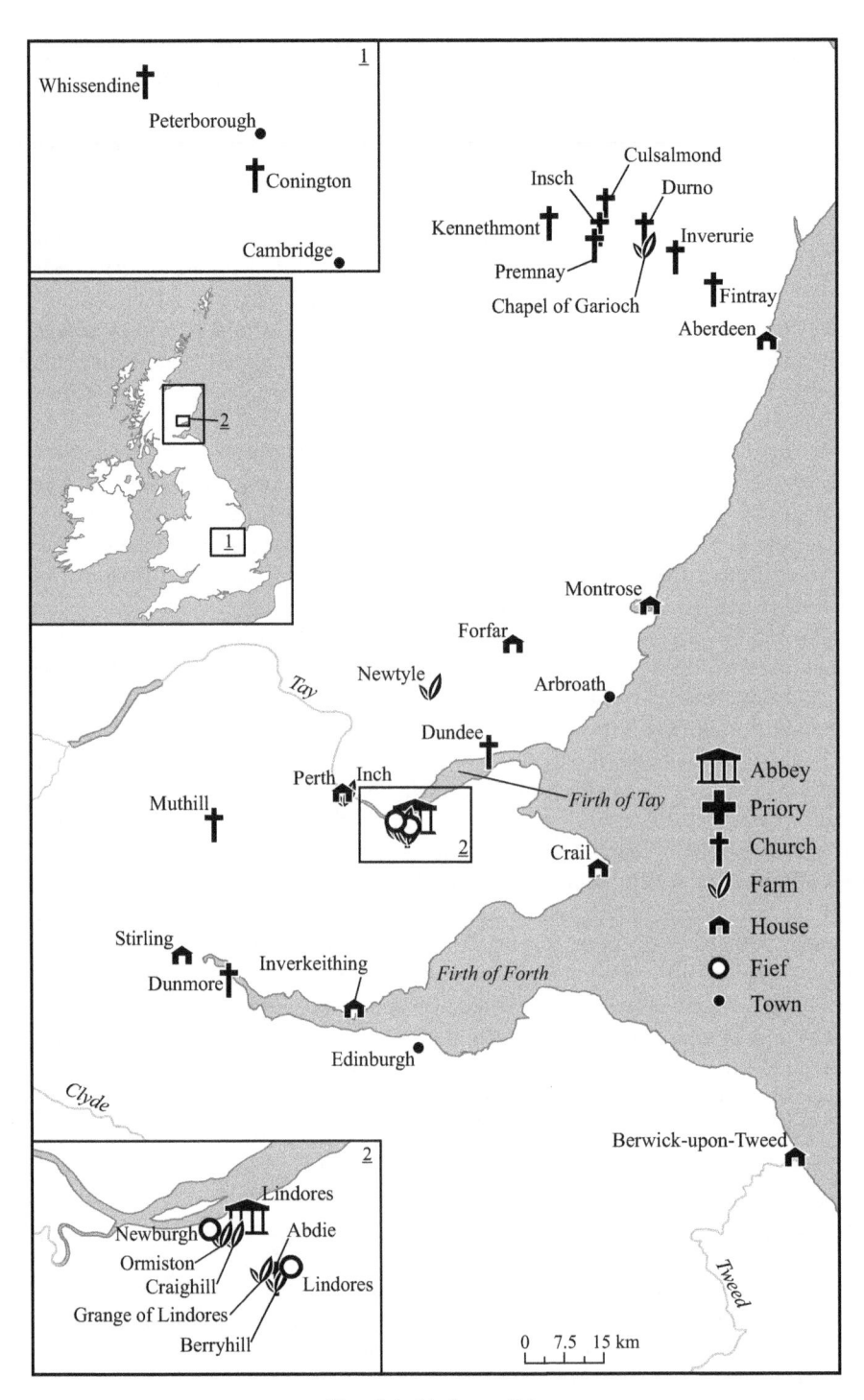

Map 6.4. Lindores Abbey

Table 6.4. Lindores Abbey

Royal Burghs **Berwick-upon-Tweed**; house; <1195; William I **Crail**; house; <1195; William I **Inverkeithing**; house; <1195; Robert of London **Stirling**; house; <1195; William I **Dundee**; church+house; <1195; David II, earl of Huntingdon **Perth**; house of Everard Fleming; David II, earl of Huntingdon+William I **Forfar**; house; <1195; William I **Montrose**; house; <1195; William I **Aberdeen**; house; <1195; William I
Lindores Abbey to Perth **Lindores**; abbey; 1178–1181; David II, earl of Huntingdon **Mugdrum Island "Redinche"**;<1195; David II, earl of Huntingdon **Dunmore**, Lindores; church; 1198; David II, earl of Huntingdon; conf. Innocent III **Lindores**; fief **Grange of Lindores**; farm **Abdie**; church **Berryhill**; farm **Newburgh**; fief **Ormison**; farm **Craighill**; farm **Inch of Perth**; farm **Muthill** (Strathearn, Perth); (church Célidé); 1198; David II, earl of Huntingdon; conf. Innocent III **Newtyle**; farm; 1198; Ada, dau. of David II, earl of Huntingdon; conf. Innocent III *Lindores is 65 km N of Edinburgh and 53 km SW of Arbroath via Dundee* Overland routes from Berwick-upon-Tweed would be difficult; maritime routes would be preferable. A land route from Stirling to Aberdeen would be feasible *Stirling, N 24 km to Muthill, E 20 km to Perth, SE 24 km to Lindores, NE 29 km to Dundee, N 18 km to Newtyle, NE 14 km to Glamis, NE 9 km to Forfar, SE 25 km to Arbroath, NE 21 km to Montrose, NE 67 km to Aberdeen*
Aberdeen inland to Kennethmont **Fintray**; church; <1195; David II, earl of Huntingdon **Inverurie**; church with chapel of Monkeigie/Keithhall (unidentified Rothketh); <1195; David II, earl of Huntingdon **Chapel of Garioch**; farm+unidentified Letgavel+Malinth; <1195; David, earl of Huntingdon **Durno**; church; <1195; David II, earl of Huntingdon **Insch**; church;<1195; David II, earl of Huntingdon **Culsalmond**; church; <1195; David II, earl of Huntingdon **Premnay**; church; <1195; David II, earl of Huntingdon **Kennethmont**; churches of Kennethmont +Christ's Kirk on the Green/Radmuriel; <1195; David II, earl of Huntingdon

(*continued*)

Table 6.4. (Cont.)

Aberdeen, NW 19 km to Fintray, NW 10 km to Inverurie, NW 8 km to Chapel of Garioch, N 5 km to Durno, NW 11 km to Insch (with Culsalmond N 6 km and Premnay S 4 km), W 11 km to Kennethmont
England **Whissendine**, Rutland; church; 1198; Innocent III **Cunington/Conington**, Cambridgeshire near Peterborough; church; 1198; Innocent III

of King David I, the earl's parents—Henry, earl of Huntingdon, and Countess Ada de Warenne (ca. 1120–1178), King William I and Queen Ermengarde and all his ancestors, and his own soul, and the souls of his wife Countess Matilda of Chester (1171–1233), David, his (natural) son, all his successors, and his brothers and sisters. Lindores was a family foundation supporting this branch of the Scottish royal family with prayers.

Lindores's holdings included thirteen churches and nine houses. The church of Lindores, dedicated to Saint Magridin (modern Abdie and Dunbog Church), was an early religious settlement of Célidé origin. Lindores extended the active exploitation of the royal demense north of the Firth of Forth, on the sheltered southern shore of the Firth of Tay. The endowment included the land and church of Lindores, north of Edinburgh and southwest of Arbroath via Dundee. The confirmation charter issued ca. 1190–1191 describes holdings extending north to Aberdeen and south to Berwick-upon-Tweed.[109]

Lindores was founded by the River Tay with offshore Mugdrum Island (also Redinche). The nearby town of Newburgh was created in 1266. The site had fine upland pasture and rich arable soil. In 1876, Laing described the property as including at least the modern local farms of Grange of Lindores, Berryhill, Ormiston, Lindores, Lindores Abbey, Craigmill, and the burgh lands of Newburgh. Water from Loch Lindores turned the abbey mill, and Earnside wood provided fuel. The abbey was granted the town churches with woods and fields. Earl David also had a mill at Lindores, and the abbey and he agreed that, if one mill was not working, grain could be ground at the other's mill free of multure. Laing states that the monks all but despoiled the church of Lindores of its revenues to endow the abbey.[110]

Lindores, credited with introducing mechanized grain-grinding to replace the handmill or quern, was also noted for its orchards, particularly apples and the Bon-Chrétien and Bergamot pear trees of old French monastic stock.[111] Lindores is considered

---

[109] *Acts of William I*, 357–59, no. 363 (ca. 1190–1191).

[110] Laing, *Lindores Abbey*, 68–69.

[111] Laing, *Lindores Abbey*, 48–49, 59n1, 60, 552–59. Nineteenth-century botanists attempted to document the folk belief of the monks as importers of continental plants by cataloging the non-indigenous plants growing wild near abbey ruins. Laing includes a list for Lindores in an appendix. John Smith notes over seventy non-indigenous plants growing wild in Ayrshire, fifty-one of them in Kilwinning, in *The Botany of Ayrshire (by parishes) from original investigation* (Ardrossan: Guthrie, 1896).

the birthplace of Scotch whisky because of a listing in the Exchequer Rolls for 1495 of Brother John Cor's payment of duty on eight bolls of malt to distill aqua vitae for James IV (r. 1488–1513).[112] Like other Scottish abbeys, Lindores had more labour to cultivate continental fruits and vegetables than the local peasants could expend on their gardens. Over centuries the monks held and improved vineyards and perfected the preparation of superior wine and beer as well as medicinal liqueurs.

Lindores had dwellings in the leading towns and burghs along the main ports, roads, and trade routes from Berwick-upon-Tweed and Crail northwest along the Firth of Forth to Inverkeithing and Stirling, north from Stirling to Perth on the Firth of Tay (with a meadow called Inch of Perth), and then northeast along the Firth of Tay to Dundee, inland at Forfar, and up the east coast past Arbroath and Montrose to Aberdeen. Earl David's gift of a toft and the church of Dundee to the northeast is the earliest written record of that burgh.[113] William I's son Robert of London's toft in Inverkeithing was at the crossing of the Firth of Forth to Edinburgh.[114] Earl David's son John, earl of Huntingdon (1207–1237), and the earls of Strathern are listed as donors to Lindores.[115] Grants of so many tofts at once along trade routes suggest that Lindores was also involved in trade.

Alexander Stevenson studied early medieval trade with the south and described Aberdeen and Perth as burghs without fairs.[116] Harold W. Booton studied Aberdeen's inland trade in the later Middle Ages. By 1273 Aberdeen was permitted to hold a weekly general market in Castlegate. On Moray Firth and the North Sea, Forres, Elgin, Banff, and Turriff traded with Aberdeen, as did Pitcaple near Chapel of Garioch northwest of Inverurie.[117] It is significant that Lindores's holdings were divided between southern Perth and Dundee and northern Aberdeen. Stringer has studied the concentration of Lindores's holdings in the vale of Garioch 130 kilometres to the northeast, described as the "north Abbacy of Lindores," and states that Fintray was Lindores's northern administrative base.[118]

Northwest of Aberdeen, Lindores had a chain of churches and tofts running 52 kilometres along the road to Kennethmont. The route ran to the land and church of Fintray and on to the church of Inverurie with the chapel of Monkeigie and all its appurtenances. Northwest of Inverurie Lindores owned the land in Chapel of Garioch (with nearby vanished properties named Lethgavel and Malinth) and the church of Durno. The route continued to the church of Insch, with the nearby churches of Culsalmond and Premnay. The town of Kennethmont was to the west, where the abbey was given Christ's Kirk on the Green, with chapels, lands, and tithes. Christ's Kirk was

---

[112] *Rotuli scaccarii regum Scotorum: The Exchequer Rolls of Scotland*, ed. John Stuart and George Burnett, 23 vols. (Edinburgh: General Register House, 1878–1910), 10:487, no. 292 [306].

[113] *Lindores Cart.*, no. 1 n. Dunde p. 230.

[114] *Lindores Cart.*, 104, no. 93.

[115] *Lindores Cart.*, 18–25, nos. 15–20 (Earl John) and 27–37, nos. 24–35 (Earls of Strathern).

[116] Stevenson, "Trade with the South," 183.

[117] Harold W. Booton, "Inland Trade: A Study of Aberdeen in the Later Middle Ages," in *The Scottish Medieval Town*, ed. Michael Lynch et al. (Edinburgh: Donald, 1988), 149, 153.

[118] Stringer, *Earl David of Huntingdon*, 98–100.

the site of Christ's Fair or Sleepy Market, which began at sundown. Kennethmont had its fair, called Trewel Fair, at Kirkhall.[119] The short distances suggest foot traffic and hauling from Aberdeen to the Kennethmont market and fair.

Celestine III confirmed the property of Lindores in a bull dated March 8, 1194–1195, and Pope Innocent III (r. 1198–1216) confirmed its expanded property on March 20, 1198.[120] Both bulls established Lindores as under the *Rule* and directly accountable to the papacy. The monks might choose their own abbot. The bulls confirm a free court and firm peace in Lindores, the easements of the island called Redinche (Mugdrum), which the abbey shared with the earl, the fishing station in the Tay, and the mill and multure in Lindores. The privilege of Innocent III adds the chapel of Dunmore on the Firth of Forth southwest of Stirling, property in Newtyle and Perth, the church of Muthill a day's ride southwest of Perth, and the distant church of Whissendine in Rutland to the church of Cunington/Conington in Cambridgeshire near Peterborough and Huntington. In these bulls Lindores was given an incentive to reclaim wasteland by acquiring exemption from paying tithes on the crops of fallow lands (*novalia*) which they had brought into cultivation either by the actual labour of the monks themselves or at their charge. The abbey was exempt from the tithe of all its cattle, sheep, and horses.[121] Lindores was entitled to receive and retain as lay brothers any laymen or clerks who wished to place themselves under monastic rule, provided that they were freemen or formally released from serfdom. The monks were forbidden to leave the house without the permission of the abbot and only to join a house with a stricter rule. Lindores Abbey had the privilege of celebrating divine offices during an interdict and the right to afford sepulture to anyone not excommunicated or under interdict who wished to be buried in the monastery. It was also entitled to burial fees, the best beast or, for the poor, the best garment, and a portion of the movable goods of the deceased after payment of debts and provision for the widow and children.[122]

Arbroath and Lindores were in the same diocese and complemented one another, for Lindores was inland on the Firth of Tay and engaged in horticulture and Arbroath was coastal and engaged in marketing and trade. Both abbeys gravitated toward Dundee and Aberdeen, with Lindores's holdings divided between the Firth of Tay and the Dee. Lindores became noted for apples and pears and Arbroath for cabbage and smoked haddock. The monks of both abbeys supplanted the Célidé by establishing continental Benedictine monasticism in older sites and became important centres near the North Sea.

Kilwinning Abbey extended the active exploitation of the royal demesne to the west coast below the Firth of Clyde. Kilwinning was founded by the Morvilles, a powerful Anglo-Norman family with lands in England and Scotland. David I endowed Hugh I de Morville (d. 1162), lord of Cunningham, the founder of Dryburgh Abbey, with lands in Lauderdale and the Tweed Valley.[123] According to Timothy Pont, a topographer and

---

[119] www.kinnethmont.co.uk/history.htm
[120] *Lindores Cart.*, 102–7, no. 93 (1195) and 107–11, no. 94, abstract 111–12 (1199), Great Privilege of Innocent III.
[121] *Lindores Cart.*, lxxviii–lxxix.
[122] Laing, *Lindores Abbey*, 74–75.
[123] Owen, *William the Lion,* 117.

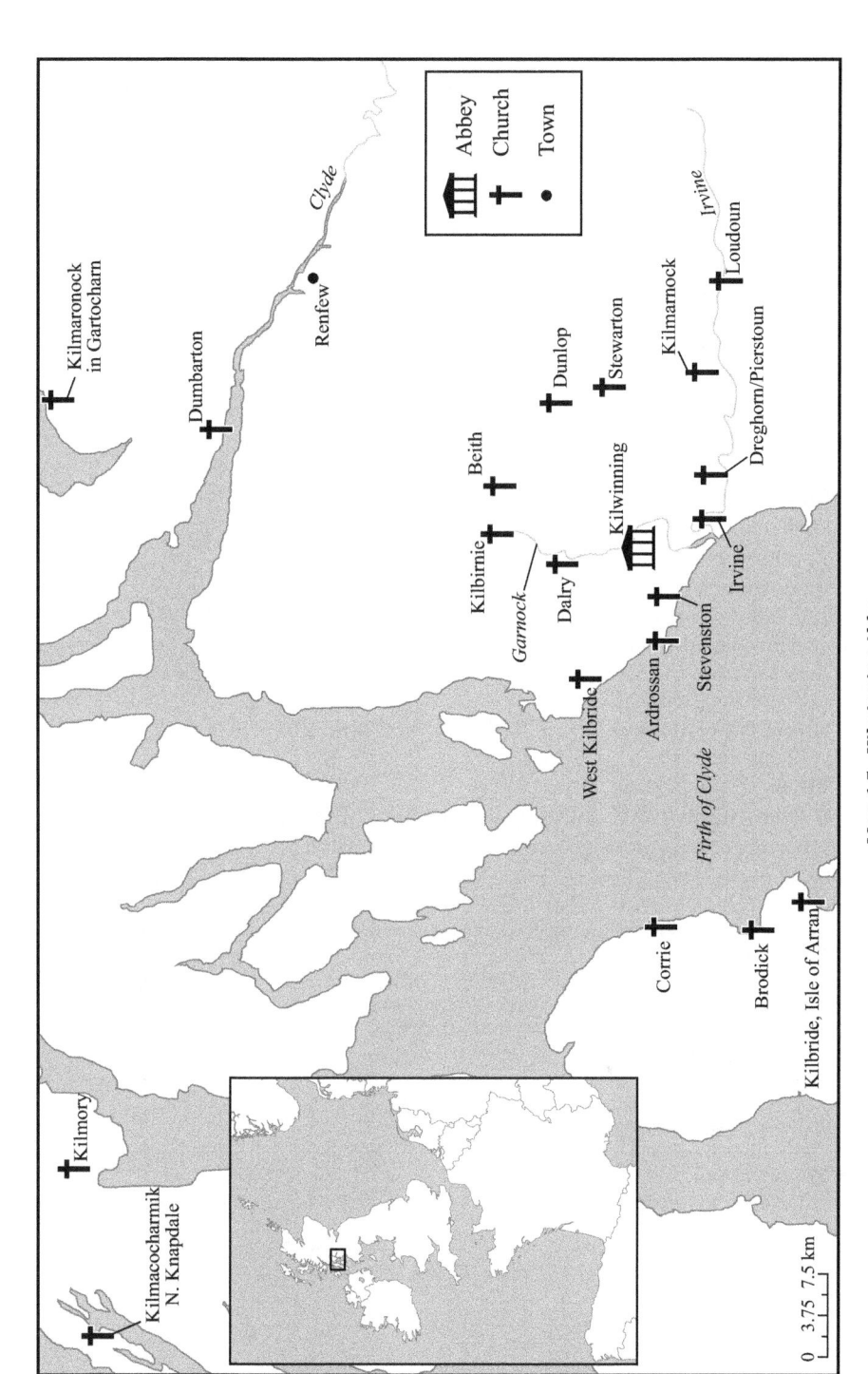

Map 6.5. Kilwinning Abbey

Table 6.5. Kilwinning Abbey

Kilwinning; abbey; 1191; Richard de Moreville, lord of Cunningham, Largs, and Lauderdale   **Irvine**; church; <1562   **Dreghorn/Pierstoun**; church; <1562   **Stevenston**; church; <1562   **Ardrossan**; church; <1562   **West Kilbride**; church; <1562   **Kilmarnock**; church; Wisheart, bishop of Glasgow (d. 1319)   **Loudoun**; church; <1562   **Dalry**; church; <1562   **Kilbirnie**; church; <1562   **Beith**; church; Robert II lands and multure of Kilwinning and Beith; church Wisheart, bishop of Glasgow (d. 1319)   **Dunlop**; church; <1562   **Stewarton**; church; <1562   **Dumbarton**; church; <1562   **Kilmaronock in Gartocharn**; church; <1562; Dumbartonshire   **Kilbride**, Isle of Arran; church+villages of Brodick and Corrie; 1357; John of Menteath, Lord of Arran and Knapdale; <1562   **Brodick**, Isle of Arran; church; 1357; John of Menteath, Lord of Arran and Knapdale; <1562   **Corrie**, Isle of Arran; church; 1357; John of Menteath, Lord of Arran and Knapdale; <1562   **Kilmory**; church; <1562; Isle of Arran   **Kilmacocharmik**, N. Knapdale; church; +S. Knapdale <1562 Argyll and Bute   **Liberton**; church, Edinburgh; ca. 1357; John of Maxwell (not mapped)   Kilwinning, N 6 km to Dalry, N 6 km to Kilbirnie, NE 7 km to Beith, N 20 km to Paisley, N 20 km to Dumbarton, N 15 km to Kilmaronock in Gartocharn   Kilwinning, NE 15 km to Dunlop, S 4 km to Stewarton, S 8 km to Kilmarnock, E 9 km to Loudoun
Firth of Clyde   Kilwinning, S 6 km to Irvine, E 4 km to Dreghorn   Kilwinning, W 4 km to Stevenston, W 4 km to Ardrossan, NW 7 km to West Kilbride
Isle of Arran   *Kilmory is 23 km SW of Kilbride*
Argyll and Bute   *South and North Knapdale are 99 km NW of Kilwinning. Liberton, Edinburgh is 94 km NE of Kilwinning*

clergyman writing ca. 1608 who was the last person to have recorded what he had seen in its lost charters,[124] Hugh's son Richard de Morville, lord of Cunningham, Largs, and Lauderdale, founded St. Thomas of Kilwinning in 1191 in repentance for the involvement of his brother Hugh II de Morville (d. ca. 1202), lord of Westmorland, in Becket's murder. This date is disputed, and the foundation has been dated as early as 1140–1162. Both Kilwinning and Arbroath were originally known as "Segdoune" or "Segton," a corruption of *sanctoun*, which indicates an earlier religious foundation at the site.[125]

Kilwinning Abbey is believed to be the work of European freemasons, and the town is the site of the Lodge Mother Kilwinning No. 0, the Mother Lodge of Scotland. It was settled by monks of Kelso, an abbey with its own builders. Its excellent water supply included St. Winning's well, whose water ran blood when war was near. A pipe running from the abbey to the nearby Kyle's Well in town was discovered in 1826 and may account for the discoloration.[126] Kilwinning is located 6 kilometres from the sea on the River Garnock. Dairy farming was the main concern in the area, and oats, hay, and vegetables were grown for farm consumption. Irvine, a busy port on the Firth of Clyde, was downriver to the south.

Pont states that Richard de Morville built the choir or chancel of the abbey church and endowed it with land and woodland rights at Kilwinning. His wife Avicia Loncaster endowed Kilwinning with the lands of Bytth Batth and Threppe-wood. Their daughter Dorothea completed the construction, and their grandson Lord Walter de Horsey confirmed the property of the monastery.

Kilwinning held at least eighteen parish churches, mainly local but some offshore on the Isle of Arran and in Argyll and Bute.[127] The abbey had the patronage and tithes (teinds) of the parishes of Kilwinning and of the churches in the coastal towns of Irvine south on Irvine Bay, Dreghorn, Stevenston, Ardrossan, and West Kilbride, all on the Firth of Clyde. To the east it had the patronage and tithes of Kilmarnock and Loudoun. To the north on the road to Paisley west of Glasgow, it had the patronage and tithes of the churches of Dalry, Kilbirnie, Beith and, in Dunbartonshire, Dumbarton and Kilmaronock in Gartocharn (near Ross Priory on Loch Lomond). On the road northeast between Kilwinning and Glasgow, Kilwinning had the patronage of the churches of Dunlop and Stewarton. On the Isle of Arran, Kilwinning had the tithes and patronage of the parish of Kilbride, encompassing the villages of Brodick and Corrie on the east coast, and of Kilmory to the southwest on the south coast.[128] It had the same privileges in South and North Knapdale (including Kilmacocharmik) in Argyll and Bute, northwest of Kilwinning, crossing the Isle of Arran, Kilbrannan Sound, and W. Loch Tarbert at Tarbert. These properties are concentrated at the mouth of the Clyde, and the distant ones came under closer supervision. Kilwinning

---

[124] Robin McLaren, "Father Thomas Innes," citing Thomas Hearne's diary, February 26, 1721, *Reliquiae Hearnianae*, 2nd ed., 2:126, in *The Innes Review* 5, no. 1 (1954), 78.

[125] *Cuninghame*, 254–55, "Heir it is remarkable yat this Monastery wes foundit in A° 1191 and destroyed in A° 1591." Ker, *Kilwinning Abbey*, 45–47.

[126] Ker, *Kilwinning Abbey*, 33–35, 54.

[127] Ker, *Kilwinning Abbey*, 102–4.

[128] *Cuninghame*, 268.

also had the church of Liberton in Edinburgh, a useful base. Pont refers to papal, royal, and episcopal confirmations that seem misdated. He states that Kilwinning had great revenues from its own land. When Kilwinning was destroyed, it owned valuable lands in Cunningham and had an estimated annual revenue of £20,000 sterling.[129]

In Wales and Scotland, the Tironensian "French" or "grey" monks were deeply engaged in their communities and retained their Tironensian identity for centuries. Tiron's emphasis on education, construction, crafts, and farming meant that its foundations brought economic improvement and important skills to small communities. Its simpler rule drew Celtic hermits toward a more continental form of monasticism. Its willingness to run markets and engage in trade and commerce supported an important sector of the British economy. Its ability to win the support of all parties in border situations fitted it well for expansion in the Celtic fringe of the British Isles. In this manner Tiron played an important role in the Normanization of the British Isles.

In conclusion, in the British Isles Tiron's expansion patterns entailed limited growth in England and substantial growth in Wales and Scotland. In England lack of royal patronage inhibited Tiron's growth, exacerbated by the civil war between rival claimants to the throne. As in France, the older English Benedictine orders owned the best land, and the Cistercians were willing to accept and farm poorer land, breeding sheep and developing high-grade wool for commerce and trade. The Tironensians adapted to their situation and turned to the sea. Almost all Tironensian British foundations were on or near the Channel, the Atlantic Coast, or the North Sea. In southern England their coastal properties facilitated traffic between Normandy, Brittany, and Southampton. Coastal foundations in Wales included Caldey Island on Camarthan Bay, the future harbour of Milford Haven, and a western abbey extending traffic to Ireland. Foundations in Scotland facilitated western traffic near Glasgow and to the offshore islands and eastern traffic from Berwick-upon-Tweed to Dundee, Perth, Aberdeen, and Banff. Tiron's development is consistent with the long history of the British Isles' participation in maritime commerce and trade.

Tiron's coalescence into an international congregation and adaptation to Kelso's separation as an independent congregation are noteworthy. Inevitably Tironensian overseas foundations came under the control of the local nobility, who ensured that their kin became abbots. Many Kers held abbacies at Kelso, Beatons at Arbroath, and Hamiltons at Kilwinning. Political assertions of national independence were accompanied by similar religious assertions, first by Kelso in relation to Tiron, and then by Kelso's daughter foundations. Thompson notes that Arbroath, "by far the richest abbey in Scotland," was built by monks of Kelso but was freed from obedience and obligation to that monastery.[130] Tiron's response was realistic and flexible. As Tiron established relations of confraternity with houses of other orders, it established procurial and business relations with its formerly dependent foundations. Procurial relations with Tiron were maintained for several centuries because of their mutual profitability, uncomplicated by assertions of independence. The accommodation was a productive adaptation to changed circumstances.

---

129 *Cuninghame*, 255–57, 267. Ker, *Kilwinning Abbey*, 50–51.

130 Thompson, *The Monks of Tiron*, 176n95, citing n95 *Liber S. Thome de Aberbrothoc*, no. 2, and n96 citing Stringer, "Arbroath Abbey in context," in *The Declaration of Arbroath: History, Significance, Setting*, ed. Geoffrey Barrow (Edinburgh: Society of Antiquaries of Scotland, 2003), 116–42.

Chapter 7

THE LATER HISTORY

BY THE END of the twelfth century the congregation of Tiron extended into the Angevin Empire or trade area, an overly large and diverse region that gradually broke apart under King John and his successors. While Tiron Abbey lost effective control of the foundations in its Celtic periphery, it had a headquarters in Paris and retained centralized control over its French daughter abbeys through annual general chapters and recourse to the papacy to quash assertions of independence, in a way that mirrored the emerging French nation. In France and Britain, monasteries accumulated wealth through gifts of inalienable property exempt from feudal incidents and inheritance taxes (mortmain). Consequently they were targeted during periods of instability and underwent lengthy recuperation of their assets and properties. During the Wars of Scottish Independence 1296–1357, the Hundred Years' War 1337–1453, the English Reformation 1536–1547, the French Wars of Religion 1562–1598, and the French Revolution 1789–1799, religious foundations were bombarded, commandeered, looted, burned, and ultimately secularized. Many did not survive, and Tiron was no exception.

Despite its strong eremitical traditions, Tiron became considered part of the Benedictine order it had been founded to reform.[1] After the Fourth Lateran Council of 1215, papal bulls, confirmations, and communications often describe Tiron Abbey as Benedictine rather than Tironensian.[2] Thus its distinctiveness became less apparent in France.

Over the twelfth and thirteenth centuries, Tiron moved from the poverty and hospitality of its founder toward a more prosperous and exclusive lifestyle.[3] Abbot John II of Chartres was a forceful administrator who regally imposed centralized control and discipline over Tiron and its daughter abbeys. He installed abbots duly elected by the chapter and conducted visitations.[4] He rebuilt many buildings in the monastery, including the cloister and a large chapter room by the apse of the church, where he was buried.[5] During his tenure 1290–1297 Pignore de Vallea copied the *Vita Bernardi* by Geoffrey Grossus, probably supplemented with other materials about Tiron's saintly founder and foundation legend. In 1291 the chapter of Chartres complained during litigation with Tiron that John II appeared in public surrounded with men-at-arms

---

1 In 1205, a charter recognizing the rights of Hamelin, bishop of Le Mans, stipulated that the election of the abbot of La Pelice should be held in his presence and that of the abbot of Tiron (Hervé) according to the *Rule*. T2:120–21, no. 345.

2 T2:171–72, no. 382, ibid., 2:181, no. 389; ibid., 2:195–99, nos. 401, 403–4; ibid., 2:203–4, no. 409.

3 A bull issued by Gregory X (r. 1271–1276) allowed the monks of Tiron to own all the things that they were given, without being obliged to sell them. IS-ADEL, 8:159, H 1384 (1273).

4 John II visited Le Tronchet in 1282 and 1294. Tresvaux, *l'Église de Bretagne*, 481–87, specifically 482.

5 GC, 8:1265.

bearing white staffs. This complaint is supported by a 1291 manuscript containing a miniature showing this abbot of Tiron entering Chartres Cathedral preceded by six laymen with staffs raised, followed by four clerics. John II's tombstone was found in 1840 and is displayed in the church. His ornate crozier is in the Musée des Beaux-Arts of Chartres.[6]

Because of their prominence and strategic locations, Tironensian abbots became involved in the political movements of their time. Tiron was introduced to Scotland as part of the Normanization process, and some Scottish abbots were statesmen. Herbert had a long and distinguished career as abbot of Selkirk/Kelso and as bishop of Glasgow, appearing frequently to witness charters as part of the *curia regis*. David I had both a chancellor and a chamberlain named Herbert, so the abbot's political role has sometimes been exaggerated. Herbert opposed the rebellion of Somerled, thane of Argyll, against Anglo-Norman Malcolm IV. In 1164, Somerled collected a fleet of 160 ships and landed with an army at Renfrew, where he and his fellow raiders were slain by the sheriff and few loyal locals.[7] Herbert's name passed into song: the *Carmen de Morte Sumerledi* describes his intercessory prayers to Saint Kentigern (d. 612) and his travel to Glasgow to rally its defenders. When Herbert accepted Somerled's head, he thanked the Scottish saints, and attributed the victory to Kentigern.[8] This pious tale presented the Tironensian bishop as courageous and revered and lent the support of Glasgow's patron saint to the king and the Normanization process.

During the reign of Edward I (b. 1239, r. 1272–1307) English domination in Scotland was countered by nationalist movements, resulting in the Wars of Scottish Independence. Like other abbots and bishops, the Tironensians were threatened with replacement by Englishmen and played important roles. Lindores's hospitality was severely tested by visitors on all sides. King Alexander III visited Lindores in March 1265,[9] and in 1281 and 1284 the abbey had the sad honour of being the deathplace of his two sons.[10] His successor was his granddaughter Margaret, the Maid of Norway (b. 1283, r. 1286–1290). Upon her death the claimants were Robert I (Bruce), fifth lord of Annandale (b. 1274, r. 1306–1329), and John Balliol, lord of Galloway (ca. 1250–1314, r. 1292–1296). To avoid civil war, Edward I of England was asked to come north to arbitrate. He insisted on the status of Lord Paramount and required the homage of all Scotsmen. Richard, abbot of Kelso (r. 1285–1299), was one of the commissioners chosen by Balliol to examine the claims of the competitors for the throne. In 1291 Edward I came to Lindores Abbey, and Abbot John (r. 1287–1291) was among the Scottish leaders who swore allegiance to him. In 1292, Balliol became king and swore allegiance to Edward I. In 1294 Balliol visited Lindores with his officers of state and issued a charter. That same year the

---

6 Guillemin, *Thiron, abbaye médiévale*, 25, 73.
7 *Acts of Malcolm IV*, 8–20 (introduction).
8 ES, 2:256–58.
9 Laing, *Lindores Abbey*, 78–79.
10 David (1272–1281) and Alexander (1264–1284) died at Lindores and were buried at Dunfermline. ES, 2:669, 683–84.

English king required troops and funds to invade France. A parliament was convened, and Scotland allied with France against England. During this period Abbot William of Arbroath (r. 1276–1284) became bishop of Dunblane (r. 1284–1292x1296). The First War of Independence (1296–1328) began when Edward I invaded Scotland and sacked Berwick. Henry, abbot of Arbroath (r. 1285–1296) was the courageous and loyal man chosen to deliver the instrument renouncing King John Balliol's allegiance to the English monarch.[11] After Scottish defeats Edward I compelled Balliol to abdicate, and the king visited Arbroath and Lindores on his royal progress through Scotland. He compelled all classes to assemble and swear allegiance to him, and the abbots of Kelso and Kilwinning signed loyalty oaths.[12] On his departure he removed the Stone of Destiny from Scone Abbey to Westminster.

William Wallace (d. 1305) fought for independence from 1297 until Scottish submission in 1304. Wallace fought a battle near Lindores in the forest of Earnside in 1298, and his men returned victorious to the abbey for rest and refreshment.[13] Robert the Bruce's campaign began in 1306 and ended with his victory at Bannockburn in 1314, whereafter he ruled as king 1314–1328. Bernard, abbot of Kilwinning in 1296, then chancellor of Scotland 1308–1328 and abbot of Arbroath 1310, and bishop of the Isles 1328–1331, drafted the letter known as the Scottish Declaration of Independence which the Scottish nobles, assembled in Arbroath Abbey, sent to Pope John XXII (r. 1316–1334) in Avignon on April 5, 1320.[14] The Edinburgh–Northampton Treaty of 1328 affirmed Scottish independence.

During the Second War of Scottish Independence (1332–1356), Edward III, king of England, the grandson of Edward I, had rival claims to the French throne, which he asserted in 1337 when waging war against Scotland to support the succession of King John's son Edward Balliol (r. August–December 1332 and for periods during 1333–1346). Kelso was so damaged by fire and despoiled that its monks were forced to beg for their food and clothing among other religious houses in Scotland.[15] Lesmahagow obtained a charter from David II (r. 1329–1371) confirming its liberties and privileges and became a refuge for monks of Kelso. In 1335 Edward III's brother John of Eltham, earl of Cornwall (1316–1336), burned Lesmahagow and fired the church in which its inhabitants had taken refuge, violating the sanctuary accorded to that priory.[16] The abbots of Arbroath received the pontificals sometime after 1268.[17] The abbot of Lindores never did, but the monks acquired the papal privilege of wearing caps in a cold climate in

---

11 Abbot Henry established a reputation for tyranny and prodigality that by 1290 caused Pope Nicholas IV to direct William Fraser, bishop of St. Andrews (r. 1279–1297), to investigate and reform Arbroath. ES, 2:686n3, citing Theiner, no. 338.

12 Laing, *Lindores Abbey*, 84–85.

13 *Blind Harry's Wallace*, trans. Hamilton of Gilbertfield, 10.2, 157.

14 Hay, *History of Arbroath*, 62.

15 *Kelso Liber*, 1:xii, and 249–50, no. 309.

16 Greenshields, *Annals of the Parish of Lesmahagow*, 12–13.

17 Hay, *History of Arbroath*, 50.

1289.[18] The Tironensian abbots' roles in the Scottish nationalist movements were inevitable given their status and location but reflect considerable engagement in high-level politics.

South of the border, Tiron's English foundations were affected by the Hundred Years' War (1337–1453), a century of military conflict interrupted by truces between the Plantagenet and Capetian rulers over the succession to the French throne. Decades of major English victories in France were succeeded in 1429 by conclusive French victories resulting in England's loss of Gascony and other continental territory. Before and during these wars, French alien priories were suspected of espionage and collusion with the enemy. Titley, St. Cross, Isle of Wight, Hamble, and Andwell were among the alien priories seized by Edward II (r. 1307–1327) in 1324 and restored by Edward III in 1327.[19] During the Edwardian War (1137–1360), in 1341 the priors of Andwell and Hamble were summoned before the council at Westminster "to account for payments they owed for custody of their priories, which were taken into the king's hand by reason of the war with France and afterward committed to the prior of Bristall." Similar notice was given to the proctor of the abbess of Fontevraud and the proctors of the abbots of Cluny, Séez, and Fécamp, among others.[20] Andwell was charged with espionage in 1342, and the abbot of Tiron, "who is of the king's enmity of France," was accused of sending the prior "to spy upon the secrets of the land of England and transmit them to him."[21] During the Caroline War (1369–1389), the French Navy attacked the English coast. In 1390, like many French abbeys, Tiron had wearied of the repeated seizures of its alien priories. In April 1391, William of Wykeham, bishop of Winchester (r. 1366–1404), purchased Hamble, Andwell, St. Cross, Isle of Wight, and Titley, together with the advowsons of the churches of Hamble, Hound, and West Worldham, for 1300 francs. Both parties sent agents to Paris to conclude the sale. Tiron appointed the priors of La Tréhoudière and Jardy as its proctors. The properties became part of the endowment of Winchester College.[22] Thus Tiron's English priories were sold or incorporated into other institutions at the end of the fourteenth century.

During the Lancastrian War (1415–1453), after the French defeat at Agincourt (1415), Henry V of England (b. 1386, r. 1413–1422) and his heirs were established as successors to the French throne. The Dauphin Charles (b. 1403), son of Charles VI (b. 1368, r. 1380–1422), was disinherited and subsequently the infant Henry VI of England (b. 1421, r. 1422–1461, 1470–1471) was crowned king of France (r. 1422–1453). Tiron Abbey was targeted because of its location on the border of Normandy and was pillaged

---

18 Laing, *Lindores Abbey*, 474 (appendix), no. 18

19 New, "History of the Alien Priories in England," 61–64. *Calendar of the Close Rolls of Edward III*, vol. 1 (London: Rolls Series, 1896), 18–19, 1, Edward III, 1, m 22 (February 4, 1327, Westminster).

20 *Calendar of the Close Rolls of Edward III*, Vol. 6 (London: Rolls Series, 1902), 358–62, 15, Edward III, 3. m 6 (December 6, 1341, Newcastle-upon-Tyne).

21 New, "History of the Alien Priories in England," 75. *Calendar of Close Rolls of Edward III*, 6:638, 16 Edward III, 2, m 34 (July 29, 1342, Westminster).

22 New, "History of the Alien Priories in England," 80–81. WCM, 2:431–32, nos. 10693–94.

and burned on June 13, 1428 by Thomas de Montague, earl of Salisbury (b. 1388, r. 1421–1428) and governor of the Chartrain region. Salisbury went to Abbot Michel Houssard (r. 1426–1431) and demanded his life or four thousand écus in silver coin and jewels. Houssard paid the ransom, but Salisbury took the horses, set fire to the abbey, and left a rear guard to prevent the monks from fighting the fire. The monastery buildings were destroyed, except for the church.[23] Salisbury behaved with exceptional cruelty even for the times, which suggests that Tiron was strategically important. Reduced circumstances followed, and the behavior of the unsupervised, newly poor monks became distinctly unmonastic. Since the scriptorium was destroyed, they forged charters to reconstitute their archives. Their attempts to obtain more income and exemptions from oversight embroiled them in lengthy litigation with the chapter of Chartres.[24]

Joan of Arc (1412–1431) had the dauphin crowned as Charles VII (r. 1422–1461) in 1429. By 1453 the English had been expelled from France except for Calais. William and his nephew Léonet Grimault, abbots of Tiron 1431–1453 and 1453–1498 respectively, instituted reforms and began to rebuild the ruined abbey. Reforms stipulated in contemporary general chapters seek to remedy recourse to violence, women, taverns, and secular dress.[25] Summarized records of later general chapters (1481–1559, 1496–1550) present exceptional matters first, such as the abbot's sentencing of two monks of La Pelice to prison in Tiron Abbey for fighting to the point of bloodshed in 1484. They proceed to assignments of benefices, leases for sharecropping farms, reports of visits to abbeys and priories, oaths given to the abbot of Tiron, and then other business.[26] By 1507–1508 Tiron's relations with the chapter of Chartres had deteriorated to cattle-raiding.[27] These charters support the centralized control of the abbot and general chapter of Tiron over the congregation well into the fifteenth century.

Hostilities continued between England and Scotland during the reign of Henry VIII. William Bunche, abbot of Kilwinning (r. 1474–1513), was one of four churchmen who fell at the battle of Flodden in 1513, where the invading Scots were disastrously defeated.[28] Henry VIII conducted a war with Scotland known as the Rough Wooing (1543–1551) to force a marriage between the infant Mary, queen of Scots (b. 1542, r. 1542–1567), and his son Edward VI (b. 1537, r. 1547–1553) and to destroy Scotland's "Auld Alliance" with France.

The Protestant Reformation emerged from earlier religious reform movements with the Ninety-five Theses posted by Martin Luther (1483–1546) in 1517, challenging many doctrines of the Roman Catholic Church and the authority of the papacy. The English Reformation (1536–1547) began with Henry VIII's declaring himself head of

---

23 Guillaumin, "Thiron, son Abbaye," 29.
24 T1:xviii–lviii.
25 Another reform mentioned in 1483 required the commemoration of the feast of Saint Bernard. IS-ADEL 8:163–64, H 1423 (1481–1559).
26 IS-ADEL, 8:163–66, H 1423 (1481–1559) to 1424 (1496–1550).
27 IS-ADEL 8:183, H 1610 (1507–1542).
28 *Cuninghame*, 261–62.

the English church in order to annul his first marriage. He claimed church property for the crown, and monasteries were dissolved throughout Britain. Young King James III (b. 1452, r. 1460–1488) was crowned at Kelso, but the abbey was destroyed in 1545 and disestablished by 1560. Arbroath also declined after the Reformation in 1560. Kilwinning was pillaged by Protestant bands in 1561 and was destroyed by 1591.[29] St. Dogmaels was destroyed at the beginning of the sixteenth century. Caldey remained a priory until the dissolution of the monasteries 1536–1541, when it was purchased, became secular property, and was restored as a Cistercian abbey in 1929.[30]

A similar movement occurred in France in the mid-sixteenth century. The monasteries were not dissolved, but the crown appropriated their income. The long line of thirty regular abbots of Tiron ended with the death of Geoffrey II Laubier in 1551. Thereafter Tiron was ruled by commendatory abbots, who might not be in religious orders or reside in the abbey but who enjoyed two-thirds of the abbey income without any obligation because of their royal appointment.[31] Tiron's income in 1573 was derived from three sources: census and rents owed to Tiron Abbey (2231 livres plus 422 chickens); income at Yron from the Beauce (16–1800 livres); and census and rents in Paris (5000 livres), amounting to 8831–10,831 livres annually.[32] While Tiron was not among the wealthiest abbeys in France, its holdings were substantial.

Many Tironensian commendatory abbots were prominent personages and important political figures.[33] The statesman Jean IV du Bellay (1492–1560), cardinal, bishop of Paris and Ostia, archbishop of Bordeaux, held the abbacy 1551–1560. Ippolito II d'Este (1509–1572), son of Lucrezia Borgia, cardinal of Ferrara and archbishop of Milan, Lyon, Auch, Narbonne, and Arles, together with other bishoprics, was commendatory abbot of Jumièges, Chaalis, Lyre, Boscherville, Flavigny, Pontigny, and Tiron (r. 1561–1563).[34] Charles de Ronsard, abbot of Tiron (r. 1564–1575), the brother of the poet Pierre de Ronsard (1524–1585), and René I de Laubier (r. 1575–1578) attempted restoration.

During the Wars of Religion between Catholics and Huguenots (1562–1598) Tiron Abbey, including its church, statues, and treasury, was pillaged March 19–22, 1562 by bands of Germans joining Louis, prince of Condé (1530–1569). Three monks were killed. The church was used as a stable; the statues of the Holy Trinity, Our Lady of Pity, and the Crucifix were broken; the altars of Saint Martin and Saint Eloi/Eligius were devastated; and shots were fired through the stained-glass windows. The most precious objects, sacred vases in gold and silver, relics of Saint Agapet and Saint Vincent, priestly ornaments, particularly Bernard's chasuble and mitre, were hidden in a wall near the chapter room but were found by the invaders.[35] Guillemin states that a sixteenth-century

---

29 *Cuninghame*, 263–67.
30 Howells, *Caldey*, 41.
31 Guillaumin, "Thiron, son Abbaye," 32.
32 IS-ADEL 8:168, H 1438 (1573).
33 GC, 8:1262–68.
34 Ippolito II d'Este gave the monastery a large gilded cross and a bell called la Ferrée in his honour. Guillaumin, "Thiron, son Abbaye," 32.
35 Guillaumin, "Thiron, son Abbaye," 32–33.

inventory described bejewelled silk chasubles, vases, censors, and other gold and silver objects set with precious stones.[36] They reflect Tiron's wealth and were stolen at this time.

The next commendatory abbot was Cardinal René I de Birague (1506–1583, r. 1578–1582), counsellor of the Parlement of Paris, Superintendent of Finances, Keeper of the Seals, and an instigator of the Saint Bartholomew's Day massacre (August 24, 1572). In 1583 Henry III (r. 1574–1589) appointed his official poet Philippe Desportes (1546–1606) abbot of Tiron (r. 1583–1606). Both did little for Tiron Abbey. In 1589, a battle at La Croix du Perche between the Royalists and the members of the Catholic League was fought about 3 kilometres southeast of Tiron. Because of its location in the border region, Tiron continued to be affected by wars throughout its long history.

Henry de Bourbon, king of Navarre, became Henry IV of France (r. 1589–1610). He ended the Wars of Religion by granting the Huguenots rights set forth in the Edict of Nantes in 1598. His natural son Henry II de Bourbon (b. 1601–1682), duke of Verneuil, bishop of Metz, became abbot of Tiron (r. 1607–1668) and of Saint-Germain-des-Prés. As an adult, he undertook the reform of Tiron, which had sunk into such corruption by 1626 that it was considered perhaps the most in need of reform of all the abbeys of France. The duke's agents requested Léonore d'Etampes de Valençay, bishop of Chartres (1620–1641) to make an unofficial visit, since Tiron, as head of an order, was exempt from episcopal visitation. The bishop was reluctantly admitted and found such disorder that he asked the monks what order they followed. They replied it was the order of Tiron. When the bishop asked what rule was set forth in their wording of profession, they were so ignorant that they had to look it up in a book. It was the same as any other Benedictine order. Henry II de Bourbon obtained papal authorization for the bishop to enter the monastery on an official visit as an apostolic commissioner. After the dormitory and refectory were repaired, in 1629 Tiron was incorporated into the Benedictine congregation of Saint-Maur, with its headquarters at Saint-Germain-des-Prés.[37] The Maurist architect Dom Hilaire Pinet (1611–1675), drew up the plan of Tiron with proposed architectural projects, contained in *Monasticon Gallicanum*, no. 58. Saint-Maur opened a *collège* for classical education in the abbot's house at Tiron in 1630, described as prominent ca. 1739.[38]

Henry IV's successor Louis XIII (b. 1601, r. 1610–1643) and Anne of Austria (1601–1666) had two sons: Louis XIV (b. 1638, r. 1643–1715) and Philip I, duke of Orléans (Monsieur) (1640–1701). Louis XIV's eldest son and heir was Louis, le Grand Dauphin (Monseigneur) (1661–1711), and his grandson was Louis de France (1682–1712), duke of Burgundy and later Dauphin of France. A measles epidemic in 1711–1712 killed his son and grandson; his great-grandson and successor was Louis XV (b. 1710, r. 1715–1774). In 1698 Michel-André Joubert de Bouville compiled a mémoire for the duke of Burgundy of the Intendance of Orléans. The relationship of the duke's uncle, Philip I, duke of Orléans,

---

36 Guillaumin, *Thiron, son abbaye, son collège militaire, guide*, 74–75.
37 Martène, *Histoire de la congrégation de Saint-Maur*, 1:265–67.
38 *Pouillé du diocèse de Chartres* (Chartres: Doublet, 1738), 24, accessible online at https://books.google.com/books?id=6ZNUl01WoR4C.

with Philippe II de Lorraine d'Harcourt (le Chevalier de Lorraine) (1643–1702) became public in 1667. Monsieur made his minion commendatory abbot of several abbeys to which he had the right of presentment: Tiron with its abbatial mense (abbot's share of the revenue) of over 10,000 livres in 1672, Fleury (20,000 livres), and Saint-Père-en-Vallée-de-Chartres (15,000 livres).[39] Guillaumin states that the Chevalier de Lorraine had Tiron's nearly ruined cloister repaired[40] and that in 1740 Elisabeth Charlotte, née Princess Palatine, duchess of Orléans (1652–1722), gave wood panelling and stalls for the choir. The amounts indicate that Tiron was sufficiently prestigious to be in the portfolio of the brother of the king of France.

Upon his marriage Henry II de Bourbon was succeeded as abbot of Tiron by Jean-Casimir Vasa (r. 1669–1672), king of Poland 1648–1668. Other commendatory abbots of Tiron included Charles II Irénée Castel de Saint Pierre (b. 1658, r. 1703–1743), a member of the Académie Française; Antoine de Malherbe (r. 1743–1771), a canon of Notre-Dame-de-Paris and vicar general of Rouen; and Mathieu-Jacques de Vermond (1735–1806) (r. 1771–1782), a librarian at the Collège Mazarin and a reader to Marie-Antoinette. Most commendatory abbots collected their share of the income, allowed the buildings to fall into disrepair, and ignored Tiron's religious life.

Louis, duke of Burgundy and father of Louis XV, ordered an overview of France before his death in 1712, which was edited by Henri de Boulainvilliers and published in London 1727–1728. The extract for the Généralité of Paris shows the income of the bishop of Chartres (18,000 livres) and of the Chartrain abbeys of Saint-Père-en-Vallée (1,500 livres), Tiron (14,000 livres), Josaphat (10,000 livres), Saint-Jean-en-Vallée-lès-Chartres (15,000 livres). The wealthier abbeys in Paris were Sainte-Geneviève (70,000 livres), Saint-Germain-des-Prés (172,000 livres), and Saint-Victor (35,000 livres).[41] In 1746 a statement of the income and expenses of Tiron's dependent priories totaled 7,778 livres in income less 2,538 livres in expenses or 5,240 livres net income. Les Châtaigniers and Bouche d'Aigre had the highest incomes and expenses.[42]

In 1776 the Collège de Tiron became a royal military school. The enrolment varied but averaged about fifty king's scholars and as many ordinary boarders. With three rates of 250, 350, and 400 livres, the school provided an income of 25,000–40,000 livres excluding expenses. A kitchen fire spread December 22–23, 1786 and destroyed the west wing of the abbey. The archives and over five thousand valuable volumes were saved, but magnificent paintings and sculptures and other volumes were destroyed. Religious

---

39 *L'Intendance d'Orléans à la fin du XVIIe siècle: mémoire pour l'instruction du duc de Bourgogne*, ed. Michel-André Jubert de Bouville et al. (Paris: Editions du Comité des travaux historiques et scientifiques, 1989), 155–56n19 and 174n121, refers to Tiron's fourteen abbeys, particular observances, and abbatial mense of about 8000 livres.

40 Guillaumin, "Thiron, son Abbaye", 34. Guillaumin, *Thiron, son abbaye, son collège militaire, guide*, 13.

41 *Etat de la France*, ed. Henri de Boulainvilliers, 3 vols. (London: Wood and Palmer, 1727–1728), vol. 2.2: *Etat de France considerée dans sa généralité: Extrait du Mémoire de la Généralité de Paris*, 135 (Chartres), 2 (Paris).

42 IS-ADEL 8:196, H 1779 (1746).

orders were suppressed in 1790: the abbey was closed by 1791 and the school by 1792. Part of the library was sold by unpaid staff and suppliers, and the abbey was pillaged by squatters. In 1817, the choir of the abbatial church of Tiron collapsed. Local efforts to preserve the history and ruins of the abbey persisted through the ensuing centuries.

The Tironensian daughter abbeys survived for centuries, with the same pattern of commendatory abbots and wartime devastation. Arcisses passed under commendatory abbots in 1547 and survived until 1627.[43] Ferrières, a prosperous abbey, was burned and devastated in 1338 during the Hundred Years' War. In 1570, Asnières and Ferrières were burned and pillaged by the Huguenot army. Asnières survived until 1746.[44] Ferrières experienced another fire in 1569.[45] Le Gué-de-Launay had only three monks in 1461 and five in 1483. Commendatory abbots held it 1544–1790, and it was also invaded by Calvinists.[46] Joug-Dieu resisted royal pressure to install commendatory abbots in 1477, so its abbots were elected by the abbot and monks of Tiron until that date at least. Louis de Crevant (r. 1511–1515) was simultaneously abbot of Tiron and abbot of Joug-Dieu. Joug-Dieu's last recorded abbot was in 1713.[47] La Pelice survived until 1731, but only five monks were living there in 1697.[48] Le Tronchet was involved in frequent disputes with Tiron in 1399. The fathers of the British Benedictine congregation took over Le Tronchet in 1607.[49] The ruins of these foundations are beautiful and of architectural interest.

The dissolution process mirrored the early expansion process. When abbeys were dissolved, their cut stone, lead, books, and valuables were claimed by their creditors or looted, and their lands and farms were sold. When monastic stone buildings were abandoned or collapsed, some ruins were incorporated into new buildings or became archeological sites. While the community may have preserved and used the priory church, the priories were often broken up and sold as dwellings and farmland. Their urban property was sold to private owners, and some demolitions are recalled in street and site names.

In modern times, some properties have been restored or are privately owned; some ruins are national monuments, and many church vocables have endured for centuries. The Tironensian churches are its architectural legacy. They dominate the skylines of many small towns and hamlets. Frequently their histories refer to the original eleventh- or twelfth-century building and its incorporation into a later structure. Without a worshipping community many churches became landmarks, monuments, festival halls, community and cultural centres. Churchyard ruins endured because of a reluctance to disturb graves or to build on them. Much of the congregation of Tiron survives today in memory and commemoration.

---

43 GC, 8:1302–3.
44 GC, 14:693–95.
45 GC, 8:1268–69.
46 GC, 14:496–98
47 GC, 4:281–83, and 8:1272–77.
48 GC, 14:498–501.
49 GC, 14:1074–79.

In the modern region between Chartres and Blois, Tiron's architectural legacy is evident. The basilica church nave is a parish church and museum, and the pond and workrooms endure. The Association de l'Ordre de Tiron is attempting to restore the network of subordinate foundations of Tiron and to contact the towns where its priories were located.[50] No properties remain in the wheat region southeast of Châteaudun or east of Orléans. In modern northern France Tiron has no abbeys, but its architectural legacy of churches is substantial. In west France Tiron's architectural legacy matches its legacy in the Chartres-Blois region. The Beck family is restoring Hambye, and the chapter house is completed. Le Tronchet has been renovated as a hotel. In south France Tiron's architectural legacy is mainly confined to its abbeys near the Loire; few of its churches have survived. Bois-Aubry became a farm and then was purchased by the Société Civile de l'Eglise Orthodoxe de France and the Association Culturelle Catholique et Orthodoxe de l'Abbaye Saint-Michel et Saint Martin in 1978.[51] When Yul Brynner (1920–1985) died, his widow eventually entrusted his ashes to a family friend who was an orthodox monk at Bois-Aubry, where a special cemetery was created and dedicated to the actor. The property was purchased by Marc-Olivier Gribomont in 2006.[52] Asnières, privately owned since 2014 by Alain Suguenot, is a former monument that can be visited. The choir and transepts of the abbey church survive and are fine examples of Angevin gothic architecture. The sculptures in the north transept depict the Last Judgement and a scene of the life of Saint Martin.[53] In east France Tiron's architectural legacy is minimal.

In England Tiron's architectural legacy resembles its legacy in Chartres-Blois and west France, with many active churches and landmarks or monuments. Owing to declining church membership, several churches may support a benefice for a single vicar, or one congregation may worship in rotation in several churches within its modern parish. The parishioners of the Priory Church of St. Andrew of Hamble-le-Rice recently made a pilgrimage to Tiron.[54] In south Wales, Tiron's architectural legacy in Pembrokeshire is evident. St. Dogmaels Abbey is a monument.[55] Caldey is an active Cistercian monastery and an important pilgrimage centre.[56] The ruins of Pill Priory near Milford Haven are an archeological site.[57] Many parish churches continue to be used as worship centres.

In Scotland Tiron's rich architectural legacy was shaped by its incorporation of centres of pre-Christian worship, hermitages, and Célidé communities. The quality of

---

50 www.ordre-tiron.com/association.html; www.perchethironnais.com/images/pages/BULLETIN_ADHESION_ORDRE_de_TIRON.pdf

51 www.abbayedeboisaubry.fr/fr/histoire.php

52 www.francebleu.fr/infos/culture-loisirs/yul-brynner-30-ans-apres-sa-mort-l-abbaye-de-bois-aubry-se-souvient-1444405538

53 www.maine-et-loire.fr/fileadmin/user_upload/internet/actions/educ_cult_sport/culture/patrimoine/fiches_reflet/asnieres.pdf

54 www.st-andrew-hamble.org.uk/

55 http://cadw.wales.gov.uk/daysout/stdogmaelsabbeyandcoachhouse/?lang=en

56 www.caldey-island.co.uk

57 www.pillpriory.co.uk/files/history.asp

the construction was complemented by centuries of local attachment to the site. In south Scotland, the abbey of Kelso is a monument that merits greater attention because of its historical importance in the Borders.[58] In Edinburgh, Arthur's Seat with St. Anthony's Chapel is part of Holyrood Park.[59] In the northeast, Arbroath Abbey is an important monument.[60] The priory of Fyvie has vanished, except for a Celtic cross.[61] Many of Arbroath's churches remain parish churches, although none survive west of Montrose or south of Glasgow. Arbroath's Northumberland property—Haltwhistle, modern Holy Cross—is a parish church.[62] Lindores's architectural legacy is less abundant; its ruins are privately owned.[63] In 2013 Andrew McKenzie Smith planned its restoration as the birthplace of whisky distillation.[64] The Newburgh Orchard Group recounts that the monks' orchards in modern Newburgh were rented to the town residents, have survived, and produce many varieties of apples, pears, and other fruit.[65] Lindores's English properties, Whissendine and Cunington/Conington, survive as parish churches. In west Scotland, Kilwinning was a smaller foundation, but its architectural legacy is similar to that of Arbroath, with many parish churches. The abbey of Kilwinning is a monument, and the Old Parish Church is an active parish.[66] The Tironensian monks are remembered locally as Frenchmen and healers. The abbey is associated with Freemasonry, the Knights Templar, and witch-burnings in popular fiction.

The disintegration and dissolution of the Angevin Empire and the congregation of Tiron were inevitable; only an exceptional leader could rule so vast an area. Nonetheless, their creation was remarkable, and religious developments often anticipated secular developments at that time. Tiron preceded the Angevin Empire and the Cistercian congregation and deserves a place in monastic studies for that reason. Tiron's survival as a large religious congregation from ca. 1107 until 1792, almost seven centuries, establishes it as an important religious order deserving further research and scholarship.

This study continues research begun for my translation of the *Vita Bernardi*. It focuses mainly on Tiron's foundation and growth in its first century of existence, and yet the possibilities for that narrow range are far from exhausted. This study tentatively contextualizes Tiron in the history of reformed Benedictine and eremetical congregations. Tiron's claim to historical importance has numerous bases. It was the

---

58 www.visitscotland.com/en-us/info/see-do/kelso-abbey-p247581
59 www.visitscotland.com/en-us/info/see-do/holyrood-park-and-arthurs-seat-p914341
60 www.historic-scotland.gov.uk/index/places/propertyresults/propertyoverview.htm?PropID=PL_013
61 www.scottishchurches.org.uk/sites/site/id/3720/name/Fyvie+Priory+Fyvie+Grampian
62 www.docbrown.info/docspics/northeast/nutpage46.htm
63 http://en.wikipedia.org/wiki/Lindores_Abbey
64 www.scotsman.com/heritage/people-places/5m-move-to-revive-whisky-birthplace-lindores-abbey-1-3117289
65 www.newburghorchards.org.uk/page4.html
66 www.historic-scotland.gov.uk/propertyresults/propertydetail.htm?PropID=PL_184
    http://kilwinningoldparish.co.uk

first of the new orders to establish foundations in the British Isles as well as on the continent. It was among the first to rule those foundations through a centralized administrative system and an annual general chapter. It was among the first to establish granges as an alternative to sharecropping farms, contemporary with the Premonstratensians and preceding the Cistercians.[67] It established a centre of crafts and trade in Chartres, bred horses, furthered the coastal–inland salt–wine–grain trade that nourished the new towns, supported pilgrimages, and may have engaged in organized trading with the British Isles. In Scotland the Tironensian houses were actively involved in trade and construction, in addition to the usual monastic contributions to spiritual life and to agriculture, education, medicine, and law. As religious centres they were instrumental in the Normanization process in Scotland and Wales. They also incorporated or supplanted the earlier religious leaders of those countries in an extension of continental monasticism. As foundations with strong eremitical roots and traditions, they were particularly suited to assume the mantle of the Célidé of Abernethy and other French and Celtic hermits. The Tironensian abbots were national leaders who became actively involved in the independence of the Scottish church and state from English domination. They left an architectural legacy of great beauty, even in ruin.

There has been little study of Tiron's early expansion in France and in Scotland. Owing to the language barrier, similar patterns have hitherto gone unremarked. Medieval Britain was less populated and had fewer monasteries, towns, and roads than medieval France in the twelfth century, so the pattern was clearer. The British royal and noble founders deliberately endowed Tironensian monasteries with the properties they required for income, trade, and communication. In France Tiron and its daughter abbeys deliberately acquired the properties they needed for the same purpose through negotiation in competitive situations. An important finding is that studies of monastic congregations should include mapping of abbeys, priories, churches, property agglomerations, and town houses. Roads, waterways, and pilgrimage routes must be taken into consideration. The meticulous process involved is time-consuming, and patterns emerge only gradually. In Tiron's case mapping reveals careful planning and purposeful acquisition patterns for trade and communication. Mapping Tiron uncovers the order's expansion process.

One result is that Abbot William of Tiron emerges from obscurity as a skilled and vigourous administrator and an implementer of Bernard's visionary ideas. He associated with English and French royalty, the nobility, and important bishops. He was a shrewd negotiator and developed a business model that profited from the rise of towns. The study sheds light on his tremendous accomplishments in building up the network of Tironensian foundations and centralizing their administration through an annual general chapter. Yet his identity is unknown, and he is not mentioned in the *Vita Bernardi*. Perhaps future scholars will learn more about this remarkable man.

This study examines a few knotty problems and special features. It contextualizes Tiron among the few twelfth-century foundations involved in trade. It offers new insights into the lost "rule of Tiron." It corrects numerous inaccuracies and misconceptions about

---

67 Constable, *The Reformation of the Twelfth Century,* 220.

the founder and the congregation. It offers local information about Bernard's origins, establishes his death date, and suggests that he died from ergot poisoning or erysipelas. It clarifies the tensions of encroachment by Cluny and competition from Cîteaux. It also sheds new light on the motivations of many prominent secular leaders who chose to fund, support, and advance the Tironensian monks. It presents Berman's suspicions about the foundation charter of St. Dogmaels dated 1120 and provides evidence for its backdating a decade later. It examines the issuance of a *filia specialis* bull to Kelso in 1165 without the customary phrase *nullo medio/mediante* at a time when another papal bull affirmed Tiron's superiority over Kelso and postulates nominal assertions of dependence to establish proctorship in a mutually beneficial business arrangement. Most importantly, this study maps the Tironensian network, discerns regional patterns, and describes the objectives, deals, and disputes inherent in the expansion process.

This study of the congregation of Tiron in the twelfth century covers merely a portion of its history. Yet it deepens contemporary understanding of the variety of reformed Benedictine orders and shows that they did not all follow the Cistercian model. Insofar as Tiron began its development prior to and then contemporaneously with the Cistercian order, it followed its own unique path and may have influenced other religious foundations. The Tironensian monasteries were prosperous, and while they were eremitical in tradition and language, there is no evidence that their members were noted for their austerity, spirituality, or antifeminism. This book is intended to rescue a lost congregation from obscurity and break ground for future research on many aspects of its history.

Appendix I

COMPARISON OF THE PAPAL CONFIRMATIONS

TIRON, LIKE OTHER religious congregations, prepared and paid for papal confirmations of its most important properties. Tiron obtained papal protection of its properties in 1119 and prepared lists for papal confirmations in 1132, 1147, and 1175. This study relies heavily on three papal confirmations of 1132 (fol. 1v), 1147 (fol. 90r), and 1175 (fol. 58) that were copied into the manuscript cartulary by twelfth-century scribes. In these confirmations the properties are listed by diocese. Not all properties were confirmed; other charters show Tironensian monks in residence in towns and farms but not organized into priories. A second parchment version of the 1147 confirmation in the departmental archives (ADEL, H 1378) differs from the cartulary version, but almost all the properties listed in 1147 are also listed in 1175. The 1175 confirmation shows little additional expansion in France. Tiron prepared an inventory of the abbey's income ca. 1250, which supplements these confirmations.

Tiron formally obtained papal protection from Callistus II at Reims in 1119.[1] In 1132 Innocent II travelled from Rome to France, and Abbot William of Tiron, Abbot Bernard of Clairvaux, and Geoffrey II, bishop of Chartres, sought papal confirmations.[2] On 16 March 1132/1133, at Valence, Innocent II issued a confirmation of the possessions of Tiron Abbey at the petition of Abbot William. Copied at the beginning of the Tironensian manuscript cartulary, the confirmation categorizes the properties as *abbatia* and *ecclesia*.

Wales: St. Dogmaels
Scotland: Kelso
Chartres: St.-Jean-et-St.-Paul-de-Bouche-d'Aigre, St.-Gilles-des-Châtaigniers
Poitiers and Angers: St.-Léonard-de-Ferrières, ND-d'Asnières, ND-de-Sainte-Croix-du-Teil-aux-Moines
Le Mans: St.-Laurent-du-Gué-de-Launay, St.-Pierre-de-Louïe
Evreux: St.-Martin-d'Heudreville-sur-Eure
Paris: La-Madeleine-de-Jardy
Le Mans: ND-de-l'Eguillé
Chartres: St.-Jean-des-Murgers
Winchester: St. Andrew of Hamble

---

[1] T1:36–37, no. 20.

[2] In 1132 Innocent II held a synod at Reims at which he anathematized antipope Anacletus II (1130–1138) and crowned the French king's heir. J. N. D. Kelly, *Oxford Dictionary of Popes* (Oxford: Oxford University Press, 1996), 167–68. On February 17 at Lyon, as he moved toward Rome, Innocent II confirmed the possessions and privileges of the monastery of Notre Dame de Clairvaux at the petition of Abbot Bernard. *Regesta Pontificorum Romanorum*, ed. Jaffé, 1:854, no. 7544. Tiron's confirmation is listed in ibid., 1:855, no. 7557. The next bull, no. 7558, issued on March 22 at Avignon, confirmed the goods and privileges of the cathedral of Notre Dame de Chartres at the request of Bishop Geoffrey II.

The confirmation contains a *sane laborum* clause allowing Tiron to keep the tithes on its own products, produce, and livestock, an issue when monasteries acquired properties whose tenants owed parish tithes or cleared new land and put it under cultivation.[3]

This central north–south axis of expansion of the congregation of Tiron mainly corresponded to domains controlled by the kinship group of Henry I: his brother-in-law David I of Scotland, his royal domains in Wales and England, his dukedom of Normandy, his nephew Thibaut II's domain of Blois and Chartres, and his legitimate children's alliances with the counts of Anjou. Abbot William and Rotrou II, count of the Perche, knew this axis through their travels.[4] The congregation of Tiron expanded around the periphery of this central core of development: to the west into Lower Normandy, Brittany, Maine, and Anjou, to the south into Poitou and Aquitaine, and to the east in the vicinity of Paris and more distant foundations in Champagne and Beaujolais.

Fifteen years later, with England ravaged by the civil war during the reign of King Stephen, at the instigation of Pope Eugenius III, Bernard of Clairvaux preached the Second Crusade at an assembly in Vézelay at Easter 1146.[5] Tiron Abbey acquired property from local crusaders in pledge or for cash and grain, and Abbot William sought confirmation of Tiron's greatly expanded holdings. Eugenius III issued a confirmation of Tiron's property in Paris on May 30, 1147.[6] Two versions have survived with significant discrepancies.

The first copy of the confirmation, in the Archives Départementales d'Eure-et-Loir, categorizes the properties as *abbatia*, *ecclesia*, *capella*, *granea*, and *locus*, and follows the order of the 1132 confirmation, beginning with the British abbeys in Wales and Scotland. Near the Loire, the abbey of Bois-Aubry in Tours is inserted as Saint-Michel-de-Luzé after Asnières. New priories in Winchester are added after Hamble. New northern properties in the dioceses of Rouen and Evreux are listed next, followed by new properties in the diocese of Chartres, including twelve granaries or granges, and the diocese of Sées to the west. The next properties are in the diocese of Bayeux northwest of Sées, followed by a church in the diocese of Meaux east of Paris. The next properties are in the diocese of Poitiers to the south, and the diocese of Nantes, south of the Loire, followed by properties in the dioceses of Angers and Le Mans, in Anjou. The confirmation ends with scattered properties in Chartres, Tours, Paris, and the distant abbey of Joug-Dieu in the diocese of Lyon.[7]

---

[3] T1:201–3, no. 182, specifically 202: *Decimas sane laborum quos propriis manibus aut sumptibus colitis, seu etiam vestrorum animalium, absque alicujus contradiction, vobis concedimus possidendas.*

[4] Rotrou II had journeyed as far as north as Woodstock, Oxfordshire, England in 1126 and 1139, and as far south as Tudela and Aragon in Spain. Thompson, *Power and Border Lordship*, 71–81; idem, "Affairs of State," 147, citing n89, BL Cotton Vespasian MS F xv, fol. 171v.

[5] Hallam, *Capetian France*, 122.

[6] T2:60–67, nos. 291–92. *Regesta Pontificorum Romanorum*, ed. Jaffé, 2:43, no. 9065.

[7] T2:60–63, no. 291.

This approximately north–south view of the Tironensian properties corresponds to a portion of one of the ancient pilgrimage routes to the shrine of Saint James of Compostela in Galicia. Pilgrims in southern England travelled from London to Brighton, and crossed the Channel to Dieppe or Caen. Pilgrims at Dieppe then chose one of two routes south to Tours and continued south to Poitiers and Saintes and on to Spain. There were secondary pilgrim routes, some along rivers, which linked seemingly isolated Tironensian priories. These pilgrimage roads, regarded as paths for the transmission of culture, were also well-established trade routes and channels of communication. Tiron's properties were located near many of these towns, and ordering them roughly north to south would have seemed natural to a religious community in the earlier twelfth century.

The second copy of the confirmation in the Tironensian manuscript cartulary is more accurate than the first and reflects a very different world view. The confirmation categorizes most properties as *ecclesia* or *locum*, although some are simply named. It begins with the extensive old and new properties in the diocese of Chartres, two new properties in the archdiocese of Sens and other old and new properties in the vicinity of Paris in the dioceses of Paris, Meaux, Soissans, and Orléans. Then it lists old and new properties to the northwest of Tiron Abbey in the dioceses of Evreux, Sées, Lisieux, and the archdiocese of Rouen, followed by southern properties in the diocese of Poitiers. It continues with properties near the Loire in the dioceses of Nantes, Tours, and Angers, new properties in the archdiocese of Bourges and the diocese of Clermont-Ferrand, Joug-Dieu on a highway to the Loire near Lyon in that archdiocese, and new properties in Saintes. The extensive Angevin holdings in the archdiocese of Le Mans are listed next to last, and the list ends with English properties in the dioceses of Winchester and Hereford, the distant abbeys of St. Dogmaels and Kelso, and income in Salisbury. The *Vita Bernardi* configures the geography of Bernard's reputation similarly.[8] This perspective, from the centre radiating out, suggests that Tiron Abbey's world view changed markedly during the Civil War in England, while Geoffrey V of Anjou completed his conquest of Normandy by 1144. The abbey came to view its properties as centred primarily around Chartres, Paris, and the Beauce, with outlying properties in Anjou and Normandy, and distant properties in the British Isles. In this particular configuration, the Loire, a great thoroughfare to the Atlantic, both divided the Tironensian properties and connected them.

Thompson considers the first copy of confirmation of 1147 (no. 291) to predate the second (no. 292), which after the early 1160s "was rearranged by diocese and copied onto a new parchment gathering that was kept with the original cartulary."[9] Her explanation accounts for the existence of two copies and the greater comprehensiveness of the second copy (no. 292), but the differences are not limited to the properties. No. 291 concludes with a single "Amen" and no. 292 concludes with "Amen Amen Amen."

---

8 "Not only was he acclaimed throughout the nearby parts of the region of Gaul but his praise was conveyed to the farthest parts of Burgundy, the Midi [Alani], and Aquitaine; it spread to the Anglo-Norman and British borders and went as far as Albania of the Scots [...]." VB, 11.95, AASS, Apr. 2: 0245C–E; VB, trans. Cline, 101.

9 Thompson, *The Monks of Tiron*, 176.

No. 292 has two witnesses not listed in no. 291: Odo, Cardinal-deacon of San Giorgio in Velabro, altered to Velum Aureum in the Middle Ages, and Guido, cardinal-priest titular of San Crisogono (sometimes spelled Grisogono). Since the witness list for no. 292 is very similar to the list of the next confirmation of the monastic property of Saint-Denis of Montmartre issued at Paris on June 7, 1147,[10] either its copier post-1160 had additional knowledge of the papal entourage in Paris in 1147 or no. 292 is based on another original. Raoul de Saint-Venant supposed that the abbot of Tiron went to Paris, compiled a list of the properties in no. 291 in haste and from memory, got it signed, realized the omissions, and had no. 292 composed as a replacement and issued in Paris under the original date.[11] His explanation would account for the greater accuracy and additional witnesses in the cartulary copy of the 1160s.

The most striking difference, however, is the *sane laborum* clause covering the extent of the exemption from tithes. No. 291 reads "no one shall presume to exact tithes from you from the produce that you raise by your own hands or for your own use or from the food of your animals or to exact dues paid for ministrations by the parish priest from your *servientes*."[12] No. 292 reads "no one shall presume to exact tithes from you from the produce that you raise by your own hands or for your own use or from the food of your animals."[13] The second clause uses the standard wording, and the parish dues exemption in the first clause is an aberration.

Giles Constable has covered the century of deliberations about whether monks could function as priests when they acquired property with *servientes* who had previously paid dues to the parish or whether they could collect tithes from the work of others. The papal formula for exemption evolved from limiting exemption to tithes on the monks' own produce, not that of their *servientes*, to limiting exemption to noval tithes, or "tithes from their new lands which they cultivated by their own hands and for their own use, from the food of their animals, and from their gardens." By the 1180s generally the Cistercians and military orders were exempt from tithes and other monks and canons were exempt only from noval tithes,[14] but the exemptions were negotiable when Tiron was expanding.[15]

A computer search of the acts of Eugenius III yielded numerous tithe exemption clauses identical to the one in the second confirmation of Tironensian property

---

[10] PL 180:1236C–39A, 193, Confirmation after Tiron, June 7, 1147.

[11] M. R. de Saint-Venant, "La Paroisse de la Chapelle-Vicomtesse et sa Fondation," *Bulletin de la Société archéologique, scientifique, et littéraire du Vendômois* 39, no. 3 (1900): 162–94, specifically 185–86.

[12] "*sane laborum quos propiis manibus aut sumptibus colitis, sive de nutrimentis vestrorum animalium, nullus a vobis decimas nec a servientibus vestris parrochialia exigere presumat*," T2:62, no. 291. English translation based on Constable, *Monastic Tithes from their Origins to the Twelfth Century*, 296.

[13] "*sane laborum vestrorum quos propiis manibus aut sumptibus colitis, sive de nutrimentis vestrorum animalium, nullus a vobis decimas exigere presumat*," T2:66, no. 292.

[14] Constable, *Monastic Tithes from their Origins to the Twelfth Century*, 304.

[15] Constable, *Monastic Tithes from their Origins to the Twelfth Century*, 299.

(no. 292). Searches using the keywords *servientibus* and *parochialia* in the first confirmation (no. 291) showed that, of the corpus of 591 acts of Eugenius III, Tiron obtained the only confirmation exempting *servientes* from payment of dues for ministrations by the parish priest.[16] In Paris, Tiron's confirmation was preceded by a papal confirmation for the monastery of Notre-Dame de Soissans on May 25, 1147 and followed by the aforementioned confirmation for the monastery of Saint-Denis of Montmartre on June 7, 1147.[17] Both contain the standard *sane laborum* clause, and it seems unlikely that a single exception was made for Tiron. Perhaps no. 291 reflects what Tiron hoped to confirm and no. 292 copied into the cartulary reflects what was actually confirmed in Paris in 1147.

A comparison of the 1147 and 1175/1176 confirmations shows that Tiron's rapid expansion in France did not continue. Abbot Stephan I obtained a papal confirmation from Alexander III misdated 1175–1176, before 1173, almost thirty years later, which was copied into the Tironensian manuscript cartulary. It categorizes the properties as *ecclesia* and shows limited growth. In the diocese of Chartres, the church of Saint-Médard-de-Viabon is added to the Voves cluster, and the farm of Sancheville is added to the Bonneval cluster. In the archdiocese of Rouen it lists the new church and priory of Saint-Martin-de-Crasville. In the diocese of Bayeux it lists the new priory of Saint-Antonin-de-Montargis and the church of Crèvecoeur-en-Auge. In Brittany, in the diocese of Nantes, it lists the church of Saint-Nicolas-de-Redon near the port of Saint-Nazaire. In the archdiocese of Dol it lists the future abbey of Le Tronchet near Plerguer and the port of Saint-Malo. Although not listed, the abbeys of Hambye near Coutances and Saint-Méen near Rennes became part of the congregation of Tiron. In the diocese of Le Mans, it lists the churches of Saint-Pierre-de-Ternay near Montoire-sur-le-Loir, and Saint-Pierre-d'Arçonnay, the tithes of Chérancé near Mamers, and the tithes of Grandchamp, and Rosay in the Saint-Paterne cluster near Alençon. In the diocese of Salesbury the new churches of Bradford Peverell and Stratton are listed. The standard *sane laborum* clause is changed to *sane novalium*, limiting exemption to noval tithes from new lands brought under cultivation, used throughout the papal charters of Alexander III.[18] This expansion in Angevin and Breton lands controlled by Henry II suggests continued support for Tiron by the Plantagenet king and his nobles and is consistent with the confirmation of Tiron's annual twenty marks from the Exchequer by his successors.

---

16 http://pld.chadwyck.com.proxy.library.georgetown.edu/all/fulltext?ALL=Y&ACTION=byid&warn=N&div=3&id=Z300106900&FILE=../session/1427824650_25475&CURDB=pld

17 PL 180:1223B–25B, no. 182, specifically 1224C (Notre-Dame-de-Soissons); PL 180:1236C–39A, no. 193, specifically 1238B (Saint-Denis of Montmartre)

18 T2:98–102, no. 326, specifically 101, *Sane novalium vestrorum que propriis manibus aut sumptibus colitis, sive de nutrimentis vestrorum animalium, nullus a vobis decimas exigere presumat.* PL 200:0086C, no. 17, and elsewhere.

Appendix 2

DISPUTES

DURING THE EXPANSION process the Tironensians had their share of disputes. Some were local. Some involved conflicting claims by other priories, monasteries, or religious organizations. The worst disputes were in the Beauce, where the wheat fields were valuable and local wars were being waged. One dispute occurred as far away as London, concerning overdue annual payments from the Exchequer. They ensued because the congregation was acquiring strategic and valuable properties together with regional authority and seigneurial rights. Many were resolved by the local lord or bishop. In dispute resolution the Tironensians were resourceful negotiators.

Tiron attempted to avoid disputes by clarifying rights and boundaries at the time of acquisition. The priory of Bacqueville-en-Caux included three churches. For the church of Notre-Dame-de-Bacqueville Hugh III, archbishop of Rouen, specified that the priory was not to interfere with the Cistercian foundation of Le Pin, also given by William Martel. For the church of Saint-Pierre-de-Bacqueville, he excluded the property of the monks of Saint-Wandrille-de-Fontonelle. The third church of Saint-Jean-Baptiste-d'Imbleville, a day's journey south on the Saâne River, was given without restrictions.[1] When a new monk gave land and tithes (listed as fruit, wool, lambs, piglets, and coins) to Saint-Barthélemy-du-Vieux-Charencey, nearby land given to the monks of Saint-Père-de-Chartres was specifically excluded.[2] When Le Tronchet was founded, agreements were concluded with the abbeys of Saint-Melanie and Saint-Jacut-de-la-Mer.[3] Asnières was founded on land originally given to the monks of Saint-Nicolas d'Angers, who neglected it and then demanded a settlement for their rights in 1137.[4] The Tironensians were settling in areas where earlier religious foundations were established and attempted to avert disputes by detailed agreements with witnesses.

During the twelfth century Tiron Abbey established its outlying farms and priories.[5] Locally, the generosity of Rotrou II and his family toward Tiron was counterbalanced by the competitiveness of the Cluniac priory of Saint-Denis-de-Nogent-le-Rotrou and its powerful international congregation. A dispute arose over property that a knight named Robert Judas (f. ca. 1118–1130) granted to Saint-Denis in 1118, before accompanying Rotrou II to Spain. Upon his return Robert granted the same property to Tiron

---

[1] T1:203–5, no. 183 (1133).

[2] T1:168, no. 143 (ca. 1130).

[3] Brébel, *Essai historique sur Pleudihen*, 301.

[4] *Dictionnaire historique, géographique et bibliographique de Maine-et-Loire et de l'ancienne province d'Anjou*, ed. Célestin Port, 4 vols. (Angers: Siraudeau, 1874–1878; repr. 1965), 1:189.

[5] The farms of Les Aulnays, Coudelée, Bois-aux-Clercs, la Vallée at Thiron, Bouchage, Gauleries, and Petit Gaufleville at Saint Denis-d'Authou were at a convenient distance from the abbey. Guillemin, *Thiron, abbaye médiévale*, 62–63.

Abbey. Rotrou II requested the monks of Saint-Denis to grant Tiron tithes at "Old Tiron" in order to obtain Robert's initial grant. The tithes were probably the ones Saint-Denis had claimed in 1113 on the first Tironensian foundation of Tiron-Brunelles, forcing Abbot Bernard to move his foundation out of the parish.[6] With the count's assistance an old score was settled. Resolving another local dispute with the monks, Hugh of Crignon relinquished his claims to the dams of the mills of Espal near Arcisses in exchange for income.[7] By that time the Tironensians often settled disputes with cash payments.

When Tiron and the nearby hamlet of Gardais to the east on the Thironne River grew sufficiently to achieve the status of towns, and a mayor was appointed for Gardais,[8] a dispute that arose between William, the mayor, and the abbey about their respective rights was resolved by an agreement. In the presence of the seneschal of Perche, William and his son Peter, who had been harassing the abbot and monks of Tiron about the mayorship, relinquished whatever right they claimed before the church altar.[9] Tiron Abbey was next involved in a dispute over the ecclesiastical jurisdiction of Gardais and the borough of the monks of Tiron. Henry, archdeacon of Chartres, ruled that although the town of Gardais was among his temporals and part of his prebend, the ecclesiastical jurisdiction belonged to the chapter of Chartres. Merlet notes that Tiron barely consented to allow the supremacy of the chapter and did not want to be subject to the archdiocese.[10]

A dispute between Tiron and the chapter of Chartres over a distant property occurred ca. 1140. The mill at Mazangé was a day's journey west of Vendôme near the confluence of the Boulon and Loir Rivers. The property consisted of the mill, land owned by the chapter of Chartres, and a field. The knight Hubert Tortus of Mondoubleau, a new monk, gave the mill, field, and his land in free and perpetual alms in the chapter of Tiron Abbey.[11] After some years the chapter of Chartres disputed the gift and demanded half the mill and field. An agreement was reached concerning the division of the property and the annual census income owed to Chartres.[12] The church of Bouffry was divided between Tiron Abbey and the chapter of Chartres. Tiron was to convey the tithes and other income to Richard Dunois the archdeacon until his death, and thereafter the abbey and chapter were to share the revenue. Tiron's tenants at Fontaine-Raoul and Fouteaux were exempt except for the obligation of paying tithes to Bouffry.[13] Parishioners might be buried with the Tironensian monks, and Tiron's dependants who ate at table were exempt from parish jurisdiction.

---

[6] T1:139–40, no. 118 (1129–1130).

[7] T2:2–3, no. 228 (ca. 1140); ibid. 2:273.

[8] Chédeville, *Chartres et ses campagnes*, 219, states that the mayor until the thirteenth century, on ecclesiastical lands, was the indispensable intermediary between the lord and the tenants, and was chosen by the lord, often with a hereditary office.

[9] T2:125, no. 350 (1208).

[10] T2:127, no. 352 (1212).

[11] T1:174–75, no. 151 (1131).

[12] T2:9–10, no. 235 (ca. 1140).

[13] T1:215–16, no. 189 (1133–1147).

A further dispute between Tiron and the chapter of Chartres arose concerning jurisdiction (including high and low justice) over the land and town of Tiron. The agreement was that Tiron Abbey had secular jurisdiction over the carucate of land given by the chapter and in the town above said carucate, except for the men and tenants (*hospites*) of the chapter and in any other dispute there.[14] These disputes and their resolutions delineating jurisdiction over the abbey land and expanding town reflected Tiron's growth during the twelfth century.

A dispute occurred ca. 1130 between the Benedictine monks of Saint-Père of Chartres and the Tironensian monks living with male and female dependants at Bois Ruffin near Arrou on the Yerre route to Châteaudun. Jeremias de l'Ile/Insula had given the Tironensian monks land and woods at Bois Ruffin ca. 1114, and ca. 1120 Ursio of Fréteval made a similar gift at Bois-Ruffin to the abbey of Saint-Père of Chartres, which owned the parish of Saint Léobin d'Arrou. Bishop Geoffrey II achieved a settlement that divided the tithes on livestock, allowed dependent non-parishioners to marry elsewhere than Saint Léobin, and upheld the Tironensian woodland rights excluding pasturage and pannage.[15] Both monasteries considered holdings at Bois Ruffin desirable.

Disputes were heard and resolved in both religious and secular courts. A gift of land at Coudray to the monks of Saint-Gilles-des-Châtaigniers was disputed and conceded to the monks in the court of William Gouet III, lord of Montmirail.[16] A challenge by Simon de Pontpinçon to a gift of tithes of animals and land to the monks of Saint-Rémy-de-Néron was pled and abandoned before Bishop Geoffrey II.[17] A dispute between Nicolas de la Bruyère and the monks of Tiron at Le Méleray in Margon north of Nogent-le-Rotrou was heard and resolved at Brou a day's ride southeast because monks of Brou were dwelling in Margon. The respective rights of the monks of Brou and of Tiron were specified.[18] A gift of tithes at Cintry/Saintry was disputed and confirmed in the castle of Beaugency by John II, bishop of Orléans (r. 1096–ca. 1125), in the presence of Ralph of Beaugency.[19] Bishop Geoffrey II also settled a dispute between Tiron Abbey and the canons regular of the church of La-Madeleine-de-Châteaudun over the deserted church of Ruan-sur-Egvonne. The bishop awarded the church to Tiron and confirmed other Tironensian holdings, income, and farms in the vicinity.[20] Odo Craton disputed a gift of land to the priory of Villandon near Voves but abandoned his claim in return for payment by Prior Robert.[21] Gauslen Gallus and his family gave Villandon land that Raginaud of Brétigny forced the monks to exchange for other land, and the monks paid cash to have the original land restored. The case was investigated by religious judges according to church

---

14 T2:165–67, no. 378 (1252).
15 T1:16, no. 5 (ca. 1114); ibid., 1:155–57, no. 130 (ca. 1130).
16 T1:77–79, no. 57 (ca. 1124).
17 T1:88–91, no. 71 (ca. 1125).
18 T1:96, no. 77 (ca. 1125).
19 T1:61–62, no. 41 (1120–1126).
20 T1:208–11, no. 186 (1133).
21 T1:153–54, no. 128 bis (ca. 1130).

law, who found that the dispute was motivated by greedy ambition and litigiousness and forced the litigants to withdraw their claim.[22] Count Thibaut II intervened in a dispute concerning a gift between Tiron and the canons of Saint-Calais of Blois.[23] A disputed gift of land to Saint-Gilles-des-Châtaigniers was heard in the secular court of William Gouet III.[24] When Geoffroy of Ouzouer's brother Robert, who was departing for Jerusalem, pledged land at Saintes-Vallées, Geoffrey's ownership thereof was disputed, and Simon, seigneur de Beaugency (d. 1153), ruled in Geoffrey's favour.[25] Much later, an agreement was reached in 1263 between the monks of Tiron and the priors of Saint-Gilles-des-Châtaigniers, la Chapelle-Vicomtesse, Saint-Nicolas-des-Fouteaux, Notre-Dame-d'Yron, Saint-Jean-et-Saint-Paul-de-Bouche-d'Aigre, Notre-Dame-de-Riboeuf, Saint-André d'Ecoman, and Tironneau concerning visitation rights, which was confirmed by Matthew des Champs, bishop of Chartres (r. 1247–1259).[26] The same pattern of resolution by overlord and bishop occurred south of the Loire. Aimeri V of Thouars and Agnès presided over the settlement of a dispute between the priory of Ferrières and Pagan Cabut.[27] Bernard, the first abbot of Asnières, had a dispute over the church of Mosterou with John, abbot of Saint-Nicholas d'Angers, which was terminated by William Adelelme, bishop of Poitiers (r. 1124–1140) in 1136.[28] Whether a dispute fell within secular or ecclesiastical jurisdiction determined the mediator. The overlords seem more involved in land transactions than the bishops, except for church property. Tiron offered cash and countergifts to validate transfers or sales, to settle disputes, or to secure or reward compliance. The countergifts show that what the Tironensians were producing was of exceptional value.

Disputed sales were sufficiently serious for Tiron to demand payment of the tithe income on the purchased property until the dispute was settled and to insist on guarantors for the tithe income. A sale of land at an unidentified Argentela near Augerville-les-Malades executed in the bishop's hall in Chartres stipulated that the monks were to have the entire tithe income of Augerville in two instalments pending resolution of any dispute. The seller's brothers and all their children were named, but Merlet did not identify the family. The brothers were guarantors of one payment and three different men were guarantors for the other payment.[29] Sellers of land at an unidentified Groselle near Chartres did not have guarantors and were required to pledge their house on the rue Muret. Merlet notes that the land was not delivered to the monks, who owned the house until the French Revolution.[30] A charter recording a gift of land at Villandon in exchange

---

22 T1:251–52, no. 223 (ca. 1138).
23 T1:68–69, no. 48 (ca. 1121).
24 T1:77, no. 57 (ca. 1124).
25 T2:57–58, no. 289 (ca. 1146).
26 IS-ADEL, 8:195, H 1772 (1263), conf. Matthew, bishop of Chartres (r. 1247–1259).
27 T1:172, no. 148 (ca. 1130).
28 GC, 14:693–95.
29 T1:158–59, no. 132 (ca. 1130).
30 T2:7, no. 233 (ca. 1140).

for a cash countergift stipulated that if any dispute arose the donor was to give grain from his tithes at Theuville until he ended the dispute.[31]

Since Tironensian foundations in the Beauce produced valuable foodstuffs and livestock, they were vulnerable to wartime depredations, when donor families appropriated livestock and supplies. Commandeering resources was considered requisitioning by the overlords and theft by the monks. Abbot William's charters record consent, payments, and gifts to the major claimants and fiefholders to avoid disputes. He provided for contingencies and exchanges of land in the event of unfavourable outcomes of pending litigation. After raids, he paid when necessary and evoked the support of the local bishops in restoring property. Otherwise, he obtained an acknowledgement of indebtedness for wrongdoing for future leverage. Significantly, the dates were the periods of unrest in 1135–1136 and 1145–1146.

Peter of Péronville was the overlord of that town on the Conie where Tiron owned the church of Secourray, the granaries of Péronville and Puerthe, and the priory of Tironneau. These riverine priories and granaries near the road to Patay and Orléans were located on divided land, funded by divided tithes and land-rents, and heavily contested. Peter of Péronville gave Tiron land in nearby Villequoy and accepted cash and a horse as countergifts. The canons of the cathedral of Sainte-Croix d'Orléans and the Benedictine monks of Saint-Florentinus' Abbey of Bonneval disputed this gift, and the Tironensians arranged a contingency for compensation.[32] A serious dispute with mutual accusations of theft was settled between Peter of Péronville and the monks of Tiron by an agreement reiterating previous donations and specifying the share of tithes and crops to be divided between Peter and the monks. Peter also gave land at Puerthe on behalf of his uncle Girard, a new monk, and accepted cash and a palfrey as a charitable gift of the monks.[33] In another agreement ca. 1135 Peter returned to the Tironensian monks the tracts he had taken from them during various disputes at Vilerfreslengis near Villequoy, Puerthe, and Le Marais.[34]

In 1136 Geoffrey III, viscount of Châteaudun, waged war with his cousin Ursio of Fréteval, who took the viscount prisoner. The viscount's son Hugh of Montluiser obtained his release with the assistance of the chapter of Tiron Abbey, Geoffrey III, count of Vendôme (1102–1137), and Bishop Geoffrey II. In an effective cooperative effort Bishop Geoffrey II, who had excommunicated Geoffrey III, viscount of Châteaudun, for the wrongs he had done to him and to the monks of Tiron, obtained satisfaction for himself and the monks. Bishop Geoffrey II and Archdeacon Richard Dunois reached an agreement with Geoffrey III's son and widow—Viscount Hugh III, and Viscountess Helvisa—regarding their family's thefts of money, oats, grain, hay, oxen, sheep, and other livestock from Yron, La Crotte, and Riboeuf. Geoffrey III received deathbed clothing and monastic burial at Tiron Abbey ca. 1150, so this charter is probably backdated to 1145.[35]

---

31 T2:45–46, no. 275 (ca. 1145).
32 T1:177–78, no. 155 (ca. 1131).
33 T1:220–22, no. 193 (1135).
34 T1:230–31, no. 202 (ca. 1135).
35 T2:38–40, no. 269 (1145). Livingstone, *Out of Love for my Kin*, 197–98, 238.

Amy Livingstone has analyzed the Fréteval family's generosity to the church and to Tiron Abbey in support of ecclesiastical reform in the first part of the twelfth century, which led to their impoverishment and conflicting claims about the restoration of such gifts by the mid-twelfth century.[36] In 1146 Ursio of Fréteval, seeking a deathbed indulgence from Bishop Geoffrey II and repentant of the many wrongs he had done to Tiron Abbey, returned property he had usurped: the wood of Pautoneria near Mondoubleau, property in Villeneuve, the crops of the monks of Fontaine-Raoul, and land at Prénouvellon which his sons had attacked.[37]

Saint-Georges-de-Cintry/Saintry was involved in local disputes ca. 1135 and 1146. Roschus of Beaugency and others surrendered to Tiron Abbey the tithes of Cintry/Saintry together with gifts of land to expand the priory and its vineyard ca. 1135.[38] The monks of Croixval near Vendôme reached an agreement ca. 1130 with Girard, dean of Ternay, who had purchased land at Ternay that the monks had hoped to buy. The monks paid Girard cash to ensure that the land would come to them upon his death.[39] Odo of Acre, a knight of Ternay and new monk of Croixval, gave the priory lands at Fains and a portion of the tithes of the fief of Chervigny. The monks agreed to payments to Odo's kin for their consent.[40] In 1204 the priory of la Chapelle-Vicomtesse was involved in a property dispute between the monks of Tiron and the canons regular of La Madeleine of Châteaudun.[41] There are other examples of Tiron's ability to reach a settlement.

The disputes extended beyond the Beauce. The town of Pithiviers northeast of Orléans, on a water route to Paris, is on the Oeuf River near its confluence with the Essonne. At Saint-Laurent-des-Coutures, a dispute arose with Simon, the son of the overlord Beroardus of Pithiviers, who plundered the monks' cattle but returned them and settled the dispute through a cash gift in the presence of Abbot William and Osbert, the prior of Coutures, in the Cluniac house at Pithiviers.[42] Manassès of Tournan-en-Brie reneged on his gift of income to the priory of Saint-Ouen-de-Tournan east of Paris but restored it when he fell ill. The Tironensian monks gave him a countergift of wine but ensured he confirmed the restored income in Abbot William's presence.[43] Alan of La Chapelle and his brothers made gifts to Le Tronchet in the presence of the chapter of Dol ca. 1200. Alan witnessed a transfer of the Saffredi domain to the abbey to cover its cash outlay to remedy his crimes and pillaging. Le Tronchet promised to reserve a chapel for him, to celebrate mass therein, to pay annual income to him and his kin, and to admit and support one monk from his family,[44] in order to obtain this valuable property.

---

36 Livingstone, "Kith and Kin," 424–28.
37 T2:59, no. 290 (ca. 1146).
38 T1:232–33, no. 205. Livingstone, *Out of Love for my Kin*, 93.
39 T1:166–67, no. 141 (ca. 1130).
40 T1:237–38, no. 209 (ca. 1135).
41 T2:120, no. 344 (1204).
42 T1:183–84, no. 160 (1131–1145). The presence of Cluny in Pithiviers shows the large abbey's presence in a significant town.
43 T1:197–98, nos. 177–78 (ca. 1132).
44 Brébel, *Essai historique sur Pleudihen*, 294.

In his study of the Benedictine abbey of Saint-Pierre-de-la-Couture, Alain Dieuleveult refers to an annual gathering of Benedictine abbots at the cathedral of Le Mans for the feast of Saint Julien on January 27, including the abbots of Le Gué-de-Launay and La Pelice. He mentions some conflicts between La Couture and Tiron and a brief issued in 1258 by Pope Alexander IV (r. 1254–1261) requesting the abbot of La Couture to protect Tiron's property, although Tiron was not an actual dependency of the abbey.[45]

Several abbots of Tiron travelled to England and appeared before the royal court at Westminster to endeavour to obtain legal settlements. Tiron Abbey attached great importance to the annual cash payment of twenty marks from the English Exchequer,[46] fifteen marks granted by Henry I and increased by five marks by Empress Matilda and their descendants through Edward III. During the periods of warfare between England and France the money was not paid. In 1268 Stephan II, abbot of Tiron, obtained an acknowledgement from the court of Henry III (b. 1207, r. 1216–1272) at Westminster that the king owed Tiron Abbey 280 marks in arrears, together with a promise to repay it in two lump sums at Easter and Michaelmas.[47] On February 9, 1293 before the court of Edward I, John II of Chartres relinquished the advowson of the church of Kington to Humphrey (VI) de Bohun, earl of Hereford and Essex (ca. 1249–1298). In a charter dated February 10, 1293, Humphrey de Bohun granted to the abbot of Tiron and his successors an annual pension of three and one-half marks from the church of Kington, which the abbot and his predecessors had received in times past.[48] In 1331 at Westminster the abbot of Tiron (probably Nicholas, r. 1320 and 1338) petitioned to apply the king's arrears of twenty marks per year, detained by reason of the war with France, to the abbot's arrears to the Exchequer. The cash payment of twenty marks sterling was still owed in 1362.[49] Tiron had extensive holdings in Hampshire but none near London, so dealings with the court at Westminster were exceptional.

The creation of a hierarchy of abbeys and priories subject ultimately to Tiron entailed disputes. Tiron had distant abbeys and priories by ca. 1119, and eventually issues arose about their subjection to Tiron or independence therefrom. Geoffrey Grossus describes the process by which Tironensian priories were expanded and enriched until they were elevated into daughter abbeys subject to the laws and regulations of the mother house.

> "After the death of the man of God, some of those who had already built priories enriched those priories though more taxes and income as well as real estate out of reverence for him, to such an extent that, at their request, we appointed abbots for them. Nonetheless we elevated them on the condition that they and their successors would obey our orders in all things and not refuse to comply with our customs in any way. Just as priors had formerly ruled those

---

45 De Dieuleveult, *La Couture, une abbaye mancelle au Moyen Age*, 137–40.
46 T1:43, no. 27 (1119–1126); ibid., 1:107–8, no. 87 (1127); ibid., 1:109, no. 88 (1127); ibid., 2:37–38, no. 268 (1142–1154); ibid., 2:82–83, no. 309 (1154–1165); ibid., 2:108, no. 331 (1188).
47 *Calendar of the Patent Rolls of Henry III 1266–1272*, Rolls Series 160 (1913), 228, m 15.
48 WCM, 2:209, no. 4280b; ibid., 3:952, no. 18930.
49 WCM, 2:430, no. 10682.

priories, these abbots would be subject to laws and regulations instituted by our authority in everything."[50]

Geoffrey Grossus also describes St. Dogmaels as a priory subsequently elevated to an abbey (1121) and Selkirk as a priory elevated to an abbey shortly after Bernard's death in 1116.[51] He emphasizes that the abbot of Tiron chose the abbots of the daughter abbeys of the mother house. Although accurate about France, he may be reacting to moves toward independence by Tiron's British abbeys on the periphery of the Tironensian network.

In the thirteenth century, when the authority of the abbot of Tiron was challenged, Gregory IX (r. 1227–1241) issued a brief confirming that the abbot of Tiron (Gervais, r. 1233–1252) had the right of correction over his monks, and all appeals were quashed.[52] Subsequently, serious quarrels occurred between the abbeys of Joug-Dieu and Tiron. The monks of Joug-Dieu attempted to elect their own abbot in 1249, were excommunicated, appealed to Rome, and ultimately recognized the authority of the abbey of Tiron in an instrument signed on May 15, 1257.[53] A dispute occurred in 1206 between Abbot Barthélemy II of Bois-Aubry and the abbot of Tiron. The decision upheld the elevation charter of 1138: the abbot of Tiron had the right of punishment, correction, visitation, reform, ordination, publication of statutes, and immediate superiority. Thus the supremacy of the abbot of Tiron over Bois-Aubry was asserted.[54] In 1298 Simon, abbot of Tiron (r. 1297–1313), obtained a recognition of his visitation right in the abbey of Arcisses, which implies that it was questioned.[55] Ferrières' submission to Tiron caused continuous disputes.[56] Sauzé de L'houmeau states that Ferrières owed obedience to the mother house, and the abbot of Tiron had the right to change the monks, administer justice, visit the monastery, and correct the monks.[57] The abbey of Le Tronchet seems to have periodically challenged Tiron's oversight. While William I was abbot of Le Tronchet ca. 1170–1179, Alexander III confirmed that Le Tronchet was among the abbeys subordinate to Tiron ca. 1173–1176.[58] In the thirteenth century Le Tronchet attempted to relax or eliminate its subjection to Tiron Abbey.[59] The archdeacon of Dol obtained a papal bull suppressing Tiron's rights over Le Tronchet in 1258, but Nicolas, abbot of

---

50 VB, 11.98, AASS, Apr. 2:245F–46A; VB, trans. Cline, 105–6.

51 VB, 11.99, AASS, Apr. 2:0246B–C; VB, trans. Cline, 106–7.

52 T2:146, no. 368 (1238).

53 GC, 8:1273B.

54 L.A. Bosseboeuf, "L'Abbaye Bénédictine de Bois-Aubry," *Bulletin Trimestriel de la Société Archéologique de Touraine*, Vol. 12 (1st quarter 1899) (Tours: Pericat, 1899), 239, 243.

55 T2: 201–2, no. 407.

56 GC, 8:1268–69.

57 Sauzé de L'houmeau, *L'Abbaye de Saint Léonard de Ferrières*, 19.

58 GC, 14:1074–79. T2:92–93, no. 320 (1165–1173). *Regesta Pontificorum Romanorum*, ed. Jaffé, 2:293, no. 12640, dated 1173–1176.

59 Walter II was abbot 1207. John I was abbot 1228–1246.

Le Tronchet at the time, officially recognized Tiron's claims.[60] Robert Pépin, abbot of Le Tronchet (r. 1378–1383), was forced to recognize the supremacy of the abbey of Tiron in 1378. The charter includes the obligation to attend the general chapter at Tiron every year, and the right of the abbot of Tiron to visit, correct, discipline, and have precedence in the abbey of Le Tronchet.[61]

Only the abbey of La Pelice was not solely dependent on Tiron: the rights of Hamelin, bishop of Le Mans, with regard to La Pelice are contained in a charter to Abbot Hervé of Tiron.[62] Another charter dated 1231 shows an agreement between Maurice, bishop of Le Mans (r. 1215–1231), and Thibaut, abbot of Tiron (r. 1224–ca. 1229/1231), on the procedure for the election of the abbot of La Pelice. The document refers to an earlier agreement on a panel of three electors, one nominated by the abbot of Tiron, one by the bishop of Le Mans, and one by the abbey of La Pelice,[63] so Tiron's authority was not absolute. A White Book contains oaths of submission to the abbot from 1479 to 1558. Oaths were made and signed by the abbots of Asnières, Bois-Aubry, La Pelice, Joug-Dieu, Ferrières, Le Gué-de-Launay, and Arcisses.[64] Another charter summons these abbots, among others, to the general chapter at Tiron 1537–1548.[65] Thus the supremacy of the abbot of Tiron over the French abbeys was contended but confirmed into the sixteenth century.

Tiron's disputes partly reflect a shift from an agricultural economic basis, with seasonal tithe income and a long-standing tradition of possession, to a commercial basis requiring a clear title to ownership and specific agreements about delivery dates and payment terms. Collecting a tithe of livestock and crops required less expertise than running a fair with variable weights, measures, and exchange rates and specific delivery conditions. Written records were essential, leading to an early scriptorium to organize records and provide binding legal language. The Tironensians endeavoured to avoid disputes through witnesses and countergifts, and to resolve disputes by negotiated settlements. When such endeavours failed, they placed their cases before local secular and religious courts and ultimately before the papal court, where the justice of their cause usually prevailed.

---

60 Rocher and Trevinal, "Notre-Dame du Tronchet," 300.

61 T2:204–6, no. 410 (1378).

62 T2:120–21, no. 345 (1205). GC, 14:498–99.

63 T2:138–39, no. 361 (1231).

64 T2:234–35, no. 419 (1516).

65 IS-ADEL 8:164–66, specifically 165, H 1424 (1496–1550). The abbots of Rathaburgo/Roxburgh (St. Andrews), Catmeis (St. Davids), St. Cross, Isle of Wight (Winchester), Saint-Méen (Saint-Malo), St. Dogmaels (Wales), Selkirk (Cumberland, Scotland), and Mortui Maris (Rouen).

SELECT BIBLIOGRAPHY

A bibliography of works cited on several occasions in the notes above and other important studies.

Primary Sources

Acta Sanctorum quotquot toto orbe coluntur, vel à catholicis scriptoribus celebrantur [...]. 67 vols. in 68. Antwerp: Mevrsium, 1643–1940. Available online as Acta Sanctorum Database, 1999–2006 (citations by the saint's feast-day are from this resource).

Acts of Malcolm IV, King of Scots 1153–1165. Edited by G. W. S. Barrow. Regesta Regum Scottorum 1. Edinburgh: Edinburgh University Press, 1960.

Acts of William I, King of Scots, 1165–1214. Edited by G. W. S. Barrow. Regesta Regum Scottorum 2. Edinburgh: Edinburgh University Press, 1971.

Andreas of Fontevraud. *Vita Altera* of Robert of Arbrissel. AASS Feb. 3:0608D–16E.

Benedict of Monte Cassino. *The Rule of Saint Benedict*. Edited by Timothy Fry. Collegeville: Liturgical Press, 1981.

Blind Harry's Wallace. Translated by William Hamilton of Gilbertfield. Edinburgh: Luath, 1958.

Bullarium sacri ordinis Cluniacensis: complectens plurima privilegia per summos pontifices [...] concessa. Lyon: Julliéron, 1680. Available online as www.uni-muenster.de/Fruehmittelalter/Projekte/Cluny/Bullarium.

Cartulaire de l'Abbaye de Saint-Cyprien de Poitiers. Edited by Louis Rédet. Poitiers: Oudin, 1874.

Cartulaire de l'Abbaye de la Sainte-Trinité de Tiron. Edited by Lucien Merlet. 2 vols. Chartres: Garnier, 1883.

Cartulaire de Notre Dame de Chartres. Edited by E. Lépinois and Lucien Merlet. 3 vols. Chartres: Garnier, 1862–65.

Chartulary of the Abbey of Lindores 1195–1479. Edited by John Dowden. Publications of the Scottish Historical Society 42. Edinburgh: Edinburgh University Press, 1903.

Cuninghame, Topographized by Timothy Pont 1604–1608. Edited by John Shedden Dobie. Glasgow: Tweed, 1876.

Early Sources of Scottish History, A.D. 500 to 1286. Edited by Alan Orr Anderson. 2 vols. Edinburgh: Oliver & Boyd, 1922; repr. Stamford: Watkins, 1990.

Farrer, William. *An Outline Itinerary of King Henry I*. Oxford: Oxford University Press, 1920.

Geoffrey Grossus. *The Life of Blessed Bernard of Tiron*. Translated with an introduction and notes by Ruth Harwood Cline. Washington, DC: Catholic University of America Press, 2009.

———. *Vita beati Bernardi Tironiensis autore Gaufredo Grosso*, AASS, Apr. 2:0222C–55A.

Inventaire sommaire des archives départementales antérieures à 1790. Eure-et-Loir. 9 vols. Vol. 8, *Archives ecclésiastiques, série H.* Ed. René Merlet. Chartres: Garnier, 1897.

Liber S. Marie de Calchou, Registrum Cartarum Abbacie Tironensis de Kelso 1113–1567. Edited by Cosmo Innes. 2 vols. Edinburgh: Bannatyne Club, 1846.

Liber S. Thome de Aberbrothoc. Edited by Cosmo Innes. 2 vols. Vol. 1, *Pars Prior, Regestrum Vetus, 1178–1329.* Edinburgh: Bannatyne Club, 1848–56.

Monasticon Anglicanum. Edited by William Dugdale. 6 vols. London: Longman, Hurst, Rees, Orme & Brown, 1817–30.

Orderic Vitalis. *Historia ecclesiastica; The Ecclesiastical History of Orderic Vitalis.* Edited and translated by Marjorie Chibnall. 6 vols. Oxford: Clarendon Press, 1969–80.

Patrologiae cursus completus: sive bibliotheca universalis, integra, uniformis, commoda, oeconomica, omnium ss. patrum, doctorum scriptorumque ecclesiasticorum [...]. Edited by J. P. Migne. 221 vols. Paris: Migne, 1844–65. Available online as Patrologia Latina Database. http://pld.chadwyck.co.uk.

Recueil des historiens des Gaules et de la France. Edited by Michel-Jean-Joseph Brial. New ed. 24 vols. Paris: Palmé, 1877. Available online at BnF Gallica. https://gallica.bnf.fr.

Regesta Pontificorum Romanorum. Edited by Philippus Jaffé, 2nd. ed. 2 vols. Leipzig: 1885–88.

Robert of Torigny. *Tractatus de immutatione ordinis monachorum.* In *Recueil des historiens des Gaules et de la France.* Edited by Michel-Jean-Joseph Brial. New ed. vol. 14, 381–89. Paris: Palmé, 1877. Also see PL 202:309–20.

Winchester College Muniments. Compiled by Sheila Himsworth. 3 vols. Chichester: Phillimore, 1984.

Secondary Sources

Adamo, Philip C. *New Monks in Old Habits: The Formation of the Caulite Monastic Order, 1193–1267.* Toronto: Pontifical Institute of Mediaeval Studies, 2014.

Barrow, Horst. *Roads and Bridges of the Roman Empire.* Stuttgart: Menges, 2013.

Bascher, Jacques de. "L'abbaye et l'ordre de Thiron: la Réforme Mauriste." *Cahiers Percherons* (1992–93): 17–47.

———. "La 'Vita' de Saint Bernard d'Abbeville, Abbé de Saint-Cyprien de Poitiers et de Tiron." *Revue Mabillon* 59 (1975–80): 411–50.

Beck, Bernard. *Saint-Bernard de Tiron: l'ermite, le moine et le monde.* Cormelles-le-Royal: Mandragore, 1998.

Berman, Constance Hoffman. *The Cistercian Evolution: The Invention of a Religious Order in Twelfth-Century Europe.* Philadelphia: University of Pennsylvania Press, 2000.

———. "Medieval Agriculture, the Southern French Countryside, and the Early Cistercians. A Study of Forty-Three Monasteries." *Transactions of the American Philosophical Society* 76, no. 5. Philadelphia: American Philosophical Society, 1986.

———. "Were There Twelfth-Century Cistercian Nuns?" *Church History* 68, no. 4 (December 1999): 824–64.

Bezant, Jemma. "Travel and Communication." In *Monastic Wales: New Approaches*, edited by Janet Burton and Karen Stöber, 133–46. Cardiff: University of Wales Press, 2013.

Bom, Myra Miranda. *Women in the Military Orders of the Crusades.* New York: Palgrave Macmillan, 2012.

Bouchard, Constance Brittain. *Holy Entrepreneurs: Cistercians, Knights, and Economic Exchange in Twelfth-Century Burgundy.* Ithaca: Cornell University Press, 1991.

———. "Monastic Cartularies: Organizing Eternity." In *Charters, Cartularies, and Archives: The Preservation and Transmission of Documents in the Medieval West.* Proceedings of a Colloquium of the Commission internationale de diplomatique, Princeton and New York, 16–18 September 1999, edited by Anders Winroth and Adam J. Kosto, 22–32. Toronto: Pontifical Institute of Mediaeval Studies, 2002.

———. *Sword, Miter, and Cloister: Nobility and the Church in Burgundy, 980–1198.* Ithaca: Cornell University Press, 1982.

Brébel, Eugène. *Essai historique sur Pleudihen.* Rennes: Simon, 1916.

Brooks, George. "The 'Vitruvian Mill' in Roman and Medieval Europe." In *Wind and Water in the Middle Ages: Fluid Technologies from Antiquity to the Renaissance*, edited by Steven A. Walton, 1–38. Tempe: Arizona Center for Medieval and Renaissance Studies, 2006.

Burton, Janet E., and Julie Kerr. *The Cistercians in the Middle Ages.* Woodbridge: Boydell, 2011.

Cabanes, Michel, and Jean Yves Lagrange. *Tiron et Molineuf: abbayes et prieurés du Perche au Val de Loire, et à bien d'autres lieux; vie de Saint Bernard de Tiron.* Dourdan: Vial, 1982.

Chédeville, André. *Chartres et ses campagnes (XIe-XIIIe s.).* Paris: Klincksieck, 1973; repr. Paris: Garnier, 1991.

Cline, Ruth Harwood. "Abbot Hugh: An Overlooked Brother of Henry I, Count of Champagne." *The Catholic Historical Review* 93, no. 3 (July 2007): 501–16.

———. "The Congregation of Tiron in the Twelfth Century: Foundation and Expansion." PhD diss., Georgetown University, 2000.

———. "Mutatis Mutandis: Borrowings from Jerome's Letter to Eustochium and Others in the *Life of Blessed Bernard of Tiron* by Geoffrey Grossus." *Haskins Society Journal* 21 (2009): 125–46.

Constable, Giles. "From Cluny to Cîteaux." In Constable, *The Abbey of Cluny: A Collection of Essays to Mark the Eleven-Hundredth Anniversary of its Foundation*, 235–39. Münster: LIT, 2010.

———. *Monastic Tithes from their Origins to the Twelfth Century.* Cambridge: Cambridge University Press, 1964.

———. *The Reformation of the Twelfth Century.* Cambridge: Cambridge University Press, 1996.

Cowan, Ian B., and David E. Easson. *Medieval Religious Houses: Scotland,* with an Appendix on the Houses in the Isle of Man. 2nd ed. London: Longman, 1976.

Cowley, F. G. *The Monastic Order in South Wales, 1066–1349.* Cardiff: University of Wales Press, 1977.

Crouch, David. *The Beaumont Twins: The Roots and Branches of Power in the Twelfth Century.* Cambridge: Cambridge University Press, 1986.
Cunningham, William. *The Growth of English Industry and Commerce during the Early and Middle Ages.* New York: Kelley, 1968.
Dieuleveult, Alain de. *La Couture, une abbaye mancelle au Moyen Age.* Le Mans: Vilaine, 1963.
Duby, Georges. *La société aux XIe et XIIe siècles dans la region mâconnaise.* Bibliothèque générale de l'Ecole Pratique des Hautes Etudes, 6e Section. Paris: Colin, 1953.
Ekelund, Robert B. Jr., Robert F. Hébert, Robert D. Tollison, Gary M. Anderson, Audrey B. Davidson. *Sacred Trust: The Medieval Church as an Economic Firm.* New York: Oxford University Press, 1996.
Everard, Judith A. *Brittany and the Angevins: Province and Empire 1158–1203.* Cambridge: Cambridge University Press, 2000.
———. "Le duché de Bretagne et la politique Plantagenêt aux XIIe et XIIe siècles: perspective maritime." In *Plantagenêt et Capétiens: confrontations et heritages*, edited by Martin Aurell and Noël-Ives Tonnere, 193–210. Turnhout: Brépols, 2006.
Evergates, Theodore. *The Aristocracy in the County of Champagne, 1100–1300.* The Middle Ages Series. Philadelphia: University of Pennsylvania Press, 2007.
Gazeau, Roger. "La clôture des moniales au XIIe siècle en France." *Revue Mabillon* 58 (1974): 293–94.
Gilbert, Christian. "Une abbaye tironienne en Touraine: Saint-Michel de Bois-Aubry au XXe siècle." *Bulletin Monumental* 151, no. 1 (1993): 139–67.
Gillingham, John. *The Angevin Empire.* New York: Holmes & Meier, 2000.
Grant, Lindy. "Arnulf's Mentor: Geoffrey of Lèves, Bishop of Chartres." In *Writing Medieval Biography 750–1250: Essays in Honour of Frank Barlow*, edited by David Bates, Julia Crick, and Sarah Hamilton, 173–84. Woodbridge: Boydell, 2006.
———. "Geoffrey of Lèves, Bishop of Chartres: 'Famous Wheeler and Dealer in Secular Business.'" *Suger en question: regards croisés sur Saint-Denis.* Edited by Rolf Große. Munich: Oldenburg, 2004.
Greenshields, J. B. *Annals of the Parish of Lesmahagow.* Edinburgh: Caledonian Press, 1864.
Guillaumin, André. "Thiron, son Abbaye, son collège militaire." *Cahiers Percherons* 9 (January–March 1959): 22–43.
———. *Thiron, son abbaye, son collège militaire, guide illustré avec plan.* Nogent-le-Rotrou: Fauquet, 1929.
Guillemin, Denis. *Thiron, abbaye médiévale.* Montrouge: Amis du Perche, 1999.
Guillois, Roger. *Histoire des rues de Chartres.* Chartres: L'Echo Républicain, 1978.
Gwynn, A., and R. Neville Hadcock. *Medieval Religious Houses: Ireland.* London: Longman, 1970.
Hallam, Elizabeth M. *Capetian France, 987–1328.* London: Longman, 1980.
Hay, George. *History of Arbroath.* Arbroath: Thomas Buncle, 1876.
Hillairet, Jacques. *Dictionnaire historique des rues de Paris.* 2 vols. Paris: Minuit, 1964.
A History of the County of Hampshire and the Isle of Wight. 6 vols. Edited by H. A. Doubleday and William Page. London: Constable, 1900–14.
Hockey, S. F. *Insula Vecta.* Andover: Phillimore, 1982.

---. *Quarr Abbey and its Lands 1132-1631.* Leicester: Leicester University Press, 1970.
Hollister, C. Warren. *Henry I.* Edited by Amanda Clark Frost. Yale English Monarchs. New Haven: Yale University Press, 2001.
Howells, Roscoe. *Caldey.* Llandysul: Gomer Press, 1984.
Ker, William Lee. *Kilwinning Abbey: The Church of St. Winning.* Ardrossan: Guthrie, 1900.
Knowles, David. *The Religious Orders in England.* 3 vols. Cambridge: Cambridge University Press, 1948-59.
Knowles, David, and R. Neville Hadcock. *Medieval Religious Houses: England and Wales.* London: Longmans, Green, 1953; New York: St. Martin's, 1972.
Laing, Alexander. *Lindores Abbey and its Burgh of Newburgh.* Edinburgh: Edmonston and Douglas, 1876.
Lalizel, Henri. *Abbaye royale d'Arcisses.* Chartres: n.p., 1900.
Lawrence, C. H. *Medieval Monasticism: Forms of Religious Life in Western Europe in the Middle Ages.* 4th ed. London: Longman, 1984; London: Routledge, 2015 (pagination from the latter).
Leyser, Henrietta. *Hermits and the New Monasticism: A Study of Religious Communities in Western Europe, 1000-1150.* New York: St. Martin's, 1984.
Livingstone, Amy. "Kith and Kin: Kinship and Family Structure of the Nobility of Eleventh- and Twelfth-Century Blois-Chartres." *French Historical Studies* 20, no. 3 (Summer 1997): 419-59.
---. *Out of Love for my Kin: Aristocratic Family Life in the Lands of the Loire, 1000-1200.* Ithaca: Cornell University Press, 2010.
Lucas, Adam. "The Role of the Monasteries in the Development of Medieval Milling." In *Wind and Water in the Middle Ages: Fluid Technologies from Antiquity to the Renaissance,* edited by Steven A. Walton, 89-127. Tempe: Arizona Center for Medieval and Renaissance Studies, 2006.
Ludlow, N. D., with R. S. F. Ramsey and D. E. Schlee. "Pill Priory, 1996-1999: Recent Work at a Tironian House in Pembrokeshire." *Medieval Archaeology,* 46 (2002): 41-80.
Martène, Edmond. *Histoire de la congrégation de Saint-Maur.* 7 vols. Ligugé, Vienne: Abbaye Saint-Martin/Paris: Picard, 1928-37.
Martin, Colin, and Richard Oram. "Medieval Roxburgh: A Preliminary Assessment of the Burgh and Its Locality." *Proceedings of the Society of Antiquaries of Scotland* 137 (2007): 357-444.
Mazel, Florian. *L'évêque et le territoire: l'invention médiévale de l'espace.* Paris: Seuil, 2016.
Moffat, Alistair. *Kelsae, A History of Kelso from Earliest Times.* Edinburgh: Mainstream, 1985.
Monastic Wales: New Approaches. Edited by Janet Burton and Karen Stöber. Cardiff: University of Wales Press, 2013.
Naud, Gérard. *Guide des archives de la Sarthe.* Le Mans: Les Archives, 1983.
New, Chester William. "History of the Alien Priories in England to the Confiscation of Henry V." PhD diss., University of Chicago, 1916.
Oram, Richard. *David I: The King who Made Scotland.* Stroud: Tempus, 2004; Stroud: History Press, 2008.

Owen, D. D. R. *William the Lion, 1143–1214: Kingship and Culture.* East Linton: Tuckwell, 1997.
Platt, Colin. *The Abbeys and Priories of Medieval England.* New York: Fordham University Press, 1984.
Power, Daniel. *The Norman Frontier in the Twelfth and Early Thirteenth Centuries.* Cambridge: Cambridge University Press, 2004.
Pritchard, Emily M. *The History of St. Dogmael's Abbey.* London: Blades, East & Blades, 1907.
Les réligieuses en France au XIIIe siècle. Edited by Michel Parisse. Nancy: Presses Universitaires de Nancy, 1985.
Robinson, I. S. *The Papacy 1073–1198: Continuity and Change.* Cambridge: Cambridge University Press, 1990.
Rocher, François, and Maurice Trevinal. "Notre-Dame du Tronchet." In *Les Abbayes bretonnes,* edited by Daniel Andrejewski. Nantes: Biennale des Abbayes Bretonnes/ Paris: Fayard, 1983.
Rosenwein, Barbara. *To Be the Neighbor of Saint Peter: The Social Meaning of Cluny's Property 909–1049.* Ithaca: Cornell University Press, 1989.
Sauzé de l'Houmeau, Charles. *L'Abbaye de Saint Léonard de Ferrières.* Paris: Picard, 1925.
Seale, Yvonne. "Ten Thousand Women: Gender, Affinity, and the Development of the Praemonstratensian Order in Medieval France." PhD diss., University of Iowa, 2016.
Stevenson, Alexander. "Trade with the South 1070–1513." In *The Scottish Medieval Town,* edited by Michael Lynch, Michael Spearman, and Geoffrey Stell. Edinburgh: Donaldson, 1988.
Stringer, K. J. *Earl David of Huntingdon 1152–1219.* Edinburgh: Edinburgh University Press, 1985.
Thompson, Kathleen. "Affairs of State: The Illegitimate Children of Henry I." *Journal of Medieval History* 29, no. 2 (June 2003): 129–51.
——. "The Cartulary of the Monastery of Tiron." *Tabularia "Etudes"* 13 (2013): 65–123.
——. "The First Hundred Years of the Abbey of Tiron: Institutionalizing the Reform of the Forest Hermits." *Anglo-Norman Studies* 31 (2008): 104–17.
——. *The Monks of Tiron: A Monastic Community and Religious Reform in the Twelfth Century.* Cambridge: Cambridge University Press, 2014.
——. *Power and Border Lordship in Medieval France, The County of the Perche 1000–1226.* The Royal Historical Society. Woodbridge: Boydell, 2002.
Thompson, Sally. *Women Religious: The Founding of English Nunneries after the Norman Conquest.* Oxford: Clarendon Press, 1991.
Tresvaux, Abbé [François-Marie]. *L'eglise de Bretagne depuis ses commencements jusqu'à nos jours.* Paris: Méquignon, 1839.
Ultee, Maarten. *The Abbey of St. Germain des Prés in the Seventeenth Century.* New Haven: Yale University Press, 1981.
Vernon, Jean. *Travel in the Middle Ages.* Translated by George Holoch. Notre Dame: University of Notre Dame Press, 2003.
Vincent, Nicholas. "Patronage, Politics and Piety in the Charters of Eleanor of Aquitaine." In *Plantagenêts et Capétiens: confrontations et heritages,* edited by Martin Aurell and Noël Tonnerre, 17–60. Turnhout: Brepols, 2006.

GENERAL INDEX

Adela, countess of Blois and Chartres, 20, 38, 41, 48, 70, 74, 80
Adjutor of Vernon, 19, 47, 60, 94–96
Alexander III, pope, 72, 92, 104, 121, 147–48, 185, 194
Angevin Empire/trading zone, 12, 30, 72–73, 98, 103, 141, 167, 177
Augustinians, 2, 69, 85, 116, 141
Anjou, 17, 27, 30, 40, 47–49, 64, 68, 73–75, 88, 97
    rulers of, see Fulk V, Geoffrey V, Henry II
Aquitaine, 7, 9–10, 61–62, 64, 73, 88–90, 108, 114, 182–83

Beatrix of Montdidier-Roucy, countess of the Perche, 21, 24, 38, 41
Beauce, 11, 17, 25–26, 28, 47–50, 54, 57, 68, 73, 75, 84–86, 89, 106–8, 119, 172, 183, 187, 191–92
Benedict, Saint, *Rule* of see Rule of Saint Benedict
Benedictine monasticism, 2, 5, 7–9, 15, 17, 45, 57–58, 64, 139, 141, 162, 166–67, 173
Bernard of Abbeville, abbot of Tiron
  Abbeville, family, 34, 39–40, 45
  abbot, abbacies, 5, 9–10, 17–18, 35–36, 38, 111
  contemporary records, 9–11
  death, 9–12, 18, 21, 24, 43–44, 48, 50, 55, 59, 65, 111–12, 115, 179, 193–94
  education, erudition, 12, 17–23, 22, 30–31, 34, 38
  hermit periods, 35–38, 69
    Chennedet, 37, 39
    Chausey Island, 36–37, 39
    Fontaine-Géhard, 24, 37, 39, 103
    Fougères, 36–37, 39, 103–4
    Saint-Médard, 36
  hospitality, 24, 27
  Mary, vision/veneration, 17, 19, 45
  miracles, 42
  mitre, 42, 172
  poverty, love of, 18, 33, 40, 43, 55, 56, 60, 66, 167
  preaching, 8–9, 33, 36–38, 43
  pirates, 23, 36
  prisoners, release of, 38, 40, 47, 60
  prophecies, xi, 11, 14, 17, 35, 41
  reform, 1–2, 5, 8–9, 11, 30–31, 33–35, 37–38, 44–45
  rule of Tiron, 17–19, 33, 45, 64, 173, 178
  Saint-Cyprien of Poitiers, monk, abbot, 9–10, 33–37, 39, 54, 111
    Council of Poitiers, 10, 35
    Rome, defense, 9, 36
  Saint-Savin-sur-Gartempe, claustral prior, 19, 34–36, 39
  travels, 9, 111
  Vita B. Bernardi Tironiensis, 2–3, 11–12, 18, 21–23, 33–35, 40, 42–43, 45, 53, 59–60, 69, 75, 86, 115, 139, 167, 177–78, 183
  women, acceptance of, 1, 5, 17, 20–22, 31, 33, 37, 43–44, 59, 69
  woodworking, 24
Bernard of Clairvaux, 10, 12, 14, 19, 33, 45, 47, 50, 52, 58, 61–62, 64, 71, 114, 127, 181–82
Blois, 9, 17, 39, 43, 49, 52, 76, 80, 86–88, 99, 106, 116
  counts of, see Stephen-Henry, Thibaut II, Thibaut V
Brice of Le Chillou, 70, 110, 112

Caulite Order, Val-des-Choux, 11
Celtic church, célidé, 7, 12, 20, 144, 151, 155, 160, 162, 166, 177, 178
La Chaise-Dieu, Casadéens, 8, 34–35, 39

Champagne, xi, 17, 73–74, 89, 108, 113, 118, 122–23
Champagne, counts of, see Thibaut II, Henry II
Channel/English Channel, 2, 17, 28–30, 39, 44, 47–49, 51, 64, 72, 86, 89–93, 95–97, 103–5, 114, 128, 130, 136–39, 166, 183
Chartres, 9, 19, 22, 27–30, 38–40, 42, 48–51, 55–56, 61–64, 73–84, 97, 117–19, 128, 148, 181–83
  bishops, 30, 68, 173–74, 190, see also Ivo, Geoffrey II of Lèves
  Bretons, 38, 83
  cathedral, 19, 22, 41, 61–62, 68, 168
  chapter, 3, 19, 30, 33, 41–42, 44, 56, 61, 107, 167, 171, 188–89
  Chartres, Tironensian priory, 61–64, 145
  Josaphat, 43, 148, 174
  Saint-Père-en-Vallée, 33, 61, 69, 83, 148, 174, 187, 189
Chartreuse, La Grande, Carthusians, 1, 8, 10, 56
Cîteaux, Cistercians, xi, xii, 1–2, 5, 8–15, 18–19, 22, 30, 38–39, 45, 47, 49–50, 52, 54, 56–58, 60, 64, 67, 72, 82, 115–16, 125, 127–28, 138, 141, 144, 149, 166, 172, 176–79, 184
Cistercian abbeys
  L'Aumône, 49, 52, 128
  Beaulieu, 128
  Dore, 128
  Forde, 128
  Fountains, 128
  Netley, 128
  Quarr, 128, 137
  Rievaulx, 128, 144
  Tintern, 52, 128
  Waverley, 49, 52, 128
Cîteaux–Cluny contrast, 1–2, 5
Cîteaux–Tiron contrast, 13–15, 45, 47, 52, 56, 64, 67, 72, 125, 127–28, 179
Cluny, Cluniacs, 1–2, 5, 7–11, 13–14, 22, 29–30, 33–36, 38–39, 41, 45, 49, 58, 66, 69, 108, 111, 115–16, 170, 179, 192
Cluniac foundations
  Saint-Denis-de-Nogent-le-Rotrou, 36, 38, 41, 56, 75, 187–88
  Saint-Pierre-de-Pithiviers, 88, 192
  Sainte-Geneviève-de-Paris, 120, 122, 174
coinage, mint, money, 8, 24, 49, 60, 62–63, 75, 82–83, 85, 97, 108, 120, 171, 187, 191, 193
community life, cenobitic monasticism, 8–9, 11, 15, 17–19, 33, 36–38, 43, 45
Conan III, duke of Brittany, 54, 71, 90, 97, 110, 113
crafts, xii, 1, 5, 11, 13–15, 17–18, 22, 24–26, 31, 38, 40, 44, 56, 58, 60, 62–64, 69, 75, 149, 166, 178
crusades, crusaders, 24, 35, 38, 47, 60, 64, 67, 182

David I, prince of the Cumbrians, earl of Huntingdon, king of Scotland, 16, 23, 42, 44, 53, 55, 60–61, 64–66, 70–71, 92, 128, 136, 141, 143–46, 148–49, 160, 162, 168–69, 182
David II, earl of Huntingdon, 70, 153, 157, 159–61, 171
Deheubarth, princes of, 66–67, 70, 128, 138–39
desert, desert fathers, 8, 15, 17
dissolution of the monasteries, 30, 140, 172, 175

Edward I, king of England, 168–69, 193
Edward III, king of England, 129, 169–70
Eleanor, duchess of Aquitaine, queen of France and England, xi, 21, 52–54, 90, 114, 120
England, civil wars, 90, 127–28, 139, 166, 168, 182–83
England, Tironensian foundations, see Hamble, Andwell, St. Cross, Isle of Wight, Titley
eremetical life, see hermitages

Ermine Street, Old North Road, Great North Road, 55, 104, 136
espionage, see intelligence-gathering

fairs, 14, 23, 27, 40–41, 73, 77, 95, 97, 104, 108, 115, 118, 120, 145, 161–62, 195
famine, 11, 14–15, 20, 30, 40, 47, 68
filia specialis, 147–48, 179
Fontgombaud, Etoile, 36, 39
Fontevraud, Fontevraudians, 1–2, 9–10, 22, 29, 39, 53, 111, 170
forest economy, 11, 15, 28, 38, 60–61, 73, 75, 98, 141
France, French nation-building, 12, 30, 72–73, 121, 125, 167
Franciscans, friars, 33, 40
Fulchard, abbot of St. Dogmael, 64–66, 139
Fulk V, count of Anjou, king of Jerusalem, 25, 38, 40–41, 48, 58, 64, 69–70, 90, 98, 110, 114

Gaul, *Gallia*, 7, 12, 28, 40, 50, 116, 183
Geoffrey Grossus, 3, 10, 27, 33, 36–37, 43–45, 60, 65, 167, 193–94
Geoffrey II of Lèves, provost and bishop of Chartres, 2, 33, 41–43, 52, 54–55, 61–62, 64, 71, 77–78, 80, 85, 88, 114, 118, 120, 127, 181, 189, 191–92
Geoffrey III, viscount of Châteaudun, 26, 70, 80, 85–86, 191
Geoffrey V Plantagenet, count of Anjou, duke of Normandy, 69–70, 88, 90, 98, 114, 183
Girard II Berlay of Montreuil-Bellay, 70, 110, 112
grange, granger, granary, 12, 14, 16, 26, 29, 31, 54, 57, 60, 72, 74–75, 78–79, 84–86, 88, 146, 159–60, 178, 182, 191
Guichard III, seigneur de Beaujeu, 70, 111, 115–16
Guy II of Montlhéry, count of Rochefort, 50, 70, 115, 118

Henry I, duke of Normandy, king of England, 11, 13, 17, 20, 24, 38, 40–43, 53–55, 58, 64–66, 69–71, 74, 90–91, 95–98, 127, 129–30, 135–36, 138–39, 182
Henry I de Beaumont, seigneur of Le Neubourg, earl of Warwick, lord of Gower, 70, 90
Henry II, count of Anjou, duke of Normandy, king of England, xi, 30, 70–71, 73, 90, 97–98, 103–4, 127, 130, 149, 157, 185, 193
Henry II, count of Champagne, xi, 54, 127
Henry II de Bourbon, natural son of Henry IV, commendatory abbot, 173–74
Henry of Blois, bishop of Winchester, xi, 127, 132, 137
Herbert, abbot of Selkirk/Kelso, bishop of Glasgow, 72, 128–29, 147, 168
hermitages, hermits, eremitism, célidé, xi, 1–2, 8–9, 10, 17, 19–20, 24, 27–28, 33, 35–38, 45, 69, 72, 94–95, 100, 103–6, 110–12, 114, 125, 127, 146, 149, 155, 157, 160, 162, 166, 167, 176–78
horses, horse breeding, 31, 48, 60, 67, 74–75, 81, 89, 104, 115, 138, 146, 162, 171, 178, 191
Hugh, abbot of Cluny, 22, 35–36
Hugh, interim abbot of Tiron, 10, 44, 50
Hugh of Blois, xi, 24, 54, 120, 123
Hundred Years' War, 4, 30, 167, 170, 175

intelligence-gathering, espionage, 16, 129, 170
Ivo, bishop of Chartres, 10, 24, 38, 40–42, 66, 69

John, bishop of Glasgow, 60–61, 72, 128–29, 141, 143, 146
John I, king of England, 121, 157, 167
John II of Chartres, abbot of Tiron, 3, 45, 167–68
Juliana of the Perche, 21, 24, 38, 41, 67, 90
justice, high and low, 87, 189

kinship groups and networks, 8, 13, 17, 53, 68–71, 74, 98, 182

leatherwork, footwear, tanning, 15, 44, 48, 60–61, 69, 74–75, 83, 89, 91, 115, 130
Louis VI, king of France, 17, 35, 41–43, 50, 55, 58, 60–62, 64–65, 69, 71, 79, 86, 88, 90, 106, 118, 120
Louis VII, king of France, xi, 21, 54, 58, 61, 64, 69, 71–72, 83, 88–89, 112, 119–20, 149

Malcolm IV, king of Scotland, 145, 148–49, 157, 168
Matilda, Empress, 60–61, 70, 74, 90, 128, 132, 135, 193
Melrose Abbey, 142–44
mills, new technology, 25–26, 31, 68, 80, 88
Mont-Saint-Michel, 37, 39, 71, 99–100, 103, 105, 125

Normanization process, 69, 166, 168, 178
nunnery, nuns, 22, 43

papal protection and confirmations, 3, 29, 42, 45, 50, 56–57, 66, 92, 103, 116, 123, 129, 136–37, 166–67, 179, 181–85
Paris, 39, 49–52, 54, 62, 73, 87–90, 116–23, 172, 181–85
  Chardonnet, 121–22
  Groslay fief, 117, 119–20
  Hôtel de Tiron, 119–21
  Notre-Dame-de-Paris, 19, 122, 174
  Saint-Germain-des-Prés, 119–20, 173–74
  Saint-Maur, 173
  Saint-Victor-de-Paris, 66, 120, 122, 174
  Sainte-Geneviève-de-Paris, 120, 122, 174
Peter II, bishop of Poitiers, 35, 53
Philip I, king of France, 7, 35, 71
Philip I, duke of Orléans, 173–74
Philip II Augustus, king of France, 30, 118, 121

Philippe II de Lorraine d'Harcourt, commendatory abbot, 174
Pignore de Vallea, Jean, 3, 33, 167
pilgrims, pilgrimage, 5, 13, 17, 19, 24, 27–29, 31, 37, 48, 62–63, 72, 75, 78, 80, 85–89, 108, 111, 114–15, 118, 122, 144, 146, 176, 178, 183
Pithiviers, 57–58, 76, 88, 117, 125, 192
Prémontré, Premonstratensians, 1, 22, 57, 178
preachers, itinerant, 8–9, 33

Ralph, abbot of Selkirk and Tiron, 10, 44, 50, 54–55, 141
Reformation, Protestant/English, 141, 167, 171–72
Robert I de Beaumont, count of Meulan, earl of Leicester, 70–71, 90, 96
Robert II de Beaumont, seigneur of Le Neubourg, earl of Leicester, 58, 71, 90–92
Robert of Arbrissel, 9–10, 12, 22, 35–38, 43, 45, 53
Robert of Bellême, lord of Shrewsbury, 38, 40–41, 55, 74
Robert of London, 153–55, 161
Robert Colaws, 133, 137–38
Robert FitzMartin, 65, 70, 91, 133, 135, 138–39
Robert FitzRoy of Caen, earl of Gloucester, lord of Glamorgan, 70, 135, 139
Rotrou II, count of the Perche, 13–14, 38, 40–41, 47, 54, 67, 70–71, 74–75, 77–78, 82, 90, 182, 187–88
Roxburgh, 23, 129, 141–43, 145, 149–51, 157, 195
Rule of Saint Benedict, 7–9, 17, 35, 56, 64, 147, 162, 167

salt trade, 29–30, 49, 54, 60, 68–69, 73, 75, 85, 89, 97–98, 103, 108, 113–15, 152, 155, 157, 178
La Sauve Majeure, 11, 25
Savigny, Savignacs, xi, 1–2, 9–10, 22, 37–39, 127–28, 138

Scotland, politics, 1, 7, 64, 72-73, 168-71
Auld Alliance, 1, 72, 171
Scotland, Tironensian foundations, see Selkirk, Kelso, Arbroath, Lindores, Kilwinning, Fyvie
shipping, 5, 14, 17, 28-30, 61, 89, 92, 97-98, 115, 119, 128-30, 136, 140-41, 143, 145-46, 149
Somerled, *Carmen de Morte Sumerledi*, 168
Stephen-Henry, count of Blois, 63
Stephan I, abbot of Tiron, 27, 52, 72, 104, 147, 185
Stephen I, king of England, xi, 54, 61, 90, 127-28, 135-37, 182

Thibaut II, count of Blois-Champagne, IV, count of Blois and Chartres, II, count of Champagne and Brie, xi, 24, 26, 42-43, 52, 54, 56, 61-62, 64, 69-70, 74, 79-80, 82-83, 113, 115, 120, 123, 127, 182, 190
Thibaut V, count of Blois, 79
Tiron Abbey, foundation 15, 24, 38-39, 41-42
Tiron Abbey, layout
  basilica church, 24, 176
  cemetery, 10, 44, 66
  chapter, 5, 18, 20, 33, 44, 48, 58-59, 107, 139, 167, 172, 188, 191
  cloister, 167, 174
  dormitory, 24, 69, 173
  fires, 3, 30, 42, 167, 170-71, 174
  guesthouse, 27, 59, 75
  infirmary, 23-24, 43
  library, 41, 175
  refectory, 66, 173
  schools, 18, 22, 43-44, 61, 75, 174-75
  scriptorium, 59-61, 74-75
  workrooms, 15, 18, 24, 42, 61, 75, 176
Tiron Abbey, community, 58-60, 68-69
  female members, 21-22, 43-44
  grey monks, 2, 166
Tiron, congregation/order of
  administration, 58-59, 67, 125
  alien priories, 4, 11, 127-30, 148, 170
  architectural legacy, 26, 173, 175-77
  Cartulaire de Tiron, ed. Merlet, 3-4
  cartulary, manuscript, 3, 12, 23, 29, 49, 181, 183-85
  charters of elevation, 23, 64-67, 194
  charters, forged, 3, 60, 63, 67, 92, 106, 115, 118, 121, 171
  commendatory abbots, 18, 30, 172-75
  confraternity, 20, 22, 47, 92, 97, 108, 122, 166
  construction/building, 9-10, 14-15, 24-27, 30, 40, 45, 49, 50, 56, 60, 69, 106, 114, 116, 122, 140, 155, 165-166, 174-75, 177-78
  dispute resolution, xii, 3-4, 8, 15, 21, 30-31, 36, 38, 43, 48, 58, 60, 62, 72, 74-75, 84, 107, 116, 122, 125, 144, 147, 149, 175, 179, 187-195
  expansion patterns, 11, 67-69
  general chapters, 2, 14, 29, 33, 64, 66-67, 125, 128-29, 148, 167, 171, 178, 195
  mobility, 17, 28, 67
  proctors, 140-41, 147, 148, 170, 179
  travel, 15-16, 27-31, 39, 54-55, 58, 67-68, 108, 118

Ursio of Fréteval, 85-86, 189, 191-92

Vallombrosa Abbey, Vallombrosans, 8, 10
Vital of Mortain, abbot of Savigny, 9-10, 22, 36-38, 44-45, 52, 69

Waleran II of Meulan, seigneur of Pont Audemer, 58, 64, 71, 90-92, 97, 120
Wales, Tironensian foundations, see St. Dogmaels, Caldey, Pill
Wars of Religion, 30, 167, 172-73
White Ship, 38, 62, 66, 70, 130
William I the Conqueror, king of England, 7, 138
William I the Lion, king of Scotland, 20, 70-71, 143-45, 149, 151-57, 159-61

William II, count of Nevers, 40, 43, 54, 56, 70
William VIII, duke of Aquitaine, 34
William IX, duke of Aquitaine, 52–54, 69, 113
William X, duke of Aquitaine, 53, 69, 88, 114, 120
William, son of Thibaut, grammaticus, *prévôt* of William IX, 53–54
William of Poitiers, abbot of Selkirk and Tiron, passim
  identity, 52–54
  death, 71, 129
William Atheling, 43, 55, 65–66, 70, 90

INDEX OF TIRONENSIAN PLACES

Note: the Latin names are the forms used in Lucien Merlet's index entitled "Dictionnaire Topographique," T2, 255–313, which indicates the communes, cantons, and arrondissements in 1883 and the charter numbers in T1 and T2.

To aid the reader with localization, monastic sites in France are provided the modern settlement and postcode (e.g., Saint-Arnoulten-Yvelines 78730) and those in Britain are provided the first half of the modern postcode (e.g., AB10 for Aberdeen 10).

Abbotshall AB15, 150, 153, 156
Aberchirder AB54, 150, 153, 156
Aberdeen AB10–13, 149–62
Aberkerdo, Kildrummy AB33, 150, 153, 156
Abernethy PH2, 20, 150–51, 155, 178
Ablis (*Sanctus-Ispanus*), Saint-Arnoult-en-Yvelines 78730, 49–51, 76, 79, 84, 117–18
Airoux (*Sancta-Maria-juxta-Forestam*), La Ferrière-Airoux 86160, 109–10, 114
Andwell/Mapledurwell, RG25 (*Mapedroella*), 128, 131–33, 135–36, 140, 148, 170
Arable (*Sancta-Maria-de-Arablo*), Dormans 51700, xi, 117, 119, 122–23
Arbirlot DD11, 150–51, 155
Arbroath DD11, 16, 20, 23, 70, 128, 149–58, 162, 165–66, 169, 172, 177
Arcisses (*Arsiciae*), Brunelles 28400, 38, 41, 47, 51, 74–77, 81, 99, 148, 175, 188, 194, 195
Arçonnay 72610 (*Archenaium*), 99, 101, 105, 185
Ardoch, Bridge of Gairn AB35, 150, 153, 156
Ardrossan KA22, 163–65, 201
Argenvilliers 28420 (*Argenvillarium*), 76, 78, 84
Arley, Lower Arley, Old Arley CV7, 131, 133, 136
Asnières (Clairefontaine) (*Asneriae*) Cizay-la-Madeleine 49700, 23,
48–49, 51, 67, 98, 108–12, 147, 175–76, 181–82, 187, 190, 195
Auchenblae AB30, 150, 153, 155
Auchterhead Muir, Cambusnethan ML2, 150, 54, 157
Augerville-les-Malades (*Ogerivilla*), Prunay-le-Gillon 28360, 51, 57, 76, 79, 84–85, 88, 190
Augerville-la-Rivière 45330 (*Ogerii-Villa*), 80, 84–85, 88
Auvilliers (*Orviler*), Ozoir-le-Breuil 28200, 76, 79, 86
Ayr KA7, 150–51

Bacqueville-en-Caux 76730 (*Baschevilla*) 3, 93–97, 187
Balfeith AB30, 150, 153, 155
Ballegillegrand in Bolshan DD11, 150, 152, 155
Banchory AB31, 150, 153, 156
Banff AB45, 150, 153–54, 156, 161
Beaulieu (*Bellus-Locus*), Auvers-sous-Montfaucon 72540, 99, 101, 106
Beaumont-Pied-du-Boeuf 72500 (*Passus-Bovis*), 99, 102, 107
Beith KA14–15, 163–65
Belhomert, Belhomert-Guéhouville 28240, 76–77, 81, 124
Berkeley, Odiham RG29, 131–32, 135
Berwick-upon-Tweed TD15, 141–43, 145, 150–51, 157–61
Beverton, Barton, Kington HR4, 136
Béville-le-Comte 28700 (*Boovilla-Comitis*) 76, 79, 84, 117–19

Blémars (*Blimartium*), Saint-Etienne-des-Guérets 41190, 76, 80, 88
Bois-Aubry (*Sanctus-Michael-Lucizensis*) Luzé 37120, 19, 23, 54, 67, 88, 98, 109–14, 147, 176, 182, 194–95
Bois Ruffin (*Boscus-Rufini*) (Les Mellerets), Arrou 28290, 76, 78, 84, 189
Boissy-sur-Damville (*Busseium*), Buis-sur-Damville 27240, 92–94
Bosc-Roger (*Boscus-Rogerii*), Gisay-la-Coudre 27330, 93, 95, 97
Bouche d'Aigre (*Bucca-Ogrie*), Romilly-sur-Aigre 28220, 48, 51, 76, 80, 84, 86–87, 174, 181, 190
Bouffry 41270 (*Castrum-Goferi*), 76, 80, 83, 87, 188
Bouligneau (*Bollonellum*), Saint-Fargeau Villages 77310, 54, 177, 119–20
La Bourgonnière (*Burgunneria*), La Chapelle-Fortin 28340, 98–100
Bowden TD6, 142–43, 145
Bradford Peverell DT2 (*Bradefort*), 128, 131–33, 136, 185
Brading, Brading Sandown PO36, 131, 133, 138
Bray 27170 (*Braia*), 93, 95, 97
Bréau 77720 (*Broilum*), 54, 117, 119, 123
Brechin DD10, 27, 150, 152, 155
La Bretonnerie (*Bretoneria*), Chartres 28000, 76, 78, 82–83
Le Breuil (*Brolium*), Fléac-sur-Seugne 17800, 76, 79, 85, 109, 111, 114–15
Brodick KA27, 163–65
Brunelles 28400 (*Brenella*), 24, 38, 41, 47, 75–77, 81–82, 188
Bursledon SO31, 131–32, 134

Caldey, Tenby SA70, 19, 29, 114, 130–31, 133–34, 139–41, 166, 172, 176
Cambusnethan ML2, 142–43, 146, 150, 154, 157
Carmyllie DD11, 150–51, 155
Carse in/of Stirling FK7–9, 150, 152, 157

Catterline AB39, 150–51, 169
Chartres 28000 (*Carnotum*), 9–11, 17, 19, 22, 25–30, 33, 38–45, 48–52, 55–56, 58, 61–64, 68–84, 88–92, 97–98, 117–20, 122, 128, 145, 174, 178, 181–83
Châtaigniers (*Castaneae*) Soizé 28330, 48, 51, 76, 78–80, 84–85, 87, 174, 181, 189–90, 124
Chavigny-Bailleul 27220 (*Chavigneium*), 92–94
Chérancé 72170 (*Charenceium*), 101, 105, 185
Choudri (*Choudre*), Prénouvellon 41240, 57, 76, 79, 86
Cintry/Saintry/Saint-Georges d'Orléans 45130 (*Cintreium*), 48, 50–51, 57, 76, 79–80, 86, 88, 189, 192
Clémas (*Climart*), Le Favril 28190, 50–51, 76–78, 82
Clères 76690 (*Sanctus-Silvester*), 93–94, 96
Cockington TQ2, 131, 133, 139
Cohardon (*Cohardum*), Fyé 72610, 24–25, 48, 50–51, 99, 101, 105
Combres 28480 (*Cumbrae*), 76, 78, 82
Corbeil/Tigery 91250 (*Tigerium*), 54, 117, 119–20
Corrie KA27, 163–65
Corsept 44560 (*Corseth*), 24, 54, 71, 109–10, 113
Coulaines 72190 (*Colonia*), 99, 101–2, 106
Coull in Mar in Tarland AB34, 150, 153, 156
Coulonges-les-Sablons 6111) (*Colungae*), 76–77, 82
Couptrain (*Cortpoltrein*)/Saint-Maurice de René (*Resneum*) 53250, 99–100, 103
Courgeoût 61560 (*Corthgehout*), 99–100, 103
Les Coutures (*Cultura*), Mareau-aux-Bois 45300, 25, 57–58, 76, 80, 88, 117, 119, 192
Crail KY10, 150–51, 157–59, 161

INDEX OF TIRONENSIAN PLACES 205

Crasville (*Crasvilla*), Crasville-la-Rocquefort 76740, 93–96, 185
Crèvecoeur-en-Auge 14340 (*Crevecor*), 93, 95, 97, 185
Croixval (*Crucis-Vallis*), Ternay 41800, 99, 102, 107, 192
La Crotte (*Gurgites*), Cloyes-sur-le-Loir 28220, 76, 80, 85, 87, 191
Le Crouais 35290, 105, 124
Culsalmond AB52, 150, 153, 156, 158–61
Cunington/Conington, Peterborough PE7, 160, 162, 177

Dalry KA24, 163–65
Danguern Guer, Saint-Servan-sur-Mer 35400, 105, 124
La Draire (*Daria*), Azay-sur-Thouet 79130, 109–10, 114
Dreghorn KA11/Pierstoun, 163–65
Duddingston EH15/Trauerlen, 142, 144, 146, 157
Dumbarton G82, 163–65
Dumfries DG1/2, 150–51, 154, 157
Dun and Hedderwick, Montrose DD10, 150, 152, 155
Dundee DD1–5, 23, 150–52, 155, 157–62
Dunfermline KY12, 150–51, 157, 168
Dunlop KA3, 163–65
Dunmore FK2, 158–59, 162
Dunnichen DD8, 150, 152, 155
Durno AB51, 158–61

Eastrop, Worting, Basingstoke RG23, 131–32, 135
Ecoman 41290/Saint-André-de-la-Forêt-Longue (*Sanctus-Andreas-de-Seveliona*), 48, 51–52, 76, 80, 84, 87, 124, 190
Edinburgh EH1, 51, 142, 144–46, 150–51, 154, 157–58
Edinburgh, Arthur's Seat Holyrood Park EH8, 142, 144, 146, 177
Edzell DD9, 150, 152, 155
Eguillé (*Sancta-Maria-de-Aguille*), Pruillé-l'Eguillé 72150, 99, 101–2, 107, 181

Eildon TD6, 142–43
Elgin IV30, 150–51, 154, 156, 161
Escalmento (*Escalmento*), Ecoman 41290, 76, 80, 87
Ethie, Inverkeilor, Arbroath DD11, 150, 152, 155

Fernhill Winkton, Christchurch BH23, 131–32, 136
Ferrières (*Ferrariae*), Bouillé-Loretz 79290, 53, 98, 109–14, 175, 181, 190, 194–95
Fethmuref/Barry DD7, 150–51, 155
Fintray, Hatton of Fintray AB21, 158–61
Fogo TD11, 141–43, 145
Fontaine-Raoul 41270 (*Fons-Radulfi*), 76, 80, 87, 188, 192
Fordoun AB30, 150, 153, 155
La Forêt-sur-Sèvre 79380 (*Foresta*), 109–10, 114–15
Forfar DD8, 150–52, 155, 158–59, 156
Forglen AB53, 20, 150, 153–54, 160
Forres IV36, 150, 153, 156, 161
Fosse-Bellay, Cizay-la-Madeleine 49700, 112, 124
Fouteaux (*Footelli*), Bouffry 41270, 76, 80, 84, 87, 124, 188, 190
Frétigny 28480 (*Fractigneium*), 76–77, 82, 91
Freystrop SA62, 131, 134, 140
Fyvie AB53, 150, 153–54, 156, 177
Fyvie, St. Peter AB53, 150, 153

Gamrie AB45, 150, 153–54, 156
Garioch, Chapel of AB51, 158–61
Gast, Tanville 61500, 99–100, 102
Gatcombe PO30, 131, 133, 137–38
Gâtine (*Sanctus-Laurentius-de-Gastina*), Les Corvées-des-Yys 28240, 76, 78, 82
Gémigny 45310 (*Geminiacum*), 57, 76, 79–80, 86, 88
La Génevraie 61240, 104
Glamis DD8, 150, 152, 155, 159
Glascarrig WX, 131, 134, 140–41
Glaskeler in Catterline AB39, 150, 153, 155

Gourdez (*Gorzeiae*), Morancez 28630, 76, 78, 83
Grandry (*Grandis-Rivus*), Fontaine-les-Coteaux 41800, 107, 124
Great Balhill (Seaclose) Newport PO30, 131, 133, 137
Greenlaw TD10, 142–43, 145
Grémonville, see Saint-Blaise-de-Luy
La Grézillé 49320, 112, 124
Le Gué-Brunet (*Vadum-Bruneti*), Parigné-l'Evêque 72250, 99, 101–2
Le Gué-de-Launay (*Sanctus-Laurentius-de-Vado-Alneti*), Vibraye 72320, 19, 26, 84, 98–99, 101–2, 106–7, 124, 147, 175, 181, 193, 195
Guémançais, Rouperroux-le-Coquet 72110, 106, 124
Gurnard PO31, Northwood, 133, 137
Guthrie DD8, 150, 152, 155

Hadden TD5, 142–43, 145
Haddington EH41, 142, 144, 146, 150–51, 157
Hallais, Bellou-le-Trichard 61130, 106, 124
Haltwhistle Tynedale NE49, 150, 154, 157, 177
Hamble (*Sanctus-Andreas-de-Hamla*), Hamble-le-Rice SO31, 11, 29, 43, 49, 51, 96, 128–34, 136, 140–41, 170, 176, 181–82
Hambye 50450, 55, 71, 98–100, 103–4, 124, 136, 176, 185
Hardingstone NN4 St. Edmund, 142, 144, 147
Heudreville (*Hildrevilla*), Heudreville-sur-Eure 27400, 92–94, 98, 181
La Heulière (*Hurelière*)+la Bretonnerie (*Bretonnière*), Happonvilliers 28480, 76, 78, 82
La Huanière (*Huaneria*), Le Plessis-Ste.-Opportune 27170, 93, 95, 97
Hubberston SA73, 131, 133–34, 140
Huest 27930 (*Guest*), 93–95
Humberston, Church Lane, Cleethorpes DN36, 104, 131–33, 136
Hume TD5, 142–43, 145
Hunny Hill PO30, 131, 133, 137
Hunton SO21, 131–32, 134

Imbleville 76890 (*Wimbelevilla*), 93–96, 187
Insch AB52, 158–61
Inverboyndie AB45, 150, 153–54, 156
Inverkeilor DD11, 150, 152, 155
Inverkeithing KY11, 150–51, 157–59, 161
Inverlunan DD11, 150, 152, 155
Inverness IV1, 149–50, 154, 156
Inverpeffer DD11, 150–51, 155
Inverugie AB42, 150, 154, 156
Inverurie AB51, 158–61
Irvine KA11–12, 163–65

Jardy (*Jarzia*), Marnes-la-Coquette 92430, 117–19, 170, 181
Jarrie (*Jarreia*), Chédigny 37310, 109–12
Jedburgh TD8, 141–43, 145
Johnston SA62, 131, 134, 140
Joug-Dieu (*Jugum-Dei*), Pré-de-Joug, Ave. de Joux, rue de l'Abbaye, Arnas 69400, 11, 39, 43, 49, 51, 64, 68, 88–89, 108–9, 111, 114–16, 147, 175, 182–83, 194–95

Keith-Hervey, Humbie EH36, 142, 144, 146
Kelso TD5/Roxburgh (*Rochaburgum*), 16, 19, 22–23, 27, 49, 70, 72, 92, 128–29, 141–49, 154, 157, 165–66, 168–69, 172, 177, 179, 181, 183
Kennethmont AB54, 150, 153, 156, 158–62
Kilbirnie KA25, 163–65
Kilbride KA27, 163–65
Kilmacocharmik, N.+S. Knapdale PA31, 163–65
Kilmarnock KA1, 163–65
Kilmaronock in Gartocharn G83, 163–65
Kilmory KA27, 163–65
Kilwinning KA13, 16, 20, 128, 160, 162–66, 169, 171–72, 177, 201
Kinblethmont DD11, 150, 152, 155

INDEX OF TIRONENSIAN PLACES

Kincorth AB12, 150, 153, 156
Kingoldrum DD8, 150, 152, 155
Kingsmuir DD8, 150, 152, 155
Kington HR5 (*Chintona*), 49, 128, 131, 133, 136, 193
Kinnell DD11, 150, 152, 155
Kinnernie (Old) AB32, 150, 153, 156
Kirkton of Culsalmond AB52, 150, 153, 156
Kirriemuir DD8, 150, 152, 155

Lamyatt, Somerset BA4, 131–32, 134
Lanark ML11, 142–43, 146, 150–51, 157
Lanthenac, La Chèze 22210, 104
Laugerie (*Laugueria*), La Puye 86260, 109–10, 114
Ledo (Le Loir) (*Ledum*), Le Thieulin 28240, 76, 78, 82
Léry 27690 (*Erilliacum*), 93–94, 96
Lesmahagow ML11, 27, 70, 128, 141–43, 146, 169
Liberton EH16, 164, 166
Lièvreville (*Leporisvilla*), Challet 28300, 57, 76, 78, 83
Lillemer 35111, 105, 124
Lilliesleaf TD6, 142–43, 145
Lindores KY14, 16, 20, 23, 70, 128, 149, 154–62, 168–70, 177
Linlithgow EH49, 150–51, 157
Little Newcastle SA62, Pill church, 131, 134, 140
Littlecote Hungerford RG17, 131–32, 134
Livet-en-Saosnois 72610 (*Livetum*), church, 99, 101, 105
Llys Prawst (Newton), Walwyn's Castle Haverfordwest SA62, 131, 133, 140
Lorelium (*Lorelium*), Bourges 18000, 109, 111, 114–15
Loudon (*Losdonum*), Parigné-l'Evêque 72250, 99, 101–2, 107
Loudoun KA4, 163–65
Louïe (*Audita*), La-Fresnaye-sur-Chédouet 72600, 99–101, 103, 181
Lower Arley, Church Lane Arley CV7, 131, 133, 136

La Madeleine-près-Bréval, also Petit-Tiron (*Sancta-Maria-Magdalena-juxta-Berelelval*), Bonnières-sur-Seine 78270, 93–95
La-Madeleine-sur-Seine (*Sancta-Maria-Magdalena-super-Sequanam*), Pressagny l'Orgueilleux 27510, 19, 93–95
Mains DD4, 150–52, 155
Makerstoun TD5, 142–43, 145
Le Mans 72000, 21, 39, 50–52, 74–75, 86, 98–99, 101–2, 105–6, 108–9, 181–83, 193, 195
Mapledurwell RG27/Up Nately/Newnham, 131–32, 135
Marlborough SN8 (*Melleburga*), 131, 135
Marolles (*Mairoliae*), Marolles-les-Buis 28400, 76–77, 82
Martigny (*Martigneium*), Saint-Germain-de-Martigny 61560, 99–100, 102
Mattingley RG27, 131–32, 135
Maxwellheugh, Kelso TD5, 142–43, 145
Mazangé 41100 (*Masengiacum*), 99, 102, 107, 188
Le Méleray (*Melereiz*), Margon 28400, 24, 49–51, 76–77, 81, 84, 189
Melrose TD6, 141–44, 155
Membrolles 41240 (*Memberolae*), 76, 79–80, 85–87
Meonstoke SO32, 131–32, 134
Merchingley, Slaley/Riding Mill NE44, 19, 141–42, 144, 146, 157
Le Merlerault 61240, 104
Le Mesnil (*Mesnil-Bertre*), Lieury 14170, 93, 95, 97
Midlem TD7, 142–43, 145
Mirablesland Niton, Ventnor PO38, 131, 133, 138
Mondoubleau 41170 (*Mons-Dublellus*), 28, 76, 80, 86–88, 98–99, 101–2, 106–7, 188, 192
Mondynes Fordoun Laurencekirk AB30, 150, 153, 155
Monifieth DD5, 150–51
Monikie DD5, 150–51, 155

INDEX OF TIRONENSIAN PLACES

Monrion (*Mons-Rion*), Cellettes 41120, 26, 49, 51, 76, 80, 88
Montaillé 72650 (*Mons-Allerii*), 99, 101, 105–6
Montargis (*Sanctus-Antoninus[de Montehargis]*), Cambremer 14340, 93, 95, 97, 185
Montchevrel 61170 (*Mons-Capreoli*), 99–100, 102
Montcollain/Montcolin, Saint-Georges-du-Rosay 72110, 107, 124
Montgauger/Montgorger, Saint-Epain 37800, 112, 124
Montgé-en-Goële/Saint-Sépulcre-d'Allemagne (*Mons-Gehier*), 77230, 117, 119, 122
Montigny-le-Gannelon 28220 (*Montiniacum*), 50, 74, 84, 87
Montluiser/Mons-Lusellus (*Mons-Luiserni*), Bouffry 41270, 80, 87
Montmerle-du-Val-Saint-Etienne, Saint-Julien-sur-Reyssouze 01560, 116, 124
Montrose (Old) DD10, 150–53, 155, 158–59, 161
Montrouveau 41800 (*Mons-Rivelli*), 99, 102, 107
Morebattle TD5 (Mow), 142–43, 145
Mortagne-au-Perche 61400 (*Mauritania*), 39, 76–77, 98–103
Mougon 86240 (*Maguntum*), 109–10, 114
La Mouise 45310 (*Maisia*), 76, 79, 86
Le Moulin-Neuf (*Molendinum-Novum*), Molineuf 41190, 26, 76, 80, 88
Moussay (*Murciacum*), Vouneuil-sur-Vienne 86210, 19, 109–10, 114
Moutiers 28150 (*Monasteria*), 76, 79, 85
Moylgrove SA43, 131, 133, 139
Muckleford, Bradford Peverell DT2, 131–32, 136
Mugdrum Island "Redinche", Newburgh KY14, 159–60, 162
Mundurno AB23, 150, 153–54, 156
Murgers (*Murgeriae*), Meaucé 28240, 76–77, 82, 181

Murroes DD4, 150–51, 155
Muthill PH5, 158–59, 162
Mynachlogddu SA66, 131, 133, 139

Nazareth-de-Nogent-le-Rotrou 28400, rue de Nazareth, 77, 81, 124
Nenthorn+St. Mary's TD5, 142–43, 145
Néron 28210 (*Sanctus-Remigius-de-Nerone*), 26, 76, 78, 83, 189
Neuilly-sur-Eure 61290 (*Nuilleium*), 76–77, 82
New Moat SA63, 131, 134, 140
Newport PO30, 133, 137
Newtyle PH12, 150, 152, 155, 158–59, 162
Nigg AB12, 150, 153, 156
Nogent-le-Rotrou 28400 (*Nogentum*), 39, 49–50, 73–78, 81–82, 84, 87–89
Nolton, Nolton and Roch SA62, 131, 134, 140
Nonvilliers-Grandhoux 28120 (*Longum-Villare*), 51, 75–76, 78, 82
Northampton NN1–7, 55, 141–42, 144, 147
North Esk, Montrose DD10, 152, 155
Notre-Dame-d'Estrées 14340 (*Sancta-Maria-de-Strata*), 93, 95, 97
Notre-Dame-des-Houlettes, Les Moûtiers-Hubert 14140, 104
Notre-Dame-/Saint-Pierre-du-Val 27210 (*Sancta-Maria-de-Vallibus*), 93, 95

Oisème (*Oiseamum*), Gasville-Oisème 28300, 76, 78, 83
Oisonnière (*Oseleria*), Montigny-le-Chartif 28120, 76, 78, 82
Orgeville (*Orgeville-soubz-Passy*), Caillouet-Orgeville 27120, 93–95
Ormoy 91540 (*Ulmeium*), 54, 58, 117, 119–20
Orsemont (*Orsemont*), Chaussy 95710, 93–94, 96

Panbride DD7, 150–51, 155
Paris 75004/75005 (*Parisius*), 22, 29, 39, 49–51, 54, 58, 62, 73, 80, 87–90, 95, 116–23, 170, 172–74, 181–85, 192
Peebles EH45, 142–44, 146

Peglait (*Sanctus-Georgius-de-Peglait*), Saint-Avertin 37550, 19, 109–11
La Pelice (*Pellicia*), Cherreau 72400, 84, 98–99, 101–2, 106, 167, 171, 175, 193, 195
La Pépinière (*Pepineria*), La Bazoche-Gouet 28330, 76, 78, 84
Péronville 28140 (*Spesovilla*), 25, 57, 76, 79, 84, 86, 88, 191
Perth PH1–2, 92, 128, 149–52, 155, 158–59, 161–62
Pill, Lower Priory, Milford Haven SA70, 29, 128, 130–31, 133–34, 140–41, 176
Plains (*Plani*)/Chapelle-Vicomtesse 41270 (*Capella-Viconteisse*), 76, 80, 84, 87, 124, 190, 192
Pont-Rousseau (*Pons-Roselli*), Rezé 44400, 71, 109–10, 113
Portincraig Broughty Ferry DD5, 150–51, 155
Pouzioux-La Jarrie 86580 (*Puteolae*), 109–10, 114
Premnay AB52, 158–61
Les Prés-Morin (*Prata-Comitis*), Condé-sur-Huisne 61110, 76–77, 81
Prunay-le-Gillon 28630 (*Pruneium*), 76, 78, 83
Puerthe (*Pertae*), Péronville 28140, 57, 76, 79, 86, 191

Le Raincy 93340 (*Rainseium*), 25, 117, 119, 122
Rath in Catterline AB39, 150, 153
Rattery TQ10, 131, 133, 139
Redden Farm TD5, Sprouston, Kelso farm, 142–43, 145
Redeland, Chineham Redlands, Basingstoke RG34, 131–32, 134
Redon, Saint-Nicolas-de, 44460 (*Rumphu*), 99, 102, 108, 185
Renfrew PA4, 142–43, 145–46
Réno, La-Madeleine-de- 61290 (*Reisnou*), 76–77, 82
Reuzé (*Rusaium*), priory, Orches 86230, 25, 109–10, 114

Ribeuf-sur-Mer (*Risus-Bovis-Supra-Mare*), Ambrumesnil 76550, 93–96
Riboeuf (*Risus-Bovis*), Romilly-sur-Aigre 28220, 26, 76, 80, 84, 87, 124, 190–91
Roch SA62, 131, 134, 140
Rosay, Saint-Georges-du- 72110 (*Roseium*), 107, 185
Rossay, La-Madeleine-de-Rossay, Changé 72560, 107, 124
Rossie Ochil Estate PH2, 150, 152, 155
Rotundum-Donum, Clermont-Ferrand 63000, 109, 111, 114–15
La Roussière (*Rungeria*), Godisson 61240, 99–100, 102
Roxburgh TD5, 23, 129, 141–43, 145, 149–51, 157, 195
Ruan-sur-Egvonne 41270 (*Rotomagum*), 76, 80, 87, 189
Rutherglen G73, 150–51, 157
Ruthven AB54, 150, 152, 155

Saint-Antoine, Montmirail 72320 (*Sanctus Antonius*), 107, 124
Saint-Antoine, Thorigné-sur-Dué 72160, 107, 124
Saint-Barthélemy-du-Vieux-Charencey (*Sanctus-Bartholomeus-de-Cherentheio*), priory, Saint-Maurice-lès-Charencey 61190, 21, 98–100, 187
Saint-Blaise-de-Luy (*Sanctus-Blasius-de-Luy*), Grémonville 76970, 48, 51, 93–97
Saint-Blaise-des-Vignes, Yvré-l'Evêque 72530, 106, 124
Saint-Blaise-en-Gaudrée, Luzé 37120, 112, 124
Saint-Colomban-de-la-Mare-Ferron, Miniac-Morvan 35540, 105, 124
St. Cross, Isle of Wight (*Sancta-Crux-de-Insula*), Newport PO30, 128, 131, 133–38, 140–41, 148, 170, 195
Saint-Clémentin-de-la-Tisonnière, Noirterre 79300, 113, 124
Saint-Denis-de-La-Roche-Montbourcher, Cuguen 35270, 105, 124

St. Dogmaels, St. Mary of Cemaes (*Cameae, Galse, Sanctus-Dogmael*), Cardigan SA43, 2, 4, 11, 19, 49, 51, 64–67, 70–71, 127–31, 133–34, 136, 138–41, 147–48, 172, 176, 179, 181, 183, 194–95

Saint-Georges-de-Cloyes-sur-le-Loir 28220 (*Sanctus-Georgius-de-Cloia*), 48, 50–51, 76, 80, 87

Saint-Germain-sur-Avre 27320 (*Sanctus-Germanus-super-Arvam*), 92–94, 98–99

Saint-Gilles-de-Contres, Saint Rémy-des-Monts 72600, 106, 124

St. Helens, Bembridge PO35, 131, 133, 138

Saint-Jacques-de-la-Bruère/de-la-Lande, Neuilly-le-Brignon 37160, 112, 124

Saint-Jouin-de-Blavou 61360 (*Sanctus-Jovinus*), 99–100, 103

Saint-Julien-de-la-Chattière, Tremblay 35460, 105, 124

Saint-Julien-sur-Sarthe 61170 (*Sanctus-Julianus*), 99, 100, 103

Saint-Laurent-des-Près, Quettreville-sur-Sienne 50660, 104

St. Lawrence of Berwick-upon-Tweed TD15, 142–43, 145

St. Lawrence, Winchester SO23 (*Sanctus-Laurentius*) 131–32, 134

Saint-Lubin-de-Cloyes-sur-le Loir 28220 (*Sanctus-Leobinus*), 76, 80, 87

Saint-Lubin-des-Cinq-Fonts 28330 (*Sanctus-Leobinus-de-Quinque-Fontibus*), 42, 76, 78, 84

Saint-Lunaire-de-l'Hostellerie, Pleudihen-sur-Rance 22690, 105, 124

Saint-Lunaire-de-La Barre, Plerguer 35540, 105, 124

Saint-Marc-de-Primart, Saint Clémentin 79150, 113, 124

Saint-Maurice-lès-Charencey 61190 (*Sanctus-Mauricius[-de-Charenthaio]*), 98–100

Saint-Maxime/le Breuil-Saint-Mesme (*Sanctus-Maximus*), Trizay-lès-Bonneval 28800, 76, 79, 85

Saint-Méen-du-Cellier 44850, 105, 124

Saint-Méen-le-Grand 35290 (*Sanctus-Menenius*), 98–100, 103, 105, 185

Saint-Michel-du-Tertre (*Sanctus-Michael-de-Colle*), Ancinnes 72610, 99, 101, 105

Saint-Nicolas-de-Buron, Saint-Contest 14280, 104

Saint-Nicolas-du-Vieux-Castel, Saint-Coulomb 35350, 105, 124

Saint-Nicolas-en-Loire/des-Défunts (*Sancti-Nicholai,Oratorium*), Corsept 44560, 24, 113

Saint-Pair-du-Mont 14340 (*Sanctus-Paternus*), 93, 95, 97

Saint-Petreuc, Plerguer 35540, 105, 124

Saint-Pierre-et-Saint-Paul-de-Roz-Landrieux 35120, 105, 124

Saint-Sauveur, Vibraye 72320, 107, 124

Saint-Sauveur-de-la-Guichardière, Saint Hilaire du Bois 49310, 113, 124

Saint-Séverin-de-Cloyes-sur-le-Loir 28220 (*Sanctus-Severinus*), 76, 80, 87

Saint-Sulpice-en-Pail, also Saint-Sulpice-des-Chèvres (*Sanctus-Sulpicius-in-Paillo*), Gesvres 53370, 19, 99–100, 103

St. Ternan in Mar, Banchory Ternan AB31, 150, 153, 156

St. Vigeans DD11, 150, 152, 155

Saint-Vu or -Leu, Saint Rémy-des-Monts 72600, 106, 124

Sainte-Marie-de-Longues-sur-Mer 14400, 104

Sainte-Sabine-sur-Longève 72380 (*Sancta-Sabrina*), 99, 101, 105

Saintes-Vallées (*Sanctae-Valles*), Ouzouer-le-Marché 41240, 57, 76, 79, 190

Sancheville 28800 (*Sanchevilla*), 76, 79, 85, 185

Sandown PO36, 131, 133, 138

La Saulaye (*Saulaya*), La Cornuaille 49440, 99, 102, 108

Secreu (*Secreu/Secroio*) [not indexed in T2:304], Aillant-sur-Tholon 89110, 117, 119, 123

INDEX OF TIRONENSIAN PLACES

Seillon, Bourg-en-Bresse 01000, 116, 124
Selkirk TD7, 11, 16, 42, 44, 49–51, 53–55, 64–65, 70–72, 128–29, 141–46, 168, 194–95
Sept-Faux (*Septem-Fagi*), Arthon-en-Retz 44320, 71, 109–10, 113
Séresville (*Ceresvilla*), Mainvilliers 28300, 76, 78, 83
Shide PO30, 131, 133, 137
Shorwell PO30, 131, 133, 137–38
Simprim TD12, 142–43, 145
Soberton SO32, 131–32, 134
Soizé 28330 (*Soisaium*), 51, 76, 78, 81, 84, 87–88
South Brent TQ10, 131, 133, 139
Sprouston TD5, 142–45
Stanton, St. Bernard SN8, 131–32, 134–35
Stevenston KA20, 163–65
Stewarton KA3, 163–65
Steynton SA73, 131, 133–34, 140
Stirling FK7, 150–52, 157–59, 161–62
Stracathro DD9, 150, 152, 155
Stratton DT2 (*Strettuna*), 131–32, 136, 185
Sydling St. Nicholas DT2, 131–32, 136

Tarves, Fernmartyn AB41, 150, 153–54, 156
Le Teil-aux-Moines/Grand-Teil (*Tiliolum*), Chapelle-Viviers 86300, 109–10, 114–15, 181
Ternay 41800 (*Turneium*), 99, 102, 107, 185, 192
Le Theil-sur-Huisne 61260 (*Tilia*), church, 42, 99, 101, 106
Tiron (*Tiro*), Thiron-Gardais 28480, passim
Tiron, Hôtel de Tiron, Paris 75004, 117, 119, 121
Tironneau 28140 (*Tironellum*), 76, 79, 84, 86, 124, 190–91
Titley HR5 (*Titileia*), 128, 131–33, 136, 140, 148, 170
Torry AB11, 150–51, 153–54, 156
Tournan-en-Brie 77220 (*Sanctus-Audoenus*), 58, 117, 119, 122–23, 192

Trahant, Tréhiant, 100, 102
La Trappe or La Moinerie (*Trapa*), Millac 86150, 38, 109–10, 114
Tréhet 41800 (*Treiet*), 99, 101–2, 107
La Tréhoudière (*Trehoderia*), priory, Tourny 27510, 25, 93–94, 96, 170
Le Tronchet 35540 (*Tronchetum*), 19, 71, 98–100, 103–5, 147, 167, 175–76, 185, 187, 192, 194–95
La Troussaie (*Troseia*), Céaux-en-Couhé 86700, 109–10, 114
Trustach, Kincardine O'Neil AB34, 150, 153, 156
Turriff AB53, 150, 153–54, 156, 161

Vaast (*Sanctus-Vedastus*), Vaas 72500, 99, 101–2, 107–8
Le-Val-Saint-Aignan (*Vallis-Sancti-Aniani*), Châteaudun 28200, 24–25, 76, 79, 85
Valmont, Notre-Dame-du-Pré-de-Valmont 76540, 104
Vert-en-Drouais 28500 (*Ver*), 92–94, 98–99
Viabon 28150 (*Viabun*), 76, 79, 85, 185
Villandon (*Villa-Abdonis*), Montainville 28150, 57, 76, 79, 85, 189–90
Villemafroi (*Villarium-Mafredi*), Membrolles 41240, 57, 76, 79

Waltham, St. Peter, Bishop's Waltham SO32, 130–32, 134, 136
West Kilbride KA23, 163–65
West Linton EH46, 42, 144, 146
West Standen, Newport PO30, 131, 133, 137–38
West Worldham GU34, 131–32, 134, 170
Whissendine LE15, 158, 160, 162, 177
Whitlaw TD7, 142–43, 145
Whitmuir TD7, 142–43, 145
Wiston ML12, 142–43, 146

Yron (*Yronium*), Cloyes-sur-le-Loir 28220, 48, 51, 74, 76, 80, 84, 87, 124, 172, 190–91